D0580930

Slang Down the Ages

Also by Jonathon Green

The Dictionary of Contemporary Slang
Newspeak
The Slang Thesaurus
The Dictionary of Jargon
Neologisms

Slang
Down the
Ages

The Historical Development of Slang

Jonathon Green

Kyle Cathie Limited

First published 1993 in Great Britain
by Kyle Cathie Limited
7/8 Hatherley Street, London SW1P 2QT

ISBN 1 85626 115 8

A Cataloguing in Publication record for this title
is available from the British Library.

Printed and bound in Great Britain by
Biddles Ltd, Guildford and King's Lynn

INTRODUCTION

The aim of this book is to provide what might best be termed a history of slang by default. Curtailed as is inevitable in any but the most all-encompassing of lexicographical works by the imperatives of practical publishing, it is not, alas, a full history — such a tome would have run to at least three times the size — but within its pages there should still be a sufficiency of those central strands of the slang vocabulary, apostrophised some fifty years ago in the *Edinburgh Review* as 'sex, money and intoxicating liquor'. Indeed, it may even be felt that, along with the proliferation of bodily parts and functions, these entries tend overly much to emphasise the sordid, or to be kinder the racier side of life at the expense of the more quotidian, let alone the respectable. If such a criticism is to be levelled, then so be it. Such is the nature, and surely amongst the appeals of this particular lexical beast.

In all probability slang is as old as human speech. The character of slang — on the one hand its essential linguistic playfulness, and on the other its use as a 'secret' speech — makes it clear that as long as people have spoken formal 'standard' languages, so too have they created informal alternatives. In his *Slang Dictionary* (1866) John Camden Hotten mused on the potentially slangy 'bloods' of ancient Nineveh, while his successor Eric Partridge (in *Slang Today and Yesterday* [1933]) acknowledged the likelihood of slang's existence in the lost empires of China, Phoenicia and Central America, not to mention its well-documented appearance in classical Greece and Rome. But such vocabularies are finally no more than fragments: recorded English-language slang, with which I deal here, is a far more recent phenomenon.

The materials upon which I have drawn cover some four centuries of a developing, ever-diversifying vocabulary. The language, of course, is much older, but slang lexicography dates only to the 16th century and the appearance of Thomas Harman's *Caveat for Common Cursetours* (1565). Harman was not the first slang compiler — Robert Copland's *The Hye Waye to the Spittel House* (c.1537) and the printer John Awdelay's *Fraternitye of Vagabondes* (1561) preceded him —but 'honest Harman' as Partridge named him, is the foremost of his period and remains, along with his successors Francis Grose, Hotten, John S. Farmer and W. E. Henley and of course Partridge himself, one of the masters of the genre.

What I have attempted is to take a variety of standard English words and phrases and look at the slang terminology that has grown up to parallel them. The areas on which I have concentrated are primarily concrete: typically parts of the body, sex and the 'sex industry', food, drink and drinking, men and women, money, crime; only occasionally, as in terms meaning goodness and excellence, have I strayed into the abstract. For all (or as many as possible) of the terms involved, I have attempted to trace an approximate earliest use (always debatable given slang's origins as a spoken rather than written language), the etymology and, perhaps most interestingly, the way in which a term is linked to others, especially earlier or later uses, and the way in which, to a sometimes surprising extent, slang survives.

As I stress above, there are unavoidable gaps. Drug terminology, for instance, is absent. Given the contemporary importance of such terms I particularly regret this, but would suggest in mitigation that much of the drug lexicon is jargon —the 'professional' slang of the user — rather than less specific general slang. Among other regretted absentees are the many terms that describe individuals — parasites and meddlers, cowards and heroes, the greedy and the generous and so on. Space, as ever, precluded unrestricted selection. I trust, nonetheless, that what does follow will both inform and entertain the many amateurs of slang, a lexicon that, however old its roots, remains the most persistently 'living' of languages.

Finally my thanks to all concerned with the production of this book, notably Kyle Cathie, Beverley Cousins and Jim Pope, and especially to Lucien Green, for his invaluable help on the index.

Jonathon Green

MEN

Among the oldest slang terms meaning man is **cove**, with its 18C feminine **covess** and its 19C diminutive **covey** (as used in Dickens' *Oliver Twist*). Given its alternative spelling of **cofe**, it is presumed that the word is identical with the contemporary Scots *cofe*: a chapman or pedlar. In turn it may, like a number of 16C cant terms, come from Romany, in this case *cova* or *covo*, both meaning man. Whichever its origins, **cove** appears in a number of combinations, notably the **cove of the dossing ken**: the landlord of a lodging house, the **cove of the ken**: the master of the house, a **cross-cove★**: a robber, a **kinchin-cove★**: a little man or a child brought up as a thief; a **flogging-cove**: a beadle, a **smacking-cove★**: a coachman; a **topping-cove★** or **nubbing cove★**: a hangman; an **abram-cove★**: a beggar, a **queer-cove**: a rogue, a **gentry-cove**: a gentleman, a **downy-cove**: a shrewd man and a **rum cove** which, given the shift in meaning of **rum★**, moved from the 17C great, i.e. successful, rogue, to the 19C odd character. The 17C **cuffin** is a variation on **cove**. The image of man as consumer lies behind **customer** (which still survives in such combinations as **ugly customer** and **queer customer** and **merchant**, typically as **meat-merchant★** or **petticoat-merchant★**. A **shaver** was literally one who shaves, and has thus reached manhood, although the term remains best known as part of **young shaver** (usually referring to a younger person), while a **gaffer**, properly the abbrev. of granfer or grandfather, came to mean husband in the 18C and boss or master a century later. The female equivalent is **gammer** (fr. grandmother).

The 17C **cull** or **cully**, typically found in **cramping cull★** or **cross-biting cully★**, initially meant a constable, but was soon extended to meaning a man. especially a foolish one. The latter definition leads to claims that the term is linked to the Italian *coglione*: a dolt, but as plain man it may well come from the Spanish Gypsy *chulai* or Turkish Gypsy *khulai*, both meaning man or possibly from the French *couillon*: testicles; certainly **culls** meant testicles. The 17C also offers **Johnnie** (its descendent **John** emerged in the 19C), **cock**, which also meant a plucky fighter, **damber**, which possible abbreviated **damme-boy** (cf. **roaring boy**) and **party**, still found in **old party**, and the basis of such legal terms as the guilty party, and being a party to. **Bugger**, coined in the 16C as SE for sodomite, joined the general terms for man by the 18C. Its contemporaries included **fish** (especially in **odd fish** or **queer fish**), **gloak** (18C, see THIEF for etymology) and the ever-popular **chap**, an abbreviation of the 16C *chapman*: a customer and as such relates to **cove**. However an alternative etymology links it to the Romany *chavo* or *chavi*: a child, and thus places it as the antecedent of the 19C **kiddy**, which also meant a small-time, if flashy, thief or pimp.

The 19C brings **bloke**, either from Shelta (cf. **gloak**) or from Romany. In either case the term seems based in the Hindi *loke*: a man although there is also a case for the Dutch *blok*: a fool (thus blockhead). Other extant 19C terms are **joker**, **cuss** (originally US; either from **customer** or possibly from **cuss**: curse), **dude** (coined in New York c.1883; either from **duds***: clothing, or an abbreviation of attitude) and **geezer** (1885) for which the *OED* claims origins in the dialect pronunciation of the 15C *guiser*: a mummer; but Partridge wonders whether Wellington's troops might not have picked it up from the Basque *giza*: a man, during the Peninsula War. **Moosh** or **mush** meant first mouth, then face and finally man; both come from the Romany *moosh*: a man. Less well-known today are **kivey** (presumably a diminutive of **cove**, though possibly linked to the Latin *civis*: a citizen), the backslang **nam** (19C, cf. **namesclop***: policeman), **omee**, **omer**, **omey**, **homey** and **homee** (all Parlyaree) and **homo** (lingua franca). **Put** had meant a rustic in the 17C (especially as a **country put**) and **file** a pickpocket in the 18C. Finally **wallah**, imported from India by British servicemen. Despite its almost invariable translation as man, and its common use as such, **wallah** is in fact a suffix, the Hindi *wala*: pertaining to or connected with, and comes in turn from the Arabic *wali*: proximity. It is the equivalent, therefore, of the Latin *-arius*. Although found today as a single term, its 19C uses tended to be in combinations: **Agra wallah**: a native of Agra, **banghy-wallah**: a porter who carries loads with a **banghy** or shoulder-yoke, **howdah-wallah**, an elephant accustomed to carry a howdah, and the Anglo-Indian **competition wallah**: those who entered the Civil Service competitive exams, established in 1856 to replace the old system of personal patronage.

Regular Joe, **sport**, **artist** (another term more commonly found in combinations, e.g. **piss artist***: a drunkard) and the rhyming slang **ice cream freezer** (**geezer**) are all 20C, as are the Spanish imports **hombre**, known since the 19C as a Spanish term but adopted more recently as part of the popularity of Hollywood Westerns, and **bozo**, with an overtone of clownishness; the Spanish term means the light beard of adolescence, known in slang as **bumfluff**. One last combination seems to have proved itself impervious to chronology. Phrases based on 'old' begin with Shakespeare and nearly all are still in use. **Old lad**, more usually associated with the late Tony Hancock, can be found in Shakespeare in 1588, as can **old boy** (although the association with specifically old men does not arrive until 19C). Other such terms include **old cock** (18C); **old top**, **old man**, **old chap**, **old horse**, and **old fellow** (all 19C); **old bastard**, **old bean**, **old egg**, **old socks** and **old sport** (all 20C).

THE IMPORTANT MAN

If 'old' creates the most combinations in the realm of the general, the big, logically, plays a similar role in denoting the important man. The first such term is the 18C **big wig** (fr. the hairpiece), followed by the **big cheese** (19C, see GOOD for etymology) and thus **the stilton**; more 19C variations are **big gun** or **great gun**, **big bug** (fr. 18C **bug**: an important fellow), **big people**, **big pot** (originally referring to Oxford University dons), the **big dog of the tanyard** or the **big dog with the brass collar** (especially in a business context) and the **biggest toad in the puddle**. The 20C has a **big deal** (although it is more usually found as a deflatory response to some supposedly dramatic statement), a **big fish** (fr. **fish**: a fellow), the **big chief** or **big white chief**, **big noise**, **big stuff** (originally describing World War I artillery shells), **biggie** and **BMOC** (US college use: big man on campus). **Mr. Big**, **big shot** and **big wheel** all came from 1930s gangland (or from the journalists who reported it), while a **big enchilada** (fr. Spanish *enchilar*: to season with chili and thus a tortilla served with a chili sauce) appeared during the Watergate scandal, c. 1974; its origins, presumably, lie in **big cheese**.

Amongst other terms are **topper** (18C) and a number from the 19C: **gaffer** and **governor** or **guvnor** (both meaning the boss, although **governor** could also mean one's father), **stunner** (anyone expert in their own skill), **cock of the walk**, **head cook and bottle-washer**, **high-up** and **his nibs** (fr. **nib**: a gentleman or **nibs**: a well-dressed workman). The US **high mucky-muck** or **high monkey-monk** probably came from the Chinook jargon *hiu muckamuck*: literally plenty food, denoting a powerful member of a tribe; **pooh-bah** originated in Gilbert and Sullivan's Savoy Opera *The Mikado* (1885) in which 'Ko-Ko' is 'Lord High Executioner of Titipu' and 'Poo-Ba' is 'Lord High Everything Else'. Another US term **sachem** means specifically a political leader and comes from the Algonquin Indian name for a supreme chief. A **nob** (originally meaning head) gave the **Nob's House**: the House of Parliament and the **Nob's Nob**: King George IV. The **nob** was a less ostentatious version of the **swell**, their differences defined thus in Jon Bee's *Dictionary* (1823): 'the swell...makes a show of his finery...the nob, relying upon intrinsic worth, or bona fide property, or intellectual ability, is clad in plain-ness.'

Aside from the various terms based on 'big', the 20C has **celeb** (abbrev. celebrity) and **headliner** (both from show business) and **heavyweight** (fr. sport). **Honcho** (fr. the Japanese *han'cho*: a group leader) came back with the US forces from the Korean War while **hot-shot** dates back to the 17C, when a **hot-shot** was one who discharged his firearm too enthusiastically; parallel terms were to **be a hot-shot indeed**, or to **be a hot shot in a mustard-pot (when both heels stand right up)**; all such terms carry a degree of sexual innuendo; all are essentially dismissive). Yiddish gives a **mensch** (fr. the German *mensch*: a person), a term that emphasises character as much if not more than it does any practical achievement, as well as **shtarka** (fr. the German *stark*: strong), for whom menace and aggression are the main attributes. The **men in suits** are senior managers, although the term tends to mean money-men rather than their creative (and perhaps more excitingly dressed) peers, as well as a political use: the senior members of the Conservative party who traditionally 'take the soundings' of party opinion, Another term rooted in politics, this time American, is **kingfish**, originally the nickname of Senator Huey P Long of Louisiana the epitome of the populist orator come to power. H. G. Wells called him 'A Winston Churchill who has never been at Harrow', a New Orleans paper preferred 'The Prince of Piffle' and everyone else opted for 'demagogue', but Huey Long called himself 'The Kingfish', a term in which he revelled until his assassination, aged 38, in 1935. Australian rhy. sl. gives **pitch and toss** (the boss), while **top dog** and **top cat** and **gorilla** continue the animal motif.

Main man is originally Afro-American, as are **Boss Charlie** (from **Mr Charlie**: a white man) and a **hammer man** (either from 19C **hammer**: a strong puncher, or 20C **hammer**: penis). Finally **the man** gains his exclusiveness from the definite article; given the context the term can also mean a drug dealer or a policeman.

THE PROMISCUOUS MAN

The promiscuous man, or the whoremonger as he has been characterised since the early 16C, has attracted a wide range of slang for what are still considered as his enviable attainments. The *monger* (fr. Latin *mango*: a dealer or trafficker) element of the term gives **mutton-monger** (16C, from **mutton**: a prostitute or the vagina), **fishmonger** (17C, from **fish**: vagina or prostitute) and **fleshmonger** (17C, also meaning whore), and **meat-monger** (18C, from **meat**: vagina). **Lusty-guts** is 16C as is **lusty lawrence** (possibly punning on *lazy Lawrence*: the epitome of laziness; based on the probably apocryphal tale of the martyred St Lawrence who refused to make a sound as he was roasted to death, causing his executioner to suggest that far from being stoic, he was too lazy to move). On a more general level the 17C has **bull** or **town bull** and **cavaulter** (both **bull** and **cavault** mean to copulate), **jumbler** (cf. **jumble-giblets***), **knocker, beard-splitter, beard-jammer, quim-**

sticker and **rump-splitter** (all meaning the penis) and **thrumster** (fr. **thrum**: to thrash). The 18C introduces **bum-faker, bum-tickler, bum-ranger, bum-worker** and **bum-fighter, gapstopper, leather-stretcher** (also meaning penis; fr. **leather**: the vagina) and **leglifter** (fr. **lift the leg**: to copulate). The fecund 19C adds many new terms. The world of nature has **bird of the game** and **cock of the game**, (19C) (although SE *cock of the game* means the champion), **bird's-nester** (doubly punning on **bird**: woman and **nest**: vagina), **gamecock** and **cock-fighter** (both drawn from the cock-pit), **goat, horseman** (who 'rides'), **muttoner** (cf. **mutton-monger**) and **ling-grappler** (fr. **ling***: vagina). A **carrion-hunter** refers to **carrion**: body although the 18C use meant an undertaker. The respective male and female genitals give **ballocks** (a slang term by the 19C, but SE from the 11C), **Bluebeard** (also the penis), **prick-scourer, button-hole worker** (fr. **button-hole**: vagina), **striker** and **tummy tickler** (cf. **tummy banana**). Sexual excitement counts for **hot member, hot 'un, warm member** (all of which can apply to either sex), **rattle-cap**, (fr. **have a rattle**: to copulate), **sharpshooter** and **rifle-man** (who 'shoot') and **scorcher. Chauvering-cove** and **chauverer** come from **charver**: to copulate, **fuckster** is bluntly self-explanatory, while **performer** and **servant** (one who 'services') are euphemistic, as is the **high priest of Paphos** (see PROSTITUTION for etymology). **Mormon** and **Solomon** both refer to the multiplicity of wives permitted both to the religious cult and the Biblical monarch, **Mr Horner** puns on whore, a **petticoat merchant** trades in females while a **smell-smock** is based on **smock**: an immoral woman. The **sportsman** plays his own sort of game while a **Corinthian** (which would also come to mean an idealised form of sportsman, this time in the field rather than the bedroom) comes from the 17C term meaning 'elegant dissipation'. The term was widely popularised with the publication in 1821 of Pierce Egan's *Life in London; the Day and Night Scenes of Jerry Hawthorne and his Elegant Friend, Corinthian Tom*, the original Tom and Jerry and thus fathers to the eponymous Warner Bros. cartoon and the male leads of the television series *The Good Life*. Other 19C figures include the **grouser, john among the maids, molrower** (which also means to caterwaul and thus compares the whoremonger's seductions to the howling of amatory cats), the **belly-bumper** (a back formation of **get a belly-bumper**: to be made pregnant), the **king of clubs** (fr. **club**: penis) and the **ladies' tailor** (fr. the in-and-out 'sewing' motion of intercourse; cf. **needle, needle-woman** and **sew**). A **billy-noodle** (US 19C, Aus 20C) is not a real ladies' man, but firmly believes, evidence notwithstanding, that no woman can resist his charms.

The equation of the penis and its user continues into the 20C with such terms as **stickman, swordsman, cocksman** and **cockhound** while the animal kingdom gives **stallion, stud** (fr. stallion at stud; an available mistress can be a **stud mare**), **wolf** (presumably from the Big Bad Wolf), **rooster** and **alligator** (both Afro-American). Other terms include **fast worker, heaver** (ΛΛ), **makeout artist, saloon-bar cowboy, come-freak** or **cum-freak** (both from **come** or **cum**: semen or ejaculation) and **swinger**, which has a secondary meaning as being a fan of what, in the 1970s was more usually known as 'wife-swapping'. US teenagers profess themselves members of the **4-F club**: 'find 'em, feel 'em, fuck 'em and forget 'em'. While most studs are omnivorous, some tie themselves to specific parts of the female body: the **fat-fancier** (19C), **fat-monger** (19C) and **figure-fancier** (19C, from **figure**: large) all prefer what the retail trade calls the 'fuller figure', as does the 20C **chubby-chaser**. The modern **arse man, leg man** and **tit man** should need no amplification. Last of all is the man who is **no better than he should be** and who, in his successful career has **had more arse than a toilet seat**.

WOMEN

Writing in *Womanwords* (1989), her invaluable lexicon of terms used to describe women, the majority of which have been coined in a less than complimentary manner by men, Jane Mills notes that so substantial is the slang vocabulary, especially that which equates 'woman' with 'slut' or its synonyms, that she 'had to draw an arbitrary line lest [the book] turned into a dictionary of slang.' As these entries bear out, her findings are all too accurate. Women fare less than well. Slang is the essence of 'man-made language', created by man and largely spoken by him too. Thus it has been, still is, and shows every sign of remaining.

WOMAN AS A SEX OBJECT

Of the various slang terms for woman a large number, no doubt unsurprisingly, see the woman as no more than a sex object and as such derive purely and simply from terms that otherwise mean the vagina. For the relevant etymologies the reader should look under Vagina. Alternatively, the sex, as it were, is muted and the object takes centre stage. This construction lies behind one of the oldest such terms, **piece**, which entered the language during the 14C, and remained SE for the next three to four hundred years, after which, in such combinations as **piece of stuff** (17C), **piece of ass★**, **piece of tail★** and **piece of stray** (all 20C), it became a staple of such dismissive descriptions. Parallel terms head by **a bit of...** took up a similar role from the 19C onwards. Additional 'bits' include a **bit of muslin** (19C), a **bit of ebony** (a black girl) and a **bit of crackling** (a mix of **cracker**, **crack**: vagina, and roast pork skin). Most 'bits' implied an attractive woman, although a **bit of mutton** or a **piece of mutton** (fr. **mutton**: vagina or prostitute, especially as in **laced mutton★**) implied in this context a woman dressing younger than her years. As well as the well-known **mutton dressed as lamb**, such a supposedly anachronistic figure was also known as a **peg puff**, a **phizgig** (possibly related to its alternative definition: a pile of moistened gunpowder which when lit fails to flash) and a **mutton cove**.

Other early description include **pussy** (17C), **flat-cock** (18C), **gusset** and **placket** (both 17C), all of which are purely anatomical. However the point of view was not wholly masculine: **gobble-prick** (18C a 'rampant, lustful' woman, Grose), **staff breaker** and **staff climber** (19C, from **staff of life**: penis), were somewhat back-handed compliments, but did admit to some degree of female sexuality. The 19C added **fish** and **oyster** (both nodding to the vagina as fish metaphor) plus **fluff** (fr. **fluff**: pubic hair). The 20C **tuna** provides another 'fish' image.

More recent terms, all of which equate vagina with woman include the Afro-American **booty** and **butter** (both from **butt**: posterior), **cock** (usually found as the masculine penis, but meaning vagina in the Caribbean and the Southern States of the US; possibly from 17C **cockles**: labia minora), **coño** (fr. Spanish), **cookie**, **coot** and **cooze** (all euphemisms of **cunt***, **crack**, **crotch**, **gash** (as simple anatomy 18C, but the derogatory use is 20C and possibly comes fr. **gash**: spare, waste), **quiff**, **slit**, **snatch**, **hair** (thus **get one's hair cut**: to visit a woman for sex), **kitty-cat** (cf. **pussy**) and **minge bag** (fr. **minge***). Finally, definitively, comes **cunt*** itself.

THE PROMISCUOUS WOMAN

Given the nature of this area of slang, the line between a 'neutral' woman and one who is deemed promiscuous is at times almost invisible. The terms that follow, some of which overlap with other sections, may be presumed to have a higher 'promiscuity' content than their peers. Readers should check PROSTITUTION for cognate vocabulary. Virtually all are 20C coinages, although on occasion their origins may lie somewhat earlier.

Of all the various 20C terms one stands out above all: **bimbo**, with its less common abbreviation **bim**, has become (and to a great extent remains) the ultimate description of a certain type of contemporary young woman. Such a figure is often seen as something of a **gold-digger** (her 1930s equivalent) and indulged as such by rich and/or powerful older men and the media to whom she tells or sells her tale. The earliest use of **bimbo** is found c.1900 in America, where it was synonymous with **bozo** to mean a tough guy. A parallel use was that to mean 'baby', abbreviated from the Italian *bambino*. By the 1920s the word meant young woman, often a prostitute. The current use stems from the revelations of a 'model', of her relationship with a millionaire businessman. Bimbos may also be masculine, and as such are synonymous with the slightly older **toyboy**, the modern synonym for the older **gigolo★**. Another masculine synonym is **himbo**.

A number of terms simply equate sexually active women with dirt: thus **dirty leg**, **dirt-bag** and **shagbag** (fr. **shag★**), **grubber**, **scab**, **scuzz**, **sleaze**, **snot** (19C, usually nasal mucus, although 19C Scots cant defined **snot** as 'a gentleman'), **sweat hog**, **pig**, **scrubber** (a military coinage of the 1920s, but obviously linked to the 18C **scrub**: a cheap whore; cf. **scrubbing brush★**), **slag** (fr. SE *slack*; its earlier, 18C use meant coward; Robin Cook's novel *The Crust On Its Uppers* [1962] defines **the slag** as 'young third-rate grafters, male or female, unwashed, useless') and **whore** (but with no commercial overtones) itself. Predictable, easy availability underlines **dead cert**, **lay**, **easy lay** or **easy ride**, **free for all**, **gin-and-fuck-it** (pun on gin-and-tonic), **pushover** and the cognate **Little Miss Roundheels** (cf. 19C **lift the heels**: to copulate), **quickie**, **right sort** (also 19C: gin), **motorcycle** (AA), **town bicycle**, **town pump**, **town punch** and **bike**, while a **carpenter's dream** is 'flat as a board and easy to screw'. **Paraffin lamp** is rhy. sl. for **tramp** and its cognate **bum**. **Knock** and **leg** both come from earlier terms meaning sexual intercourse, respectively **knock** (16C) and **leg business** (19C); **goer** (orig. 19C racing use: a good runner), **hot-bot** (cf. 17C **hot-arsed**, **hot-backed**), **screamer and creamer**, **lust dog**, **nympho** and **nymph** (both from SE *nymphomaniac*; cf. 18C **nymph of darkness**, **nymph of delight**: a prostitute) all suggest an insatiable woman; a **shack job**, **shack-up** or **sleepy-time girl** are good for a brief relationship. The **floosie** or **floozie** comes from the dial. *floosy*: flossy, thus soft, while **punch** originates in the 18C SE verb *punch*: to pierce. **Broad** (possibly from a woman's physique, though most contexts ignore such a possibility) remains primarily US, while the sexually generous **charity girl** and **chippie** usually mean prostitute.

Parasites include the **groupie** or **band rat** and the **snow bunny** (specialising respectively in rock groups and skiers); a **splash** is a victim of gang rape, while a **buttered bun** (**butter**: semen, **buns**: buttocks) is one who has sex with several men in succession. The term was first coined to describe the 16C courtesan Louise de Quérouaille; the current use dates from the 17C. The **Mayfair**

Merc or **Mayfair mercenary** (coined as the somewhat tartier cousin of the **Sloane Ranger**) is one happy to use sex as a launchpad for social success. Finally, the girl who is 'no better than she should be' is one who has had **more pricks than a second-hand dart-board**.

ANIMALS AND FOOD

A less aggressive, but barely more complimentary group of terms position women as animals, or even food. **Bitch** had moved on from its 14C SE origins as meaning a female dog to becoming a prostitute by the 15C; that aspect vanished but the term has remained generally derogative since the 18C; **bitch party** is a synonym of **hen party**. **Bird**, still extant today, appeared a century ago; other birds include **biddy** which began life in the 16C meaning a chicken, became a young girl in the 18C and has meant any woman since the 19C; if anything the 20C meaning, often with the adjective 'old' has made the logical last leap and means an old woman. **Hen** is an early 17C term, while **chick**, a byword for the politically incorrect, is 20C, although it has been used as an affectionate description of a child since the Middle Ages, as has the synonymous **chickabiddy**, which was coined by London coster-mongers during the 19C. **Quail**, **pheasant** and **plover** all started life in the 17C, when they generally meant prostitute, but became generalised terms by the 19C; of the three **quail** is the survivor – still widely used in the US – and the **San Quentin quail** is a synonym for **jailbait**, i.e. such a youngster can send a man to the San Quentin (or any other) prison. **Poultry** (19C) meant women in general and **wool**, like **fluff**, also means pubic hair while **dish** invariably implies good looks.

Like **pussy**, **cat** has a lengthy pedigree: whore in the 16C, argumentative termagent in the 19C and gossip since the 1920s. **Mare** is a 20C term, and like the similar **moo** gained wide currency during the successful 1960s' television series, *Till Death Us Do Part*. Either term is open to affectionate as well as derogatory use; **cow** (17C) may have begun life as a neutral term but its modern use is strictly negative. **Filly** is 17C, as is the male pursuit of **filly-hunt-**

ing, **haybag** (upon which one lies) is 19C, while **fox** is the current Afro-American term of approval. To move from animals to food, **trout** (18C) is another play on the 'fish' image, but originally **trout** = truth = honest, and thus implied the trustiness of the woman, rather than anything offensive. The **jelly** (19C) was a buxom and pretty girl, the **cherry** or **cherry ripe** (19C) and the **cherry pie** (20C) is a virgin; a **potato** (a term much beloved of Damon Runyon's fictional Broadway hustlers), is in fact Australian rhy. sl: **potato peeler: sheila★**.

More recent 'food' terms include the Afro-American **cookie** (US: biscuit), **banana** (possibly for a 'yellow' girl), **butter baby**, **pound-cake** (cf. **eat poundcake★**), **sweet potato pie**, **tootsie roll** (fr. a well-known US sweet), and **candy** (a sexually desirable person of either sex; cf. **sweetmeat**). **Cheesecake** (while commonly used as a synonym for pinup or **Page Three girl**, is also a richer version of the commonplace **tart**); similar are **creamie**, **crumpet**, **cup-cake**, **dish**, **honey**, **jam** (also meaning semen), **pancake**, **peach**, **pie**, **sweetie** (although this is generally the abbrev. of sweetheart), **tomato** and the all-encompassing **yummy**.

THE ATTRACTIVE WOMAN

Nowhere is the male-orientated dimension of this particular area of slang so prevalent than in the terms to describe attractive women or girls and, in the following section, those who are considered less physically favoured. A mix of lasciviousness and patronage infuses virtually every term. Once again some words overlap with more general uses, meaning simply 'woman'.

Among the most popular of today's terms is **stunner** or **stunnah** (as spelt by tabloid sub-editors). It is, in fact, a 19C coinage and can be found in *The Adventures of Mr Verdant Green* (1853) by 'Cuthbert Bede' (the Rev. Edward Bradley 1827-89). The **stunner's** peer, the **Page Three girl**, is all 20C, an invention of the *Sun* newspaper of the late 1970s, which started featuring scantily clad pin-ups on page three. Other popular terms include **lovely**, **dreamboat** (equally common as a description of an attractive male), **eyeful**, **glamour puss**, **charmer** (usually as **little charmer**), **classy chassis**, and

cracker or **little cracker**. Slightly more exciting are **scorcher**, **sexpot** and **hot number**. America offers **babe** and **real babe**, **cutes**, **cutesie-pie** and **cutie** (plus **cute chick***), **looker**, **nifty** and **nifty piece**, **patootie** (possibly from **potato***), **toots**, **little pretty** and **star**. A **ten** is a girl who rates at ten out of ten on any scale of male appreciation, the term comes from the eponymously titled film of 1979, starring Bo Derek. Back in Britain **doll*** is compounded as **doll city**, **dollface** and **dolly**, an **angel** was originally a prostitute working near the Angel public house in Islington; the **talent** is a general term for pretty girls, e.g. 'Any talent about?' **Donah** is virtually defunct, but was a classic 19C term, a Parlyaree word that came from the Italian *donna*: a woman, and is enshrined in the music hall couplet (usually attributed to Gus Elen): 'Never introduce your donah to a pal / For the odds is ten to one he nicks your gal. '

Australia adds **beaut** and **grouse gear** (both of which can simply mean good) and the surfers' **ginch**. Afro-American terms include **poodle** (an unusually complimentary twist on the negative **dog***), **Porsche** and **Mercedes** (both luxury motorcars), **melted butter** (a light-skinned girl), **mink**, **brickhouse**, **fleshpot**, **hamma** or **hammer**, **sleek lady**, **thoroughbred black** and the sexually paradoxical **stallion** (she gives a good ride?). Finally a **Barbie Doll** (fr. the trade-marked toy) is pretty but ultra-conventional and **all tits and teeth** describes a girl who is blatantly sexual, if less than notably bright.

THE UNATTRACTIVE WOMAN

Cow meant simply woman in the 18C, but acquired the image of prostitution in the 19C; modern uses tend to be as combinations —typically **stupid cow**, **ugly cow** and Nell Dunn's book title: *Poor Cow*. **Crow** comes from **chromo**, both of which can also mean whore (see PROSTITUTION for etymology); **dog**, **dogface** (also a soldier) and **doggie** are common US pejoratives, all of which are presumably rooted in the earlier **bitch**, although **dog** is a general negative, as often found in non-sexual contexts. Other terms include **cull bird** (possibly fr. 18C farming use, *cull*: an animal too

old for breeding), **bat** (often as **old bat** and originally, 18C, a
prostitute), **buzzard** (an ignorant and gullible person since 14C),
hedgehog, heifer (19C, cf. **cow**), **hog** (fr. 20C **hog**: to copulate)
and **mule** (which can also mean an impotent male). Other put-
downs include **bad news, bag, double-bagger** and **douchebag**
(US; Aus. has **Douche Can Alley**: Palmer Street, the red light area
of Sydney), **drack** (Aus., possibly from Dracula), **hairbag, pitch**
and **skank**. Black America has its share: **bear, chicken** and **thunder chicken** represent the animal kingdom, while **B.B. head,
nailhead, ragmop** and **tackhead** all equate ill-kempt or unfash-
ionable hair with an unappetising person. A **welfare mother**
extends the condemnation to poverty, while a **skeeza** (fr. **skeeze**:
to have sex; beloved of **rap*** lyricists) is not merely ugly but
promiscuous with it. The acronym **PTA** stands for **pussy, tits** and
armpits – all of which allegedly smell.

Finally a fat woman is variously a **Bahama mama** (AA, con-
trasting supposedly overweight West Indians with sleek US girls),
a **butterball, Judy with the big booty** (AA; fr **judy**: a woman,
and **booty**: the behind), a **pig, pigger** or **pigmouth**, a **shuttle-
butt**, or a **teddybear** (AA); the 19C, slightly less cruel, opts for
feather-bed and pillows.

GENERAL TERMS

Of general terms for women, **mot** or **mort, blowse** or **blouse**
and **gixie** (16C) have also been stolen to mean prostitute and their
etymologies can be consulted in the relevant section. The 17C
blowen has had a similar treatment. Other 17C terms include
apron (cf. **apron squire***), **smock** (cf. **skirt**) and **cooler** (fr. the
assumption that passion cools after sex; cf **wife in water colour***).
Like the generic **smock**, which can be used to mean woman in a
variety of contexts, usually those injurious to her reputation,
petticoat appears in a number of combinations: **petticoat government** (female rule in the home, a precursor of the 20C
pussy-whipped), a **petticoat merchant*** (a whoremonger), a
squire of the petticoat (a pimp, cf. **apple squire***), and **petticoat led** (one who is infatuated). A **gig** is a flighty woman while

a **crackish** one (fr. **crack**: vagina) is a 'wanton' ; a **faggot** is synonymous with a **baggage★** (which has strong overtones of promiscuity): both are something to be borne or carried. The 18C borrows from Scots dialect to add **dame** and from the Latin for man — *homo* — to obtain **homoney**. **Moll** is yet another term that serves equally as whore, while a **catamaran** is a play on **cat★**, or possibly puns on the 19C SE use of catamaran: a **fireship★**). The suffix **-widow**, meaning any woman whose husband is occupied elsewhere, emerged in the 18C, typically as **grass widow** or **widow bewitched**; such combinations as **golf widow** or **cricket widow** are 20C coinages.

Doll, the ancestor of the 1960s **dolly** and **dollybird** appears in the mid-19C, while **hairy** ('a hatless slum girl in Glasgow') and its adverbial form **hairy** (sexually alluring) is a contemporary. **Judy**, possibly from Punch and Judy shows, appears c.1810; other 19C terms include **mivvy** (possibly from **mivey**: a landlady), **polone** (a Parlyaree term that echoes the older **blowen★**), the generic **skirt** (often as in a **bit of skirt**), **totty** (fr. the proper name Dorothy or from **titty★**; originally a high class whore, by the 20C it was used without pejorative overtones) and **crumb** or **crummy** (a pretty, plumpish woman; the term comes from the crumb of a risen loaf), **sister** and the great Australian feminine: **sheila**. **Sheila**, usually spelt **shaler** until c.1900, has no easy etymology. As a name it is all-purpose for an Irish girl, the female equivalent of **paddy★**, which has come to mean any Irishman; both terms appear in that context in 19C Australia. Hotten suggests that it is the 'corrupt form of Gaelic, *caille*, a young woman.' The drift from Irish girl to any girl approximately parallels the **shaler/sheila** spelling change; by 1919 the writer W. H. Downing defines it simply as 'a girl' in his *Digger Dialects* .

Modern terms include **babe**, **frail** (now US, although the 'frail sisterhood' was used in the UK c.1830 to mean prostitutes. albeit classy ones) and **jane** (cf. **judy**, **sheila**), all primarily US and all still smacking of the pulp novels wherein they first saw the lexical light. More recent Americanisms are the Afro-American **band** (used in Aus. to mean a whore), **rag baby**, **real woman** and **one good woman**. The UK has **tart** (with its implication of promiscuity),

nammo or **nemmo** (both backslang), and the rhy. sl.**twist** (**twist and twirl**: girl) and **cuddle and kiss** (miss), **sort** (coined in Aus. c.1910 it appeared in the 'old country' thirty years later); the term was briefly popularised c.1970 as the invariable name of the girls who associated with skinhead boys. **Mystery** describes young girls who had run away to London; thus **mystery mad** or **mystery punter**: a man who specialises in the pursuit of such girls. Finally a party of women can be a **fool's wedding** (19C), a **hen party** (19C), **bitch-party**, **cat-party** or **tabby-party**.

THE BODY

THE BODY IN GENERAL

Thomas Harman, composing in his *Caveat* (1567) a fictitious dialogue between a couple of villains as a means of illustrating the canting vocabulary, has the one greet the other: 'Bene Lightmans to thy quarromes...' and translates this as 'Good morrow to thy bodye...' **Quarromes**, sometimes found as **quarroms**, or **quarron** must thus stand as the earliest slang term for the body. It comes, like a number of cant terms, from Europe, in this case from the Italian *carogna* or the French *charogne*, both meaning flesh. Subsequent terms include **bacon** (used by Falstaff in *I Henry IV* [1596] when he urges 'On,! Bacons, on!', and is the basis for the phrase 'save one's bacon' and the rude gesture of **pull bacon** or **long-bacon** – cocking a snook or thumbing one's nose), the 18C **soul-case**, which still survives in the modern Australian **belt**, **worry** or **work the soul-case out of** (to work to exhaustion), and **apple-cart** (although this is probably not the same conveyance found in 'upset the apple-cart'), and the 19th's **bone-house**. A single bone was known as a **tot** (fr. the German *todt*, meaning dead.) Modern terms include the abbreviated **bod**, the mechanistic **chassis** and, specifically applied to women viewed strictly as sex-objects: **shaft**. A pair of terms meaning skin reduce the human to his/her animal basics: **hide** and **pelt**.

THE HAIR

Hair offers two pieces of 19C rhy. sl.: **fanny blair** (which has not survived) and **barnet fair** (still extant, usually abbreviated to **barnet**; it is known as **bonny fair** in US), as well as the agricultural **top dressing** (19C), **strommel** (16C: straw), **nob thatch** (19C **nob**: head, thus **strommel-faker** and **nob-thatcher**:wig-maker), **thatch** and the Afro American **righteous moss** (**moss** originally meaning lead). Still in vegetable mode, red hair, logically, is **carrots**, as well as **ginger** and **flames**. **Turnip-pated** meant white-haired. A bald man was the **Marquis of Granby**, and his modern-day equivalent a **skinhead** or **baldie**. The potential problems of dirty hair are found in the 18C **louse trap** (a comb), **lousewalk** (a back hair parting) and **louse bag** (a wig or bag over the hair) as well as the **louse ladder** (1920 side whiskers). False hair was a **tower** (19C), a predecessor of today's **rug** or **wool**. Newgate, the best-known City jail, from whence so many felons went to the gallows, was especially productive of hair-related terms. The **Newgate knocker** (19C) was a lock of hair shaped like the figure 6, and twisted from temple back towards ear; the grimmer aspects of the jail were further reflected in the **Newgate ring** and **Newgate collar**, respectively a moustache and beard worn as one without whiskers and a collar-like beard worn under chin, both of which were fancifully reminiscent of the hangman's noose.

Other popular hairstyles were the **heartbreaker** (16C, a curled love-lock), the **aggerawator** (a coster-monger speciality comprising a well greased lock of hair twisted and pointing either at the corner of an eye or at an ear), the **meat-hook** (another coster favourite and shaped as it would seem), the **beau-catcher** or **bow catcher** (19C, both equivalent to the modern kiss-curl), and **love-curls** (late 19C, hair cut short and worn low over forehead). **Knockers**, usually meaning breasts (qv), were small curls worn flat on the temples. Apart from the **DA** (UK: **duck's arse**) or **duck tail** (US) cuts beloved of the 1950s' Teddy Boys, rockers and greasers, and the **skinhead** and **suedehead** crops of their 1970s successors, the gaudiest of modern styles remains the punks' **mo-**

hican (whether plain or coloured). The term was by no means new in slang: coined c. 1960 for hair (though popularised in the late 1970s) and related to the Mohican Indians, or at least their Hollywood incarnation, a century earlier it indicated 'a very heavy man that rides a long way in an omnibus for sixpence'.

Apart from the two Newgate-generated phrases above, terms for facial hair – a beard or moustache – include **stache** and **tash**, **face fungus**, **fungus**, and **face fins** (all 20C), **mouser** (19C), also meaning the female pubic hair, as do **muff** (19C) and **beaver** (20C, especially as in the street game when children would compete to be the first to spot a bearded man and signify their success by shouting, 'Beaver!'). A bearded man was also a **billy-goat** (19C); one who needed a shave oyster-faced, and light adolescent fuzz merely **bum-fluff**.

THE HEAD

Logically enough the head, with its uppermost position on the body, takes its slang names from the heights, human and otherwise. Such terms include **attic** (1823, with its extension **queer in the attic**, meaning both mad and drunk arriving in 1870; craziness is also implicit in the 20C **rats in the attic**), **cockloft** (17C) and **garret** (18C), **belfry** (19C, in which of course one may be **bats**). Others include **dome** (19C UK, 20C mainly US), **topknot**, **top piece** (1830s), **topflat**, **top end**, **top** story and **upper story**, **upper extremity**, **upper apartment** and **upper crust** (all 19C), **weathercock**, **gable** (1870), and **wig**.

The essentially global shape of the head, plus the desire of slang coiners to relate it to a variety of edibles, lends itself to a second set of slang terms; readers of P. G. Wodehouse may find many of them familiar. Apart from **crust** and **loaf** (both rhy. sl.: **crust / loaf of bread**: head) and **twopenny** (loaf: loaf of bread: head), they include **biscuit**, **crumpet** (19C), **scone** (Aus.), **bean** (19C), **coconut** and its abbreviation **coco** (1830), **turnip** (19C; a popular bet was 'all one's head to a turnip') and **swede** (20C), **onion** (19C; an eccentric is 'off his onion'), **costard** (16C, meaning a large apple as such the root of that prime user of Cockney slang, the costard or coster-monger), and **pumpkin** (19C). **Gourd** also means pumpkin, as does **calabash**, a term based in the Levant, with roots in the Persian *kharbuz*, or *kharbuza*, meaning melon', and occasionally 'water-melon', from which came the Arabic *khirbiz*, melon, and *kirbiz*, pumpkin or gourd. Other linguistic links can be found in Spain, Sicily, Turkey, Albania, Greece and Serbia. Gourd further serves to mean the mind, as do **thinker** and **upstairs**. **Nut** and **nutcracker** (both 19C) imply the head in the context of violence, thus the verb to **nut**, meaning to use the head as a weapon.

Harman lists **nab** (as **nabe**) in 1567; **nob** follows a century later; its later use as a synonym for **toff** emerges c.1800. **Noll** (SE from 9C–18C, but henceforth slang) leads on to **noddle** (18C, but SE in 15C when it meant the back of the head), **noodle**, and **nuddikin** (19C; from noodle-ken).

Finally a random group: **block** (17C, extant only in 'knock one's block off'), **boko** (in 20C Australia a horse with only one eye), **bonce** (otherwise meaning a large marble), **chump** (1860), **conk** (more commonly nose, but head in Aus. since 1920), **deache** (backslang); **pimple** (thus **pimple cover**: hat), **napper** (18C, also meaning hat) and **hat peg**; **poundrel** (17C, the SE word means scales); **canister, brainpan** and **knowledge box**; **lolly** (19C), **lob** (mid-19C, originally a snuff-box), the punning **Crown office**, **billiard ball** (presumably of a bald person), **holus bolus** (19C), **jolly** (abbrev. for **jolly nob**); a last trio, **sconce** (16C), **noggin** (19C) and **mazzard** (fr SE mazer 16C) also meant a drinking cup.

THE FACE

The face is particularly susceptible to rhyming slang. Such terms include **airs and graces** (20C), **roach and dace** (1874), **boat** (1946, **boat-race**: face), **chevy chase** (1859), and **Jem Mace** (fr. the 19C prize-fighter). The jaw is similar creative, with **jackdaw** (1857) and **rabbit's paw** (1930, but more often **rabbit★** means talk or speech, in which context **jaw★** means to converse and dates to the mid-18C). Other terms include **muns** (17C, cf **mun**, below), **whisker-bed, beezer** (usually meaning nose, qv), **clock** (1870) and **dial** (1830), **esaff** (backsl.), **kisser** (1860) and **smiler** (20C);

frontage, **frontispiece**, **map** (20C), and **signboard**; **mug** (1708, possibly from the Toby-Jug-like mugs designed as grotesque faces), **mush** (fr. the skin's softness), **pan** (20C), **phiz** and **phizog** (fr. SE *physiognomy*), **puss** (often implying ugliness) and **gills** (thus 'green about the gills': looking poorly). A light complexion is **furmity-faced** (fr. frumenty: hulled wheat – Latin *frumentum* – boiled in milk), a broad face is a **splatter face**. Freckles are **angel kisses**.

The chin is variously the **button** (orig. prize-fighting jargon), and the rhy. sl. **Errol Flynn** or **Gunga Din**. The 19C **nutcracker** denoted a Mr Punch-like profile with a curving nose and protruding chin. Cosmetics, with which the face is adorned include **lippy** (20C, lipstick), **slap** (19C, theatrical) and **war paint** (20C).

THE MOUTH AND THROAT

The earliest recorded non-standard term for mouth is **neb**, otherwise meaning beak, which dates back to the *Ancren Riwle,* a devotional work composed c.1225. It was followed, c.1300, by **mun** or **munn**, a direct loan from the Norwegian dialect term for mouth, and 150 years later, by **gob** (still going strong, especially as in the dismissive phrase 'Shut your gob!'), possibly rooted in the Irish term meaning beak. The unconnected **gan**, possibly from the Scottish *gane*, is cited by Harman. **Gans**, the plural, means lips. By the 18C **gab**, another Scottish term, joined the lexicon, with its extension **gob-box**. Other general terms include **moey** (19C, fr. Romany *mooi*: mouth), **trap** (19C, usually as in another putdown: 'Shut your trap'). Further general terms include a quartet of rhy. sl.: **East and South**, **sunny south**, **North and South** and **salmon and trout**; **mizzard** (fr. *mazzard*: face), **dubber** (18C), **mummer** (fr. **mun**), **rag-box** (**rag**: tongue), **bazoo** (fr. the Dutch *bazu(in)*: trumpet; cf. **trumpeter**: one who has bad breath). Specific terms include **gig** (1871, possibly fr. **gibface** meaning a heavy lower jaw and thus an ugly person), and two meaning a large mouth: **oven** (18C) and **sparrow-mouth** (19C, 'one whose mouth cannot be enlarged without removing the ears' Grose).

Other terms reflect the various functions of the mouth as a hole or passageway, as a container for the teeth, or as a means of eating,

speaking or kissing. **Chops** (18C), **puss** (see above at face) and
muzzle all hark back to one's essential animality, while **hole**, **gash**
(US, 1852), **hatchway** (1820), **hopper** (19C), and **maw** all underline the mouth's physical shape and purpose. The use of the
mouth for speech can be seen in **yap** (with further animal overtones), **blabber** (16C, from **blab***), **blubber** (18C, also meaning
breasts), **chaffer** (19C, from **chaff**: to banter with), **chirper** (19C),
clacker and **clack-box** (19C), **flapper** (one 'flaps one's lips'),
prater (fr. 15C SE, meaning talker) and **prattler**; **respirator** and
lung-box point up its breathing role. **Kisser** and **kissing-trap** are
self-evident, although both originated in the jargon of the 19th
century prize-ring rather than that of the romance. **Dribbler**
implies less than perfect manners; **fly-trap**, **fly-catcher** (both late
18C) imply the open mouth of stupidity, and **flatter-trap** (1840)
marks the toady.

As a container for the teeth, the mouth appears as a **bone-box**
(18C), **box of dominoes** (c.1822), **ivory box** (19C), **box of
worries** (19C: worries is surely a mispronunciation of ivories),
spoke-box, and **graveyard** (19C, the teeth resemble tombstones,
a term that itself meant a discoloured and projecting tooth);
coffee-mill (1800) implies not so much the consumption of the
drink, as the grinding of teeth; as a facility for eating terms include
gobbler (19C), **dining room** (1820), **cakehole** (1936 and per-
ennially popular), **potato-box**, **potato-jaw** and **potato-trap** (all
19C), **rattletrap** (1820), **rat-trap** (1920s), **mousetrap** (19C,
mouse appeared briefly too in the 1890s), **sauce-box** (19C,
though the implication might be not of food, but of sauce meaning
cheek), **sewer**, **sink** (also meaning throat) and **coffer**.

Grub, meaning food and rooted in the Dutch *grubbelen*, and hence
the verb form of *grave*, meaning to bury, offers a variety of similar
terms: **grub-trap**, **grub-box**, **grub-shop** and **grubbery** (all
19C). Terms related to drinking include **Gin Lane** (1830, also the
throat, and presumably offering a tip of the hat to William Hogarth's
celebrated engraving of 1751), **grog-shop** (1840), **jug**, **sluice-
house** (1840) and **sluicery** (1820, usually a public house).

Terms for the throat, which often crossed over into those for
mouth (and vice versa), include **gutter alley** and **gutter lane**

(19C, the former also meaning urinal), **Beer Street** (19C, see **Gin Lane**, above), **common sewer** and **drain** (both 19C), **funnel** (18C), **gully hole** (19C), **Holloway** (19C, the punning 'hollow way'; it also meant the vagina, and as **Holloway, Middlesex**, the lower bowel), **Peck Alley** (fr. **peck**: food), **red lane** (18C), **Red Sea**, **Spew Alley** (spew:vomit), **swallow**, **thropple** or **throttle** (14C, Northern dial.), **whistle** (especially as in 'wet one's whistle'), **spud-grinder** and **wicket** (SE for gate).

THE TEETH AND TONGUE

Terms for the teeth include **choppers** (1950), **eating** or **laughing tackle**, **Hampsteads** (1830, rhy. sl. **Hampstead Heath**: teeth; the term outlasted its once equally popular 19C peer **Hounslow Heath**), **pearlies** (19C), and the children's **toothy pegs** (1828). Earlier slang offered **crashing cheats** (16C, **cheat** or **chete**:thing), **rattlers** (19C) **grinders** (17C), **bones** (19C), **dining room furniture** (cf. **dining room**), **munpins** or **mompyns** (15C, 'mouth-pin'), and **nut crackers** (19C). Notably clean teeth were **ivories** (1780), while dirty or discoloured ones were **dominoes** (1820), a **tombstone** was a snaggle-tooth, as is a **snag** (Aus. 20C; thus **snag-catcher**: dentist).

Harman offers **prating cheat** and **pratling cheat** (cf. **crashing cheat**) for the tongue, terms preceded only by the *Ancren Riwle's* **clap** (c.1225). Subsequent terms includer **clapper** (1638) and **clack** (16C), **rag** (1825), **red rag** (17C) and **red flannel** (19C), **dubber** (also mouth), **manchester** (1812, possibly fr. *mang*, meaning talk in Scots dial. and/or fr. Romany *mag*: beg), **glib** (19C, orig. ribbon), **velvet** (17C, particularly in 'tip the velvet', a staple phrase of 19C pornography), **jibb** (19C, fr. Romany *jib* or *chib*, and still found in the phrase **jibb in**: talk one's way in), and **quail pipe** (17C, fr. a pipe used to decoy quail). Farmer and Henley also put forward **toloben** or **tullibon** but Partridge rejects this: the term comes from Romany *tullipen* meaning lard or grease, and at best can be seen as meaning 'paint' (for the face), a theory that becomes more acceptable when one remembers that **ham**, a bad actor, comes from **ham-fatter**, and refers to the those second-rate and thus impoverished actors who were forced to rub hamfat over their faces, as a base for the powder that was then applied, rather than being able to afford sweeter smelling oils.

THE NOSE

As far as slang is concerned, the human nose has two primary functions: sticking out in front of the face, and facilitating the sense of smell. The first area, dominating the terminology, thus gives us **beak** (used by Thackeray in 1854, but probably much earlier: in 1598 the writer John Florio [1553?-1625] defined *Naso adunco* as 'a beake-nose.'), **beezer** (20C, also the name of a popular comic of the 1950s), **conk** or **konk,** (both fr L. *concha*, meaning big nose and immortalised by the nickname Conchy, bestowed upon the suitably adorned Duke of Wellington); the rhy. sl. **I suppose** (mid-19C); **schnozzle, schnozzola, schnoz, snoz, snozzle,** (all from Yid. / Ger. *schnauze*: snout and famously personified by the US comedian Jimmy 'Schnozzle' Durante [1893-1980]); other snout images include **snoot** (20C), **snout** (18C), **snitch** (17C), **nozzle** (1755, from the SE, itself is a diminutive of *nose*), **bowsprit** and **proboscis** (both from SE), **peak** (19C), **gig** (18C), and **leading article** (19C). Sneezing or blowing the nose gives **bugle, honker, horn** and **hooter** (all 20C), **post-horn, paste-horn** and **trumpet** (19C), and of course **sneezer** (1820).

The sense of smell gives the punning **snuff-box** (1853), **snuffler** (19C), **snorter** (1860), **mell** (either from a childish mispronunciation of smell or SE *mell*: club), **smelling-cheat** and **smeller** (both also meaning garden and dated respectively 16C and 17C), **snotter** and **snottle-box** (19C, from **snot**: mucus) and **candlestick** (a runny nose). **Snorer,** while not strictly a 'breathing' term, (1840) is self-evident.

A particularly prominent nose was a **cheesecutter** (19C) and a red-nosed man boasted a **lighthouse** (19C). The prize-ring underlines its particular interest with **claret-jug** (1840, claret:blood). Perhaps the only solo performer is **boco** or **boko** (19C), but then only if one discards the obvious link to **beak**, whether or not combined, as some claim, with **coconut** and turn instead to the alternative etymology: the clown Joseph Grimaldi's [1779-1837] trademark tapping of his nose with the comment, *'C'est beaucoup'*.

THE EARS

Ears are relatively under-represented in slang. **Lug** and **lughole** both stem from 16C Scottish dialect, while **flaps** (20C, occasionally used as a nickname) hints at their shape. A trio of other popular terms are **cauliflowers** (20C, ears deformed through boxing, hence the 1930s boxing term 'cauliflowered and mashed': squashed ears and mashed nose); **tin ear** (20C, no ear for music) and **cloth ears** (20C, unhearing, whether deliberately or otherwise).

THE EYES

16C villains, according to Thomas Harman, called their eyes **glasyers** or **glaziers,** and another old cant word **glim,** meaning light or fire, gives **glims** (18C, although the singular **glim** is still used by market traders today). Later terms include **lamps** (16C), **peepers** (17C) and **ogles** (17C, with its variations **queer ogles**: cross eyes, and **rum ogles**: bright eyes) **daylights** (18C), **optics** (18C) and **killers** (late 18C), and two examples of 19C rhy. sl.: **mutton-pies** (now defunct), and **mince pies** (these days almost invariably known as **minces**). Other 18th and 19th century terms, some of which are still current today, offer **toplights** (18C), **deadlights** (19C), **twinklers** (19C), **front windows** and **windows** (19C), **gagers** (19C US), **blinkers** (18C), **orbs, seer** and **sees** (19C), **winkers** and **spy**. Technological advance gives the 20C **headlights** (more often as spectacles); the modern **babyblues** are generic, the colour of the eyes so described is irrelevant.

Squinting eyes, in an era when physical deformity was openly mocked, bring : **squinters, squinny-eyes, squin-eyes, squint-a-pipes** and **squint-a-fuego** (a pun, presumably, on the 17C **cacafuego★** and on fire, as in **glims★**). **Chaney-eyed** (fr. China or china) meant either small-eyed (the inference is of a China doll), or glass-eyed (china being the original material used for such eyes).

The black eye, given its occurrence in the rough and tumble of the ring or of street life, generated its own small lexicon. The eye itself was a **mouse** (19C), a **shiner** or a **stinker** (19C), while the sufferer had or wore **a full suit of mourning** (both eyes), or of **half-mourning** (one eye). He might also be carrying the **Northumberland arms** (fr. the red and black spectacle-like badge that is basis of Percy arms), a **painted peeper**, or **peepers in mourning**. Bags under the eyes, occasioned not by violence but by tiredness or excess, were **luggage**.

THE NECK

Other than three pieces of rhy. sl. — **three quarters of a peck**, **Gregory Peck**, and **bushel and peck** — terms for the neck include the venerable **colquarron** (16C, presumably from a combination of **col**: neck plus **quarrom***: body) and **scrag** (18C), engendering a number of terms relating to judicial hanging, e.g. **scragging** (hanging), **scrag 'em fair** (the execution), **scrag-boy** (the hangman) and **scragging post** (the gallows). **Squeezer** (1840) has similar overtones of the gallows; indeed an alternative meaning is the noose. Similarly **nub** (c.1670) carries its own grim lexicon: as a verb (and possibly slightly earlier) it means to hang; **nubbing** (hanging), **nubbing-cheat** (the gallows) and **nubbing-cove** (the hangman); the **nubbing-ken** (lit. hanging room) is the sessions house, a cynically fatalistic reflection on the likely outcome of one's appearance there.

THE BREASTS

For the purposes of slang, men have no breasts. Body-builders boast of their **pecs**, from Latin *pectus* and thus the pectoral muscles, but beyond such jargon, the concept is essentially meaningless. Thus the words the words that follow, with careless ideological impurity, refer exclusively to the female.

Perhaps the most common of all 'breast-slang' is **tits** (fr. *teats*, and thus technically referring to nipples — known in slang as **eyes** — but generally used for the whole breast, and latterly even for the whole woman, eg. 'a nice bit of tit'), with such variations as **titty** and **diddies**, but this is surprisngly modern, dating only to the 19C. **Tit**, meaning a young girl, is older, originating in the 16C, but the transference had to wait. Older are **bubs** and **bubbies** (17C, either from Latin *bibere*: to drink, or possibly – in the way that some claim that SE *pap* is onomatopoeic, stemming from the infant's sucking lips – from the hungry child's cries of 'Bub, bub!'). The modern versions – **boobs** and **boobies** – are almost equally as popular as **tits**, although perhaps more so in America.

The SE *bosom*, a word that may be rooted in an Old Aryan term meaning arm, and thus implying the space between the arms, gives a variety of terms that are more or less variations on the basic theme: mainly 20C, they include **bazoom, bazooms, bazoomas, bazongas, gazungas** or **gazongas** and possibly **ballons**.

Among further general terms are **tremblers, hangers** (US), **wallopies** (20C US, especially when large), **chichis** (20C, Mexican), **lungs** (20C), **mams** (20C, from SE mammaries and particularly popular in those soft-core men's maagzines devoted to the 'mature figure'), **Mary Poppins** (20C poss. a nonce use by the writer Tom Wolfe, teasing the otherwise squeaky-clean image of the fictional nanny), **nay-nays** and **ninnies** (possibly from the Spanish *niño*: child, or indeed from nanny), **mountains, globes** (19C), **racks** (of meat), **meat market, blubber, blubber-bags** and **poonts** (1870, possibly from font or even fountain). The protruberance of the breasts give **bumpers, headlights, knobs, knockers** (originally Aus. UK since 1950s), as well as **top bollocks** (20C) and **forebuttocks** (coined by Alexander Pope c.1727). **Cupid's kettledrum** (18C) and **maracas** (20C) presumably hint at the (rough) handling of the breasts.

Rhyming slang has offered **cabman's rests** (breasts), **brace and bits** and **threepenny bits** (tits), **Bristols** (either **Bristol bits**: tits or **Bristol City**: titty), **Manchesters, Jerseys,** (both with the unspoken **City**: titty), **cats and kitties** (titties), **charlies** (Aus.: **Charlie Wheeler: Sheila**★: female, thus objectified as breasts); **gib tesurbs** is backslang for big breasts while **berkeleys** (as opposed to the more common **berkeley**★: vagina), comes from the Romany *berk*, meaning breast. Breasts have also spawned three acronyms: **BSHs** (British Standard Handfuls), **TNT** (two nifty tits), and, much beloved by the US world of burlesque, **T and A** (tits and ass).

While most terms relate to the breasts as objects, sexual or otherwise, their role as the providers of milk has attracted a number of synonyms. **Dairies** (18C, with the phrases to **sport** or **air the dairy**: flash one's breasts), **dugs** and **udders** (19C, both from SE), **milk bottles** (20C, Aus.), **milkwalk, milkshop** and **milky way** (all 19C), **milkers, feeding bottles, pap feeder,** jujubes (20C), **jugs** and **cream-jugs** (originally Aus. c.1920) and **norks**, an Australian term, taken from Norco Co-Operative Ltd, a butter manufacturer of New South Wales.

Finally, the 'edibility' of the breasts gives **apples** (20C), **cakes** (20C, probably from **cheesecake**: pin-ups), **cupcakes, grapes** and **grapefruits, lollies, dumplings**, and **catheads** (US, a type of biscuit). The roundness of all these foods also underlines their supposed resemblance to the breast.

THE STOMACH

Harman's 16th century 'canting crew', usually adept in their adoption of the cant vocabulary, made no such provision for the stomach. They called it a *belly* (rom a variety of European roots, all meaning bag or sack) as did the general populace. Entering the language in the 10C it satisfied such literary authorities as Wyclif and Shakespeare until, c. 1840, Victorian prudishness drove it, if not underground, then into the shadowy borders of colloqualism and slang. There it remains, giving the rhy. sl.: **Auntie Nelly, Darby** or **Derby Kelly, Ned Kelly** (all 20C), **Newington Butts** (guts) and the rarer backsl.: **elly-bay** and **yellib**.

Alternative terms focus on the stomach's capacity, typically as a **victualling office** or **department** (19C), **dumpling-depot** (19C), **breadbasket** (18C), **bread-bag** (19C), **meatbag** (19C), **beer barrel** (19C, also meaning the body as a whole; **beer-belly** means simply a paunch), **porridge bowl** (19C, although **porridge-hole** means the mouth) and **water-butt** (19C). **Tummy, tum** and **tum-tum** (once the nickname of the corpulent King Edward VII) originate in the nursery and generally remain there. The more recent **gizzard** (20C) comes from the 10C SE, used variously to describe animal or insect stomachs, which in turn comes from the Latin *gicerium*: the cooked entrails of a fowl.

Other intestinal terms include **gormy-ruddles** (19C, from *gormy ruttles* = 'the strangles' = horses' quinsies [or tonsilitis]), **kishkes** (a Yiddishism based on the Russian word for intestines), **trankle-ment** or **trollobubs**, (19C), and **pudding** or **pudding-house** (18C) with the combination **pudding-belly** meaning fat, al-though the cant **pudding-ken**, which 'translates' as pudding house, is in fact a cookshop. **Wiffle-woffle** (19C) was a stomach ache.

A fat stomach could be a **bow window** (19C) or a **corporation** (c.1750). This latter, while owing something to the SE 'corpulent', is a dig at the self-indulgent gluttony of the Corporation of the City of London. Thus an **alderman**: a turkey, and an **alderman in chains**: a turkey garlanded with sausages.

The ribs, adjacent to the stomach, are **slats** (20C, first US, then Aus. and finally UK), while the heart can be a **pump** (19C), a **raspberry tart** (rhy. sl.) or a **ticker.** The womb was once known as a **kidney,** while the lungs were **bellows** or **bellers** (19C); thus an earlier version of 'blow one out' was 'give one the bellows'.

THE ARM

Compared with the hands and fingers to which it is attached, the arm has relatively few slang synonyms. Those that do exist, include **props** (19C, also meaning crutches); the rhyming slang **Chalk Farm** (19C) and **false alarm** (20C, mainly military) **bender** (19C, also used for elbow), **hoop stick** (19C), and two terms also used for hand: **fin** (19C) and **daddle** (18C, possibly from **paddle**). The shoulder has a single backslang form: **redloch**.

THE HANDS, FISTS AND FINGERS

Given their interchangeability in standard English, the slang terms for hands, fists and fingers similarly provide a good deal of crossover. It is thus simplest to take them in a single section. Harman gives **fambles** (16C) for hands, and throws in **fambling cheat** (a ring). Half a century later (c.1600) a new term, **goll**, appeared, followed c. 1690 by **fam** and **fem** (both from Romany and presumably abbreviations of **famble**). **Fin** and **daddle** (both of which can also mean arm and finger) are 18C, as is **mauley** (often found in the prize-ring context, and either from SE *maul*, or the Gaelic *lamh*, the Shelta *malya* or the Romany *mylier* – each of which means hand). **Mauler** and **maulers** (fingers) arrived in the 19C.

Slang terms for the hand often compare it to an animal appendage: typically, **paw** and **forefoot** (both 16C, the latter popularised by Shakespeare), **flipper** (19C), **mitten** (19C) and **mitt** (US 19C, adopted in the UK 20C), **pud** and **pudsey** (17C, both possibly from Dutch *poot*: paw).

The grabbing potential of the hand is found in **cornstealer**, **picker**, **clutch**, **feeler** (19C), in which context the terms elide with those for fingers and can also be found defined as such. Further terms, ostensibly for fingers but equally feasible for hand include **claws** (thus the 17C phrase: 'claw me and I'll claw thee', a precursor of the modern 'scratch my back...'), **paddle** (19C), **fives, forks** (18C, specifically the middle and forefingers), **flappers, grapplers, grappling irons, gropers, hooks, lunch-hooks, meathooks** (19C), **cunt-hooks** (20C) **divers, pickers and stealers** (17C, from the mid-16C catechism: 'To keep my hands from picking and stealing'), **Ten Commandments** (15C, especially of a woman), **ten bones, ticklers, pinkies** (19C, Scots dial. a single **pinky** is the little finger), **muck-forks** (mid-19C), **bunch of fives** (19C), **bunch of sprouts** (thus a **sprout** means a beating). In rhy. sl. **lean and lingers** (20C) and **bell ringers** (19C) denote fingers, while **Mary Anns, German bands** (a 19C term that vanished abruptly with the declaration of World War I, and the departure of the once popular German bands from British streets) and the backslang **deenach** mean hands.

Terms mainly applicable to the fists include **dukes** (19C, either from rhy. sl. **Duke of York**: fork, or from the Romany *dukker*, meaning tell a fortune, probably through palmistry); dukes generate such popular phrases as 'put up one's dukes' (prepare to fight with the fists) and 'grease the dukes' (to bribe). A further pugnacious term is **raw-'uns**. (19C). Finally, phrases for shaking hands include **tip a daddle, tip the fives, tip the gripes in a dangle, fam-grasp** and **sling one's mauley**.

THE LEGS

The first recorded slang term for legs is **stamps** (1567), taken directly from their function; it was followed by **pins** (16C, from the primary meaning of *pin* as a peg, and gave such phrases as 'on ones pins': to be feeling well, or in good form) and then by **gams** (1780, from French *jambes*, thus 'flutter a gam': to dance), and **hams** (fr. the 10C SE *ham*: the bend in the back of knee, then, in the 16C, the buttock and upper thigh taken together and thence, somewhat imprecisely, the whole leg). **Hams** thus creates the 18C **ham-cases**: trousers, poss fr. Rom. *hamyas*: knee breeches, **ham-bags**: girls' drawers (c.1900, and presumably a pun on *handbags*) and **ham frills** (c.1925 girls' running shorts). **Ham hocks** and **hammers** are 20C developments. Rhyming slang for legs, possibly coincidentally, offers **ham and eggs** (19C), **bacon and eggs**, **scotch eggs** or **scotch pegs** (19C, now found either as **scotches**, or **pegs**).

Other terms include **drivers**, **drumsticks** (19C), **shanks' pony**, **mare** or **nag** (1795, punning on **shanks**: legs), **stumps** (19C, and now found mainly in the phrase 'stir one's stumps'), **cabbage stumps** (19C), **timbers** (18C, originally a wooden leg but soon any leg), **sticks** (19C), **trams** (20C), **trespassers** (19C), the punning **understandings** (19C) and the literal **underpinners** (19C) and **pods** (19C, esp. of children's legs; thus **podding**: toddling).

The shape of legs accounted for a number of specific terms. **Doog gels** meant good legs, but most terms were derogatory: **cheese-cutters** (1820, bandy legs), **calves gone to grass**, **spindle shanks** and **trapsticks** (all meaning thin legs; the latter taken from the stick used in a popular game); **marley stopper** (fr. the image of stopping a **marley** – a marble – with one's foot; thus splayfooted), **skew-the-dew** (splay footed); **spiddock pot legs** (ungainly; from their supposedly resembling a spigot) and **Irish arms** (thick legs). Knees were **marrowbones** or the rhyming **biscuits and cheese**; **baker-kneed** and **cross-legged** all meant knock-kneed.

THE FOOT

Like much early slang, the first terms for feet reflected the animal kingdom, i.e. **hoofs** (16C), **trotters** (17C) although **trots** did not appear until the 20C. **Dew beaters** arrived in the 18C; similar terms were **dew-dusters**, **dew-treaders**; all also used to describe pedestrians who take dawn strolls — when the dew was still on the grass. Other early usages were **ards** (an old cant term, possibly related to the Nordic *ard*: plough, and which by the 17C and in the singular meant hot, presumably from the French *ardent*), and **hocks** (late 18C and another reference to the farmyard).

The 19C produced **creepers**, **kickers**, **trampers**, **beetle-crushers** (the latter enthusiastically popularised by the still new *Punch*; especially in reference to large feet, and of the shoes that encase them), **understandings**, **tootsies** (nursery use), **boot-trees**, **double-breasters** (19C, specifically when referring to a club foot), **pridseys***, **crabs** (originally shoes), **goers**, **mud flaps**, **plates of meat** (rhy. sl.; the singular **plate of meat**, however, meant street). The 20C has seen a couple of canine additions: **dogs** (US) and **puppies**.

THE VAGINA

Other than terms for drinking, which run substantially over 2,000 according to one recent compiler, and those for sexual intercourse the slang terms for the vagina outstrip any rivals, and certainly those for the penis. There are nearly 900 listed below, and there are doubtless others. They encompass what is generally acknowledged as the most injurious of monosyllablic epithets, and run the course through to some of the most floridly convoluted of literary euphemisms. Aside from general terms there are at least twenty sub-sections into which the larger vocabulary may be grouped. They range through rural-agricultural, antagonistic, terms that see the vagina as food, the many that see it as an entrance, a hole or a slit, those that equate it with places and things and proper names, the coarse, the crude and the romantic. As with any section of this book, many are dead, but a surprising number flourish on. Men think of sex, it is claimed, every eight seconds; the slang lexicon, if nothing else, gives them plenty of terms in which to couch their repetitive mental obsession. If such a mass of terms appears to prove yet again feminism's contention that men see women primarily as sex objects, then so be it. If slang is indeed the most 'man-made' of languages then it is never more so than when dealing with the female genitals.

THE MONOSYLLABLE

The **monosyllable**, a term possibly coined in 1714 but first set down specifically in Frances Grose's *Classical Dictionary of the Vulgar Tongue* (1785), is of course the primary euphemism for that ultimate in four-letter words: **cunt**. Cunt itself 'a nasty word for a nasty thing', as Grose dismisses it, appears as 'C—t', although he offers roots in the Greek *konnos* and the Latin *cunnus*, and lists the French synonym *con*. This reticence was by no means limited to Grose (who, a single entry earlier, was perfectly happy to list **cunny-thumbed**: 'to double one's fist, with the thumb inwards, like a woman): not until its supplement of 1972 did the *OED* (albeit unphased by **prick★**) list the term, and other, lesser dictionaries, on both sides of the Atlantic, showed themselves equally coy. Many otherwise authoritative American tomes, hamstrung either by the religious right or the politically correct left, have yet to break the taboo. Yet as Eric Partridge, writing in 1931 (six years before the term would be included in the *DSUE*), put it, 'to ignore a very frequently used word – one indeed used by a large proportion, though not the majority, of the white population of the British Empire – is to ignore a basic part of the English language.'

The first use the *OED* can find for the term appears c.1230 when *Gropecuntelane* is listed among the streets that made up the **stews** or brothel area of Southwark. Given the environment, it must be assumed that the term was already in general use; it would also appear from subsequent early citations that the term, while vulgar, was descriptive rather than obscene. Lanfranc, for instance, used it while writing on surgery around 1400. But by the end of the 15C cunt had gone off-limits. Two centuries later it was deemed legally obscene: to print the word in full rendered one liable to prosecution. It's most notorious appearance in the dock came in 1960 when it featured as the most abhorrent of those alleged obscenities enunciated so lovingly by the prosecuting counsel in the trial of *Lady Chatterley's Lover*. It has yet, if ever, to return to grace.

As Grose suggested, the word can be traced back to the Greek, although Partridge disputes whether *konnus* – a trinket, a beard, or the wearing of the hair in a tuft – is actually linked to the Latin *cunnus* which meant both vagina and, like such English terms as **crack**, **slit** and **pussy**, the woman (especially if seen as promiscuous) who possesses it. More likely Greek roots are *kusos* and *kusthos*, which are both related to the earlier Sanskrit *cushi*, meaning ditch. *Cunnus* itself, setting a pattern for its descendant, was already outlawed as obscene in Rome. Horace used it, Cicero did not.

While the French, more heavily influenced by Latin, have *con* (and the Spanish *coño*), with its obvious links to *cunnus*, the English **cunt** or *cunte*, as found in Middle English, takes its inspiration from a variety of German (*kunte*) and Scandinavian (*kunta, kunte*) terms. It would appear, in this form, to be a combination of the ultimate root *cu* (which also lies at the basis of cow), which appears to imply quintessential femininity and the *nt* of the European synonyms.

Aside from such obvious diminutives as **cunny**, **cunnikin**, **cuntkin** and **cuntlet**, and such variations as the rhyming slang **Berkeley** (or **Berkshire**, hence the pejorative **berk**) **Hunt**, **sharp and blunt** or **grumble and grunt** (all 19C) and the backslang **tenuc**, directly cognate with **cunt** are **coynte**, **queynte** and **quaint** (which last persisted in Northern dialect until the late 19C). Similar, although linked not to Scandinavia but to Wales, where *awm* means valley (cf. *cushi*, above) are **quim**, **quem** and **quimsby**, the first of which at least is still widely used. **Quiff**, a contemporary back-formation from the 18C **quiffing**: copulation, may well be related, as presumably is **whim-wham** (18C).

Among other 'non-specific' terms for vagina the old Romany *minj*, transformed via Suffolk dialect into the general slang **minge** survives in wide usage, as does **fanny** (plus **fan** and the backsl. **naf**; US **fanny** means only buttocks), a 19C coinage of no discernible etymology, although some theories would link it to John Cleland's mid-18C novel *Fanny Hill* (see **engine** for *Fanny Hill* as a double pun). Combinations with **fanny** give the defunct **fanny-artful** and **fanny-fair**. Other terms include **chuff** (also meaning backside), and the older **cornucopia** (19C, fount of all good things) and **gallimaufry**, (19C, from the 17C SE: mess or jumble and the 17C slang: mistress). **Conjuring book** (with overtones of SE *conjugal*) and **conundrum** presumably stem from the basic **cunt**.

The US has a number of homegrown terms. Foremost among them is **poon** or **poontang** (both 20C), which some attribute to a perversion of the French *putain*: prostitute, while others, Partridge among them, opt for pidgin, from the Chinese, which also has the variants *poong tai* and *poong kai*. **Vag** is an obvious abbreviation, **ginch** (1950s) may be linked to an earlier, British use of **ginch** meaning class or elegance (thus **ginchy**: excellent), while **trim** (20C) parallels the pickpockets' use of the word to mean a back pocket. Seemingly paradoxical is the use of **cock**, otherwise one of the most widely used words for penis, to mean vagina. Restricted to the US South and the islands of the Caribbean, the term may be related to the 18C British term *cockles*, meaning labia. Similarly defiant of a clear etymology are **cooch**, **coot, cooze, cou** and **cuzzy** (all US 20C). They all would appear to be related to **cunt** or even **cock**, but in quite what way remains unknown.

EUPHEMISM

Before moving on to the realms of pure literature, in which one will encounter some of the most elaborate attempts to bypass the naming of the vagina, there are a number of terms of non-literary euphemism, some of which stem from the nursery, and others simply from the strictures of embarrassment. Aside from Grose's **monosyllable, nonny-no** (16C, also a general term for sex) and **naughty** (19C, thus **do the naughty**: to copulate), the squeamish continue to offer the careful Victorian vagueness of **thingamy, thingumabob, thingumajig, what-do-you-call-it, you-know-what, you-know-where, the place, it, that, the thing, that there, the ineffable, the name it not** and **the nameless. Down there, Downshire** and **downstairs** at least point in the right direction, while **scabbard, quiver** and sheath are translations of the Latin *vagina*. **Commodity** and **novelty** (both 18C) return readers to the opaque, while **love-flesh** could be anywhere. Only with **where the monkey sleeps** (19C, an earlier version of the coarser **where the monkey shoves his nuts**: the anus) and **where Uncle's doodle goes** (19C, reflecting Victorian pornography's fascination with incest) acknowledge a less determinedly 'innocent' terminology.

Other euphemisms, or otherwise unquanitifiable terms include **bumbo** (18C, from the West Indies), **cloth, catherine wheel**, **cogie** (Scots), **forge** (19C), **fobus** (late 19C), **agility** (as in 'show one's agility': for a woman inadvertently to reveal her vagina), **tivvy**, (19C, from SE *activity*), **fancy-bit, funny bit** and **funniment** (19C), **fie for shame** (19C schoolgirls' use), the **fleshly part, jewel** (19C, cf. **family jewels**), **knick-knack** (19C) **masterpiece** (18C, cf.16C 'to be hit on the master vein': to conceive), **lea-rigs, never-out** (19C), **non[e]such** (18C), **Number-Nip** (19C), **ware, rest and be thankful** (19C), **old ding** (fr. **ding**: to strike?) and **poor man's blessing** (19C).

LITERARY EUPHEMISM

It is perhaps in literature that one finds the most elaborate of euphemisms to describe sex in general, and the sexual organs in particular. The modern era, sedulously rejecting euphemism for harder-edged narrative offers few such alternatives, but a more mannered world made up for such 20C shortcomings.

With *The Memoirs of a Woman of Pleasure* (1749, better known as *Fanny Hill*) John Cleland (1709-89) managed, quite deliberately, to produce a major pornographic work — one that stood virtually unrivalled until today's mass-market porn boom began in the Holywell Street shops of the mid-19C — without using a single obscenity. His terms for what a contemporary called the **agreeable ruts of life** (punning on both senses of *rut*) included the **cleft (of flesh)**, the **cloven spot, etcetera**, the **central furrow** and the **treasure of love**.

Shakespeare used a wide variety of bawdy, although by no means all of his own creation. Such terms as do appear to be his invention include **circle, commodity** and **dearest bodily part**. More prolific by far was Britain's first translator of Rabelais, the Scot Sir Thomas Urquhart (1611-60). As well as the unparallelled **aphrodisiacal tennis court** (a precursor of the later **gymnasium**) Urquhart offered **callibistry** (fr. **callibisters**: testicles and the suffix -*try*: place of), the **carnal-trap, contrapunctum** (literally *counterpoint*: the penis being the 'point' in question), **cunny-barrow** (punning on **cunny** = **coney** = rabbit), **Hans Carvel's Ring** (a name taken from a popular and bawdy tale by Poggio and Ariosto among others), the **hypogastrian cranny** (fr. the Greek *hypogastrium*: that section of the body below the belly and above the privates), **justum, skincoat** and **leather** (although this last was in general use by the 16C, and had meant *skin* in SE since the 14C).

Robert Burns (1759-96), whose more reputable poetry was balanced, to the delight of some and the horror of others by his collection of what can best be seen as proto-type 'rugby songs' *The Merry Muses of Caledonia* (c.1800). His contributions to the vaginal vocabulary include **canister, Cupid's furrow**, the **gate of life**, **gyvel, mill, nest in the bush, spleuchan, tirly-whirly** and **wame** (fr. womb).

Equally prolific was the 17C playwright and songsmith Thomas D'Urfey or Durfey (1653-1723), author of many satires, melodramas, farces and other tales. His coinages tend to reflect the image of the vagina as receptacle and include **toll dish** (used to measure grain at a mill), the **mouth that cannot bite**, the **placket-box** (fr. SE *placket*: a slit in a petticoat), **sack, kettle** and **copyhold** ('the tenure of lands being parcel of a manor, at the will of the lord according to the custom of the manor'), as well as **weather gig, hone** (a whetstone used to grind knives, as was the 17C **whetting corn**) and the **mark of the beast**.

Geoffrey Chaucer (c.1343-1400) has the delicate **belle-chose** and the much more vulgar **nether end, nether eye** and **nether lips**, while John Donne (1572-1631) opts for both the **best** and the **worst part**, the **exchequer** (prefiguring a number of later vagina as money coinages) and a **part of India** (a geographical reference echoed in **antipodes**, qv). G. A. Stevens opted for lengthier phrases, amongst which are the **eye that weeps most** when best pleased, the mouth that says no words, life's dainty and the book-binder's wife (a pun on her pastime: 'manufacturing in sheets').

Lord Rochester, who shocked the public and outraged the courts when, in defiance of law he spelt out the word 'cunt' in a number of writings, and whose *Poems on Several Occasions* (1680) and play *Sodom:or the Quintesence of Debauchery* (1684) made him the frankest writer on sex until the 20C, still allowed himself some euphemisms. Those for vagina included the kennel, the best in Christendom, the bull's eye (cf. target) and the crown of sense.

Many other writers have added their contribution. The American Walt Whitman (1819-92) has the bath of birth and the lady flower; Thomas Carew (1594-1640) used the slang term Cyprian, meaning whore, to create Cyprian arbour, Cyprian-cave and Cyprian strait as well as the very flowery grove of Eglantine; John Florio (c.1553-1625), translator, tutor and courtier, as well as editor in 1598 of the Italian dictionary *A Worlde of Wordes*, has gear (equally, and more generally applicable to a man) and the positively bodice-ripping Mount-Faulcon; the romantic poet Robert Herrick (1591-1674) has living fountain while Sir Walter Scott (1771-1832) adds the mouth thankless.

Bereft of such pedigrees, the line between simple euphemism and its literary peers is a fine one and dependent as much as anything on the richness of the language involved. On that basis, and on no other, the following terms are included here: Venus's Secret Cell, Venus's Highway, Venus's Honeypot, Venus's Mark, Cupid's Alley, Cupid's anvil, Cupid's arbour, Cupid's cave, Cupid's cloister, Cupid's corner and Cupid's cupboard; the hogstye of Venus may refer to the Homeric goddess Circe, who turned men into swine. Also the ABC, (19C, the start of things, i.e. life), Alpha and Omega, (the beginning and end and thus the ultimate in pleasure), Abraham's bosom (upon which one rests); Adam's own altar, the altar of hymen, the altar of love and the altar of pleasure; lamp of love, love's harbour and love's paradise; the treasure and the mine of pleasure; leading article (19C), almanack (19C), amulet and everlasting wound.

NAMES

Setting aside the pet names that some people create for their sexual organs, slang references to the vagina include a number of proper names. Among them are **Aunt Maria** (1903), a **Dutch clock** (a term taken from the rhy. sl. **Dutch★** = **duchess of Fife** = wife, and which also means a bedpan), **Jacob's ladder** (19C, up which one climbs) **madge** and **Madge Howlett** (18C, also dialect for a barn owl), **maddikin** (possibly from **madge-ken**), **Mary Jane** (19C), the punning **Miss Brown** and **Miss Laycock** (18C), **Molly's Hole,** (19C, from **molly★**: a compliant girl) the **Mother of All Saints**, the **Mother of All Souls** and the **Mother of St Patrick** (all 18C) and **tu quoque** (18C, from the Latin 'you also' and defined by Grose as 'The mother of all saints'). Perhaps the most fascinating is the otherwise impenetrable **Buckinger's boot**, which refers to the hapless Matthew Buckinger (fl.1750) who was born limbless 'notwithstanding which', remarks Grose, 'he drew coats of arms very neatly and could write the Lord's Prayer within the compass of one shilling'; thus for him a boot could only fit his **third leg★**, his penis.

A PLACE FOR THE PENIS

If in slang the male genitals are seen most basically as an object to be placed, thrust or otherwise introduced into the vagina, then a number of complementary terms exist that categorise the vagina as no more than a receptacle for the penis. Many, such as the **confessional** and **Bluebeard's closet** (where respectively **father confessor★** and **Bluebeard★** mean penis) simply reverse or revise the original phallic term. Others of this type include **penwiper**, (19C), **pintlecase** (19C), **pin-case** and **pin-cushion** (17C), **needlecase** (19C, hence **needlewoman★**: a whore), **toolbox** and **tool chest; cuckoo's nest, goldfinch's nest** (1827), **phoenix nest** and **bird's nest**. Even more direct are **pole hole** (20C), **niche-cock** (18C), **prickholder, cock-chafer, cock-holder, the Cock Inn, cock-loft, cock-pit, Cock-Shire,** and **cock-shy**. **Diddly** and **diddly pout** (mid-19C) combine **diddle**: penis and **pouter**: vagina. In **doodle case** and **doodle sack** doodle is the penis. **Naggie** (19C) is the passive element of a set which includes the 17C **nag**: penis and **nags**: testicles. Similar passivity can be deduced from **quarry** (18C), **factotum** and **ornament**.

Less direct are **cradle**, **tickle Thomas** (19C), **standing room for one** (19C) and the **custom house** (**customs officer***: penis), **Eve's custom-house** and the **receipt of custom** (in all of which institutions 'Adam made the first entry'). Finally a group of 'technological' terms involving locks and keys: **machine** (19C, also the penis), **keyhole** (19C), **lock**, **locker** and **lock of locks** (all 18C), and **jigger** (19C, from **jigger**: lock, although elsewhere it means key and thus also penis). Other receptacles include **pitcher** (17C), **pipkin** (17C, from SE for a small earthenware jug; thus **crack a pipkin**: to deflower), **cellar**, **cellarage**, **cellar-door** (19C), **corner-cupboard** (the 'corner' being the fork of the legs), **bucket**, **caldron**, **mortar**, (19C, the opposite of the phallic **pestle***), **box** (20C), **fuzzy cup** (20C), **bag of tricks** (19C, also used for the penis and testes) and **lucky bag**, the 19C fairground equivalent of the latterday *lucky dip*.

SEMEN

If the vagina is a receptacle for the penis, then, logically, it exists equally to extract and receive semen. As with the penis there are very few terms relating to procreation − only the somewhat contrived **certificate of birth** and **brat-getting place** − but several which deal with ejaculation and its product. As well as the punning **seminary** (19C), they include **lather-maker** (19C), **butter-boat** and **melting pot** (**butter** and **melted butter**: semen), **hive** and **beehive** (**honey**: semen) and **honeypot** (17C, but popularised in Terry Southern's *Candy* [1958]), the **cream jug** (cf. **creamstick***) and the **churn** (which 'turns milk into butter'). Semen as 'milk' reappears in **milking pail** and **milk pan**, while **milt market** refers to **milt**, or fish eggs, another term for semen.

PUBIC HAIR

Slang is no great respecter of physiology, and while the pubic hair is not the vagina itself, the terminology happily elides the two.

Terms include **bun** (17C, also meaning squirrel and rabbit, which has strong sexual overtones), **broom**, **busby** (otherwise referring to a military fur cap), the **crown and feathers** (19C), **black bess** and **black jock** (though **jock★** or **jockum★** both mean penis too), **ace** and **ace of spades** (19C, thus 'play the ace and take the Jack': for a woman to receive a man). The **red ace**, **red C** (19C) and **rufus** (19C, from SE *rufous*: reddish) transfer the 'ace' of the hair to the actual flesh. Most obvious are a selection based on the hair itself: the **hair-court** (thus **take a turn in hair court**: to copulate), **Hairyfordshire** (19C, cf. **Downshire** and **County Down**) and the **hairy ring** and **hairy oracle** (18C). Other terms include **oracle**, **muff** (17C), **patch** (19C) and **sporran** (19C).

Natural images dominate terms for the pubic hair. **Garden** dates to the 16C, the **grove of eglantine** (also used as vagina) is 17C as is **sweet briar** (*Rosa rubiginosa*) otherwise known as the eglantine; **Parsley** is 18C, **mustard-and-cress** 19C, along with **grass** (cf. **greens★**), **lawn**, **forest**, **shrubbery**, **moss** (cf. **righteous moss**), **stubble** (giving **shoot in the stubble** and **take a turn in the stubble**: to have intercourse), **hedge on the dyke**, and the literary **boskage of Venus** and **Cupid's arbour**. **Bush**, one of the most enduring terms for male or female pubic hair, is a 19C coinage; similar terms (all 19C) include **damber-bush**, **dilberry-bush** (cf. **dilberry creek**), **gooseberry-bush** (it is this bush of course, rather than the fruiting variety, beneath which the child is allegedly born), **furze-bush**, **quim-bush**, **whin-bush** and the 20C **Fort Bushy**. **Beard** is 18C and **silent beard** 19C, while **brush** (20C) gives the **shaving brush** and the **scrubbing brush**. The animal kingdom gives **bearskin** (19C), **feather** (18C), **fluff** (19C), **fur** (18C) and the punning **fur-below** (18C, from the SE meaning of flounce or trimming). **Fud** (18C, Sc. dial.) and **scut** (16C) both reflect the SE *tail* while **tail feathers** is based on the slang **tail**: vagina, which produces such combinations as **tail fence**: hymen, **tail fruit**: children, **tail gap**, **tail gate** and **tail hole**: all vagina and **tail flowers**: menses, as well as the **tail pipe**, **tail pin**, **tail tackle** and **tail trimmer**, all of which mean penis.

The position of the pubic hair 'down there', gives **Downshire**, the **front door mat**, the **lower-wig**, the **nether eyebrow**,

nether lashes and **nether whiskers** (all 19C); its proximity to the vagina creates **belly-bristles**, **quim whiskers**, **quim-wig**, **cunnyskin**, **cunt-curtain**, **motte fleece** and **mott-carpet** (all 19C); **twatrug** is 20C. Further terms include **area** (19C, abbrev. of SE *pubic area*), **cotton and wool** (19C), **banner**, **plush**, and a **lady's low toupee**; **cuffs and collars** (20C) denotes pubic hair the same colour as head hair.

FEAR AND LOATHING

The concept of the *vagina dentata* in a physical form may have been abandoned but, as much feminist theory would claim, male fear and even hatred of the vagina persists unabated: emotions that are faithfully reflected in slang. The menace of a term such as **snatch**, with its variations **snatch-blatch** and **snatch box** (all 19C) is undeniable, as is the loathing implicit in the **parts of shame**, the **vaccuum**, the **sperm-sucker** (19C), the **suck and swallow** (19C), the **wastepipe** (19C), the **stank**, **stench trench**, **stink** and **stinkpot** (all 20C).

Similar emotions are found in **fool trap** (c.1840, which also means a whore), **flycage**, **flytrap** and **fly-catcher**, (19C, with the additional image of an open mouth catching flies) and **bite** (17C, although the term may in fact come from the Anglo-Saxon *byht*: the fork of the legs). **Magnet** (18C), **regulator** (18C: the vagina as power), **fort** and **fortress** may imply a grudging respect, but **rattlesnake canyon**, **snapper**, **snapping turtle** (**puss**) (20C), **nasty**, **bit of rough**, **touch 'em up**, **tuzzymuzzy** (1710) and **catch-em-alive-o** are unequivocally antagonistic, as are **mangle** (1860), **manhole**, **man-trap**, (18C), **eel-pot**, **eel-skinner**, **prick-skinner** and **skin-the-pizzle**, (19C) **rasp**, (19C), **rattle bollocks**, (18C), **rob the ruffian** (19C), **rough-o**, **rough-and ready** and **rough-and-tumble** (all mid-19C). Less aggressive, but certainly dismissive are various references to physical deformities, mainly coined in the 18C: **blind eye**, **dumb glutton**, **dumb oracle** and **dumb squint**. Nastiest of all are **claptrap**, **firelock**, **fireplace** and **firework**, in all of which **clap★** and **fire★** refer to venereal disease.

THE HOLE

In terms of direct language, equating hole with vagina is as basic
as one can get. Unsurprisingly such terms abound. **Hole** itself dates
to the 16C or even earlier; there are several combinations: **hole of
content** (16C), **hole of holes**, **queen of holes**, **Holloway** and
upper Holloway (twin puns from 1860), **pigeonhole**, **bunghole**
(usually found as the anus), **sportsman's gap** and **sportsman's
hole** (19C, a term that mixes the huntsman's image of a gap in a
hedge with the term **sporting house**★ meaning brothel), **touch
hole** (17C) and **sear** (16C) both referring to the touch-hole at
which the match sets off the charge in a pistol, **black hole** (19C)
and **black ring** (19C), **dark-hole** and **second hole from the
back of the neck**. **Glory hole** is 20C, although it is often found
as gay jargon, referring to holes bored in the inter-connecting walls
of public lavatory stalls. Inner depths are similarly suggested by
dark, **cave of harmony**, **bore** and **maw**, while **ring** too dates
back to 16C. Other 'holes' include **drain** and **gully** (both 19C),
grummet (19C, from the SE use to mean a ring of rope and latterly
a washer), **furry hoop** (20C) and **golden doughnut** (20C,
Australia). Finally darkness, circularity and depth combine in **pit**
(17C), **bob and hit** (rhy. sl.), **pit hole**, **pit mouth**, **pit of
darkness**, **bottomless pit** and the marginally more congratula-
tory **passion pit** (20C, but also popular as a drive-in cinema,
where, as in the synonymous **Olympic pool**, one 'does the breast
stroke'). While not specifically holes, **open C** (19C) and **open
charms** (a pun on open arms?) make their meaning obvious.

THE SLIT

As popular as **hole** is **slit**, a term that originates in the 18C and
perhaps because of the relatively greater physiological accuracy,
there are more 'slit' terms than 'hole' ones in slang. They include
chasm, **crack** (16C, personified a century later as meaning whore
as well), **cranny** (19C, thus **cranny-hunter**★: penis), **crevice**
(19C), **gap** (18C), **gape** (19C) and **gaper** (19C), **canyon**, **breach**
(19C), **ditch**, **furrow** and **one-ended furrow** (both 19C), **gulf**,
gutter (19C), **gash** (18C), **slice of life** (cf. **agreeable ruts**...),

slot, **trench** (18C), **grotto**, **harbour**, **harbour of hope** (19C), **alcove** (19C), **arbour** (19C), **chink** (18C), **dyke**, **prime cut**, **notch** (18C) and **nick in the notch** (19C). **Inglenook** means slit, while **crinkum-crankum** (1780) has an SE meaning of a narrow, winding passage (although **crinkum★** itself means venereal disease). A **dimple** draws on the SE meaning of a depression in the flesh, while **placket**, used by Shakespeare in *King Lear* (1605) is the opening or slit at the top of a skirt or petticoat, for convenience in taking it on and off.

Most 'slit' terms are relatively quotidian but one, **twat**, led to a lexicographically celebrated misunderstanding. **Twat** has meant vagina since 1656: it is related to *twachylle* or *twittle* which, as *twitchel* mean a narrow passage; a dialect usage, *twatch* means to mend a gap in a hedge; combinations include **twat-masher** and **twat-faker** (pimp) and **twat-rug** (pubic hair). None of which it turned out, was apparent to the poet Robert Browning (1812-1889) who in 1841 published *Pippa Passes*, a mainly verse 'drama' drawing on his studies of Elizabethan and Jacobean plays and known today for its blithe assurance that 'God's in His heaven, all's right with the world.' As part of his research Browning read the poem 'Vanity of Vanities' (1660), in which he found the couplet 'They talk't of his having a Cardinalls Hat, / They'd send him as soon an Old Nuns Twat.' The coarseness of the verse was lost on the poet, who simply assumed that **twat** denoted some part of a nun's attire. Thus in *Pippa Passes* he wrote blithely, 'Then, owls and bats / Cowls and twats, / Monks and nuns, in a cloister's moods, / Adjourn to the oak-stump pantry.' Others were less innocent, and the lines remained a good source of schoolroom sniggering. Browning was never to be disabused of his belief: he died in happy ignorance since no-one could find a delicate enough means of explaining his error.

PERSONIFICATIONS

As well as the proper names above, the vagina is subject to a wide variety of personifications, few of them particularly complimentary. A number of terms meant prostitute as well as vagina: notably **gigg** (18C), **fly by night** (19C), **housewife** (19C), **shakebag** (a whore in 18C, a vagina in 19C), **breadwinner, scate** and **flap** (17C), while others were alternatively used for the brothel: **button-hole,** (19C, **buttonhole factory**: a brothel, **buttonhole-worker**: a whore), **cab-mat** (**cab**: brothel), **case** or **kaze** (fr. *casa:* house and thus brothel) and **goatmilker** (c 1840, originally meaning whore, while **goat house** meant brothel). The **milliner's shop** (19C) may have referred to the real-life milliners, many of whom could found working as **dollymops**, or semi-amateur whores to supplement their meagre income.

Other terms include the 'musical' trio of **instrument, fiddle** (1800, cf: **strum**: strumpet), and **lute** (upon which one 'plays').**Itch**: sexual excitement gives **itcher** and **itching jenny** (19C) while slang's eternal propensity for puns gives **old hat** (17C, 'because it is frequently felt'), **saddle** (17C) and later **omnibus** (19C, 'everyone gets a ride'; like the 20C **town bike★ omnibus** also meant a prostitute or promiscuous amateur), and **sampler** (19C, from its image of 'needlework'). **Tile**, itself slang for hat, may be related to old hat. Further terms include **vade-mecum, wanton ace** (cf: **ace**), **jing-jang** (possibly from **jig-a-jig★** meaning copulation) **joxy** and **jock** (though **jockum★** also means penis).

Woman seen purely as a sex object, and as such personified by her vagina can be seen in **keifer** (also **kaifa, kyfer**), **booty** (20C, a synonym for US **ass★**), **futy, futz, pfotz** and **pfotze,** (19C and US 20C, all may stem from a euphemism for **fuck★**), **downybit** (19C, also an attractive girl) **coupler** (fr. SE *coupling*: sexual intercourse) and **basket-maker** (18C, **basket-making★**: copulation.)

More complimentary, or at least neutral, are **beauty, little sister** (19C), **bed fellow, brown madam** (18C), **chum, Lady Jane** (1850), **Lady Berkeley** (presumably from **Berkelely Hunt★**), **old woman** (19C, as in **old man★**: cock), and **spinning jenny** (19C, from the machine patented in 1770 by James Hargreaves).

The relations of the vagina and money, or at least its money-making potential, underpin a number of terms, although a few, notably **ha'penny** (20C) and **ninepence** (19C?), with their euphemistic use towards and amongst young girls (as is **peewee**, though with no monetary overtones) must be allowed some degree of innocence. Less naive are the openly materialistic **money-maker** and

money-spinner (both 19C), **till** and **money-box** (both 19C) and
purse (17C, also meaning scrotum). Others include **bank, bazaar**,
and **budget**. Race and geography come into the remaining terms,
of which only the first, the **Irish fortune** (19C) survives. Others
are the **Whitechapel fortune** (19C), the **Tetbury portion** (18C,
'a cunt and a clap'), the **Rochester** and **Whitechapel portions**
(17C, 'two torn smocks and what Nature gives') and the **Tippe-
rary fortune** ('two **town lands** [the breasts], **stream's town** [the
pudend] and **ballinocack** [the anus]' Grose).

PLACES

The vagina has also become identified with a number of places,
real or otherwise. **Botany Bay**, the **Antipodes** and the **South
Pole** (19C), stress 'physical' geography, as well as hinting at the 20C
go down south, meaning to perform cunnilingus. **Cape Horn**
puns on **horn***: an erection or sexual excitement, **Cape of Good
Hope** stresses expectations, while **County Down** is a double pun.

Mons Meg (19C) refers, according to Partridge, to a 15C gun
kept in Edinburgh Castle, while **Jack Straw's Castle** (19C) was
named for a leader of the Peasants' Revolt (1381) and as a pub near
Hampstead Heath latterly patronised by Charles Dickens, William
Thackeray and other Victorian literary heavyweights. The use of
Exeter Hall, better known for its temperance sermons and as the
first London home of the YMCA, was presumably a tease, while
Fumbler's Hall (18C) was a purely metaphorical image, as are
Lapland (fr. the Shakespearian **lap**: vagina), **Leather-Lane** (fr.
leather*), **Mount Pleasant** (19C) and **Shooter's Hill** (upon
which the amorously inclined might 'take a turn'). The **Nether-
lands** (18C) are, of course, synonymous with the **low countries**,
and in turn the **lowlands**. The **Thatched House (under the hill)**
may have referred marginally to the actual Thatched House Lodge
(built for the keepers of Richmond Park in 1673 and subsequently
owned by Prime Minister Sir Robert Walpole) but its real inspiration is **thatch** as in pubic hair; the cognate **house under the hill**
stresses the 'down there' aspects of the phrase, further emphasised
in the 'decadent' illustrator Aubrey Beardsley's (1872-98) title for

his sole and unfinished erotic novel *Under the Hill* (1898). The 'under' motif is also found in **under-belongings, under-dimple, under-entrance, under-world**, plus the punning **undeniable** and **undertaker**.

Less geographically specific are a number of other places, such as the **palace of pleasure** and **garden of pleasure** (hence the **garden padlock**: a menstrual cloth), **pleasure boat, pleasure ground, pleasure place** and **privy paradise** (all 19C); the **happy hunting grounds** (1870, more usually equated with death) puns on the 'Wild West' usage. The vagina could equally stand as **heaven** or **hell** (18C, thus **put the devil into hell**: a phrase taken from Bocaccio and meaning to copulate). It could also be **home sweet home** (1870), a **hotel** (19C, cf: **Cock Inn, Cupid's Arms**, etc), a **leaving shop** (19C, originally an unlicensced pawnbrokers), the **nursery** (19C), **premises** and **lodgings** (both 19C) and the ecclesiastical **pulpit** or **vestry** (thus **vestryman***: penis); finally, though physically paradoxical, it could be the **attic** (1903).

Physiologically more accurate are those terms that refer to the bodily centrality of the vagina. They include the **central office, centre of attraction** (both 19C), **centre of bliss** (18C), **centrique part** (coined by John Donne), the **Middle Kingdom** (an acknowledgement of the 19C fascination with things Egyptian), the **midlands** (19C), **middle-cut, axis** and **central cut**.

ROAD

To persist with 'geography', the vagina has also been seen as a road. Such images include **road** itself (17C), the **road to a christening**, the **road to heaven, alley, pipe, tunnel, turnpike, main avenue, covered way** (fr. SE, with a nod to the farmyard use *to cover* meaning copulate), **love-lane, smock alley** (**smock** in such contexts usually suggests female immorality) and the **crooked way** (all 19C). **Cock Alley** was imaginary, but a real **Cock Lane** (in the City) was in the 14C the only street down which London's prostitutes were licensed to ply their trade in public; the Great Fire was supposed to have stopped at its junction with Giltspur Street, while in February 1762 thousands of the curious (including Dr.

Johnson, the Duke of York and other grandees) flocked to number 33 Cock Lane to hear the scratchings and knockings of the alleged 'Cock Lane Ghost'. Modern 20C coinages add **Dead End Street**, **highway**, **joy trail** and the **red lane** (usually meaning throat).

ENTRANCE

At the end of the road lies the **front gate** or **entrance**. Front gives **front bum** (cf: **top bollocks***), **front door**, **front attic**, **front parlour**, **front window**, **front-gut** and **front garden** (all 19C) while under entrance there are **belly entrance** and **gut entrance**. Allied terms include the **ivory gate** and **Marble Arch** (1850), the **way-in** (19C), **wicket** (19C), **hatchway**, **forecaster**, **forecastle**, **fore-court**, **fore-hatch** and **fore-room** and the punning **Gate of Horn**.

NATURE

Somewhere between the elaborate constructions of literary euphemism and the various real and fictional place-names above, are terms that relate the vagina to Nature, especially in its rural embodiment. 'Country matters', as Shakespeare nudgingly puts it in *Hamlet* III ii.

Nature itself and **nature's tufted treasure** are augmented by such flowers as the **daisy** and **rose** (18C, especially of virgins), the **teazle** (19C), the fantasy **flower of chivalry** (punning on chivalry: 'riding' and thus copulation), the **moss rose** (and its peers the **mossy bank**, **mossy cell** and **mossy face**, all referring to **moss**: pubic hair, as do **Bushey Park**, **belly dale** and **belly dingle**), **evergreens** (punning on **greens***: sexual intercourse), and the **fruitful vine**, which 'bears flowers [menstruation] every month'. Such a **bower of bliss** or **beauty spot** is to be found in the **garden** (16C) or even **garden of Eden** (originally a 16-17C British euphemism, now more popular among Afro-Americans), where also can be found a **flower pot**, a **seed plot** (both 19C), a **shady spring** and a **miraculous cairn** (although the logic of cairn, meaning a hill or pile, in a context of bowers and valleys, seems obscure). Beneath the **clouds** there may be a **nettle bed**,

parsley bed or **gooseberry bush** (all traditional euphemisms for 'where babies come from', although girls, it was claimed, came from parsley, while boys owed their origin to the posionous nettle or the spiky gooseberry, a term also used in the plural to mean testicles). Finally comes the **orchard** (19C) with its allied term **get Jack in the orchard**, meaning to have sex.

WATER

Resolutely orientated towards the sexual aspects of the vagina, slang tends to sidestep the urinary aspects of 'down there'; nonetheless there remain a number of terms dependent on water, although whether this refers to urine, or to vaginal secretions or even to the common, if slandrous, identification of the organ with fish depends on the word or phrase in question.

Such terms include **pisser** (19C, also found as penis), **stream's town** (19C), **sluice** (17C), **waterbox**, **water-gap**, **water-mill** and **water-course** (all 19C) as well as **fountain of love**, **wayside fountain** and **wayside ditch**, **damp** (possibly coined by Terry Southern in *Candy*), **pump** and **pump dale** (17C) and **duck-pond**. 'Fish' terms include **fish** (19C), **tench** (19C, either from the fish's name or from an abbreviation for pentitentiary, in which the penis is 'imprisoned'), **trout**, **tuna**, **bit of fish**, **bit of skate**, **shell** (19C), **whelk**, **periwinckle** (19C), the **fish market** and the **free fishery**, **lobster pot**, and Shakespeare's **peculiar river** (*Measure for Measure* I ii., with its bizarre synonym for copulation: **groping for trouts in a peculiar river**). The **oyster** and **oyster-catcher**, are echoed in the titles of a pair of late Victorian pornographic magazines: *The Pearl* and *The Oyster*. The **bearded clam** rose to popularity through the exploits of Barry Humphries' mid-1960s creation, the Australian Candide 'Barry McKenzie'(feted in the pages of *Private Eye*), whose efforts, when not focused on alcohol were concentrated on an endlessly unrewarded quest to 'spear' the self-same bivalve.

Ling (16C UK, 20C Australia), another fish, gives **ling-grap-pling★** (intercourse) and works either as the vagina or as the female sexual odour. Thus the old music hall song, c. 1835, which tells the tale of a girl attempting to buy a fish the name of which she has forgotten and runs in part: 'Then the girl shoved her hand 'neath her clothes in a shot/And rubbed it about on a certain sweet spot;/Then, blushing so sweetly, as you may suppose, she put her hand up to the fishmonger's nose./The fishmonger smelt it, and cried with delight,/.../'I'll tell you directly, you wanted some *ling*.'

FOOD

While 'eating' in a sexual context usually refers to oral sex, the vagina offers a wide range of 'edible' terms. General concepts include a **bit of jam**, a **bit of mutton**, a **bit of meat**, a **bit of pork**, a **bit on a fork**, a **bonne-bouche** (fr. the French for 'pleasant taste', anglicised as 'tasty morsel') and **yum yum**, which can be consumed from a **lunch box** (20C), an **oven** (18C, source of the phrase a **bun in the oven**: pregnant) or the **kitchen** (1860), where the **roasting jack** 'turns the meat'. The equation of human flesh with metaphorical meat offers **meat** itself (thus **meat-merchant**: pimp, **meat-house**: brothel, **flash the meat**: expose oneself), and the **meat market** (both 16C), **mutton** (as vagina c. 1670; as whore, especially as **laced mutton**★ since 1518), **bacon sandwich** (20C, **bacon hole**, however, means mouth), the **butcher's window, chopped liver** (cf. **chitterlings**★: penis). All these are garnished at the **mustard pot** (19C). The pubic hair gives another small list, including **fud** (originally a rabbit's tail and thus doubly sexy), **furburger, fur pie, fuzzburger, hair pie** (all 20C, with the last also meaning cunnilingus). **Finger pie** (brought into the mainstream by a Beatles' lyric) means the manual stimulation of the vagina. Secretions of whatever sort give **dripping pan, gravy-giver** and **gravy-maker** (18C, **gravy**: 'spendings') while **cut and come again** was originally defined by the lexicographer John Bee as 'the meat that cries "Come eat me!". **Catsmeat** (19C) refers more to the use of **pussy**★ than to meat itself, as does the acronym **PEEP** (20C US, 'perfectly elegant eating pussy'). **G**, for goodies, may be stretched to ally it to food. Truly bizarre is **fart-daniel**, a 19C term meaning literally a sucking pig that is the youngest of a litter, a term more usually written **fare-daniel**, and therefore possibly a misprint.

Other than meat, the vagina as food encompasses **apple** (a back formation from from 16C **apple squire***: a pimp), a **medlar** (17C), a **fig** (19C and connected to the physical act of 'giving the fig', ie sticking one's thumb up between two forefingers), **groceries** and **split-apricot**, **split fig** and **split mutton** (all 18C). Vegetables include **greens** (already widely used to mean copulation and thus a pun on 'get one's greens'), a **green meadow** (1850), **cabbage, cabbage field, cabbage garden** and **cabbage patch**, **cauliflower, mushroom** (19C) and **sweet potato pie** (AA).

Finally a group of 'sweets' available, as it were, in the **coffee-shop** (more usually found meaning lavatory). They include **jam** (19C), **cookie** (US, meaning biscuit), **muffin** (20C), **pancake, jellybag** (17C), **jellybox** and **jelly roll** (20C) and **jampot** (19C, combining the image of a receptacle with two further definitions of **jam** as semen and menstrual blood). Other food receptacles are **sugar basin** (19C) and **saltcellar** from the 19C use of *salt*: lecherous, itself a development of its 17C meaning of copulation.

ANIMALS

Last, but far from least, come those words that equate the vagina with a variety of animals, most notably with the **cat**. **Pussy** must be one of the most widespread of such terms, although it appears no earlier than the 20C. **Puss**, on the other hand, dates back to the 17C, while such variations as **catty-cat, kitty, kitty-cat, chat** (fr. the French *chat* = cat = puss) and **poozle** (fr. puss?) all appear in the intervening centuries. Earliest of all are **malkin** and **rough-malkin**, from 16C Scots *malkin*, meaning cat; *grimalkin* is often the name of a witch's feline familiar, while **malkin** itself also means hare, suggesting a link to the rabbit, a traditionally 'sexy' animal, that may or may not be coincident.

Other animals that have been seconded to slang include the **cushat** (the wood pigeon or, more linguistically pertinent, the ring dove), the **mink**, the **civet** (18C), **dormouse** and **monkey** (19C US, 20C Aus). **Mouse, mouser** and **mousetrap** (all 19C) are equally valid, as is **rooster** (19C: where the cock roosts). **Tail** remains widely popular, especially in America, where **magpie's nest** (18C) has become an Afro-American term. **Mole-catcher** reflects **mole*** meaning penis, while the original use of **mumble-peg** (19C) was to mean mole-trap. Finally the pubic hair gives **fur** (18C) **fluff**, (19C), **beaver** (20C) with the porn trade jargon **split beaver** and **pink** for the wide-open vagina.

THE PENIS

THE GENITALS

Before passing on to the substantial list of individual terms, all meaning penis, one should preface this section with those terms that apply not merely to the penis, but to the whole genital area, ie. the penis and testes. Underlying a good many of these is the idea of, almost literally, a tool-box, neatly packed with what one requires for sexual and procreative efficiency. Such terms include **accoutrements, equipment, gear** (SE since the 16C, but rendered improper by the Victorian language police and thus slang since mid-19C) and **marriage gear, tackle** and **wedding tackle** (18C), **kit** (19C), **necessaries** (20C), **luggage** and **bag of tricks** (20C). **Basket** was widely popular in the gay world, thus giving the pursuit of **basketeering**: wandering the street eyeing up the groin area of passing men; any relationship to the 18C **basket-making*** (sexual intercourse) is purely coincidental. Other terms include **lady ware** (19C), **crown jewels** and **family jewels** (20C, the latter being adopted by the CIA to categorize its most secret of secrets) and **rig** (giving the term **donkey-rigged**: possessed of a notably large penis). **Nature** (19C, also **pioneer of Nature**) gives the additional **nature's scythe** (the penis), **nature's privy seal** and **nature's treasury** (the vagina), and **nature's duty** (intercourse) and **nature's founts** (female breasts).

A number of more or less humourous terms have evolved, each describing the penis and attendant testicles: **string and nuggets,**

three-piece set, meat and two veg, watch and seals (19C, this also means sheep's head and pluck or viscera), and Gore Vidal's **okra and prunes** as created for his novel *Duluth* (1983).

A final set of terms are as euphemistic as they are slang, and while by no means restricted to the nursery, bear all the signs of the childish mentality: **down there**, **genials**, **naughty bits**, **rude parts**, and **you know where**. The bulk of these are equally applicable to the vagina.

COCK, PRICK AND TOOL

Of the succession of primary slang terms for penis listed by Professor Geoffrey Hughes in his study *Swearing* (1992): **cock** (appears c.1400), while by no means the earliest coinage, has, with **tool** (1252) and **prick** (c.1592), best lasted the linguistic course and it is worth considering them as a group, before moving on to more diverse, if less instantly recognizable terms. **Weapon**, **tarse** and **limb** all appeared around the beginning of the 11C, but died out, at least in this sense, by respectively 1370, 1700 and c.1900. **Tail** also predated the survivors, appearing c.1362, but while it still plays a role in the slang lexicon — either as the buttocks, the vagina or as a generic term for women — it has not meant penis per se for some time. **Yard** (see below) also predates **cock**, **tool** and **prick**, first appearing in 1379, but it vanishes in the late 19C, and has not been in regular use for many years.

Cock comes from the Latin *cuccus*, the male domestic fowl. Thus the term has been used for any object that resembles a cock's head. As far as its use as a sexual term is concerned, **cock** here mixes the basic image of the cock as rooster (to use the 19C US euphemism) and the cock's head seen as a tap-like shape, this secondary aspect emphasized by its function in 'pouring' semen. **Dinosaur** (20C) reflects the shape of the head, while **spigot** (19C, with its companion **spigot-sucker**: fellatrix) points up the pouring aspect.

While Shakespeare, whose affection for the double entendre is almost as great as his more celebrated literary achievements, has a number of early 'cock' references in his plays, notably in *Henry VII*, i.e.: 'Pistol's cock is up and flashing fire will follow', Professor

Hughes has unearthed the early 15th century lyric, 'I have a gentle cock', which, for all that its earlier lines do appear to describe the barnyard fowl, its last verse declares with unambiguous sexuality, 'And every night he percheth him/In my lady's chamber'.

Despite the undoubted nudge-nudgery of these early uses, **cock**, like so many kindred terms, remained in perfectly standard use until Queen Victoria's coronation, shortly after which it joined the ranks of the taboo. It has yet to return to the mainstream. As far as its other slang uses are concerned, only as meaning 'man', and as such usually found as **old cock**, or as in the phrase a 'cock and bull story' (the 17C equivalent of the more recent 'shaggy dog story') is it likely to be used without at least some restraint.

Although Eric Partridge (*DSUE* 7th. edn.) suggests that **prick** is another term that started its life as SE before being dispatched to the linguistic outer darkness at the turn of the 18C, the *OED*, with its first citation in 1592, annotates it unequivocally as 'coarse slang'. Certainly this initial quote – 'The pissing Boye lift up his pricke.'(R. D. *Hypnerotomachia*) –appears coarse to modern ears, but **piss★** too was still SE at the time. It should also be noted that fifty years earlier, in 1540, **prick** was used to denote 'a pert, forward, saucy boy or youth; a conceited young fellow'; the term is defined as 'humorous or contemptuous', but not indecent. It might have referred simply to the lad's 'sharpness', but given the synonym alongside which it appears – **princock** (or prime cock) – one is inclined to opt for sexuality. Whatever the truth, **prick** had certainly declined by 1680 when it is found in Lord Rochester's devotedly pornographic *Poems on Several Occasions*. Cognate are the 18C **needle** and **wimble**, which in the 13C meant a gimlet.

While **cock** relates the human organ to the shape and sexuality of the fowl, **prick** points up the penetrative function of the penis. A number of terms based on **prick** similarly underline the role of the vagina as its receptacle: **prick-purse**, **prick-scourer**, **prick-holder** and **prick-skinner**. Thus **prick-scouring** and **prick-chinking** both mean copulation and **prick-pride** an erection. The long-defunct **pintle**, from the Anglo-Saxon *pintel* and as such SE from 1100 until 1720, was another variation on the **prick** or **pin** = penis model. **Pintle** generated a wide range of combinations between the 17C-19C including **a pintle-bit**, a **pintle-maid** or **pintle-merchant** (a mistress or whore), **pintle-blossom** (a bubo or chancre), **pintle-fever** (VD in general); **pintle-case** (vagina), **pintle-fancier** or **pintle-ranger** (a promiscuous girl) and **pintle-smith** or **pintle-tagger** (a surgeon).

Tool, with its roots in the Old Norse word *tol*, meaning to prepare or to make, and its direct ancestry in the SE term for 'an instrument of manual operation', basically echoes the penetrative imagery of **prick**. It also takes on the function of the earlier **weapon**; indeed 19-20C criminals talk of **tools** meaning weapons, and work **tooled-up** when necessary.

Cock, **prick** and **tool** have survived as the leaders, as it were, of the phallic pack, but that pack is extensive, disparate and takes in terms from four centuries of linguistic development. However, there are certain identifiable areas, some of which stem from the major terms already discussed, and prior to attempting an overview of the wider list, it is possible to assess those related groupings.

MEMBER

The term **member**, reminiscent of the defunct **limb**, a direct translation of the Latin *membrum virile*, and an abbreviation of virile or privy member, has remained SE since its first appearance in the 13C. There are, however, a number of terms that use **member** and which must be seen as slang, albeit of the heavily punning variety: **dearest member** (1740, used by Robert Burns), **jolly member** (19C), the **member for Cockshire**, (1840, with its extra pun on **cock**; cf. **County Down★**: vagina) and **master member**. The **unruly member** (19C), however, is the tongue, a phrase based on lines 5-8 of the *Epistle to St. James*.

WEAPON

'Draw thy tool; here comes two of the house of the Montagues.' warns Sampson in the first scene of Shakespeare's *Romeo and Juliet*, and receives the quick response, 'My naked weapon is out'. Along with such sexually implicit armaments as **instrument**, **sword**, **poll-axe**, and **lance**, **weapon**, as used here, underlines Shakespeare's affection for innuendo, and the role of the penis as a weapon remains central to the slang vocabulary, Shakespearian or otherwise. The terms engendered offer **arse-opener** and **arse-wedge** (both 19C), **bush-beater** and **bush-whacker** (20C, punning on **bush***: pubic hair; the term also means mugger), **battering piece**, **plug-tail**, (17C), **beard-splitter** (18C, **beard***: pubic hair), **hair divider**, **hair-splitter**, **cherry splitter** (20C, **cherry***: maidenhead), **split rump** and **rump-splitter**. **Belly-ruffian** (17C), **dong** and **ding-dong**, while not weapons as such, are undoubtedly aggressive terms. A **bow** shoots arrows (presumably of desire), although the term may refer to the sawing motion of the fiddler's bow; cf. **fiddle***: vagina. Finally **quimstake** and **quimwedge** (and the abbreviated **wedge**) play on the 17C term **quim**: vagina and are as such cognate with the Celtic *cym* and thus, like so many such terms, with the ur-slang synonym: **cunt**. More 20C terms include **chopper** (which had an earlier life meaning tail, which, with nice circularity, means both penis and vagina), **swack**, **swipe**, **twanger**, **wang**, **wanger**, **wang-tang** and **whammer**. **Helmet** (sometimes as **German helmet**, presumably of the World War I vintage, adorned with its spike or *pickelhube*), while undoubtedly part of one's armoury in standard English, and meaning glans in slang, is only a marginal contender in this section.

While the following terms too are not weapons as such, they all denote a degree of aggression. The woman, in these cases, is always on the receiving end, and pleasure, if it exists, is purely coincident: among them are **eye opener**, **girl-catcher**, **girlometer** (1870), **leather stretcher** and **leather dresser**, (19C, **leather***: vagina), **trouble-giblets**, **tickle-gizzard**, **tickle-toby**, **tickle-tail**, **tickle faggot**, **tickle thomas**, and **bum-tickler**. The Northern dialect **pillock** (sometimes known as **pillicock** or **pillicock pistol** – like **prick** and **dick** also used as a pejorative) dates back to the 14C (thus **pillicock hill**: vagina). The **placket-racket** (17C) uses placket to mean woman and thus, objectified, vagina; the penis as racket 'hits' her. **Enemy** may be purely literary; its implication is also quite unequivocal.

KNIFE AND DAGGER

Aside from the general weapons above, and echoic of the stabbing implications of **prick**, there are several terms based on a sword, knife or dagger. They include **dagger** itself, **dard** (meaning dart), **love-dart**, **lance of love**, **dirk** (18C), **bayonet** (19C), **blade**, **bodkin** (fr. SE:dagger), **butter-knife** (**butter***: semen), **bracmard** (17C, a short broad sword, from the French *braquemard*), **pike** and **pikestaff** (18C), **cutlass**, **culty-gun** and **cutty gun**, (19C, all from the Latin *cultellus*: knife), and the contemporary trio: **pork sword**, **beef bayonet** and **mutton dagger**.

GUN

'This is my rifle, this is my gun,' chant the hapless recruits drilling in America's boot camps, their M-16 clasped in one hand, their penis in the other, 'this is for fighting, this is for fun'. The penis as pistol, confirming feminism's most pessimistic stereotyping, has a venerable history: not for nothing is Shakespeare's braggart soldier, cited at **cock** above, named Pistol. Later sexual hardware includes **bazooka** (originally an anti-tank rocket launcher, first used in World War II), **cannon**, **gun**, and the Afro-American **peace-maker**, a term that springs either from the nickname of the Wild West's legendary Colt .45 revolver, or, just possibly, from the ironic nickname accorded the nuclear arsenal's MX missile.

STICK

The shape of the penis, as well as its function, gives **stick**, **blow stick**, **gutstick**, **fuckstick** (20C), **drumstick** (19C) and **shitstick**. Similar terms include **prod**, **prong**, **ramrod**, **reamer**, **rod**, **wand**, **pipe** (20C, thus to **lay some pipe**: to have intercourse), **pole** (19C, thus the US campus slang for sex education courses: **holes and poles**), **tube**, (19C) **pile-driver**, (19C) **pilgrim's staff** (18C), **sceptre**, **spindle** (19C), **staff of life** (19C, punning on the phrase's usual meaning, coined in 1638, of bread or any other staple food) **shove-straight**, **spike-faggot** (fr. the 17C use of **faggot**: woman), **wood**, **tentpeg**, **rolling-pin**, **roly-poly**, **ploughshare** and **dib-**

ble (fr. the gardening implement, a dibbler). **Copper-stick** and **coral branch** both refer as much to the organ's colour as its shape, as does **rubigo** (a Scots term of the 16C, possibly from the Latin *ruber* meaning red). The implication of **gigglestick** (technically US rhy. sl.), **joystick** and **joy prong** (all 20C) is more of pleasure than of pain and the **wriggling stick** or **pole** (18C, thus to **wriggle navels***: to have intercourse) is presumably as pleasurable as it is merely penetrative. **Broom-handle** and **clothes-prop** (both of which imply the erect organ) must be listed with the 'sticks'. Similar implements are the **gulley raker** and **kennel raker** (19C, also applied to the man who does the 'raking') and the **handstaff** (19C, from that part of a flail that is held in the hands). Less obvious is **langolee**, which Partridge surmises as being from the Welsh *trangluni*, meaning tools. **Yard**, one of the earliest slang words for penis, is rooted in a variety of terms, typically the Old Teutonic *gazdjo*, all of which mean a thin pole; the word is also possibly linked to the Latin *hasta*, meaning spear, and even to the Italian *cazzo*, also slang for penis. Certainly the 17C **gadso** and **catso** are borrowings from the Italian original and like a number of similar terms mean both penis and rogue or villain.

Alongside these 'stick' terms are a variety of 'clubs'. These include **hammer, bludgeon, club, claw-buttock, pestle** (which in other contexts meant a constable's staff, although it is found here as the logical opposite of **mortar**, meaning vagina), **life preserver** (a form of truncheon or sap) and **billy** (either from the mid-19C **billy***: truncheon or a pun on the **billycock*** hat). The **sensitive truncheon** (19C) is more usually found meaning the human nose.

HUNTER

Finally come those terms which anthropomorphise the penis as a hunter. Among them are **cunny-catcher**, punning on the 16C **coney-catcher***, a conman, itself punning on **coney**: a rabbit, **Nimrod** (19C: the 'mighty hunter' of *Genesis* with an additional punning nod towards **rod**), **crack-hunter**, **cranny-haunter** and **cracksman** (all 19C) and **hunter** itself.

FOOD

The image of the penis as food — either as a sweet or, with the obvious inference of the masculine attributes of the bull as meat — gives rise to more terms. The first category includes **yum-yum** (19C, also the vagina), **sweetmeat**, **sugarstick** (18C, and the logical opposite of **sugar basin**★: vagina), **lollipop** or **ladies' lollipop** (19C), **tummy banana** (20C), **lunch** (20C) and **pud** (thus to **pull one's pud**★: to masturbate). As well as the **pork sword**, the **beef bayonet** and the **mutton dagger** (above) meat terms include the simple **meat** itself (16C, thus **a bit of meat**★: intercourse), as well as **beef** (19C, to **do** or **have a bit of beef**★ is for a woman to have sex), **hambone**, **tubesteak** (20C), **white meat** and **dark meat** (20C, depending on race), **sausage** and **live sausage** (19C), **butcher** (thus the **butcher's shop**: the vagina), **goose's neck** and **gooser** (both 1870s) and **turkey neck** (20C, particularly favoured by the writer Charles Bukowski, but also used, albeit as a simile, by Sylvia Plath in *The Bell Jar* [1971]). The idea of a **meat cleaver** implies that here the vagina, rather than the penis, is the flesh in question. **Schnitzel** and **schnickel** come from the German, meaning a veal cutlet and usually found since the mid-19C as the *Wiener* (Viennese) *schnitzel*, coated with egg and breadcrumbs, fried and often garnished with lemon, capers, anchovies. Finally there is the **crimson chitterling**; chitterlings being the small intestines of animals, especially pigs. It may simply be coincidence that the one country house to be named in the 19C pornographic novel *The Modern Eveline* (c.1840) is called Chitterlings. More carnal treats come in **marrowbone**, **marrowbone and cleaver** and **marrow-pudding** (all 19C).

Still in the realm of the edible, we have the **creamstick** (19C), although the **cream** in question is semen, and its modern successor, the **ice cream machine**, as well as **goober** (US: peanut) and **bean** and **bean-tosser** (19C, presumably from the shape). **Gristle**, while usually inedible, falls into this section. Among Shakespeare's many euphemisms for penis is the **poperin** or **poperine pear**, which in this case lends its shape to the phallic synonym. The 'poperin' in question is the town of Poperinghe, in west Flanders. It comes in

Romeo and Juliet, that repository of so much innuendo. 'O Romeo, that she were/An open *et-caetera*/thou a poperin pear! 'says Mercutio. Indeed the term may even, as Eric Partridge suggests in *Shakespeare's Bawdy* (1947) offer a second level of doublespeak, with **poperin** punning on 'pop her in'. **Et-caetera*** is of course a literary euphemism for vagina. **Jargonelle**, an early ripening brand of pear, is another linguistic penis-substitute. It appeared in the 18C and was originally limited to what gardeners condemned as a second-rate variety; it may be pure coincidence that in French the fruit is known as *Cuisse Madame* or lady's thigh.

RHYMING SLANG

Rhyming slang terms for penis include **almond** (19C, from **almond rock**, although the plural **almond rocks*** means socks) and **dickory dock** (19C); the Irish **colleen bawn** (19C, lit. 'the fair girl') and **Marquis of Lorne** (20C, both **horn**), **Uncle Dick** (20C, **prick**, although it also means sick, thus giving **dicky*** as in **dicky ticker**: a weak heart), **mad Mick** (Australian), **Pat and Mick, stormy Dick** (US), **Hampton rock** (cock) and **Hampton Wick** (19C prick) a term that underlies the period joke, as recorded by Julian Franklyn in his *Dictionary of Rhyming Slang* (1960), concerning the young woman who claimed that her flat had been furnished by Waring and Gillows when in fact all her luxuries had been provided by *Hamptons*. Why, as Franklyn asks, East End Cockneys should opt for an outer London suburb rather than the adjacent Hackney Wick as the basis for the term remains unknown. The backslang **enob** means bone.

NAMES

Pet names for the genitals abound – they are not even attempted here. Nonetheless the penis has attracted a number of proper names, all of which can be categorised as general slang rather than bedroom intimacy. Perhaps the most obvious, even if one usually forgets that it is a name, is **dick**, the use of which is almost as widespread as **cock** or **prick**. The term emerged from the British Army around 1880, and presumably is a variation on the once

equally popular **John Thomas**, although some authorities see it as
yet another development of **dirk**★. The term soon passed into
general use, although one should note World War I's cynical
translation of the DSO (Distinguished Service Order) as 'dick shot
off'. Perhaps the most celebrated occurrence of **John Thomas**,
whose variants include **man Thomas**, **Tommy**, **Master John
Thursday**, **Master John Goodfellow**, **Julius Caesar** (19C) and
Jack Robinson, is in D. H. Lawrence's once taboo novel *Lady
Chatterley's Lover* (1928), with its bucolic couplings of 'John Thomas'
and 'Lady Jane'. The term originated c.1840 and remains in use,
albeit somewhat self-consciously; the abbreviation **JT** is also popular. Its alternative meaning, that of servant, barely survived the turn
of this century. **John Willie** is a similar term, which was taken up
as a pseudonym by one of this century's most famous and sought-
after illustrators of bondage and discipline pornography.

Other names include **Jacob**, (19C, a reference to the Biblical
Jacob's ladder — up which one climbs), **Jack in the box**, (19C, which
pops up), **Captain Standish**, (18C, who 'stands erect', and ranks
among a number of contemporary' Captains' including **Captain
Hackum**★: a thug, **Captain Cheat**: a card sharp and several more),
Don Cypriano, (17C, used by Sir Thomas Urquhart in his
translation of Rabelais, a work which included a wide variety of
new, if literary, slang coinages), **Jezabel** (19C), **Dr Johnson**, (18C;
possibly on the model of **John Thomas,** although Partridge
suggests 'there was no-one Dr Johnson was not prepared to stand
up to'). The US use of **Johnson** for penis is unlikely to stem from
the great lexicographer but relates, more probably, to the boxer Jack
Johnson (if any individual is involved), or simply as a development
of such terms as **jock**★ or **jack**★.

Little Davy and **Master Reynard** (the latter usually repre-
senting the fox) are both 19C, as is **Nebuchadnezzar** (19C, from
the Babylonian monarch's reputed appetite for grass, and thus
greens★: sexual intercourse). **Old Blind Bob** (19C), **old Horney**
and **old Hornington** (18C) and **old Rowley** (which also means
the devil) convey a certain affectionate tone. **Old Slimey** is merely
descriptive. **Peter** and **Robin** (the pet name for a servant's penis
in *The Modern Eveline*) are linked to **John Thomas**; **St Peter** 'keeps

the keys of Paradise' while **Sir Martin Wagstaffe** 'wags his staff', **Roger** (1650) also means to have intercourse, and a century later the name was one regularly given to bulls. Finally come the essentially alliterative **Percy** (best-known in the Australian phrase for urination, **point percy at the porcelain★**, although also used as the title of a deeply embarrassing film of the Sixties), while **Polyphemus** (19C) is taken from Homer's *Odyssey*, where he is a Cyclops, distinguished by his single eye and thus a distant relation to the modern **one-eyed trouser snake** and **one-eyed brother**. The **bald-headed hermit** (19C) bears a similar implication.

As well as these proper names the penis has been variously personified as an **old man** (19C), **customs officer** (he exacts his 'duty' on 'entering'), **milkman** (although this usually implies a masturbator), **rector of the females**, (17C) **ranger** (18C) and **solicitor general** (presumably a pun on SE solicit) and **vestry-man** (the vestry being positioned at the **entrance★** of the church).

NURSERY TERMS

The terms used either to or amongst children to describe the penis are, by their nature, euphemistic, but they have also entered the slang lexicon. They include **peenie**, **weenie** and **wienie** (US, from the similar term meaning sausage, and known in Britain's delicatessens as a Vienna), **willy** (the almost universal term of choice in today's schools, and thus today's homes), **winkle** and **winky** (the second of which implies the 'one-eye' of the urethra), **doodle**, (18C), **peewee** (19C) and **tinkle** (a term similarly used for urination). **Dicky** (1870) is the child's diminutive of **dick**.

GENERAL TERMS

There are many other terms for penis, a wide selection of which follows. They come in no particular order, and unlike those above often defy obvious structure; such links as do exist will be noted.

For instance the physical aspects of copulation give **jigger**, (originally meaning key but also vagina), while **jig-a-jig★** means copulation), **do-jigger**, **jiggling bone** (19C), and **driving post**, while the shape of the flaccid penis gives **flip-flap** (1650), **flapper**,

flapdoodle (17C), **floater** (19C), **crank** (20C), **derrick** (a crane)
dangler (19C, cf. **danglers**: testicles), **dingle-dangle** (19C), **pen-dulum**, (19C, which swings back and forth) and **dingaling** (best
known in rock 'n' roller Chuck Berry's song 'My Dingaling'). The
idea of the penis burrowing into some dark tunnel gives **maggot**,
ferret, (thus **ferreting**: copulation), **chutney ferret** (20C, usually
in the context of sodomy) and **mole** (which wanders around in
the dark, although a mole was for a time a promiscuous girl —
although this may well be a variation on **moll**★, and as such related
to another unlikely term, **doll**, also more usually meaning a girl)
plus its dialect cousin **mouldiworp** (literally 'earth-thrower' and
almost universal amongst the UK regions), **cunny-burrow** and
cunny-burrow ferret, and **mouse** (19C). The basic physical
connection of sexual intercourse also offers **joint**; the Northern
dialect **tadger** or **todger** may also have a similar meaning, if it
comes, as some have claimed, from the term **tadge**, meaning to
join. **Nag** and **bob-my-nag** (17C) both trade on the meaning of
nag as horse, and thus 'ride' and thus sexual congress.

Music offers **blue-veined piccolo**, **blue-veined trumpet** and
indeed **blue-veined steak**, as well as the **flute** (18/19C), best
known as the **skin flute**, the **living flute** or the **silent flute**.
Fiddle-bow may have musical overtones, but **fiddle** here means
vagina, as in the cognate **fiddle-diddle** (19C), where **diddle**
means sexual intercourse; similarly **whore-pipe** is not something
one plays upon, but simply inserts. Less tuneful, but loosely related
to the 'blue veins', are **Bluebeard** (fr. the children's story, and Henri
Landru, France's real-life seducer and serial killer who ended his
days on the guillotine) and **Blueskin** (otherwise meaning mulatto
and best-known as the nickname of an 18C villain).

Engine, much beloved of John Cleland (1709-89), whose *Mem-oirs of a Woman of Pleasure* (1748-49), better known as *Fanny Hill*
(itself quite possibly a reference to **fanny**★: vagina, and *hill* with its
implication of 'mounting') is celebrated for its being the only major
pornographic novel to have achieved its effects without the use of
obscene language (which has never, however, preserved it from
being censored for obscenity), has generated a number of allied
terms. Among them are **machine** (19C) and **love machine** (20C),

fornicating engine, fornicating tool, fornicator and **forni-cating member** (19C), **garden engine** and **gardener** (19C, from **garden***: vagina), **gaying instrument,** (19C, **gay**: sexually active) and **generation tool** (19C, **generating place**: vagina). **Tool** itself, of course, falls into this category. The size of such engines gives the modest **inch** (properly from its function of 'inching in'), the boastful **nine-inch knocker,** and **four-eleven-forty-four,** an Afro-American term that refers to supposed dimensions of four inches in circumference and eleven long. The Yiddish **schlong,** from the German *schlange:* snake) and popularised in Philip Roth's *Portnoy's Complaint* (1969) has a certain onomatopoeic heft, while **kidney wiper,** given human anatomy, presumes impressive length. The unqualified **knocker** relates to the vagina as a door, as do **key** (18C), **picklock** (17C) and **knock Andrew** (though this is more likely a misprint of **nockandro***: the buttocks). **Chink-stopper** and **gap-stopper** are self-evident. **Sky-scraper** (19C) comes from the name for the topmost sails on a large sailing boat.

Slang terms for penis can often be used as pejoratives: **prick** is an obvious example. Others include **dork, plonker** (massively popularized by the BBC-TV series *Only Fools and Horses*), **schmuck** and **putz** (both Yiddish and nearly always found as putdowns, although the former is somewhat more affectionate), **yoyo** (20C) and the allied **dorkbrain** and **dickhead,** based on dick. However in the case of **fool sticker** and **fool maker** (both 19C) the 'fool' is presumably a cuckolded husband.

Nature is represented in **stalk, tail*, root, man root, old root** and **Irish root** (1830); **Irish toothache** means an erection. Such terms should also include **bog bamboo, sensitive plant, acorn** (fr. which great oaks grow) and **arm** (notably apostrophised in the comedian Lenny Bruce's description of a large penis as 'a baby's arm with an apple in its fist'). The animal kingdom offers **worm, hog, bird, big bird, beak, white owl, cuckoo** (possibly an amplification of **cock**), **rabbit** (fr. the species' allegedly non-stop copulations) and **strunt** (1608, in SE the fleshy part of animal's tail), while human anatomy has **thumb of love, stump, big foot Joe, third leg, middle leg** and **best leg of three** (19C). An alternative version since World War I has been **short arm**, often found as 'short-arm inspection', the military inspection of the genitals for VD. **Pizzle** meant the animal penis until c.1520, when it became slang for the human variety. The etymologically puzzling **tallywag** (18C, plus **tallywagger**, **tallywhacker** and **tallywock**) may be related to **tail**, but the original tally was a notched stick, and that connection too would not be impossible. **Pecker**, if it is related as some suggest to SE *beak*, should be ranked in this section as should its derivative **pecnoster**, (a pun on **pecker** and *paternoster*).

Horn has meant sexual excitement as much as it has the penis in which it is generated, since the 18C; like **honker** it can also mean nose. The use of horns in a variety of phrases meaning cuckold, especially to **wear the horns**, while logically related to the horn as penis, apparently comes from an old German farming practice of grafting the spurs of a castrated cock on the root of the severed comb. These transplants would grow into horns, sometimes several inches long. The German word *hahnreh* or *hahnrei*, meaning cuckold, originally meant capon, a castrated cock.

Euphemistic terms, especially popular in literary use, include **Aaron's Rod** and **Adam's Arsenal**, **Father Abraham**, **father-of-all** and **father confessor** (thus the **confessional**: the vagina), the **old Adam** (19C, a standard English term for original sin), **arbor vitae** (18C, from the Latin meaning tree of life), **athenaeum**, (early 20C, from its original meaning: a group of persons meeting together for mutual improvement), **my body's captain**, (coined by the US writer Walt Whitman) and **Cupid's torch** (possibly lighting the corridors of **the Cupid's Arms** or **Cupid's Hotel**: the vagina). The best example is probably **pego** (18C), supposedly from the Greek *pege* meaning spring or fountain. Other terms include **trifle**, **toy**, **ware**, **knack** and **piece** (usually found as meaning woman). Even more euphemistic are those terms which fail even to identify the object in question. These include **it** (19C, although **it** is more widely found meaning vagina) **dingus**, **doover** (fr. *doofah*, meaning gadget or thingummy), **that**, **the Lord knows what** (17C), **what Harry gave Doll** and **what's its name**. **Affair** and **concern** (c.1840) are both suitably vague. **Privates** and **private property** (both 19C) epitomize these evasions.

While so many terms concentrate on the aggressive image of the penis, some are less devotedly macho, even if the point of view is still that of the man. Such terms include **partner, matrimonial peacemaker** (19C), the **wife's best friend** (20C), usually found in the phrase 'shake hands with...', meaning urinate), **good time** (as in 'I'll give you a good time...', although the traditional whore's come-on – 'Fancy a good time...' – obviously bears other interpretations), **ladies' delight, ladies' plaything** and **ladies' treasure, merrymaker** (19C), and **master of ceremonies. Lullaby,** which 'puts one to sleep', and **lamp of light** may be numbered amongst these gentler images. The procreative aspects of the penis are almost wholly subsumed in the sexual ones, but **child-getter, baby maker** and **brat-getter** (all 19C), pay the function at least a modicum of lip-service.

Finally in this lengthy selection are those terms that defy categorisation of any sort. **Jock,** (18C, and for the next century used to describe the female genitals as well) comes from the otherwise obscure cant term **jockum,** cited by Harman in his *Caveat* as meaning penis. Thus **jockum-cloy** meant to have intercourse and a **jock-gagger** was a man living upon the earnings of a prostitute. Other discrete terms include **end** (as in 'get your end away'), **rudder** and **sternpost** (combining the SE meaning of *end* – in this case of a boat – with the protruberant aspects of the penis), **ID** (fr. SE *identification,* as in 'let's see your ID'), **string** and **wire** (20C, thus to **pull one's wire***: to masturbate), **jammy** (20C, mainly found in the lyrics of rap music and on the streets that produce them), **woofer, yang, ying-yang** and **yutz.**

ERECTIONS, IMPOTENCE, SIZE AND CIRCUMCISION

Terms for the erect penis, other than those incidentally cited above, include **Bethlehem steel** (US) and **Britannia metal** (UK), **blue vein, bone,** and **boner, prong, scope, cockstand** (18C) and **stand** (19C), **horn** (see above), the **stiff deity, stiff and stout, jack, hard-on, bit of hard** and **hard-bit, fixed bayonet,** the **old Adam, lance in rest, spike** and **stiffie** (20C). The partially erect penis is the **lob** or **lazy lob,** while an impotent organ is an **Irish**

horse, a **dropping member, muddy waters** (AA) or **Hanging Johnny** (especially if suffering a venereal disease as well) and a **dead rabbit** (fr. **rabbit**). The **brewer's droop** refers to impotence through an excess of alcohol, while to be **piss proud** is to have an early morning erection. To achieve an erection is to **get a hard-on**, **get a stand** and so on, as well as to **be in one's Sunday best**, the Aus. **crack a fat** and the 19C **bring up by hand**.

Given male worries about such dimensions, there exist a number of terms for the large and small penis – although given the prevalence of those worries, perhaps there should be more. The small penis can be an **IBM** (not the computer firm but 'itty bitty meat') or a **puppy**; a **stringbean** is thin; large penises are **donkey-dicks**, and those who have them are **donkey-rigged**, **hung**, **well-hung** or **donkey-dicked**. If the penis is larger at the top than at the base it is **bell-topped** or **bell-swagged** and **rantallion**, according to Francis Grose describes 'one whose scrotum is relaxed as to be longer than his penis'.

As most British schoolboys learn, a circumcised penis is a **round-head**, while its uncircumcised cousin is a **cavalier**. There are other terms, especially for circumcision, many of which, unsurprisingly, feature 'Jewish' references. Among these are the **Jewish compliment** (also found as 'a large penis and no money'), **Jewish corned beef** (US, salt beef in Britain), **Jewish National** (the reference is to America's Hebrew National brand of kosher salami), **Jew's lance** and **kosher dill**. Non-Jewish terms are the **one-eyed boy with his shirtsleeves rolled up** and a **low neck and short sleeves**; a circumcised penis has been **clipped**. The foreskin is **lace curtains** or a **snapper**; the uncircumcised penis is **blind** or **near-sighted** and known, at least in gay use, as **Canadian bacon**.

TESTICLES

Of the best-known terms for the testicles, three had a lengthy career as SE until the constraints of Victorian English consigned them to the world of slang. **Ballocks** (now more generally **bollocks**) dates from 11C SE, **stones** from the 12C and **cods** (later **cobs**) (initially meaning the scrotum) from the 14C. They are followed by the 16C

culls or **cullions** (both from the French *couillons*: testicles) and the 17C **jelly-bag** (also the vagina), **nutmegs**, and **pounders**. **Nicknacks** is 18C (cf. **nick-nack**: vagina), as is **nuts** (and its 19C successors **nerds** and **nerts**); **baubles** and **bawbels** (18C, although Shakespeare uses **bauble** as the penis itself) and **bobbies** and **bobbles** (19C) see the testes as items of jewellery, and thus prefigure the 19C **trinkets** and the modern **family jewels**. The 19C has **balls**, perhaps the best-known of all such synonyms, plus **bum-balls** and **cannonballs**, **knackers** (fr. northern dialect use), **eggs in the basket**, **pills**, **clock-weights**, **bullets**, **marbles** and **pebbles**, **seals** (which 'seal' a sexual bargain) and **love-apples**. **Thingumibobs** is euphemistic and reminiscent of the 17C **whiblin** (the term vanishes after 1652), which also means thingumibob, but is defined by Farmer and Henley as a eunuch. **Dowsetts** play on the 17C SE: deer's testicles, while **goolies** was imported via the Indian army, whose soldiers drew on the Hindi *goli*: a bullet, ball, or pill. The 19C also has the rhy. sl. **tommy rollocks** (ballocks) and **Niagara Falls** plus the backslang **slabs**; 20C rhymes include **flowers and frolics** (ballocks) and **orchestra stalls**. Other 20C terms include **rocks** (as in **get one's rocks off***), **sack o'nuts**, **grand bag**, **frick and frack** (20C AA) and the Spanish **cojones**, much celebrated in Ernest Hemingway's tales of macho derring-do. To be castrated is to be **two stone under weight** or **two stone wanting** (18C), **unpaved** or **stoned**.

THE POSTERIOR

Among those words categorised as 'Anglo-Saxon' the basic slang term for the posteriors, backside or 'rear end', **arse** can rightly claim pride of place. Whether spelt a-r-s-e, or, as in America a-s-s (possibly a tribute, albeit subconscious, to lexicographer Noah Webster's 19C attempts to simplify English spelling) the term can be found in Old High German, Old Norse. and a variety of other Teutonic and Scandinavian languages. Its nearest relation is the German *arsch*.

Indeed the term goes back even further, with definite links to the Greek *orros* and *orsos*. In English it dates easily back to 1000 when it is spelt *ars*, *ears* or *ars*; the modern version appears around 300 years later. It should be noted, however, that despite the prevalence of the **arse** spelling in Britain, Shakespeare opts for **ass**, often in a punning context, on several occasions.

Like many similar terms, **arse** did not begin life as slang: until c.1660 it was quite respectable, but henceforth it entered the realms of the taboo, to be resisted in polite conversation and printed only after the exclusion of crucial consonants, typically by Francis Grose in his *Classical Dictionary of the Vulgar Tongue* (3 edn. 1796), who prefers 'a--e' to the fullblown word. It remained off-limits, at least in print, until 1930, when Frederic Manning earned himself a good deal of notoriety for spelling it out in his memoir of World War I, *Her Privates We*. Since then the word has become decreasingly terrifying, and combinations such as **arse about**, or **can't tell one's arse from one's elbow**, while yet to join standard English, can reasonably be considered as colloquialisms, rather than hard-core slang. That said, **arse/ass**, remains one of those 'filthy words' cited in 1978 by the US Federal Communications Commission as indecent, if not actually obscene.

THE ANUS

The basic term for anus remains **arse-** or **asshole** (18/19C) and it is the 'hole' element that provides a number of terms, notably **bunghole**, **cornhole** (20C, thus **cornholing**: sodomy), **porthole** (17C), **ring** (19C), **quoit** (Aus. 1920s), **round mouth** (1810, sometimes as **Brother Round Mouth**, whose 'speech', of course, is a fart, as is that of the **backdoor trumpet**), **roundeye** and the somewhat arch **monocular eyeglass** (1860). The same 'eye' is responsible for **backeye** (plus **backslice** and **backslit**) as well as **deadeye** and **blind eye**, while the shape offers a couple of fruits – **medlar** (17C) and **date** (20C, both Aus. and market traders) – as well as **freckle** and **blot** (Aus. 1930). The defecatory function of the anus is seen in terms going back to Chaucer, where **tewel** or **tuel** meant literally a pipe. More recently the image persists in the 20C **dirt chute, poop chute, shit chute** and **shitter,** as well as the 'travelling' implications of the **dirt road,** the **tan track** and the **Hershey highway** (Hershey bars being America's most popular chocolate). The **brown-eye** and **brownie** refer to the excrement itself, as does the earlier American **Brunswick** (although this may have some relation to **heinie,** meaning buttocks and similarly rooted in a German name).

The hollowness of the anus also produces **gazoo** and **kazoo,** both of which are probably rooted in **keister** or **keester.** This 19C US term also means the back pocket of a pair of trousers, a safe, and the suitcase carried by street salesmen, from which they display their wares. **Satchel,** meaning anus, is a logical extension.

Extending from hole to notch, one finds **nock** (18C) and the 17C **nockandro** (1611, possibly from notch plus the Greek *andros,* meaning man). The modern Afro-American **gripples** is rooted in the 15C when SE *gripple* meant a small ditch or trench, itself stemming from the 11C *grip,* meaning the same thing. Given its function, and slang's inevitable earthiness, there are also references to the smell, typically **spice island** (1810), **winker-stinker, stank** and **stench-trench** (all 20C) and **Roby Douglas,** an 18C reference to a hapless individual of that name, blessed with 'one eye and a stinking breath'. **Windmill** and **windward passage** both refer to unpleasant odours. Finally, of no particular grouping, are **trill** (possibly a pun on the Latin *ars musica*), **jacksie** (19C, probably from **jacksy-pardy,** also meaning anus), **dinger** (Aus. 1935, from ring or perhaps dung) and **nancy.** This last is usually found in the rudely dismissive phrase 'ask my nancy'; its relation to the same word when meaning homosexual is unproven, although they both appear around 1810.

THE BUTTOCKS

What **arsehole** is to anus, so is **bum** to buttocks. Despite popular belief, **bum** is not an abbreviation of bottom, but an onomatopoeic term, echoic of the smack of one's backside hitting a flat surface, and as such coined as early as 1387. The word is also allied to a variety of terms meaning protruberance or swelling, typically *bump.*

The actual abbreviation is **BTM**, essentially a children's euphemism. **Arse** itself is responsible for a variety of rhy. sl., notably **bottle and glass**, **khyber pass**, and the particularly complex **arris** (Aristotle = bottle = **bottle and glass** = **arse**); other rhymes include **Daily Mail (tail)**, **North Pole** and **Elephant and Castle** (both **arsehole**). Buttocks gives **butt**, the Afro-American **butter** and **booty** and the West Indian **batti**. **Kab edis** is backslang for backside while **double juggs**, has a satisfying onomatopoeia.

The shape of the buttocks offers **cheeks**, **blind cheeks**, **two fat cheeks and ne'er a nose**, and **blind Cupid**. **Ampersand** has the requisite curves but properly recalls the fact that in late 19C nursery alphabets the symbol '&' was usually printed after the twenty-six letters. **Juff** (possibly from the French *joues*: cheeks) carries on the image, as does **chuff** (Aus. then UK 20C) and **duff**.

The protruberant aspect of the buttocks offers **jutland**, **keel**, **stern** and **poop** (both referring to the rear end of a ship, although the latter has been co-opted as a nursery term for excrement), **caboose** (19C from the rear part of first a coach and then a railway train), and **tail** (standard English from 14C to 1750, thereafter more colloquial than slang, and currently more American than British). The 'seating' function of the buttocks creates the obvious **seat**, **sit-me-down**, **sit-upon** and **squatter,** as well as **parking place** (20C, reminiscent of the US radio comedian Harry Parke [1904-58] who worked under the stage name of 'Parkyakarkus'). Similar in position is **dummock** (19C, possibly from the Romany term for 'back'), as are the **seats of honour**, of **shame** and of **vengeance** (all 19C).

From Yiddish comes **tochus** (variously spelt as **tokhes**, **tokkus**, **toches** and even **tush** – they all stem from a Hebrew word meaning 'under' or 'beneath'). German offers **heinie** (stemming from the World War I nickname for the German enemy and based on Heinrich), while Spanish gives **culo**. The gay community is credited with **Dutch dumplings**, **English muffins** and the **Greek side.**

Other random terms include **prat** (cited in Harman's *Caveat* in 1567, and still the basis of show business' 'prat-fall'), **fun** (17C, from fundament), **dopey** (18C, originally a beggar's doxy), **droddum**

(19C), **corybungo** (19C, initially prize-fighters' jargon), **fanny** (US 1920, but used in Britain to mean vagina from at least 1860), **Sunday face** (19C), **Westphalia** (19C, a pun on Westphalia ham), **feak** (19C, possibly from *feague*: to thrash), **gooseberry grinder** (19C, often in the phrase 'ask Bogey the gooseberry grinder', a euphemism for 'ask my arse') and **can** (20C, also used widely to mean lavatory).

DEFECATION

EXCREMENT

Three words dominate the excretory lexicon: in order of entry into the language they are **turd**, **crap**, and **shit**, the first two of which emphasize the way that excrement is detached from the body, while the third concentrates on the idea of excrement as waste.

Unlike so many so-called 'Anglo-Saxon' words, **turd** does have a real claim to the title, stemming as it does from the old English *tord*, and indeed beyond that to an Indo-European root that means tear or split. Emerging into popular use around 1000, and as yet merely descriptive of a common bodily product, **turd** became a pejorative around 1250. By the time of Harman's *Caveat* (1567) his translation of the cant phrase 'Gerry gan the Ruffian cly thee' is 'A torde in thy mouth, the deuill take thee'. Gerry is literally **jere**, itself meaning **turd**. The phrase continues, appearing typically in Ben Jonson's *Bartholemew Fair* (1614) and elsewhere. Despite the obvious coarseness of such terms, the word, in common with many other once acceptable, if not wholly respectable words, did not become slang until the mid-18C. Unlike his predecessor Harman Frances Grose could no longer spell the word out: in his slang dictionary of 1785 it has become T—D. It has stayed off-limits ever since, although like many of what are considered as the 'milder' obscenities, it has crept gradually into spoken, if not written English, especially as where, like its cognate **shit**, it refers not to excrement, but to a human object of derision or dislike.

Like **turd crap**, with its connection to the Dutch *krappen* – to pluck off, cut off or separate – underlines the way excrement is cut off from the body. However, like **shit**, it also introduces an element of waste or rejected matter, notably in its links to the Old French *crappe*: siftings, particularly 'the grain trodden under feet in the barn, and mingled with the straw and dust', itself drawn from the medieval Latin *crappa* and *crapinum* – the smaller chaff. The modern French *crape* maintains the idea of waste, although it literally translates as 'dirt' and 'filth'. The chaff meaning appears in English c.1440; **crap** meant money to the 18C and the gallows to the early 19th, but the excretory aspects waited four centuries from that first use, before **crap** finally meant to evacuate. **Crap** as a noun waited even longer: the first citation the *OED* can produce is remarkably late, in 1898 and attributed to its appearance in Joseph Wright's *English Dialect Dictionary*.

The last of the base trio, **shit** abandons the idea of separation and concentrates fully on the waste aspects of excrement. Its roots lie in the Old English *scite* and the Middle Low German *schite*, both meaning dung, and in the modification *scitte*, also OE, meaning diarrhoea. A final form, **shite**, emerged in the 19C, but remains relatively rare, usually found in dialect and often put into the mouth of those a writer is attempting to portray as Irish. Like **turd shit** emerges early into English, the noun and verb appearing in the early 14C. As a putdown it is already popular around 1500 and by 1598 Florio, in the *Worlde of Wordes*, is comparing a 'shitten fellow' with a 'goodman turd'. By the 18C, after four hundred years of acceptance by the mainstream, **shit** joined the slang lexicon, and subsequent citations for its use, from the 18C to around thirty years ago, are careful to insert judicious hyphens when printing it.

There are many other terms. Given the importance of excrement in the juvenile mind, a number of them, which persist into many adult vocabularies, stem from the euphemisms of one's earliest years. Among them are **big jobs** (fr. the Scottish **jobby**), **number twos, poo, poop** and **poopie-plops, diddley poo, dookey, dukie, kak, ca-ca, yackum, do** (especially as applied to animals, e.g. **doggy do**) and **doo-doo**. Most if not all of these appear in the 19th and 20th centuries.

Earlier terms return us to the adult vocabulary. Defining **turd**, Grose cites **sir-reverence** (also **save-reverence**), which began life in the 14C as a formal phrase meaning 'begging your pardon' and which by the late 16C had taken on this euphemistic secondary meaning. It is thus the basis of a later, 20C euphemism for visiting the lavatory: to 'excuse oneself' and the schoolchild's cry of 'Can I be excused?' **Scumber** or **scummer** comes from the dialect for animal dung or sticky, viscous mud, **clart** (coined in 1808 as sticky mud, and often found, notably in the 1970s television series *Porridge* as 'in the clarts', an obvious euphemism for 'shits'), while in the 17C a **tantoblin** or **tantoblin tart** was not just a **turd**, but also a round sweet tart.

More recent terms include the Australian **crash**, **honey** (as in the **honey-carts** that drain off the sewage tanks of airplanes and railway trains), the **alley apple** (in the animal kingdom the **road apple**), **body wax**, **scharn**, **sozzle**, **taunty**, and the abbreviation **BM**, meaning bowel movement. Defecation of all types is particularly productive of rhyming slang, as will be seen below, doubtless through a perceived need for euphemism. Terms for excrement include **big hit** (Australian) and **tomtit** (both **shit**), **pony (pony and trap)** and **horse and trap** (both crap), **lemon (lemon curd)** and **Richard (the Third)** (both meaning **turd**).

Other excrement-related terms are **dags** (Aus.), **clinkers** and **dingleberries** (presumably from SE *dangle*), all meaning the excrement that adheres to a badly cleaned rectum (in the case of **dags** also, in Aus., to a sheep), and **skid marks** (stains on one's underwear). The sewers of the 17C produced two terms: **Gravesend sweetmeats** (solid lumps of sewage; by the 19C the term meant shrimps) and **jere-peck** (a sewer: **jere** meaning turd, **peck** a heap).

DIARRHOEA

Given the relative consequences of the two states – constipation may be painful, but it is diarrhoea that may be actively and publicly embarrassing – it is the latter condition that has attracted a far wider range of slang. Indeed constipation offers only the anti-clerical **quaker** (18C, a hard, and possibly lengthy piece of excreta; thus

bury a quaker: to defecate), plus its rhy. sl. synonym, the 19C **muffin baker**, which brings the comment, when the desire, but not the facility for defecation is on hand, 'Better let it bake.' To be constipated is to be **hard-baked** (19C) or **bunged up**.

Diarrhoea, on the other hand, is infinitely more productive. **Runs**, **scoots**, **trots**, the **backdoor trot**, **movies**, **jerry-go-nimble** (19C, like the 16C **gurry**, from **jere**), **thorough-go-nimble** (17C, also meaning inferior beer, presumably from its deleterious affects on the gut) and **wherry go nimble** (20C, possibly from 'where he go') all attest to the urgency of finding a lavatory when thus afflicted, while **squitters** and **collywobbles** describe the problems of those who are **loose in the hilt** (19C), as does the painful **ringburner** (20C). The key term is **shits**, with its rhyming slang alternatives **toms** (tomtits) and **Jimmy Britts** (both Australian), and **threepenny bits**.

The experiences of British and Americans troops in the last World War, magnified by the onset of mass tourism, with its concomitant culinary xenophobia, has created a whole sub-group of terms to describe the diarrhoea picked up by these first contacts with exotic menus. Described generally as the **touristas** or, crudely, as **wog gut**, these afflictions, depending on geography, have been named variously as the **Aztec twostep**, **Cairo crud**, **Delhi belly**, **GIs**, **Gyppy tummy**, **Hong Kong dog**, **Montezuma's revenge** and **Rangoon runs**.

TO DEFECATE

The actual act of defecation naturally uses a number of the terms above – **take a crap**, **take a shit** – as well as those for visiting a lavatory – **go to the dunnee**, **go to see one's aunt**, visit the **crapping casa**, etc. – (for which see LAVATORY below), but there are some extra words and phrases. Among them are **powder one's nose**, **cramber**, **take a dump**, **choke a darkie** (Aus.), **post a letter**, **go and sing 'sweet violets'**, **take an Irish shave**, **sit on the throne** and, when suffering from diarrhoea, to **ride the porcelain bus** or **ride the porcelain Honda**. The 'bus' in question is of course the lavatory pan. To suffer from diarrhoea is to be **caught** or **taken short**, or to be **loose-legged**.

URINE

While the major terms for excreta concern themselves with the function of actually voiding waste matter from the body, that for urine, for all it that has equally venerable roots, is simply onomatopoeic. **Piss**, with its origins in Old French and Middle English, entered the modern language around 1290 and remained, as is typical of such latterday vulgarisms, in perfectly open use for the next seven hundred years and then, as the shadows of Victorian reticence gathered, vanished into the world of the taboo. In the last twenty or thirty years it seems to have made a comeback, though strictly on colloquial, not SE terms.

The 18C brings **tea**, **long tea**, and **cold tea** (thus **tea voider**: one who is urinating), and **tail-water** (**tail★**: the genitals), and the 19C **little jobs** and **number ones**, but virtually every other term refers back to **piss**, or its modified euphemism **piddle** (18C). Thus **pee** and **wee-wee** reflect **piss**, while **widdle** echoes **piddle**. Like **wee-wee**, a nursery term, is **tinkle**, another one. The remaining terms are all rhyming slang: **rattle and hiss** (US), **cousin sis**, **snake's hiss** (Aus, 20C), **Johnny Bliss** and **Micky Bliss**; **dicky diddle** (piddle, plus **dicky★**: penis); **you and me** and **Robert E** (**Robert E. Lee**: pee). The noun-form, urinating, adds the onomatopoeic **slash** and **wazz**, plus **leak** (all 20C) and more rhy. sl.: **gypsy's** (20C, **gypsy's kiss**) and **Jimmy** or **Jerry Riddle** (19C). The 19C also provides **sweetpea**, usually with reference to a woman urinating in the open air; the term is similar to other euphemisms with which decorous picknickers would excuse themselves: **water the flowers**, **pluck the roses** and others.

TO URINATE

Inevitably the most widely used terms meaning to urinate simply take the basic words for urine or urination and add **have**, **take** or **go for a**. Alternatively the nouns simply become verbs, as in **piss** itself, **wee**, **pee**, **piddle**, **widdle** and so on. There are, however, a

number of words, and more particularly phrases, that add a colourful extra, if sometimes strainingly euphemistic vocabulary.

The oldest of these is probably **lag** (fr. the 16C term for water or
wine and one that survived among the market traders of the 20C).
The connection of urine to alcohol is maintained in **rack off**(19C,
from the wine trade jargon meaning the drawing off liquor from
the lees), **drain off** (19C), **run off** (19C) and **tap a keg** (19C,
from the beer trade). The 18C also had **pump** and **pump ship**,
only the latter has survived; similarly nautical is **scatter** (19C, the
plural **scatters** means diarrhoea). **Preeze**, a Northern dialect term
linked to the SE *pressure*, refers to ineffectual, if straining efforts to
urinate, or indeed to defecate. **Give the chinaman a music
lesson** reflects the 'China' toilet bowl, and the 'music' that is the
'tinkle' of the urine hitting it; **point percy★ at the porcelain** has
a similar reference to the receptacle itself, while **splash the boots**
implies standing at a urinal, and **spend a penny** refers to the
traditional cost of Britain's public lavatories (although the urinals,
unlike the stalls, were always free). **Visit the sand box** (an item
usually reserved for one's pet cat) and **visit Miss Murphy** also
refer to making a trip to the lavatory.

Phrases for the discharge of urine include **squeeze the lemon**
(although this usually implies sexual rather than urinary images),
bleed the liver, bleed one's turkey (punning on **turkey-cock**),
water or **drain the dragon** (19C), **strain the potatoes** or **taters,
drain** or **strain the spuds, syphon the python, drain one's
radiator, drain one's crankcase, drain one's lizard, take one's
snake for a gallop, wring the rattlesnake** and **wring the dew
off the branch**. Equally popular are **shake hands with an old
friend, shake hands with the wife's best friend, shake the
dew off the lily** and **shake a sock**.

Two especially popular euphemisms are to **see a man about a
dog** and its joking reverse to **see a dog about a man**, although
neither excuse is exclusively for urination, merely leaving the room.
Further euphemisms, mainly linked with taking an al fresco pee,
include **pick the daisies, pluck a rose, do a rural, burn the
grass, go catch a horse, go look at the crops, shoot a lion,**

water the horses, water one's pony or **one's nag, kill a snake** and **kill a tree.**

THE LAVATORY

The earliest term for privy, and as such more a euphemism than pure slang is **gong** or **gong house** (11C), which comes from the Old English *gang*, meaning the act of walking or going and is, however remotely, an ancestor of the child's plaint, 'I've got to go'. **Siege** (1400, from the Latin *sedem*: a seat) originally means a privy, although by 1515 it is simply excrement. More recognisable is the 16C **boggard**, also meaning privy, which comes from the verb form of **bog** (16C), but is itself the origin of the nouns **bog** (18C), **boghouse** (17C) and **bog shop** (19C). **Compost hole** is a 19C synonym. Other 16C terms include **jakes, Jacque's** or **jake-house**, all of which probably come from **jack's** or **jack's place**, and which must lead on to the 18C **john** (US, 1735). **Ajax**, punning on 'a jakes', appears in both Shakespeare and in *The Metamorphosis of Ajax* (1596) by Sir John Harington (c.1561–1612), a plea for the introduction of the water-closet which so displeased Queen Elizabeth I that its author was banned from Court.

The role of the lavatory as a separate place or 'house' informs many 17C terms, notably the **chapel**, the **chapel of ease**, the **place** or **house of ease** or **easement**, the **house of office**, the **place of convenience** or **of resort**, the **closet of ease** and the **stool of ease**. Similarly one 'sat' in the **House of Commons** or the **Parliament**, although the **House of Lords** (a 20C descendent) was merely a urinal. Other terms include the **draught** (1602), the **scotch ordinary** (1670) and the cod-Latin **necessarium** or **necessary-house** (in a shift of priorities to the 20C **necessaries** mean the genitals) and **cacatorium**, a pun on **caca**, from the Latin *cacare* to evacuate the bowels. Australia's 20C **dunnee** has its roots in the 17C **dunnakin** (fr. **danna**: human ordure, plus **ken**: a place or house). Its variations **donagher**, **donigan**, **dunnyken** and **dunny** all emerge over the subsequent 200 years.

Two of the most enduring terms for lavatory appear during the 18C: **john**, still an essential term in America, and **crapper**, with its variations **craphouse**, **crapping castle**, **crapping-ken**, **crapping-casa** and **crapping house**, **crappus** and **crappery** (all 18C) and the 20C market traders' coinage **crapereena**. While popular etymology links all such combinations to the 19C sanitary engineer Thomas Crapper, who did indeed pioneer the flush lavatory, the root of **crap** lies in the 15C Dutch *krappen* meaning to cut off or separate. For further details see under DEFECATION.

Other 18C terms include the coy **little house** (and its 19C descendents **little office** and **petty house**), **coffee-shop** or **coffee-house** and **spice island** (also meaning the anus and defined by the early 19C *Lexicon Balatronicum* as a 'stinkhole bay or dilberry creek'), **minor** (possibly a misreading of the 18C euphemism **my uncle's**) and **Jericho**, which in more general use meant a place of banishment. A link with **jerry**, a chamber pot, would be more satisfactory, but the place appears c.1750 while the receptacle is a coinage of 1825.

Jericho was coincidentally known as the rough quarter of Oxford, and the universities are responsible for a number of 19C terms. The fake Latin **colfabias** was popular at Trinity College, Dublin, while in Oxford Worcester College opted for **forakers**, from the Latin *forica*, a privy; **fourth** was used at Trinity, Cambridge: at that time the college privies were sited in the fourth court and thus an undergraduate who had temporarily gone there would write upon his door 'Gone[4]'.

The 19C saw the coinage of another basic term: **loo** is possibly a punning abbreviation of Waterloo, or of the French warning '*gardez l'eau*' ('mind the water', the 'water' in question being hurled into the street from a full chamber-pot) or from the 18C ladies' portable '*bordalou*' — carried in a muff, it looked like sauceboat, but was actually travelling *pissoir*. The lavatory might also been called a **dike** (fr. SE meaning pit; a predecessor of the 20C Aus. use: **vandyke**), the **quaker's burying ground** (fr. **quaker*** meaning turd), the **rear** or **rears** (punning on 'behind'), the **back**, **back-**

house or **backy** (all from the backyard privies, the sole plumbing available for many houses; such outside lavatories were and are **one-**, **two-** or **three-holers**) and the **head** or **heads** (a naval usage, taken from the position of the privy at the 'head' of a ship, near the bowsprit). **Altar**, **throne** and **temple** are a trio of euphemisms, as are **visit Sir Harry** or **visit Mrs Jones**, while **where the Queen goes on foot** or **sends nobody** maintain the elevated tone. **West Central** puns on the London postal district, WC. A **karsy** is based on the Italian *casa*, a house, while the **thunder-box** is an Indian army term; finally **dilberry creek** comes from **dingleberry***, thus **dilberry-bush**: the pubic hair.

Apart from the abbreviations **lav** and **lavvy** the 20C is a mix of euphemisms and bluntness. The former gives the quintessential **little boy's** or **little girl's room**, and **my aunt's**, with its rhyming variation **Mrs Chant's** (Mrs Ormiston Chant: a well-known moralist), both adopted by 'society' women of the 1920s. The latter is best seen in **shitter** and **shithole** (both also used for the anus), **shouse** and **shithouse** (although Partridge claims that this use is incorrect and the term should only apply to a commode [19C], a reviled person, or anywhere dirty [both 20C]). This theory is surely undermined by a pair of popular phrases: to **bang like a shithouse door in a gale** (of an sexually enthusiastic woman) and to be **built like a brick shithouse** (of a notably large or tough man). **Pisshole** and **pisshouse** are parallel terms, while **snakes' house** (Aus.) emphasises urination, with its abbreviation of the **one-eyed trouser snake***: the penis. **Leakhouse** comes from **leak**, to urinate, **kybo** either from **khyber pass*** (arse) or, possibly, from an acronym: 'keep your bowels open'. Like the earlier **john can**, for the receptacle, is primarily American, while **honey house** refers to the colour of ordure and gives the combinations **honey bucket** (for night-soil) and **honey-wagon** for taking it away. Finally **cottage**, which emerged at the turn of the century meaning urinal, predates its modern, gay use by twenty years.

The latrine man, whose task it was to empty the privies in a world before automated water closets was variously the **gold finder** (cf. **honey cart**), the **haut-boy**, **Tom Turdman** (17C, thus **Tom Turdman's fields** or **hole**: the place where nightmen deposit the soil) the **gong man** and **gong farmer** and the **night man**. To **upset Mrs Jones** (19C) was to empty the privy tub. Such emptying was always done at night, which earned it the heavily humorous description, a **wedding**.

THE CHAMBER POT

Early terms for chamber pot include the **jockum gage** (17C) from **jockum***: penis and **gage** (originally a mug holding a quart of beer) meaning a pot; **member mug** (17C) means exactly the same while a **jordan**, **jordain** or **jurden** (17C) all referred to the Biblical River of Jordan. **Oliver's skull** (c.1690) was an unashamed attack on the memory of the late Lord Protector Oliver Cromwell (1599-1658); similarly the later **twiss** (18C), an Irish coinage targeted the English writer Richard Twiss (1747-1821) who had published the highly critical *Tour in Ireland*. To take their revenge the Irish then produced a chamberpot with picture of Richard Twiss inside it, beneath which was inscribed the rhyme 'Let everyone piss/On lying Dick Twiss.'

The 18C also produced the **thunder mug** (a variation on **thunder box** and like it based on the noise of urination), the **mingo** (possibly from **ming**, meaning a stink, and thus a 'stinker'), the **pisspot** (which since its coinage in 15C had been SE, but was now exiled to the lexical margins) and the **tea voider** (fr. **tea**: urine). The **lagging gage** was based on **lag**: **water** and **gage**: mug or pot. The term survives as the market traders' 20C **lag**, urination. **Looking glass** is based on one's reflection in the urine, as well, possibly, as the attention paid by contemporary physicians to the urine itself.

The 19C saw the last real flourishing of terms for chamber-pot – other than earlier survivors and the nursery-based **pottie** the ubiquitous WC gradually rendered it redundant in a 20C household. Among the 19C terms are the Scots dialect **chantie** and **mastercan**, **it**, **jerker** and **jerry** (fr. SE *jereboam*: an outsize bottle containing the equivalent of ten or even twelve normal measures). **Po** comes from the French *pot de chambre*, a chamber pot) and **smoker** or **smokeshell** from the steam that rises from hot urine in cold weather; thus **smokehouse** meant privy. **Remedy-critch** comes from the SE *remedy* meaning ease and *critch*, an earthenware vessel; this in turn comes from *cratch*, a stable hayrack and thus a crèche; the term is used as such in early descriptions of Christ's birth. Finally, a chamber pot could also be a **bishop**, yet another assault on the episcopacy, whose character was regularly assassinated by the coiners of slang. Aside from **bang the bishop★** (to masturbate) a **bishop** could be an outsize condom or a broken signpost which 'neither points the way nor travels it', as opposed to a **parson**: a whole signpost which 'sets people on the right way'.

Lavatory paper, a modern invention, is **wipe** or **asswipe**, **bumf** and **bum-fodder**, **bogroll**, **tail timber** (19C) and **torch-cul** (loaned from the French equivalent of bum-fodder).

EXCELLENCE

EXCELLENCE

It is perhaps because of slang's origins in cant, where the single adjective **rum★** or **rome** (16C) served muster as an all-embracing term for good or excellent, that few particularly early terms of approbation have been recorded. The earliest appears to be **topper**, first recorded and still, if less commonly, to be found. It comes, naturally, from the SE *top*. The following century proves far more fruitful, offering a number of terms that have survived in more or less regular use down to the present day, as well as a number that have vanished.

Of the former group **pippin** and the abbreviation **pip** refer to the generic name for a number of species of apple, the first recorded in 1432, and more directly from the phrase 'sound as pippin' a synonym for 'sound as a bell'. **Pippin** has the added implication of physical attractiveness; such usage originates in the US around the turn of the 19C. **Daisy**, a slightly earlier US term that also looks to nature, has similar overtones of beauty. Less measured are the boldly declaratory **snorter** (mid-19C), **scorcher** (cf. **hot stuff**) and **scorch** (20C, Afro-American), **belter** (Yorks. dial: whopper) and **cracker**, which originally referred to a fast horse, a large sum and similar adjuncts of the sporting life. **Bobby dazzler** (orig. a Midlands term) has lasted the course, as has **the goods** (US 19C, UK 20C) which is usually found in the phrase to 'deliver the goods'. **Knockout** and **kayo** (KO) appear to have links to the boxing ring, but may actually stem from the 17C **knocker**, which meant a notably attractive person and is found as such in Middleton and Rowley's play *A Chaste Maid* (1628). **Out and outer** began life meaning an unscrupulous person, a meaning it still carries, but the parallel image of excellent followed soon after. **Duck soup** is really obsolete, but survives in its *locus classicus*, the title of the the Marx Brothers movie of 1933. A secondary meaning is of easiness, synonymous with the equally gustatory **piece of cake**. Its etymology remains obscure: the relation of easiness can be extended to people, making it synonymous with **pushover***. To link the soup, undoubtedly a Chinese dish, to the Chinese immigrants, generally regarded as inoffensive, is alas most likely one connection too far. **Jim-dandy** offers no such problems; coined in the US c.1887 its links to fashion make it a peer of the adjectival **swell** (19C).

Perhaps the most enduring 19C term is the phrase the **real McKay** or **real McCoy**. The origins of this venerable term of praise remain debatable. One party opts for Scotland, where it emerged in the 1880s to mean both men and whiskey of the highest quality. It has also been suggested that the clan McKay had at one period two rival chieftains, each heading their own branch. The arguments over which sub-clan, and which leader was the *real* McKay gives the phrase. The alternative version, and the alternative spelling, McCoy, as found in the US, refers to the boxer Norman Selby (1873-1940), whose ring name was Kid McCoy. Apocryphal tales had a drunk approaching the champion and demanding a fight. McCoy attempted to sidestep this foolish challenge but finally, his temper overcoming him, succumbed and floored his assailant. When the drunk recovered he supposedly announced, 'You're right, that was the real McCoy.'

Of the second category **clipper**, from the type of ship, referred first to horseflesh and then to people; **pea** had vanished in the UK by 1900, although it has had some popularity in 20C Australia; Australia also hosted **scrouger** (originally US, and similar to the SE *scrunch*), which came from *scrouge*, meaning to shove out of the way and thus, as a noun something large or forceful; **lummy** came from Yorkshire dialect, especially as in a **lummy lick**: a delicious mouthful. **Stem-winder** still survives in US politics, where it refers to a rousing speech, but has vanished as a term for excellence. Both meanings came from the then (1890s) newly invented stem-winding watch, which with its rejection of any need for the usual key, was seen as the finest example of state of the art technology.

The 20C has added a number of terms. **Bee's knees, cat's pyjamas** and **cat's whiskers** are dated – they are all 1930s' coinages – but refuse to disappear; the teenagers' **fave rave** (**fave**: favourite, **rave**: something one raves over) tends only to ironic appearances today while **Shovel City** (something one 'digs') is positively embarrassing. More popular are **lulu**, a **dilly**, **peach** (often used of a pretty girl, although equally of an idea), **hot stuff** and the coarser **hot shit, ace** or **aces** (fr. the card), **something to shout about, something to write home about** and the jazz-orientated **something else**. Australia ofers a variety, notably the stereotypical **beaut**, (c.1900, abbr. of *beautiful*), **rip-snorter** (long since exported to the UK), the lesser-known **trimmer** (fr. SE *trim*: neat) and **humdinger** which began life in the USAF meaning a fast airplane (fr. **hum**: speed, and **dinger**: something forceful) and thence moved via Australia to the UK. Other terms include the Afro-American **bells** (possibly from the approving phrase 'you ring my bell'), the **berries** (US, from **berries**: dollars, and thus something worthwhile), **big time, but good, gravy** (with its implication of a bonus) and **corker** (which has changed its meaning from the mid-19C when it meant the last word in argument and was an alternative spelling of *caulker*: a settler).

EXCELLENT AND FIRST-RATE

Sixteenth century villains, the first recorded consistent users of slang, or more properly cant, had two all-purpose words for goodness: **rum** and the slightly less common **bene**. **Rum** could

mean good, fine, excellent or great and was the antonym of the
equally widely used **queer**, meaning bad. According to Partridge,
who deals with it at length, **rum** comes most probably from Rome
(and indeed could be spelled **rome** until the 18C), which as a city
meant glory and grandeur. Other origins include the Romany *rom*,
a male gypsy, or the Turkish *Rûm*, which also meant gypsy, many
of whom passed through the Ottoman Empire. Reversing the
process, the Latin *Roma* (Rome) is cognate with the Teutonic root
hruod (fame) (as found in the names Roger and Roderick) which
appears in the German *Ruhm* (fame). Today **rum** has taken on
something of an opposite meaning, being used to mean odd,
eccentric or suspect. In that context, which appeared c.1725 (when
it was noted in the *New Canting Dictionary*) it can be seen as the
ancestor of all those bad = good constructions, typically **wicked**,
nasty and **bad** itself, so common among modern youth. As good
rum appears in many combinations, starting with Harman's 1567
listing of **rome vyle** (London), **rome mort** (Queen Elizabeth)
and **rome bouse** (wine, literally 'good drink'). Other uses of **rum**
(Partridge cites nearly one hundred), include **rum bubber** (17C,
a fellow dextrous at stealing silver tankards), **rum blowen** (18C, 'a
handsome wench'), **rum joseph** (17C, a very good cloak) and
rum prancer (17C, a very fine horse); there are many more.

   Bene, also spelt **ben** or even **bien** could be conjugated: **benar**:
better and **benat**: best, and came from the French *bon*, meaning
good. Harman offers **bene bouse** (good liquor), **bene lightmans**
(good-day, good morrow) and **bene pecke** (good meat or food).
Other combinations include **bene mort** (16C, a good, or pretty
girl), **bene darkmans** (16C, good night) and **bene feaker** (17C,
a counterfeiter, in which **bene** is synonymous with skilful).

   The 17C provides a few new terms, notably **bully,** which in the
17-18C was used only of persons but which was extended to things
as well in the 19C; used mainly in the US, perhaps its best-known
appearance was in US President Theodore 'Teddy' Roosevelt's
(1858-1919) oft-repeated dictum: 'The White House is a bully
pulpit'. **Splendacious**, which would otherwise bear all the hall-
marks of a more recent coinage, in fact appeared in the 17C, while
its descendent **splendiferous** is 19C. **Cheery** is more of an

understatement, its basic meaning remains lively or cheerful; **crack** referred to things from 1630 and to people from 1700. **Neat as ninepence** is 17C, but its derivatives **grand, nice** or **right as ninepence** are all 19C. The 18C brings **bang up** (fr. bang up to the mark?), **rich** (with an added connotation of spicy or saucy), **bobbish** (fr. the image of one who bobs up and down with barely suppressed enthusiasms), **tip-top** (cf. **topper**) and **up to the nines**, especially as in 'dressed up to the nines'. The etymology remains obscure, but may come from the role of nine (three times three) as a mystical and thus laudable number. Finally **dandy** or **d**, like the later US **swell**, reflect the relations between high fashion and supposed excellence. **Dandy** first emerged from the Scottish borders c.1800 and by 1815 was a smart London word, describing the 'exquisites' of the era. It may in turn derive from **Jack-a-dandy**, coined c.1632, which, although it began life describing 'a little pert or conceited fellow' (*OED*) and was at best a contemptuous name for a fop, the contempt passed away and the modern meaning (itself not wholly devoid of suspicion) took over. **Pink**, especially as in 'in the pink', while usually found referring to health, also began life as a description of fashionable elegance, as did **slick**, meaning especially smooth. **Dossy**, primarily meaning elegant, comes either from a **dosser**, an ornamental cloth used that covers the back of an imposing seat, or from the Comte D'Orsay: whose character and thus name epitomised the perfect gentleman. However the 20C **dossy** (and its noun-form **doss**, both of which originate in the 18C **doss**: to sleep) refers to something easy – you could 'do it with your eyes closed', i.e. asleep.

Among the many words supplied by the 19C, one of the most enduring is the term **A1**, a category applied by *Lloyd's Register* to ships in first-class condition, as to hull and stores alike. As laid down in the *Key to the Register*. 'The character A denotes New ships, or Ships Renewed or Restored. The Stores of Vessels are designated by the figures 1 and 2; 1 signifying that the Vessel is well and sufficiently found.' The category was then added to the names of ships, e.g. 'the fast-sailing ship *Sea-breeze*, A 1 at Lloyd's'. The term gradually moved, as does so much jargon, into colloquial speech to mean first-rate or prime; its first recorded citation appears in Charles Dickens' *Pickwick Papers* (1837).

Food and drink provide a number of 19C superlatives. The latter gives **all brandy,** the Aus. **double-distilled** and **creamy**; the former has **clean wheat** (presumably from commercial jargon, cf. **A1**), **good as wheat, bread** or **cheese,** and **the cheese**. This term, however, is edible only by pronunciation: its origin is most likely in the Persian and Urdu *chiz,* meaning *thing.* As Yule and Burnell put it in *Hobson-Jobson* (1886) 'The expression used to be common among Anglo-Indians, e.g. "My new Arab is the real *chiz*", i.e. "the real thing".' Hindi also offers the non-edible **first chop,** from *chhaap* meaning a print, and thus a seal, notably that which is placed on first-rate merchandise. Another Hindu term, **brahma,** was anglicized to mean both very good and, specifically, a pretty girl: like the statues of the god in question, she might well be covered in jewels. **Jammy** comes from **jam,** meaning luck, and gives **real jam** and its synonym **true marmalade,** while **plummy** derives from **plum** meaning very good, especially as in a **plum job; scrumptious** (and the much rarer **scrumdolious**) refer not so much to a specific foodstuff, but to general pleasurability. The 20C **scrummy** and **yummy** are both obvious developments. The **pick of the basket** assumes the context of food, while the **pure quill,** while non-edible, falls within this group.

As in nouns such as **scrouge** and **humdinger,** the concept of force may underline that of excellence. Hence **slapping, slashing, smashing, slap up** (fr. Northern dial.), **crushing, ripping** (redolent of the 'jolly good chaps' rhetoric of the *Boys Own Paper*), **snappy, screaming** and another schoolboy term, **tons** (among its earliest uses is that found in J M Barrie's *Peter Pan* [1904]). The world of commerce is similarly productive, giving **all wool and a yard wide** (fr. drapers' shops), **that's the ticket** (with its cousin **that's Bible**), **at par** and **above par** (both from the Stock Exchange), and **the hammer** (possibly referring to an auction house), with its variations **just the hammer** and **up to the hammer. Knocker** has overtones of physical beauty, and **up the knocker** means in the peak of condition. **Bod** and **bodacious** come from *body* and mean bodily or totally. **Boiler-plated** implies absolute dependability and consistency, and is the root of the jargon *boilerplate*: meaning those clauses that appear regularly in a set of given documents, be they legal contracts or political speeches.

Simple supremacy comes in **boss, number one** and **numero uno** (with the 20C antonym **number 10**, as used in the pidgins of the Far East), **prime** and **primo** (the latter currently jargon for high-quality drugs, especially marijuana), **first rate** and **rooter** (used of anything first class). An air of cunning and foresightedness lies behind **fly, up to Dick** and **downy** (fr. the noun **down**: alarm or suspicion); a certain understatement informs **all the go, about east, about right, all there**, and **proper**, which had been SE between the 15–19C. Other, unclassifiable terms include **classic, death** (an early example of the bad = good syndrome, with the combination **death on**: very good at or keen on), **doog** (backsl. for good), **fizzing** (seen today as a euphemism for fucking, but possibly an innocent reference to the effervescence of champagne; cf. **bobbish**), **great shakes** (usually as 'no great shakes', and taken from the shaking of dice in gambling) **hunky-dory** and **hunky** (predating its current use as the description of the kind of muscular young boys who appeal to teenage girls), **righteous** (now mainly Afro-American use), **rorty** (possibly from the Yiddish: *rorität*: anything choice or from rhy. sl.: naughty), **severely, spiffy** and **spiffing, sweet, tall** (US, from the boastful exaggeration of tall stories) and **tzing-tzing** (possibly from **chin chin**). **Nap** is another gambling term, taken from the eponymous game: each player receives five cards, and calls the number of tricks he or she expects to win; one who calls five is said to go nap, and a nap hand, which will probably take all five tricks, is the strongest.

A final selection gives **bona** (fr. Parlyaree and commonly found as the intensifying very), **splash up, down to the ground** (often as 'that suits me…', although the 17C **go down to the ground** meant to defecate), **clipping** (fr. **clipper★**), **out-and-out** (fr. **out-and-outer★**), **jonnick** (meaning brave, tough, loyal and honest) and **to rights** (fr. the legalese 'to be to rights': to have a legal case against someone; it is the basis of the police or criminal jargon **bang to rights**: legally watertight or caught without any excuse). **All Sir Garnet** refers to the military successes of Sir Garnet (later

Lord) Wolseley (1833-1923), whose reputation was further enhanced by his efforts to improve the lot of the private soldier. **All
Sir Garnet** appeared c.1885; the versions **all sirgarneo, all
sigarno** or **all Sir Garny** coming slightly later.

Given the prevalance of youth culture in the 20C it is hardly
surprising that of the most recent slang superlatives a large proportion emerge from the succession of fads and fantasies that have
sequentially overtaken teen life. In a very approximate chronological order these include the jazz-related **crazy** (although **crazy for**
had meant very enthusiastic since the 18C) and **cool**, another jazz
term (of the late 1940s) which replaced its predecessor **hot** when
bebop or bop — loosely known as progressive or modern jazz —
took over as the predominant form, ousting 'hot' jazz from fashion.
Cool, both as a superlative, and, as a noun, is the description of a
poised, distanced way of dealing with life (often underpinned by
an intake of narcotics), moved away from jazz into the mainstream
of teenage life during the 1950s and maintained its popularity until
the hippie Sixties. Other 1950s terms, culled from the less mannered world of rock'n'roll (a white world rather than jazz's essentially black or Bohemian one) include **neat, keen** (and **keeno**) and
peachy-keen, killer and **killer-diller** and **major**.

The early Sixties, with their deification of the Beatles, offered **fab**
and **gear** — both allegedly culled from the Beatles' **wacky★**
Liverpudlian vocabularies. **Fab** was simply an abbreviation of
fabulous (and could be expanded by the teen magazines into
fantabulous, while **gear** harks back to **the goods★**, as in the
phrase 'that's the gear': that's what's required, that's perfect. **Gear**
also meant clothing, as in the fictional Sixties emporium 'Fab Gear
of Tooting', created for the decidely unhip contemporary television
sitcom *Hugh and I*. Drugs, especially of the hallucinatory sort,
appeared in the later 1960s, and with them came a number of
drug-related terms: **trippy** (fr. the LSD trip), **mind-blowing,
heavy, far-out, out of sight** (often spelt **outasite**, or even **out
of state**), **too much** and **groovy. Groovy** had in fact a much
older pedigree. 19C users related it to the phrase 'in a groove', and
thus made it synonymous with conventional; 1940s jazz redefined

it in its modern context, but the hippie era saw its most pervasive flowering, typically in **groovy chick**, an attractive girl.

What rock writers termed the English invasion may have taken a few terms West along with such bands as the Beatles, the Rolling Stones and the Who, but the US remained dominant in teen culture. So did its language. The surfers of California, and their cultural cousins the Valley Girls of the early 1980s drew on the same vocabulary, introducing **awesome**, **totally, mondo** (fr. the Latin *mundus*: the world, and thus, its its meaning of all-encompassing synonymous with **bodacious***), **bitchen**, **bitchin** and the extreme **bitchin twitchin** (although **bitchin** had been an earlier 20C Aus. euphemism for fucking), **to die, massive, total blow-choice** (very appealling but finally irrelevant) and **tubular**, a degree of excellence that surpassed all others and came from the surfing jargon the **tube**: the inside curve of a good wave. Teen slang also comes up with a number of abbreviations, typically **brill** (brilliant) and **TB** (*très* brill), **cas** (casual, a deliberate understatement), **def** (definitive), **ex** (excellent), **triff** (terrific), **rad** (radical) **v.** and **vg.** (respectively very and very good), **marvy** (marvellous)and the all-purpose prefix **mega-**.

Black culture, first US and then UK, remains one of the foremost influences on all teen slang, with the white boys and girls for once finding themselves firmly at the back of the queue. Jazz came from the US black culture and today's hip-hop and rap music have created a number of terms, perhaps the classic among which is **bad** (with its intensfier **baddest**), the epitome of that vocabulary in which, whether ironically or with the age-old intention of slang – the confusion of the outsider – terms that conventionally signify bad, in fact mean good. Others include **tough, nasty, vicious, wicked** and **mean** (which has the overtone of being so good it's unfair). **Dope** comes from the generic term for drugs, and implies that the object in question has the same pleasurable effect, **cold** refers back to **cool** and has the same image of studied indifference, while **foxy** links to fox, a good-looking girl. The earlier **superfly** (1970s) referred to the name of high-quality cocaine, and served as the title of a hit film; **pimp**, at least within a certain subculture, also means first class. Finally, in what may be the ultimate in good/bad reversals (at least in religious eyes) is **sex with Jesus**.

Another major source of contemporary terms is Australia, always a leading coiner of slang, sometimes modified from English origins, but equally often brand new. Such terms include **apples** (either from the 18C **apple-pie order** or the rhy. sl. **apples and spice**: nice), **bonzer, bonza** and the cognate **boshta** (the first coined in 1904, and according to the *OED* at least, an elision of *bonanza*), **dead set, ducky, grouse** (often intensified as **extra-grouse**; in Aus. prisons a **grouse** is a tailormade, rather than a prison-issue cigarette) and **mad. Out of the box** (which parallels the phrase **happy as a box of birds** in very good spirits), **ripper** (the contemporary successor to the once all-conquering **beaut★**), **spot on** (20C superseding the earlier **bang on**), **unreal** (cf. the contemporaneous **out of sight** and **far out**), **stone** (cf. **dope**, but stone as in the SE *stone blind* or *stone deaf* dates to 19C) and the rhyming slang **Wee Georgie Wood** (good), often found in the interrogative: **any Wee Georgie?**: any good?

Adult as well as teenage America has contributed its share of words. Among them are **socko** and **boffo**, both from show business, and both featuring largely within the pages of that home of the superlative, *Variety* magazine. The former comes from **sock**, to hit, while **boffo** and its companion **boffola** both come from **boff**, meaning a belly-laugh; thus a performance that elicits such laughter from the audience may be considered a success. **Bonaroo** is a Cajun term, from Lousiana, while **copacetic**, sometimes assumed (with no apparent etymological reason) to be Yiddish, most probably comes from Chinook jargon and, as originally used on the waterways of Washington state is properly *copasenee*, meaning, like **copasetic**, everything is satisfactory. **Hellacious** is reminiscent of the earlier **bodacious★**, **high-tone** carries an air of classiness, while **hotsy-totsy**, so redolent of the roaring Twenties, is best known as the name of New York's Hotsy-Totsy Club, owned by the gangster Jack 'Legs' Diamond (1896-1931).

The grab-bag of 20C superlatives ranges far and wide. **Dynamite** came with World War I (the explosive had been patented by Nobel in 1867), **electric** followed soon afterwards; similarly forceful terms include **bang on** (abbreviating the RAF's 'bang on the target'), **blinding** (fr. **blind★**), **hot-shit** and **shit-hot**, **knockout** and **solid**. The veteran **topper★** lay behind **top drawer** (originally used in a class context: 'out of the top drawer'), **top hole**, **top notch** and **top shelf**, while a sense of fitness and satisfaction underpins the phrases **just like mother makes it**, **just the job**, **just what the doctor ordered** and **just the ticket** as well as **right up one's alley** or **right up one's street**. **Gaff** (fr. **gaffer★**) and **king** carry on the idea of leadership as already found in **boss★**; **wizard** comes from the World War II RAF use, much satirised in such phrases as 'wizard prang', while **magic** was popularised c.1975 through a television sitcom. Television has also introduced **handsome** (originally 16C), **sponditious** (fr. the comedian Lenny Henry) and **stonking** (popularised by Jonathan Ross).

Other terms include **bagged**, from **in the bag** and thus easy, **all fine and dandy** (also rhy. sl. for brandy), **good as all getout**, **irey** (Jamaican), **jolly d** (**d**.: decent), **live** (with implications of a live performance), **on the money** (gambling), **out of this world** (cf. **out of sight**), **serious** (perhaps *the* adjective of the yuppie 1980s) and **sexy** (a media, term referring not to actual sex, unless coincidentally, but to any story guaranteed to excite the readers). **Crackerjack** is a descendant of **crack★**, although its original nautical use was to describe a dish of pounded biscuit with minced salt meat.

OTHER TERMS

A few general terms round out this section of goodness and excellence. To be excellent is to **beat all** or **beat the band** (both 20C), to **go over big** (19C), to **go over like a million bucks**, to **hit the spot** and **make it big** (all 20C); to **take the cake**, to **take the biscuit** or, more elaborately, to **take the Huntley and Palmer** (a leading biscuit manufacturer) are all 19C. Partridge cites a correspondent who claims, somewhat ponderously, that the cake in question refers to the Greek *pramous*, literally a victory cake, and originally a cake of roasted wheat and honey.

Exclamations implying excellence include **encore!**, **far out!** (and **far fucking out!**), **fucking A!** and **perfecto!** (all 20C); to be quite good is **better than a thump on the back with a stone** (18C), **better than a poke in the eye with a blunt** (or **sharp** or **burnt**) **stick, a slap in the belly with a wet fish** or **wet lettuce** (all 19C); **close but no cigar** (US, from the solace offered unsuccessful punters on the carnival midway) and **not so dusty** (19C). That which is correct or done properly is **according to Cocker** (1760): Edward Cocker (1631-76), an engraver and teacher, was the writer of *Cocker's Arithmetic* (published posthumously in 1678) which dealt specifically in commercial questions. Its pre-eminence in its field lasted for at least a century, thus engendering the phrase. Americans have the parallel **according to Gunter**, referring to a similarly influential treatise. The same meaning of *comme il faut* is found in the later **according to Hoyle**: Edmund Hoyle was editor in 1752 of *The Polite Gamester*, soon retitled *Mr Hoyle's Games of Whist* (1760), then *Hoyle's Games Improved* (1786); editions continue to appear. An enthusiast is a **flamer** (a term that still persists in computer hacker jargon, where a flamer is one who waxes garrulous on an electronic Bulletin Board) while the adjective **flaming** (c.1840) remains common, especially in the term a flaming row. Finally the phrase **that's the man that married Hannah** (meaning that's good, that's as it should be) originated in Shropshire, then moved up to London.

OK

OK (and its intensifier **A-OK**) may not, strictly, be invariably used as a superlative, but as slang terms go it may well stand as the most controversial, the most argued over and the most promising candidate for ranking as what Eric Partridge, writing in fact of the word *slang* itself, as a 'prize problem word'.

Surely the lexicographers' favourite, the American scholar Allen Walker Read has indeed made something of a secondary career out of expounding upon its origins and it is Read to whom the *OED* has turned when searching out the word's etymology. That etmology, remarked Eric Partridge in *Slang* (1933) is 'hotly disputed' but finally attributes it to 'all, pron. oll, korrect' and dates it from 1840 in the US and 1880 in the UK. The *OED* fortified by Read's researches, takes it back to 1839, but otherwise concurs.

The term originated as 'orl korrect' in 1839 and was then co-incidentally used in the election campaign of US president Martin Van Buren in 1840, when it conveniently suited his nickname 'Old Kinderhook', which came from the town of his birth Kinderhook, New York. The term was further popularized by the OK Club, founded in 1840, whose members were Democrats who backed Van Buren. The first use of 'oll korrect' (still spelt in full and as yet to gain its abbreviation) came, according to one story, during another campaign – that of the Whig Presidential candidate William Henry Harrison, when a local handyman in Urbana, Ohio, was commissioned to paint a banner for Harrison's supporter John Rock, a farmer. Unfortunately the handyman, Thomas Daniels, was illiterate and his slogan read 'The People is Oll Korrect'. Unfortunately another researcher has squashed this otherwise appealing story. Such harsh demolitions mark the history of research into **OK**, but neither they nor the *OED*, whose word may be assumed to be final, have finally flattened those who love to probe the term. Alternative versions were and are legion. They are, alas for their proponents, universally wrong, but it would be churlish to ignore their optimistic inventiveness.

Among them are the railway freight agent who signed bills of lading 'OK', after his name Obadiah Kelley; an Indian chief known as Oled Keokuck whose friends abbreviated his name to OK and often said 'OK, he's all right'; Aux Kayes, a Haitian port from where the best rum came from the initials the multi-millionaire John Jacob Astor used to sign bills presented to him for credit; an invention by US telegraphers to accompany *NM* meaning 'no more', and *GA* meaning 'go ahead'; the British word 'hoackey' or 'horkey' meaning the last load brought from the fields which signified the end of the harvest and the beginning of rustic celebrations. Two particularly popular theories attributed the term to the Choctaw *okeh* meaning 'it is', or to the West African language *Wolof* , brought to the US by transported slaves.

More ideas included the French *au quai* (meaning 'on the quay' and thus either referring to goods ready for transportation, or from the quays on which French soldiers met US girls in the War of Independence in 1776); the Finnish word *oikea* meaning correct; the Orrins-Kendall company which put its initials on its boxes of crackers: of high quality and eaten widely during the US Civil War they were known to soldiers as OKs; certain bills in House of Lords had at one time be signed and initialed by Lords Onslow and Kilbracken; from the initials 'H.G.', pronounced 'hah gay' which were used by Scandinavian sailors and came from Anglo-Saxon *hofgor* meaning seaworthy; from the Greek *omega chai* a magical incantation against fleas; from the signature of the Prussian General Schliesen who initalled all official documents *Oberst Kommandant* or OK; from the Scottish 'och aye' and from the 18C French form of *oui* (meaning yes) which was pronounced *o qu oui*.

INTELLIGENCE

INTELLIGENT PERSONS

Slang being what it is, few of the terms that indicate an individual's intelligence are not tinged with a certain disdain. England's traditional fear of the overly bright (generally echoed across the Atlantic) guarantees few bouquets. The able person however, uncorrupted by suspicious intellect, receives a far more positive treatment. In either case, of course, there are but a fraction of the terms allotted to the foolish.

Earlier centuries appear virtually devoid of such terminology; fools abound but intellectuals keep their distance. The 19C sets the pattern with **know-all** and the later **know-it-all,** followed around the turn of the century by **highbrow** and its contemporary **egghead** —both terms acknowledging the belief that a large brain required a commensurately substantial forehead. **Highbrow** duly generated the gradations of **middlebrow** (1906) and **lowbrow** (1925), while **egghead** has remained popular, typically in the *Variety* magazine headline coined to celebrate the wedding of playwright Arthur Miller to superstar Marilyn Monroe: 'Egghead

Weds Hourglass'. Afro-Americans opt for **gallon-head**. The early 20C also has the unequivocal and relatively neutral **brain** (the children's **brainbox** is a development) and **longhair**, apostrophised in Sinclair Lewis' novel *Main Street* (1920): 'I'm surprised to find you talking like a New York Russian Jew, or one of these long-hairs!', a sentence that sums up the Anglo-Saxon opinion of the openly clever. **Longhair** as intellectual is somewhat dated, but the term was revived in the late 1960s to mean hippie, a member of a youth cult that exulted in its long (male) hair, and which was also tainted, in many eyes, by its apparently thinking too much. **Pointyhead**, another anatomical fantasy, was coined in 1972 by the right-wing governor of Alabama, George Wallace, who used it in his regular attacks on US liberals. England is particularly fertile in terms that basically mean too clever for your own good. They include **clever-clogs** (19C, from Northern dial.), **clever-boots, smartypants, smart arse, clever Dick** and **smart Alec**. The US equivalent is **wisenheimer** or **wise guy** (although the **wise guys** are one of many euphemisms for the US Mafia). Only the US **smart cookie, razor** (who is 'sharp') and **maven** (Yiddish, from the Hebrew *mavin*: understanding) allow the intellectual any credibility. A certain affection underlines **old dog** (AA: expert in a given field) but the usual contempt returns for **culture-vulture**, coined in the 1940s to replace the earlier **culture-hound** and **pseud** (1960s, abbrev. pseudo-intellectual); once public school slang for anyone raising their sights above the philistine, the word was adopted by the magazine *Private Eye* and enshrined in its regular column 'Pseud's Corner'.

An out-and-out scholar is a **sponge** (i.e. one who learns easily) or, if feminine a **blue**, abbreviating blue stocking. This term originated c.1750 when a coterie of intellectual ladies — Mrs. Montague, Mrs. Vesey, and Mrs. Ord — set out to replace London society's traditional post-dinner pursuits — card-playing — with more cerebral amusements. As part of the new attitudes, formal dress was no longer required and among those who attended their soirées was Benjamin Stillingfleet, who habitually wore grey or blue worsted, instead of black silk stockings. Admiral Boscawen, a staunch traditionalist, thus derided such gatherings, labelling them 'the Blue Stocking Society' and the ladies were called Blue Stock-ingers, then Blue Stocking Ladies, and finally Blue Stockings.

The able person, as suggested, receives a much more positive treatment. He or she can be a **sensation** (19C), **no slouch** or **nobody's fool** (19C), a **clever dog**, **hot stuff**, a **good head** or a **crack hand**. Earlier terms include a **long crown** (as in the proverb: 'That caps long-crown, and he capp'd the devil'), a **long ear** or a **whipster** (although the implication here is of cunning as well as ability). A **dab** or **dabster** (17C, thus **dab hand**) was originally a topflight gamester. The **natural** began life as a harlot (16C), moved on to meaning bastard (18C, from SE *natural child*, whose parents are linked by nature, not by religion) before meaning one who is naturally (by dint of nature) talented. The **ace** is a coinage of World War I, when it was used by the RFC and RAF to characterize their best fliers. Superlatives include **the tops** and a **whiz** (fr. wizard); **the cheese**, meaning the real thing, comes from India (see GOOD for its etymology). A hopeful contestant is an **up-and-comer**. Experienced figures can be **old hands** (18C), **old-timers** (19C) or **vets** (20C, from veteran). Those who make predications are **crystal-gazers**, **dopesters** and **dopers** (who **dope things out**; from **dope**: information, thus **get the dope on**: to find out about), **steerers** and **tipsters**.

INTELLECT

The abstract idea of intelligence is most famously rendered con-crete by Agatha Christie's coinage, the **little grey cells**, created for her Belgian detective Hercule Poirot in his first appearance, in *The Mysterious Affair at Styles* (1920). Her phrase drew presumably on the earlier **grey matter** (19C) which referred to the colour of the human brain. Otherwise terms have tended to the abstract. **Nous** (loosely translated as common sense, and set in opposition to actual learning) is taken from the Greek word νουσ meaning mind. Its first slang use is by Alexander Pope in *The Dunciad* (1729). Another foreign language, French, is responsible for **savvy** (18C, from *savoir*: to know or understand), and Yiddish, and before it Hebrew, give **cocum**: knowledge. **Gaum** or **gawm** come from a dialect term, defined by Grose in his *Provincial Glossary* (1787) as meaning to understand. Thus the popular belief that the similar **gorm** is a back-formation from the popular **gormless** (foolish), is negated; it is simply a mis-spelling. **Gawm** also provides the root of **gumption**, which, if Grose is correct, is merely a version of **gawmtion**. Other terms are **horse sense** (US, horses were presumed to be supplied with some natural intelligence) and **smarts**. The **smart money**, from gambling, is the sensible viewpoint. As well as **dope***, knowledge can be **know-how** and the **nitty-gritty** (originally Afro-American) with its implication of the essential.

TO BE CLEVER OR AWARE

Meliorists may choose to see the terms that follow as referring to intellect, but the qualities on offer are far more those of knowing 'what's what' than of those dependent on any academic skills. The great majority of such phrases are prefaced by 'know' (and there exists a parallel vocabulary, indicating ignorance, which simply adds 'not'). For the most part they are self-explanatory; those that are not have been amplified. In chronological order they are to **know what is what** (1400) to **know what's what** (1600), to **know A from a battledore**, to **know A from a windmill** and to **know B from a bull's foot** (15C) (all 15C), to **know B from a battledore** and to **know which way the wind blows** (both 16C). To **know a hawk from a handsaw** in which **handsaw** is generally recognised as a corruption of *heronshaw* or *hernsew* meaning a heron appears to be a phrase exclusive to Shakespeare. It is used only once, in *Hamlet* (1602): 'I am but mad North, North-West: when the Winde is Southerly, I know a Hawke from a Handsaw.' More terms include to **know how many numbers make five**, to **know how many days go to the week**, to **know how the cards are dealt**, to **know a shilling from sixpence** (all 17C); to **know a thing or two**, to **know a trick or two** to **know which way is up**, to **know up from down**, to **know great A from a bull's foot** (all 18C).

19C versions are to **know A from the gable-end**, to **know B from a broomstick**, to **know how many beans make five**, to

know one's way about, to **know something**, to **know what o'clock it is**, to **know the time of day** and to **know how many go to a dozen** and to **know the ropes** (fr. naval use). The 20C has to **know enough to come in out of the rain**, to **know one's age**, to **know one's anus from one's ankle**, to **know one's arse from a hole in the ground**, to **know one's arse from one's elbow**, (20C arse is often euphemised as 'ears'), to **know one's boxes** (fr. printers' jargon: the boxes are of metal type), to **know one's eccer** (Aus., **eccer**: exercise, or school homework), to **know one's kit** (originally military), to **know one's onions**, to **know one's stuff**, to **know more than one's prayers**, to **know what's happening**, to **know what time it is** (currently popular in the language of rap music: 'Tell them what time it is!'), to **know where one's arse hangs** (said of one who has come up in the world and is suspected of forgetting their origins), to **know whether one is Arthur or Martha** (20C Aus., the term can also be used to denote a degree of sexual ambiguity), to **know it backwards**, to **know it down to the ground**, to **know one's stuff** and to **know whether it's pancake Tuesday or half-past breakfast time**. To **know where the bodies are buried** is to have knowledge which gives one leverage over others, and is often used in a political context.

A number of similar phrases substitute 'have' for 'know'. Among them are to **have the inside track** (19C, the original meaning of **inside track**, as used by racing men, was the truth), to **have the inside running** is to have an advantage (both terms come from the race track where the inside track, nearest the rails, gives horses an advantage). To **have the goods on**, to **have dead to rights**, to **have it pegged** (fr. 19C **peg**: to work hard, to hammer it out; or from pegged down: steady) are all 19C. To **have bang to rights** means to catch in the act, especially as in (fictional) conversations between police and criminals. 20C versions are to **have a line on** (fr. marksmanship), to **have the stuff on**, to **have down cold** (**cold** has subsequently become popular as an adjective meaning extremely or very, used as such by the **rap**★ community), to **have down pat**, to **have its number** (fr. telephones) and to **have it**

straight, to **have it sussed** (fr. **suss out**: to puzzle out, in turn linked to **sus**: suspect or suspicious; thus **sus** or **sussy**: aware).

Other phrases that suggest shrewdness or native wisdom include **see with half an eye** (19C, although the phrase has origins in the 15C), **see through a mill-stone** and **see through a brick wall** (both 19C), to **be on the ball**, to **have all one's marbles** (cf. **lose one's marbles**) and to **have what it takes** (20C, orig. US, in Aus. **what it takes**: money), to **be bright as a new pin** or **bright as a button** (20C), to have a **head on one's shoulders**, to **be nobody's fool, not be born yesterday, not be as daft as one looks** or **not be as stupid as one looks**. A number of term are based on the head: **use the old bean, use the chump, use the noggin, use the loaf** and **use the turnip**. The Afro-American **graduate** means to gain knowledge, though not specifically of an academic sort. As well as such verb combinations as to **be hep★**, to **be on the inside track★**, other 20C terms include **be posted, be wise to, be up on, get next to** and **make for**.

USING ONE'S SENSE

Savvy★, seen above as a noun, is equally valid as an adverb, as is sharp which the 18C referred solely to a cheating gambler, but in the 19C had broadened into meaning one who is well informed. **Half-wide** (19C) had an earlier, 16C incarnation as immoral, both terms are abbreviations of wide-awake; **fly** (19C) comes from the 18C Scots *flee*, both terms mean aware as does the 19C phrase **no flies on…** The latter definitely refers to the insects, and the need to keep alert if one wishes to avoid them settling; the former may do as well – the image is of the difficulty of catching flies – but there are equally valid claims for a root in *fledged* or even the cant term **flash★**. Less problematic are **all there** (the root of all those phrases meaning **not all there★** and denoting stupidity or even madness), **not so dumb, not so dusty** (fr. SE *dusty*: worthless) and **down** or **down to** (all of which are 19C). An addict of what the speaker considers to be difficult words must have **swallowed the dictionary**, (19C, often abbrev. as the **dick**). **Tasty**, especially popular in television's contemporary police series, originally (18C) referred only to food, and meant simply appetising. The extension to its modern definition comes with the 19C, although the word still carries an image of being 'good enough to eat'.

Jerry (20C), an abbreviation of **in full jerry**: up to someone's tricks comes from the verb to **jerry**: to understand (19C), itself based on **jerrycumumble**, which in rhyming slang, gives both the modern **tumble** (to) or **rumble. On the beam** (20C) originated in the RAF, where the beam was that of the radar, and one could be on or off it. Other 20C terms include **there with the goods**, **smart**, **first cab off the rank** (Aus.), **quick on the trigger**, **spunko** (20C, from **spunk**: spirit) and **swift**, although the phrase **a bit swift** means unfair or taking unfair advantage. The swiftness, acceptable in oneself, becomes a negative quality in another.

Black America has **down**, **necklaced**, **ready** and **ready-eyed** and **triple hip. Hardcore**, popularised in America's black ghettoes has spread, like so much slang, to white teenagers on both sides of the Atlantic (its original meaning was extreme pornography); the same fate has been accorded **street**, with its variations **streetified**, **street smart** and **street wise**, all of which give primacy to the sort of wisdom gained surviving in the urban jungle. Earlier teen terms include **cool★**, **hep** (first used among jazz fans of the 1940s, but rooted in the 19C **hep**: shrewd which comes in turn from 'Hep!', the exhortation of the ploughman or driver urging his horses to 'Get up!' and get lively), and its successor **hip**, the beatnik's term of choice and the root, in its turn, of the *hippies* of the late 1960s. The hippies themselves had their own coinages, notably **together, turned on**, and **switched on** (all of which had a certain drug-related aura); **with it**, an early 1960s term, was, like **dolly bird★** and **groovy★**, more celebrated in the media than amongst the slang speakers. Finally the phrase **who slept in the knife box?** (and is thus 'sharp') is a slightly mocking query of those considered to be showing off their brains.

To see one's own interest is variously to **blow wise, get hep, get smart, get wise, get next to oneself, get one's head screwed on, get one's mind right** (also as come to one's senses), **get straight (to oneself), smarten up** and **wise up**. Those terms, all 20C, plus to **be jerry to**, to **be on one's wavelength**, to **have**

down, to **have one's number,** to **have one sussed,** to **know what makes one tick, know where one is at,** to **know where one is coming from** and to **know where one's head is at** (the latter pair culled from New Age psychobabble), all give the meaning of knowing another person's motives, and by implication taking care of oneself.

FOOLS

After parts of the body, or at least those that are involved in sex, states of the mind, specifically the state of foolishness, with its gradations from eccentricity to certifiable insanity generate a wide range of language. Slang, on the whole, does not immediately distinguish: the differences must be assumed from the context.

THE SIXTEENTH CENTURY

The first recorded term for a fool is **looby** (14C), a precursor of the 20C adjective **loopy** and an ancestor of the children's television character, the puppet Looby-Loo. More contemporary are **lubber** (14C, the basis of the 16C nautical **land-lubber**) and **lob** (16C), both of which, like **looby**, have the added dimension of physical slovenliness, of a hulking boor as well as a fool. **Lob** and the slightly earlier **lobcock** (of which it must thus be an abbreviation) have a further dimension, that of the relaxed or only half-erect penis (cf. **lazy lob★**) — the image is thus one of laziness, of 'hanging around'. A final development of **looby** is the 19C **lobby** (which combined with the assonant *lud* made up the name Lobby Lud, an intinerant character whose task was to boost the circulation of one Fleet Street newspaper by appearing in holiday resorts and paying out small rewards to those who recognised him from his picture in that day's edition of the paper). A **natural** (1533) has two alternative, possibly parallel sources. A natural child is a bastard, otherwise known as a **get,** which gives the 20C **get** or **git,** synonyms for fool; at the same time the natural is 'one who is by nature deficient in intelligence;

a fool or simpleton by birth.' (*OED*). The ironic **wise** may well come from the contemporary phrase 'as wise as Waltham's calf' (cf. **calf**, below) or the three wise men of Gotham, among whose idiocies was the dragging of a pond to extricate the reflected moon. A **ninny-hammer** is based on the original meaning of **ninny**: a 'canting, whining beggar'.

   Prat, still widely used, comes from the alternative meaning of the buttocks while **hoddy peak** can also mean a cuckold; **hoddy** comes from the **hoddy-dod**, a snail, and the inevitable **horns★**, the mark of a cuckold, are in this case those of the snail. Nature is at the heart of the remaining 16C terms. **Buffle**, giving the 17C variation **bufflehead** (and the 20C **boofhead**) comes, from the French *buffle* meaning buffalo; thus the *OED*, although why a buffalo was *de facto* stupid must remain debatable. A **tame goose**, a **widgeon** (Freddie Widgeon is of course one of P. G. Wodehouse's foolish Drones) and a **cuckoo** (although the cuckoo's habits seem sly rather than foolish) present a trio a foolish 'birds' (leading presumably to the later **birdbrain**). Finally come **lamb**, **calf** and **calf-lolly** (fr. **calf**, plus the nautical **loblolly**: a cadger).

THE SEVENTEENTH CENTURY

The nature motif continues into the 17C with **bullfinch** and **gawk** (whether from the Scots dial. **gowk**: cuckoo and thus fool; or from **gawk** meaning to stare at) but such terms stand alone amongst the other new coinages. A **singleton** came either from **single** meaning simple or as an elision of a 'single ten': since the ten in cards ranks one below the knave, 'he' must therefore be a fool. **Nizzie** is rooted in one of two words meaning foolish: the French *niais* or the SE *nice*. **Sop** abbreviates the derogatory SE *milksop*, while **fopdoodle** combines **doodle**, a fool, with the original, 15C meaning of **fop**: also a fool (fr. the French *fat*, and the Latin *fatuus*). The 16C SE *zany*, meaning clown (especially as one performing in the Italian *Commedia dell' arte*) and later fool, gives **sawney** (plus its verb-form, meaning to whine and wheedle, cf. **ninny-hammer**) and **yawney** (19C). A real-life clown, Jack Adams, gave his name to another 'foolish' synonym; **Jack Adam's parish** was Clerkenwell, where he presumably lived, while similar terms are **jack fool** and **jack pudding**. Another proper name, **tony**, normally an abbreviation of Anthony, also meant fool, and is used as such in Middleton's play *The Changeling* (1623). Three near-nonsense words **nimenog**, **nigmenog** and **nigit** (**an eejit** or idiot) round out the century.

THE EIGHTEENTH CENTURY

If nature characterised the 16C terminology, then foodstuffs have an influence of the 18th. **Gooseberry** may be a laboured reference to the sweet, gooseberry fool, while **cake** refers to the 'softness' of the unintelligent head. **Noodle** only sounds like a food, it is more likely to have some link to **noddle**, meaning head, which it can also mean, although the *OED* separates the two meanings. Further images of food can be found in **macaroon** or **macaroni**, but these two are red herrings: this use of **macaroni** comes from the Italian *maccherone*, meaning a blockhead, fool or mountebank and is referred to as such in Joseph Addison's *Spectator* (1711). This **macaroni** has no relationship to his dandified cousins, who won their nickname from their ostentatious consumption of what was then an exotic foodstuff: pasta. **Gawney** came from the Midlands dialect term meaning to stare vacantly; **gabes** and **gaby**, respectively from East Suffolk and Yorkshire, meant much the same. **Sumph** came from Scots dialect. A **flat** or **flattie** was a rustic or peasant, especially as seen as the target of a thief or con-man, while **tom doodle** simply extended the 17C **doodle**, **tom** being a general term meaning simply man. A **griffin** (in SE a mythical animal usually represented as having the head and wings of an eagle and the body and hind quarters of a lion) was defined by Jon Bee as 'a grinning booby who hath lost a tooth or two at top and the same at bottom' and might remind modern readers of *Mad* magazine's mascot, the irrepressibly doltish Alfred E. Neuman and his catchphrase 'What, me worry?'

THE NINETEENTH CENTURY

Many of the strains that emerged in earlier centuries reappeared in the 19th. Proper names offered **Billy Barlow** (a real-life street clown of c.1840), and **Jim Crow**, which in this context is simply rhy. sl. for *saltimbanco*, meaning a street clown, although the original (and far more extensive) use of **Jim Crow★** was based on the 'nigger minstrel' song with its refrain 'Wheel about and turn about and jump Jim Crow'. It was this version of **Jim Crow** that lay behind the 20C term that became generic for the whole apparatus of US racial discrimination. Its use as a racist epithet can be seen under RACE. Less controversial names included the dialect terms **Ralph** or **Ralph Spooner**, **Johnny**, **Johnny-cake** (cf. **cake★**) or **Johnny-raw** (all meaning a rustic simpleton as do **shaney** or **shany**; cf. **flatty**), **Toby Trot** and **Tom Tug** (rhy. sl. for **mug★**). **Rube**, from Reuben a 'typical' rural name, was especially popular among America's touring showmen, who used it as their warning cry:'Hey, Rube!' **Silly Billy**, and the abbreviated **silly**, came from a generic term for a clown, as possibly is **bozo** (20C), which means man in Spanish, but may refer to the character Bozo the Clown.

Dundreary referred to the character Lord Dundreary, a foppish fool in Tom Taylor's play *Our American Cousin*, which piece President Lincoln was watching on the night of his assassination. **Juggins** is a general term, meaning specifically one who is so foolish that he can be prevailed upon to buy every round of drinks (the term is an extension of jug) but gained greater use through the notoriety of one Henry Ernest Schlesinger Benzon, better known to London's sporting fraternity as the 'Jubilee Juggins'. Benzon, the son of a Birmingham umbrella frame maker, went through an inheritance of £250,000 (a massive sum at the time) in less than two years. His last pennies went in 1887, the year of Queen Victoria's Golden Jubilee, thus earning him his nickname. Only the kindness of his fellow patrons of the raffish Romano's Restaurant in the Strand who established a fund that sustained him on £7.00 per week for life saved him from absolute penury. Other terms for **juggins** are **jay** and **j**, while **muggins**, an extension of **mug**, obviously parallels it semantically. **Cousin Betty** referred specifically to women, and could also mean a **tart★**. Finally the phrase **he is none of John Whoball's children** means he's no fool; a convoluted confection playing on **whoaball** meaning milkmaid which in turn combines **whoa** meaning stop and **ball**: a common name for a cow.

Further dialect term include **buffer** (Scots), **doddy** (Norfolk), **gump** (Yorkshire; the 'homely, parochial, awkward, well-meaning' gump was adopted as a trademark by the 20C comedian Norman Wisdom) and **joskin** or **josser** (both from the dialect *joss*, meaning bump, itself found in the SE *bumpkin*). Nature gives **dodo**, (either from the extinct bird or from **doddy**), **cod** or **cod's head**, **lights** (more usually an animal's innards, but possibly an early version of the 20C **lights on but nobody home**★) and **jacob** (usually meaning the bird a jay, it puns on **jay** or **j** meaning **juggins**★. As well as the rustics listed above, other dupes include the **mug** (into which one can 'pour' anything), the **go-along** and the **pigeon**. The **muff**, from the softness of a real muff, is soft in the head, as is a **sammy-soft** or **softy**; a **jobbernowl** mean's literally a fool's head, from **jobbard** meaning simpleton; the **nod(ge)cock** or **noddy** wags his head foolishly while the **strut-noddy** has no idea of his own stupidity. A **stump** is, like the SE term, short and thick, while the **trunk** is all body and no head.

More 19C terms include **duffer** (otherwise a seller or maker of a variety of counterfeit goods), **gulpin** (originally a Royal Marine), **loon** or **loony** (fr. **lunar**: moonstruck) and **moony**, **tootledum-pattick**, **crack** (fr. **crackbrain**), **eejit** (phonetically mis-spelling idiot), **gooby** (possibly from **goof**), **greener**, **greenhorn** or **greenlander** (all dependent on **green**: naive). Physical inadequacies are underlined in **crock** (usually meaning injured) and **dotty** (with definite links to **doddery**, meaning weak or stumbling). **Side sim** is a simpleton, **nias** comes from the earlier **nizzie**★, and **slowcoach** is the root of the 20C US **slowpoke** and before it meant vagina, **dickey-dido** meant simply fool. Finally **mome**, **mo-mo** or **momo** come either from the French *mome*: a little child or an innocent, or from the English **mum** meaning dumb. Lewis Carroll's *mome* as in the 'mome raths outgrabe', used in 'Jabberwocky' and found in *Alice Through the Looking Glass* (1871) has no bearing on stupidity; writing in 1855 Carroll himself defines it as 'solemome' or solemn and thus grave.

THE TWENTIETH CENTURY

Reflecting, no doubt, the world about it, 20C slang adopts a harder, more combative edge than does that of earlier centuries. Thus of the modern terms meaning fool a good number are synonymous with those usually found meaning the genitals, especially the penis. Thus one finds **tool★**, **wienie★**, **pud★**, **dildo★** and **dork★**, as well as the Yiddish **schmuck** or (in its euphemised form) **schmo** (fr. the German/Yiddish term meaning jewellery or ornament and thus the penis, cf. **family jewels★**), **goober** (US, usually a peanut). **Numbnuts** combines **nuts**, meaning testicles (and crazy), with *numb*, as in braindead, while **poop** began life in the 17C as the buttocks. **Horse's arse** and **horse's hangdown** are self-evident, while in Australia a **flipwreck** is one whose idiocy is atttributed to the supposed results of excessive masturbation (cf. **flip oneself off**). Perhaps the best-known of all such 'genital' terms is **berk**, the abbreviation of **Berkeley hunt** or **Berkshire hunt**, rhy. sl. terms for **cunt**, otherwise meaning vagina, but also used as an all-purpose pejorative. A second layer of rhy. sl. is found in **Charlie Smirke**. Whether **poon** (Aus.) is related to the US **poontang★** (vagina) and is thus cognate with **berk** is debatable; the *Australian National Dictionary* (1988) gives no hint of such a relationship, although it does link **poon** and **ponce★** (which exists as a term of abuse, although with no special emphasis on stupidity).

Yiddish and Australian both make a notable contribution. If the Eskimos have an infinity of terms for snow, so do Yiddish speakers have a number for fool. They include **schlub** (not just a fool, but a coarse bumpkin too), **klutz** (fr. the German *klutz* meaning block of wood, a heavy person or a giant) and **shlemiel**, a word that comes from the proper name Shlumiel, son of the leader of the tribe of Simon (see *Numbers*, ii) and notable for his inability to win any of the battles in which he fought. Leo Rosten, writing in *The Joys of Yiddish* (1968), sets out the precise hierarchy of idiocy: 'The *schlemiel* trips and knocks down the *shlimazel*, and the *nebech* repairs the *shlimazl's* glasses'. **Schmeggege** and **schnook** sound Yiddish, but in fact, if one takes 'real' Yiddish to be that spoken in eastern Europe, they are both inventions, coined by the immigrants who flooded into the US c. 1900. Australia's contributions include **clunk**, **dill** or **dilly** (cf. **dildo**), **gig** and **tonk**. For all that popular etymology links it to Australia's Aborigines, **nong** or **ning-nong** are strictly European: the origins are either **nimenog★** or even the Latin *non compos (mentis)*. **Galah** comes from the name of the rose-breasted grey backed cockatoo 'much given to chatter', while **drongo** was originally the name of a 1920s racehorse that consistently finished last or thereabouts in all of its thirty-seven races; **Drongo** was thereupon taken up as the name for a slow-witted figure in the political cartoons appearing in *The Melbourne Herald*.

Nature has its usual say with **coot** (an allegedly stupid bird), **kook** (US, an abbreviation of **cuckoo★**), **cluck** (as in a chicken) and **dingbat** (cognate with the phrase **bats in the belfry**); **boob** is an abbreviation of the 17C **booby**, a term that meant both a fool and the *Sula fusca*, a species of gannet that was so nicknamed from its apparent willingness to let itself be caught; **noddy**, another 17C term for fool, is also a seabird, this time the tern-like *Anous stolidus*. Food gives **veg** (fr. vegetable), **fruitcake** (which is full of 'nuts'), **mutt** (either from **muttonhead★** or from the popular nickname for a dog), **lunchbox** (as in the phrase **out to lunch**) and **nana** (fr. the banana which is soft [in the head]). **Goof** and **goop** share a similar reference to softness. Simple stupidity underlines such terms as **dope** (possibly from Cumberland dialect), **ig man** and **ignant** (both Afro-American, both abbreviations of SE *ignorant*), **lame** (fr. **lamebrain**), **loogan** (US), **lunk** (fr. **lunkhead**), **simp**, **stupe**, **thickie**, **thicko** and **gink**. **Dingaling** and **ring-ding** both have the implication of the rattling within an empty head, **screwballs** have a 'screw loose', **bugs**, a term whose most celebrated exemplars are the US gangster Benjamin 'Bugsy' Siegel and the cartoon rabbit Bugs Bunny, are 'bugs in the head'. The US Army gives a **section eight** (that section of the US Military Code under which a man is discharged on the grounds of mental instability) and, from the Vietnam era, **FNG** or **effengee** (a 'fucking new guy', whose inexperience is bound to render him inadequate); **sickie** abbreviates sick in the head, while the children's term **spaz** comes from spastic and often denotes physical as well as mental problems. **Twit** and **nit** are also mainly playground terms (the former cognate with various terms based on birds, the latter coming from louse, thus **nitwit** means literally louse brained).

A **wet goose** or **wet foot** (fr. **wet**: naive plus **goose**★ and SE *tenderfoot*) is naive; **whacko** comes from the Yorkshire dial. **whacky**, meaning a dolt. **Clod** (fr. **clodhopper**) and **shitkicker** (US) both carry on the tradition of identifying the peasant with stupidity. **Dipshit**, with its euphemised form **dipstick** (as heard in television's *Only Fools And Horses*) is simply derogatory, while **Dublin University graduate** plays on the stereotype of the stupid Irishman; **Herbert**, often pronounced as **'Erbert**, is presumably a 'silly' name, while the West Indian **quashie** comes from Kwesi, a child born on a Sunday. The Afro-American **semolia** probably refers to a once-celebrated mental hospital. A **stumer** comes from **stumer** meaning a dud cheque, hence a dud anything including a person, like the **nine-bob note**, a **three-dollar bill** is abnormal while a **two-foot rule** rhymes with fool. Specific terms include **school-book chump** (AA: one who is intellectual but not intelligent) and **square-eyes** (one who watches too much TV, and is therefore considered stupid). A foolish person can look like **he wouldn't piss if his pants were on fire**; one might tell a dullard **one of these days you'll wake up dead**.

HEAD

Many terms for fool refer, quite logically, to the head. They are arranged here in approximate chronological order.

The 16C gives **block** (also meaning hard-hearted) and **block-head**, **goosecap** (fr. the 'silly' **goose** and the use of *cap* to mean head) and **calf's head** (fr. **calf**★); **beef-witted** is an adverbial form. The 17C has **clodpoll** and **clodpate** (**poll** and **pate** both meaning head; thus the epithet: **clod-skulled**), **souse-crown** (fr. **souse**: thump) **cabbage-head**, **beef-brain** and **hulverhead**, (fr. **hulver**: holly), while the 18C includes **addlepate**, **addle cove** and **addle head** (fr. SE *addle*: to confuse) **noddy pate**, **noddy-head** and **noddipol** (fr. **poll**: head) **numbskull**, **sheep's head** (also meaning garrulous) and **beefhead**. The 19C has **mutton-head**, **crackpot** (also a crank) **muddle head**, **muffin head**, **sate-poll**, **plump-**

pate (i.e. **fathead**), and **pestlehead** (fr. **pestle**: penis, thus **pestle-head** is a prototype of **dickhead**).

Most of these terms are 20C coinages, the majority of which are still in use: **airhead, boofhead, bubblehead; birdbrain; bone-head, cement-head, lamebrain, lunkhead, meathead, mus-clehead, thickhead, stupe-head; dickhead, diphead, dork-brain, fuckhead, fuckwit, poophead, toolhead; chowder-head, chucklehead** (US 20C, fr. **chuckle**: clumsy or stupid), **crapbrain, deadhead** (20C), **fathead; hammerhead** (possibly fr. **hammer**: penis, thus another **dickhead** clone), **squarebrain** and **wethead** (all Afro-American); **head-banger** (also used to describe fans of heavy metal rock music), **mental job, nutter, nutcake, puddinghead, pinhead, prawnhead** (Aus.), **zipalid** (a **lid** or head with a zip, from which the brains have been removed); **jolt(er)-head, shatterbrain, shatterpate, weather-head** (which nods from side to side like a weatherock) and **loggerhead**.

ASS

Donkeys may well be stubborn rather than stupid, but this has not spared them centuries of identification with stupidity. All that remains today is **ass**, which dates to the 18C, but earlier eras have **baldwin, cuddy, Dick, Edward, Issachar, Jack, Jenny, Neddy** (all 18C) and **moke, donkey, Jerusalem pony, longears, myla** and **softhorn** (all 19C). Perhaps the most intriguing, and a proof that in the coining of slang little really changes, is the **King of Spain's trumpeter**, a ponderous pun on the fictional aristocrat 'Don Key' and a term that, while different in meaning, in style predates by two centuries today's **Spanish archer**, the equally punning 'El Bow'.

DUMB AND TOM

Dumb has meant stupid since the 16C; its descendants and peers include **dum-dum, dumb-ass, dumb-bell, dumbellina, dumb fuck, dumbhead, dumbo, dummy** (19C) and **dumbski**. Apart from those terms including **Tom** that are cited above, slang fools include **Tom Coney** (17C, coney meaning both rabbit and the simpleton who can be gulled by the **coney-catcher***), **Tom-far-thing** (17C, **farthing** being a general term for worthless), **Tom Fool** (tom being a general term meaning man) and **Tom towly**.

INSANE AND CRAZY

As well as the many terms meaning fool or simpleton slang has a wide vocabulary for dealing with those who are deemed to have stumbled one step further from reality: the crazy or insane. Predictably, few such terms pay even lip-service to political correctness; this is not the world of the 'differently abled'. What is perhaps worthier of note is the fact that although this vocabulary stretches over four centuries, surprisingly little has been discarded.

The oldest of such terms, **cuckoo**, which can be found in Shakespeare's *Henry IV, pt. II* (1600), is a perfect exemplar. So too is **barmy** (17C), which comes from SE *barm*: yeast and implies a brain bubbling over with manic energy. **Barmy** leads in turn to the 19C **balmy**, with an additional reference to the SE *balmy*: soft. Both terms are linked in the rhy. sl. **lakes (of Killarney)**, which in turn leads to the 20C **lakesy**: mad. **Cracked** (17C) is yet another vintage term, abbreviating cracked in the head, and leading to the 20C **crackers** and **cracko**. In many ways the most interesting is **rum**, which other than in deliberate archaisms such as **rum cove** (an odd fellow) is a term that has barely survived. **Rum** began as an all-purpose 16C cant term meaning good (see GOOD for a full etymology); yet a century later, c.1774, it had been transformed into odd or eccentric. The precise reason for this reverse is debatable; Partridge suggests, plausibly, that rum, as a gypsy term and indeed in the spelling **rom** actually meaning gypsy, might have been branded with the same opprobrium as was accruing to the gypsies and thus, while the underworld might still see it as 'good', the larger world came to associate it with more negative qualities.

The prolific slang coiners of the 19C came up with a number of new terms; once again the majority are still in wide use. They included **daffy** (fr. Northern dial. **daff**: a simpleton and cognate with SE *daft*), **dotty** (fr. **dotty**: weak in the legs) with its fake-Latin intensifiers **dottima**: slightly and **dottissima**: very mad), **gaga** (first used by Rudyard Kipling in the 1880s; it comes from the French *gateux*: an old man so feeble as to be incontinent, and also means drunk), **gone** (abbr. **gone in the head**), and **half-cracked**, **half-gone** and **half-there**. **Funny** abbreviated **funny in the head**, the first instance of 'funny peculiar' rather than 'funny ha-ha'; **loco** (US), was originally applied by cowboys to cattle that had eaten **locoweed**: marijuana; its extreme version **plumb loco** played on the 15C **plumb**, from 'plum ripe', meaning completely, utterly. **Screwy** referred to the early 19C **have a screw loose**, as did **loose up top**; the 20C **unglued** merely alters the category of weakened link, **apartments to let** also implied a certain emptiness in 'the upper storey'. **Loony** (abbrev. of *lunatic*) was a forerunner of the 1980s **loony tune**: a crazy person; Loony Tunes was the name of a series of film cartoons created by the team of Hollywood animators Hanna–Barbera; fittingly the term was popularised by another Hollywood star, Ronald Reagan, to describe such figures as the Libyan leader Colonel Gaddaffi. **Loopy** played on **looby★**: a fool, or the Scots *loopy*: crafty; **non compos** abbreviated the legal term *non compos mentis* (of unsound mind), **whacky** (fr. the Yorks. dial. *whacky*: a dolt) led to the 20C **whack-a-doo**, **whacked out** and **whacko**; like its modern incarnation **kinky** meant not straight, but without the slightest sexual overtone.

'Infestation' of the brains gives a small sub-group: **bats in the belfry** (19C) generates **bathouse**, **batty**, **bats** and **batshit** (all 20C); once transported to the Antipodes the bats become **rats** (which originally meant simply *delirium tremens*, the **DTs**), as in **in the rats**, **rathouse**, **rats in the upper storey**, **rats in the garret**, **rats in the attic** and **rats in the loft**. One can also have **maggots in one's head** (19C), although **maggotty** means drunk in the UK, and irritated in Australia. The 20C **bughouse** (US) continues the imagery, with the variations **bugs**, **bugs in the brain**, **crazy as a bed-bug** and **bugsy**, a term immortalised in the nickname of gangster Benjamin 'Bugsy' Siegel (1906–47), New York hoodlum and the pioneer of Las Vegas. **Living on a worm farm** substitutes invertebrates for insects or rodents, but the meaning remains.

The 20C adds **all over the board, around the bend** with the punning **harpic** (fr. the detergent's copyline: 'clean around the bend'), **mental** (1913; fr. mental case, mental defective) with its rhy. sl. synonym **radio** (fr. **radio rental**). **Crazy-arse, crazy-ass** and **wild** and **wild-ass** and **buck-wild** (AA) all denote serious instability, as does **apeshit** (fr. **go ape**: to lose control); **bananas** (fr. **go bananas**) is a harder variation on its earlier definition: to go mushy (as in a ripe banana) with emotion and excitement. More 20C terms include **dippy** (possibly from dipsomaniac: an alcoholic), **doofus** (US), **dopey, dorky** (fr. **dork★** = **prick★** = fool), **freaky** (with the inference that the madness is drug-related), **kooky** (US), **lamebrained** (fr. **lamebrain★**: a fool), **meshugge** (Yid. fr. Heb. *meshuga*: insane), **neuro** (abbrev. neurotic) and **schitzi** (abbrev. schizophrenic, coined in 1910 and used, with little regard for its precise origins, as a blanket description of insanity). **Nuts**, a core term, is rooted in **off one's nut★** (19C, **nut**: head) and gives **nutso, nutty** and **nutty as a fruitcake** (itself a synonym). **Squirrelly** plays on nuts, and a **squirrel** was briefly US slang for a psychoanalyst: each patient is a 'nut'. **Potty** was coined in the 19C, when it meant indifferent, shaky or unpromising; the intimations of lunacy are a 20C addition. **Bonkers** was popularised in 1964, when the Tory grandee Quintin Hogg, ridiculing Labour leader Harold Wilson's much-touted proletarian origins, declared, 'If the British public falls for this, I say it will be stark, staring bonkers.' **Wig City, wigged out** and **wiggy** all come from **flip one's wig, wired** has drug overtones —one is 'strung too tight' —as do **twisted** and **weird**, while **wires crossed** refers simply to faulty electrics. **Toey** (Aus.) was originally used of an unstable horse, endlessly shuffling its feet. A **space case** refers either to one's losing a grip on down-to-earth reality (cf. **airhead★**), or the 'space' that such sufferers metaphorically have between their ears.

Colonialism and the military have a small sub-vocabulary of madness, gleaned from the overseas postings that could leave a man seriously debilitated by the tropical conditions. Thus **asiatic**, originated by the US Marine Corps, **troppo** (fr. *tropical*), an Australian invention, and, most celebrated of all, **doolally**, coined in the late 19C by Britain's Indian Army, and still extant, at least amongst Londoners. The term, in full **doolally tap** (fr. Hindi *tap*: fever), comes from the Deolali military sanitorium in Bombay, to which the mentally ill troops were sent. However, according to the veteran Frank Richards, writing in his memoir *Old Soldier Sahib* (1936) the illness came not before one arrived at Deolalie, but during one's stay there. Time-expired troops were sent to the sanatorium to await the next troop-ship home. It was during the long hot days of tedium that men, formerly first-class soldiers, might gradually go to pieces. Anyone who did 'queer things', was characterised as having the **doolally tap**. A later, and much rarer term is the **Balkan tap**, characterizing the growing, happy indolence that took over men involved in the World War I Macedonian campaign.

Other asylums give their own particular terms: **yarra** comes from the Australian institution at Yarra Bend, Victoria, **go Yarmouth** from the Royal Naval hospital at Great Yarmouth and **winnick** from the asylum at Winwick, Lancs.

The core term **not all there** (19C) has generated many synonyms, some of which, but by no means all, are listed here. They include **not quite there** (19C), **not having both oars in the water** (20C), **not playing with a full deck**, (20C) **not the full quid** (Aus.) or **ten pence short of the full quid**, **two pence short of a bob**, **five annas shot of the rupee**, **two bricks short of the load**, **two wafers short of a communion**, **only eighty pence in the pound**, **one shingle short**, the Australian equivalent of having a **tile loose** (19C), **one sandwich short of the picnic**, a **couple of chips short of a fish dinner**, **cruising with one's lights on**, (20C) **lights on but nobody home** (20C), **out to lunch**, to have **lost one's all one's marbles**, and have **a few of one's pages stuck together**.

The basic, and interchangeable terms **out of one's head** and **off one's head** give the variations **off one's bean**, **off one's chump**, **off one's trolley**, **off one's head** (19C), **off one's kadoove** (19C, an aborigine term which was taken from **cady** or **kadi**: a hat), **out of one's box**, **out of one's cake**, **out of one's chump** (19C), **out of one's gourd**, **out of one's nut** (19C), **out of one's onion**

(20C), **out of one's tree, off the rails, off one's rocker** (19C), **off the beam, off the wall, off-beat, off-brand, out of whack**, and **on the edge**. Off and out of can be substituted for each where grammatically relevant. **Out of left field** comes from the game of baseball and, like any term using 'left', implies something not quite right, or at least, given the position of left field as it relates to a right-handed batter, out of the main area of interest.

Finally, a mental hospital can be a **bin, booby hatch** (the reference to the notorious north London asylum at Colney Hatch may in fact be coincidental) or **booby hutch** (19C, the term also meant a police station), **bughouse, crazy house, funny farm, loony bin, nut hatch** or **nut house**.

SPEECH AND TALK

Other than the logical divisions by part of speech, and even these can elide, with single words serving as both noun and verb, drawing the fine lines between the way a given slang term is used in the area of speech and talk is at best difficult and at worst pointless. All is determined by context; slang by its nature is far more fluid than is standard English; never more so than in terms relating to speech.

SPEECH AND TALK

Blab and its verb forms **blab** and, apparently **blabber**, are the first slang terms relating to speech and can be found as such in the 17C. Their history, however, is somewhat older. There is even, according to the *OED*, a question over whether what appears to be an obvious link even exists. **Blab**, then spelt **blabbe** and meaning a 'chatterer' occurs in Chaucer c. 1374, **blab** meaning simply 'chatter' or 'loose talk' can be found in *The Tale of Beryn* (c.1400), but then promptly vanishes until the 16C. when it is augmented by a verb form, **blab**: to chatter (1535); this in turn creates a noun **blabber**: a chatterer. However the verb **blabber** predates all these; it occurs in *Piers Ploughman* (1362), and with its noun **blabberer** is common in the works of John Wyclif (1330-84). Thus, however tempting it may seem, one cannot simply assume that **blab** is a 14C abbreviation of **blabber**. Instead, the *OED* suggests, it is related to the noun *labbe*: a revealer of secrets' in Chaucer, and the verb *labbe* in *Piers Ploughman* and to *labbyng*: open-mouthed,' It can also be linked to the Old Dutch *labben*: to chatter. Thus **blab/blabbe** might be a mixture of *labbe* and **blabber**; but might also be simply onomatopoeic. Whatever the root, the terms appeared often during the 16C and 17C (at which point **blab** began to be rated as colloquial rather than SE), but had been consigned to slang by the 18C.

Two of the 18C's terms refer to the body: **gab** comes from **gab**, meaning mouth, which is in turn a development of the earlier **gob***; **jaw** is a variation on the SE *jaw*, and means especially a lecture; the 19C **pi-jaw**, **pi** being short for pious, is an earnest exhortation aimed at schoolchildren. The reduplicated **jaw-jaw** is a 20C creation, most famously used by the then Prime Minister Harold Macmillan who declared on January 30, 1958, 'Jaw Jaw is better than war-war', a line that echoed his predecessor Winston Churchill's comment to President Eisenhower at the White House on January 26, 1954: 'Talking jaw to jaw is better than going to war'. A third 18C term is **rap**, which originally meant to swear an oath against someone; it languished thereafter until the 1960s, when it was exhumed with a new emphasis, to speak deeply and sincerely, often of one's innermost feelings; thus a **rap session** was a form of informal therapy. Apparently consigned to the psychobabble of the New Age **rap** gained a third identity in the 1980s when it came to describe a style of Black music, also known as hip-hop, pioneered in New York and spreading to the West Coast, in which performers spoke rather than sang their lyrics (often highly political or sexual, and defined by the concerns of teenage life in the inner city ghetto) against a simple backing track.

The 19C has the rhy. sl. **Duke of York** (talk), **snaffle** (especially 'shop', and derived from the E. Anglian dial. *snaffle*: to talk nonsense), **luff**, **pishery-pashery**, and **jibb** (fr. **jibb**: the tongue, and giving the 20C **jibb in**: to talk one's way in, to gatecrash). **Gaff** meant an outcry or simply a cry, becoming a conversation in the 20C and giving the 19C **blow the gaff**: to tell a secret; **gas** carries an implication of verbosity (cf. **hot air, wind**) and gives **all gas and gaiters**, the name of a once-popular clerical sitcom. **Guff**, from the SE *guff*: a puff or whiff, and synonymous with **gush** and **tosh**, is equally skewed towards verbal nonsense; it may also relate to the Anglo-India *gup* or *gup-gup*: idle gossip, from Hindi *gap*: prattle, which borrowed in turn from the Turkish *gep* or *geb*: word, saying or talk and the Persian *guftan* or *guptan*: to say. The word made its way to England c.1868, the year in which a highly critical account of South Indian society was published, under the pseudonym of 'Gup'. The word also reached Australia, where **gup** means a fool. **Patter**, in the 18C the equivalent of *jargon* (i.e. professional and occupational slang), meant glib talk, especially that of showmen (cf. **spruik**), but could also mean a judicial summing up and theatrical lyrics.

  Rabbit (rhy. sl. **rabbit and pork**: talk) and the cognate **bunny** (rabbit) appear in the 20C, as does the backslang **kaylack, tongue-wagging, broadcasting, yap** (a development of 19C **yap**: to prattle on, cf. **waffle**) and **mouth music** (cf. **chin music**). This latter, according to Scotland Yard's then D.A.C. David Powis, writing in the glossary included in *The Signs of Crime* (1977) is also 'a taboo and gross expression meaning the practice of cunnilingus. Never used in mixed or family company'. **Crack**, usually **the crack** is an Anglo-Irish term, although it comes from the 19C Scots *crack*: a friendly chat or bragging and tends to be used in reference to the enjoyment to be gained from an event as distinct from the ostensible meaning of the event itself. Other 20C coinages are the Afro-American **ji-jibe** (fr. **jib**; unimportant chatter) and **fat lip** (unpleasant talk); a **blooper** (an embarrassing public verbal error; possibly from a mixture of **blab★** and the exclamation *oops!*); and a **beef** (a complaint), which Partridge suggests comes from the theatrical term meaning to shout or yell but the *OED* attributes to US farming, both terms appear during the 1880s.

CHATTER AND GOSSIP

Although a number of the terms listed above can mean chatter or idle talk, and are often found as such, those listed below are more specifically related to 'hot air'. The 16C **jabber**, which these days is more likely to mean unrestrained, even unintelligible talk rather than gossip comes from **jibb**: the tongue; **cackle** (17C) comes from the verb meaning to reveal secrets through indiscreet talk, **gum** (18C, fr. the gums in one's mouth and thus the mouth itself) gives the 20C combination **beat the gums**, while **mag** (18C) is an abbreviation of the 'gossipy' magpie whose chattering, according to various ancient authorities betokens evil tidings or at best the arrival of a stranger; its bad reputation (dating back at least to the Middles Ages) is based on the belief that alone of all birds the magpie did not enter the Ark with Noah, preferring instead to sit outside 'jabbering over the drowned world' (William Henderson *Notes on the Folk-Lore of the Northern Counties* [1866]). Chatter is further suggested in **wind, gas** and **hot air** (all from the emptiness of the words), **gush** (19C, words springing up like a fountain), **burble** (see verb below), **blather** (possibly fr. **blat★**), **tosh** and its probable root **bosh**, a direct borrowing of the Turk *bosh*: empty or worthless; the word became current in English after the appearance of Morier's best-selling novel *Ayesha* (1834). **Poker talk** (19C) is fireside chit-chat (fr. the poker), and **scanmag** (19C) comes from *scandalum magnum*: the 'scandal of magnates'. This old legal term dates back to a statute of King Richard II which forbade anyone from publishing a malicious report against any person holding a position of dignity.

Two musical terms have been adopted by the 20C: **jazz** (hence the phrase **all that jazz**) and slightly later **jive** both were used in a non-musical sense to mean 'misleading, untrue, empty, or pretentious' talk, a comment perhaps on the intolerance of those who failed to appreciate the musics in question. Other terms include **bull** (thus **bull session**: a male get-together; cf. **bullshit**), **dribble** (fr. SE) and **schmooze** (see verb, below). **Yack** or **yak** and **natter** have both been adopted from earlier dialect terms: **yack** (and thus **yakety-yak**) originally meant fast and meaningless talk (and is still found as such), while **natter**, now a neutral chat or discussion, comes from the 19C **gnatter**: to grumble, to complain, to be peevish or querulous; or to talk or gossip in an unfriendly manner.

SMOOTH TALK AND DECEPTION

Blarney (18C) is perhaps the epitome of slang terms meaning smooth talk. It comes from Blarney, a village near Cork in Ireland, which has a castle in which lies an inscribed stone. The stone is hard to approach and the popular belief is that any one who kisses this 'Blarney stone' will ever after be gifted with a persuasive, plausible tongue. Thus **blarney** has become synonymous with smoothly flattering or cajoling talk; it can also mean outright nonsense. Similar properties have accrued to **gammon** (possibly from the SE verb to *game*) which has also been defined as chatter (18C) and nonsense (19C). **Apple sauce** (19C) and **banana oil** (20C) are both notably smooth; **eyewash** is a former army term, meaning anything, e.g. washing the eyes, that is done for effect rather than for any practical purpose. Like **blarney bunk, bunkum, buncombe** and **bunkum** (19C, US) stem from geography in this case Buncombe County in N. Carolina. The word emerged during the debate on the 'Missouri Question' in 1821 when one Felix Walker, the member from this district rose to speak. Although the debate was due to end and members begged him to sit down, he refusing, explaining that his constituents expected it, and that he was bound 'to make a speech for Buncombe.' The term stuck, first as **buncombe**, then **bunkum**, then, as abbreviated by the satirist George Ade, **bunk**. Thus Henry Ford's celebrated dictum 'History is bunk,' and Harold Laski's mordant assessment of the obituary business: 'De mortuis nil nisi bunkum.'

The sceptical 20C has other terms. **Bullshit** is bluntest, sometimes modified to **bull** or **BS**, but it far from alone. **Chat** implies seduction, as does its coarser amplification **bumchat**; SE *chat* means simply talk and underlies another combination, **backchat**, meaning cheek or impudence. Seduction is also central to **line**, although its roots are in the SE *line of goods*, and thus presumes something to 'sell'; the **con** (fr. SE *confidence trick*) is self-explanatory, and **come-on** can apply to swindlers or **lotharios***; **soap** and **soft soap** and **flannel** all imply 'cleaning up' one's words; in the 19C **flannel** meant the ornate, scroll-ridden letterheads with which tradesmen garlanded the invoices they sent to their aristocratic clients; there is no proof that this is linked to the 20C use, albeit a similar one. **Oil** or the **old oil** makes things go more smoothly, a **snow job** blankets the hearer with a smooth coating (like untrampled snow); **spiel** is based on the German *spiel*: to talk and is synonymous with **patter** or **line**; so too is **riff** fr. SE *riff*: a simple musical phrase repeated over and over. Britain's West Indian population talk of **speeching** while Afro-Americans prefer a **spit-bit**.

Sob stuff (thus **sob sister**: agony aunt and **sob story**) is a story intended to persuade through pity and **soft sawder** (19C) means flattery; the term comes from SE *sawder*: solder, which smooths over the cracks. A number of phrases are based on the verb **come the…**; they all imply deception and often insert 'old'. Thus **come the artful** (19C, hoax, deceive), **come the acid** (exaggerate or speak sarcastically), **come the blarney over** (19C), **come the bludge on** (20C Aus, cf. **bludge**), **come the gammon** (19C, wheedle), **come the cunt** (20C, be obnoxious or obstreperous), **come the raw prawn** (Aus. 20C), **come the tin man** (20C, to deceive) and (perhaps the best known) **come the old soldier** (19C, to malinger). A number of nouns meaning smooth talk also pass muster as verbs, typically **blarney**, **oil** and **flannel**; other such verbs include **apply the oil**, **pour on the oil**, **feed a line** or **hand** and **hand out a line**, **schmooze** (Yiddish, from Hebrew: *schmuos*: things heard, thus rumours) **snow** and **snow under**.

OTHER TALK

More references to ways of speaking include **beating the gums** (20C), **going on** or **going on at** (19C) and **wanking** or **wanking on** (20C), all of which mean complaining or whingeing. A remark can be a **crack** (20C, but meant a lie in the 17C), a **wisecrack** (a joke), and three terms which imply the verbal 'trumping' of another speaker: **capper** (US 20C, which 'caps' the previous comment), **zinger** (20C, fr *zing*: energy) and **whammy** (20C, best known for the phrase **double whammy**, as touted by the British Conservative party during the General Election of 1992). Articulacy can be the **gift of the gab** (18C) a development of the **gift of the gob** (17C); the former term also meant to have a wide mouth. Finally

pipe, meaning a voice (17C) gives the verb **pipe**: to talk, **open one's pipes**: to sing, **set up one's pipes**: to yell (both 17C); **pipe down**: to be quiet or, as an exclamation be quiet! and **pipe up**: to speak more audibly (all 19C and based on the Royal Navy's use of pipes to signify orders).

THE TALKER

Tending as it does to point up one's failings rather than to laud one's virtues, slang's terms for talker emphasize the negative. It is the gossip, the bore, the slanderer and the braggart who gain slang's attention; the mellifluous orator must turn to standard English, as he or she does for their vocabulary, for suitable encomiums.

Tongue-pad (17C) is based on **footpad***, and, meaning a smooth and not wholly trustworthy talker, is about as reputable; a **tongue-padder** is a lawyer, an invariably dubious character in slang; a **blab** (17C) is likely to talk indiscreetly, and a **tub thumper** (17C), originally describing a ranting preacher, was soon extended to apply to any over-enthusiastic speaker. **Bag of wind**, **windbag**, **blowhard**, **gasbag** and **gasser** are all 19C and all mean **loudmouth** (20C). A **chaff-cutter** (19C fr. **chaff**: to boast) is a slanderer or an overly knowing talker. A **spruiker** (Aus. 20C, fr. Dutch *spreker*: to speak) is a loud talker, specifically a sideshow barker); the Afro-American **storefront preacher** (20C) preaches only to those who idle away their days outside the general store of some small US town. A **tummler** (Yiddish, fr. German *tummel*: noise, tumult) is a noisy person, thus the life and soul of the party, and specifically the paid social director of one of the Jewish hotels in what was known as the **Borscht Belt**, the Catskill Mountain resorts of New York state. The **barrack-room lawyer** or the **jailhouse lawyer** (19C) are both self-taught experts; in the larger world the terms are synonymous with whinger; the 19C **bubbly jock** rhymed with turkey cock and implied a turkey's characteristics: strutting and making too much noise; the **Bubbly Jocks** are the Royal Scots Greys, whose rival regiments equated them with the farmyard bird. **Catolla** (19C) meant a noisy person, possibly linked to *caterwaul*; a **dish queen** (20C, gay use) is a notably slanderous person while **Tom Long** (17C) is a bore, telling long and tedious stories with little point and no end. The term comes from the the proverbial figure: 'John Long (16C) or Tom Long (17C) the carrier who will never do his errand'.

Dedicated gossips include the **tattle-tale, tattle-basket, prattle-box**, the **tattlebox** or **tittle tattle** (18C), the **rattlebag, rattle-bladder, rattle-brain, rattle-cap, rattle-head, rattle-pate** and **rattle-skull** (19C); the **blabbermouth, gatemouth, motormouth, sack mouth** (AA, cf. **satchel-mouth**, the nickname of the jazz superstar Satchmo, or Louis Armstrong), **mixer, stirrer, shit-stirrer** and **shit-disturber** (all 20C). The **whistle-blower** (20C) tells very specific tales: usually those which a given authority or establishment would prefer to keep covered up; the image is of a referee, blowing the whistle to stop the game after an infringement of the rules. One who uses an excess of obscene language is a **garbage mouth** or **sewermouth** (20C); a **barker** or **pitchman** can also be a **gee man** (Aus., he gees people up) or a **spruiker** (Aus., fr. **spruik**); a teller of tales or an exaggerator is **bull artist, bullshit artist** or **bullshitter** (all 20C), a **slickster** (20C, AA), a **smoothie** (20C, fr. his smooth talk) and a **wind-up merchant** (20C, fr. the image of winding up a mechanical toy; the original 19C meaning was to get a racehorse fit for the next race). Talkative people are variously **all mouth, full of it** (it = shit*), **gabby, gassy, gobby, mouthy, yappy** and **long-tongued**.

TO TALK

Verbs meaning to talk are as dependant on context as are nouns. They are also, as has been noted, interchangeable, and in a number of cases the reader should seek the etymology above.

Aside from **blab** (which seems capable of appearing in every grammatical guise) the 16C has **blow**, meaning speak angrily and giving, a century later, **blow upon**: to inform against; **cut** (16C) has the image of cutting out a selection of words to make one's speech, thus the 19C **cut a joke. Warble** (17C) comes from the SE term meaning to swing sweetly (of birds); latterly it has meant confess, synonymous with **sing. Cackle** (17C, see noun above) gives the 20C **cackle one's fat**: to brag. **Gab**, **jaw** and **jib** (still used by black Americans) all come from the human anatomy (see nouns, above); **gas** similarly mimics its use as a noun and the subsequent career of **rap** has already been outlined. **Spin a yarn** (18C) is originally a Royal Naval term, and implies the telling of a tale, 'tall' or otherwise; **palaver** (to converse, and thus as a noun: conversation; 19C Scots defines it as a fussy person or busybody) comes either from the Portuguese *palavra* or Spanish *palabra*: both words meaning talk and first coined to describe the pidgins that were employed by early explorers to communicate with the natives of the African coast. To **palarie** comes from a mixture of **palaver** and **Parlyaree**, the Italianate stage language.

If **warble** is a term common to the sort of proto-fascist bestsellers embodied in the adventures of that clubland hero Captain Bulldog Drummond, usually attributed to whichever hapless *untermensch* the hero is currently 'persuading' to confess, then Drummond himself will never speak when he can **burble** (usually 'genially'), a term onomatopoeically although (attests the *OED*) not etymologically linked to the Italian *borbogliare*: to make a rumbling or grumbling noise. It also finds echoes in the Portuguese *borbulhar* or Spanish *borbollar*: to bubble forth. Drummond (or at least his creator) is more likely to have picked up his use from the popularity that it gathered following Lewis Carroll's *Through the Looking-Glass* (1871) in which The Jabberwock...'came whiffling through the tulgey wood, And burbled as it came!' Something, surely, of a nonce-word is **gladstonize**, meaning to evade and prevaricate, and to talk much and mean nothing. The term, cited in Farmer and Henley, derives from W. E. Gladstone (1809-98), four times Prime Minister and the 'Grand Old Man' of the Liberal Party.

More recent terms include **beat the gums** and **break one's chops**, **bat the breeze** (mid-20C Aus. although the 18C **breeze** meant an argument), the rhy. sl. **rabbit** (and thus **bunny**), **chew the fat**, **chew the rag** (fr. **rag**: tongue) and **chew the grease**, **dish** (to slander, usu. gay use) and thus today's **diss** (primarily teen use; an abbrev. of SE *disrespect*). **Go** (as in 'I go...and she goes...') can serve as say or speak, as can **spill a line** (fr. **spill**: confess), **shoot a line** and **shoot the breeze**; **sound off** means to get annoyed; its parallel use, in the US army, is to count in cadence while marching; **spiel** and **yap** are dealt with above.

To talk fast, and usually meaninglessly is to **flash the tongue** or **flash the patter** (19C), to **yaffle** (19C, from Yorks. dial. to yelp or mumble), to **talk nine words at once** (17C), to **talk nineteen to the dozen** (19C) and to **talk thirteen to the dozen**. To **talk forty to the dozen** (19C) gives the adjectives **forty-jawed** and **forty-lunged**. As well as certain terms, typically **burble, jaw, beat one's gums, gab** and **gas**, all of which have appeared in other contexts, terms meaning to talk lengthily, repetitiously and perhaps angrily include **go off (at the mouth), pop off (at), run off at the mouth, shoot blanks** (AA), and **shoot off (at one's mouth)** most of which are 19C and all of which are informed by the image of firing a gun. **Bang on,** in which tedium is substituted for anger, is equally aggressive, the Yiddish **shpritz** (fr. German *schpritz*: to spray) typifies a scattershot delivery, while **blow, blow off** and **blow off steam** (19C) refer to the the steam engine. To **go on** is just what it appears, although **bend one's ear** (20C, part-punning on *lend an ear*) is more metaphorical. **Flap at the jibs** (20C) underlines the way in which the older **jib★** is still used among Afro-Americans. **Spout** or **spout off** has elements of the unrestrained fountain (cf. **gush**), **waffle** (19C) was printers' jargon, meaning nonsense; it is also dialect for the bark of small dog (cf. **yak**), **woof** (AA) continues the canine imagery, as does **yawp** (fr. **yap**). **Talk the hind leg off a donkey** (19C) has contemporary variants: the hind legs in question are those of a cow, a bird or a horse, while a modern variation is **talk a blue streak**.

To Chatter

Cut, Duke of York, mag, pipe, rap, warble, cackle and **crack** have been considered above; and again, one must stress the invidiousness of attempting to divide chatter from 'normal' talk. Still, the terms that follow have some claim to being grouped together.

Cant, the thieves' jargon of the 16C and 17C, which has been considered elsewhere in its role as the basis of slang, has a further meaning, that of empty talk, of idle chatter. It is with reference to this type of cant that Samuel Johnson declared in May 1783, 'Clear your *mind* of cant.' In this context it has no bearing on the criminal world, but should traced back to the word's use, as early as the 12C, as a pejorative description of church services that were condemned as substituting rote mouthings for real devotion. It was this use that led to criminal use of **cant**, the language of the **canting crew★** or itinerant criminal beggars. Here **cant** echoed the whining tones in which they 'chanted' for alms. The other branch of **cant**, vapid if sententious verbiage, while certainly rooted in the same Latin *cantare*: to sing, is a later coinage, often associated with two 17C Presbyterian ministers: Andrew Cant and his son Alexander.

Gabble, coined during the 16C on the basis of **gab**: mouth, began life as SE, but had become slang by the 19C, while **jabber** (16C, a mix perhaps of **gabble** and SE *gibber*) was always slang, as were **wag the red rag** (17C, from **red rag**: tongue) and **confab** (18C). Body parts appear yet again to underpin **chin** and **chinwag** (19C) and **clack** (19C, fr. **clack**, meaning: tongue [16C], prattler and busy-body [17C] and thus the 19C **clack-box**: mouth). **Chow** (19C) was primarily theatrical. **Flam** (19C) comes from **flam**: a sham story or hoax; its 20C descendents include **flame**: to exaggerate or bore, and **flim-flam**: to trick or swindle; **flam** may also have links to the Scots *flamfeu*: a trifle). **Flummox** (19C) meaning to perplex is an abbrev. of **flummox by the lip**: to talk down. It probably comes from a dialectal origin, notably *flummocks*: to maul, mangle; *flummock*: a slovenly person or *flummock*: to make untidy, disorder, to confuse, bewilder. There is also an onomatopoeic element based on throwing down roughly and untidily; as such the term is reminiscent of *flump*: a hummock, and *slommock*: a sloven.

Other 19C terms include the verbs to **jerk chin music** (US), to **ladle** (19C theatrical: to enunciate slowly and solemnly: from ladling soup); to **mang** (fr. **mag★** and from the Romany *mang*: to beg) and **slam** (cf. **slum**) both mean additionally to boast; to **slum** is to talk nonsense (cf. **slum**: fake jewellery and **slum**: the Romany language). To **slang** was, logically, enough, to speak slang, but by the 19C it meant also to abuse, thus **slanging-match**. **Voker** and **rocker** both mean to speak, specifically to speak tramps' jargon. The words come from the Romany meaning to talk; that in turn is based on Latin *vocare*: to speak. To **give green rats** (19C) was to backbite (fr. **green** implying envy), to **chirp** (20C) is also to inform (as is **sing**), to **chuck it out** is to speak without restraint (fr. **chuck**: to vomit) and to **give some lip** is to be cheeky.

IN OTHER WORDS

Finally, a run through those types of speech hitherto left undiscussed: whispering, shouting, abusing, speaking honestly and so on.

To whisper is to **blow down one's ear**, and to **talk out of the side of one's neck** (cf. **talk out of the back of one's neck**); to speak without expression is to **deadpan** (fr. **pan**: the face). To **bloviate** (US mid-19C), **blow hard** (19C) **blow off at the mouth** (19C) and **blow off steam** all mean to talk loudly or aggressively, as do **talk big** (late 17C), **thery** (19C, presumed to be Romany, but possibly a corruption of SE *theory*), **blat** (fr. 18C **blate** or **bleet**: to roar or talk wildly), **blart** (fr. **blate** or possibly SE *blurt*), **ballyhoo** (coined early 20C to describe a fairground barker's touting speech), **broadcast** (20C), **loudmouth** (20C) and **sound off**. To make a remark, whether complimentary or otherwise, is to **crack**, **cut loose** (cf. **cut**) or **let loose**, **dish**, **out with**, **spew** or **spew out**, **shoot**, **shoot one's wad** (which also means ejaculate in a sexual sense) and **sing one's song**. To become abusive is to **curse out**, **cuss down** (late 20C), **get down dirty** (AA), **slag off** (mid-19C, cf. **slag★**); to emphasise maliciously is to **rub in**.

To talk sincerely is to **make no bones** or **make no bones about**, a phrase that originated in the 16C, as to **find no bones in this matter**; both phrases imply the absence of bones in a soup or stew; similar examples of straight talk can be found in **come flat out with** (fr. SE *come out with*), **come out strong** (19C), **be one hundred per cent** (20C), **get down to brass tacks** (early 20C, probably from rhy. sl. **brass tacks**: facts), **pull no punches** and **take the gloves off** (20C, from boxing), **put one's cards on the table** and **show one's (hole-)card** (20C, both from cards, specifically poker), **rap on the real** (AA, cf. **rap**), **shoot straight** and **shoot straight from the shoulder** (20C), **take no prisoners** (20C), **talk turkey** (the image is of a turkey being central to a

Christmas dinner, and thus to talk of the basic issue), **get down to the nitty-gritty** (20C, cf. **nitty-gritty***) and **touch base with**. This term, rooted in baseball, initially reflected the touching of bases as one runs between them and as such meant to encounter or meet; in this context base means the bottom or the deepest point, and thus implies talking of important matters. The phrase **on one's say-so** (19C) means on trust and comes from the 18C **on my sammy say-so**: on my word of honour.

To talk cleverly is to **come the smart arse** (20C, with negative implications, cf. **smart ass**), to **crack wise**, (20C US, cf. **crack**, **wise** and **wisecrack**), to **deliver the goods** (20C), and to **talk like a book** (20C). To **talk like the back of a cigarette card** (20C) is to pretend to greater knowledge than one has: the reference is to the cards that were once supplied in every pack of cigarettes and which carried a picture on one side and text – a description, a potted biography – on the other. To start talking, especially as an injunction to do so, is to **fire away** (18C), **out** or **out with it** or to **shoot** (20C); **shoot** has been attributed to film use, but in this context (and underlined by **fire away**) the firing of a gun would seem more likely. To interrupt is to **butt in** (19C), to **chip in** (19C, fr. putting one's gambling chips on table to signify one's joining in the round of betting) and to **pick up fag ends** (20C, fr. late 19C **fag**: a non Turkish, i.e. cheap cigarette); to **pull one's coat** (20C) is to attract someone's attention.

To **hit the button, say a mouthful, strike home**, and **touch base** all mean to to talk aptly, while the offering of an opinion generates to **cop an attitude**, to **put in one's two cents**, to **say one's piece** and to **sound off** or **sound off about**. To speak foolishly is to **go off half-cocked, put one's foot in it** (18C), **put one's foot in one's mouth** (20C, thus **foot-in-mouth disease**: a propensity for gaffes), to **shovel the shit** (20C; cf **shit-stirrer**) and to **make a bloomer** (19C, fr. **blooming error**, cf. 20C **blooper**: a blunder, usually in a media/political context). To talk nonsense is to **talk Hebrew** or to **talk Greek** (both 17C, both playing on the unintelligibility of the languages) and to **talk through the back of one's neck** or **talk through one's arse)**. To tell off, scold or reprimand is to **comb one's hair** (18C) or

comb one's noddle with a three-legged stool (16C, but usually meaning to thrash or beat and found as such in Shakespeare), to **dress down** (17C, also to beat), to **give a curtain lecture** (17C, the lecture given by a wife to her husband when they are in bed, cf. SE *curtain-sermon*; the curtain is that of their four-poster), to **give a juniper-** (17C) or **jiniper-lecture** (18C, the terms come from the sharpness of the juniper berry); to **carpet** (19C, the miscreant is standing on his or her superior's office carpet while receiving a reprimand), to **walk the carpet** (19C, servants were summoned into the parlour to be told off) and to **give a wigging** (early 19C, from **wig**: a severe reprimand). An **earwigging** was a rebuke delivered in private (19C, cf. **wigging**, and **earwig**: to whisper insinuations); a **jobation** or **jawbation** (19C, from 17C **jobe** or **job**: a tedious scolding, which comes from the lengthy scolding given to Job by his supposed 'comforters'; the word might also have links with **jaw***). To **tear a strip off** (20C) is based on the noise made when one tears off a strip of cloth; it sounds like a **raspberry** (or farting noise). To boast (see synonyms above, plus terms at braggart, below) is to **chant the poker** (19C, to exaggerate, cf. **poker talk**?) and to **vapour** (cf. **hot air**, **wind** and thus the 20C computer jargon *vapounware*: software or hardware that is announced with much publicity, but never actually appears.

To **chi–ike** (19C) is to praise in Britain but to cheek in Australia; a **gun** is a lie (17C) or a rumour (19C) and **hackslaver** (19C, fr. SE *hack*: to stammer) is to stutter. Cheek or impudence is **lip** (20C), **slack-jaw, stock** (18C, from a stock of impudence) or **sauce**; a cheeky person is a **nash-gab** (19C) from Romany *nash*: to run, and thus someone who runs off at the **gab**, or mouth) or a **saucebox** (fr. **sauce**) . Terms meaning be quiet! or shut up! include **mum's the word!** (18C, fr 16C **mum**: silence), **nantee parlaree** and **nantee palaver** (both mid 19C, from lingua franca **nantee**: none or not; itself taken from Italian *niente*: nothing).

THE BRAGGART

Defined as he is by his words, which exceed by far his non-existent deeds, the braggart is truly the word made flesh. Indeed, he is nothing more. The earliest slang synonym is **cutter** (16C, cf. **cut**, thus **swear like a cutter**) following by **roarer** (16C, fr. **roar**: to riot), **hector** (17C, fr. the Trojan hero) and **mouth** (17C) which gives its successor the **mouth almighty** (19C). With proper disrespect the braggart is linked unashamedly to excrement: the 20C has **bullshitter** and **bullshit artist**, but there are many precedents: **cacafuego** (17C, lit. shit fire), **shitefire, fire-eater** (19C), **pump-thunder** (19C, fr. **pump**: to fart) and **pissfire** (18C). **All wind and piss** (19C) comes from the 18C proverb: 'like the barber's cat: all wind and piss'); similar phrases include **all mouth and trousers** and **all prick and breeches** (both 20C). Other 17C synonyms include the literary **furioso, dammy-boy** or **damme-boy** (fr. **damme**: generic for the oaths he likes to use) and **petronel** (fr. SE *petronel*: a kind of large pistol or carbine, used in the 16C and early 17C). **Captain Grand, Captain Bounce, Captain Bluff** and **Captain Hackum** are 18C coinages; all mock the bully's military pretensions; **hackum** alone means braggart as does **bouncer** (17C, meaning liar in the 18C).

The 19C, concentrating more on his exaggerations than on his threats of violence offers **barker, blower** (Aus.), **windbag, gasser** (the 20C alternative use of **gasser**: someone or something amusing probably comes from the Irish phrase **great gas**: lots of fun), **gasman** and **gasbag, huff, huffcap** and **huffer** (thus **huffy**: angry or touchy etc and **huff**: anger or bluster). **Ramper** comes from **ramp**: to roar and rage. A **Tooley-Street tailor** supposedly refers to three tailors of Tooley Street (SE1) who supposedly put together a petition to Parliament; it carried none but their own signatures but was headed grandiosely: 'We the people of England...'. **Blatherskite** (19C, Aus) comes from the 16C **bletherskate**: a mix of **blether**: bluster and SE *skate*: to slide over. 20C Australia adds **big note artist** (fr. **big note**: to speak highly of) and **ear-basher** (also meaning a bore). Other terms include **bigmouth, loudmouth** and **fatmouth, blowhard, bilge artist** (fr. **bilge water**: nonsense), **smart arse** or **ass** and **smart guy, swellhead, wise-ass, wise guy, wisenheimer** and the **man with a paper ass** (AA).

INSULTS

With its relentless deflation of the pompous and its ribald attitude to the underpinnings of the status quo, it is unsurprising that slang lends itself enthusiastically to insults. Not all are listed here: racist slurs, criticisms of those who are, for instance, primarily drunkards or beggars can be found at the appropriate section. Certain descriptions, as in many of the terms used to describe women, are *de facto* insults. These terms may be considered both as general insults and as descriptions of those who might be termed 'unsympathetic'.

SIXTEENTH TO EIGHTEENTH CENTURIES

Aside from the ranks of thieves, mendicant criminal beggars, fornicators, and other ne'erdowells, the names of all of whom form the basis of the ur-slang cant and are duly listed elsewhere, the 16C throws up a couple of terms that have lasted until the present day. A **pettifogger** was literally a second rate lawyer, condemned by his inadequacies to dealing only in minor cases. The subterfuges used to win these cases gave such men the reputation of trickery and of sharp practice; the term duly lost its legal status, and became instead a generalised insult. The **petty** element is obvious, the **fogger** has a more complex background. It comes from the name Fugger, the great Augsburg banking family of the 15th and 16th centuries, which appears (usually with the u changed to an o) in a number of European languages meaning initially a merchant, usurer or monopolist and subsequently an avaricious rich man, a cheap huckster, and anyone who uses corrupt methods for personal gain. The term persist today: the Dutch *fokker*, the Walloon *foukeur* and Spanish *fúcar* are all contemptuous designations for a man of great wealth. Thus the **petty-** or **pettifogger** was one whose methods emulated those of the great merchants, but at the lowest level. The second 16C term is **ragamuffin**, a mix of **rag** meaning ragged or disreputable, and the suffix **-muffin**, which offers no discernible etymology; the term first appeared in the 14C as the name of a demon. By the 16C it had taken on its current meaning.

While never out of use, the term has gained a new twist in the past decade, as a successor in the West Indies and amongst British blacks to the older **rude boy**: a Jamaican street hustler who was seen, depending on one's perspective, as criminal riffraff, or a streetwise role model. The **raggamuffin** or **ragga** (the double-g making a slight reference to reggae music) plays the same role. The generic term **queer** (the opposite of **rum***) can be found in a number of combinations signifying disapproval: **queer bluffer** (a 'sneaking, sharping, Cut-throat Ale-house or Inn-keeper' Grose), **queer mort** ('a dirty Drab, a jilting Wench, a Pockey jade' Grose), **queer gill** (19C, a shabby fellow), a **queer bitch** ('an odd out of the way fellow' Grose) and so on.

Of the notable 17C coinages virtually none have survived, for all their undoubted exoticism. A **fustilugs** (literally 'dirty ears') was described as 'a Fulsom, Beastly, Nasty Woman' in B. E.'s *Dictionary of the Canting Crew* (1698?); a **pilgarlick** was an outcast, often apostrophised as 'poor pilgarlick' and as such a general term meaning a pitiful creature. The words comes from SE *peel garlic* which, on the basis of the smooth garlic clove, meant literally a bald-headed man. Similar terms, all meaning bald, include *pilcorn*, *pilledow* and *pilpate*. A **shotten herring** or **shotten soul** came from the Dutch *schoten haringh* and referred properly to any fish (especially a herring) that has spawned. Such herrings were 'empty' of their spawn and when the term was applied to human beings it meant emaciated, worthless and generally good for nothing. Like **shotten herring slubberdegullion** or **slabberdegullion** comes from the Dutch, in which the word *overslubberen* means to wade through mud and plain *slabberen* gives **slabber**, a synonym of SE *slobber*. to dribble saliva. Thus the term means a filthy, slobbering fellow. **Tarleather** is a general term of abuse directed at women; its SE meaning is of a strip of leather used in a flail; the women thus described are presumably scolds and, given that **leather** can mean vagina, the word is a distant precursor of **pussy-whipped***. It must also relate to the 19C **bulldoser** or **bulldozer**, which came from the US **bulldoze**: to whip with a strip of hide, and went on to mean one who is seen as doing that whipping: a domineering woman. **Son of a bitch**, a 17C coinage which originally meant a bastard, has survived. With such synonyms as **sonofagun**, **SOB** and **sumbitch** it is still going strong.

The 18C gives plain **animal** as well as the specific **pig**, a term that was widely assumed to have sprung fresh-minted into mid-20C life, when it was used by the radical young of the 1960s to mean a policeman, but in fact has a somewhat older pedigree. For its use meaning a policeman c.1800 see POLICE. **Thatch-gallows** was worthless person, good only for thatching a gallows (which of course had no roof) while a **slive-andrew** was composed of **slive**: to sneak away and **andrew**: a servant and meant a general lazybones. Finally a **sad man** was mischievous, troublesome and dissipated; the term has recently reappeared as part of contemporary teen vocabulary: such figures are less mischievous and dissipated than merely inadequate and it is their unfortunate ineptitude that makes them so pitiable.

NINETEENTH CENTURY

Many of the sexually-based terms that form the core of the modern vocabulary of insult emerge during the 19C. These include **arsehole***, **bugger***, **cocksucker*** (although at the time this meant merely toady and carried no sexual overtones), **cunt***, **sod*** (fr. sodomite; cf. **bugger**) and **fucker***. Aside from these are other staples: **mug** (19C, a fool or dupe into whose ear any nonsense might be 'poured'), **lummox** or **lummocks** (fr. the dial. verb **lummock**: to move heavily or clumsily; the 20C **lug** has the same image of heavy work), **sucker** (US, originally a parasite, then a dupe or innocent), a **bad egg**, **bad hat**, **bad penny** (fr. the earlier **bad halfpenny**) all of which lead to the 20C **baddy** (although this is also linked to **bad guy**), **hard** and **hard case**, **sap** or **sapskull** (a simpleton who is 'soft in the head'), **lowlife**, **yob** or **yobbo** (both of which come from the backsl. meaning boy) and **hood** or **hoodlum**. The origins of **hoodlum**, which means unpleasant person in general and thug or gangster in particular and which was coined in San Francisco c.1870-72, are lost. The term spread across the US by the end of the decade, generating a number of popular etymologies. Among them, according to H. L. Mencken, is the idea of a local newspaperman who, keen to coin a term to describe the street gangs that were plaguing the city's streets, decided simply to reverse the name of a leading gangster, one Muldoon. This created *noodlum*, and a printer's error, substituting h for n, did the rest. Other theories include a reference to a gang rallying-cry: 'Huddle 'em!', and to roots in the Bavarian dialect term *hodalump* which carries exactly the same meaning, in various terms in Spanish and among US Indian languages and the wonderfully unlikely linkage put forward by Barrère and Leland (*Slang, Jargon and Cant* [1889]) that the term is based on the pidgin English *hood lahnt*: lazy. It is tempting to bring in **hooligan**, with much the same meaning, but that word was British, and only appeared when it started finding its way into London police reports c.1898.

Two long-running Australian terms: **lare** and **larrikin**, also appear in this period. **Lare** means a loud and flashy person and is a back-formation of **lairy**, itself a variation on **leery**, both of which mean cunning, smart and 'fly'. **Lare** succeeded the earlier **cabbage-tree mob** (a type of mid-19C layabout, typified by his wearing of a cabbage-tree hat: a hat made of woven cabbage-tree or cabbage-palm leaves) and was in turn replaced by today's **larrikin** which appeared c.1870 in Melbourne. Larrikin obviously has some connection to **lare**, but it is also tied to *larking*, as in larking about, and to the Worcestershire dial. *larrikin*: a mischievous youth and the Yorkshire term *larack*: to lark about. The term may also be an abbreviation of **leary kinchen**: a 'fly' youngster.

Less well-known are such obsolete terms as **shagbag** (fr. 17C **shakebag***: a whore), **gallows**, **gallows-bird** and **slip-gibbet**, **rudesby** (SE *rude* plus the sfx. *-by*), **shicer** (either from **shice**: worthless or German *sheisse*: shit), **scurf** (which had referred to a variety of skin diseases since the 11C), **scrub** (spec. a shabby fellow, or one who doesn't pay his round at a tavern), **seek-sorrow** (a whining malcontent), **slamtrash**, **slamkin** or **slammocks** (all based on the dial. *slam*: an ill-shaped person; cf. **lummocks**), **slobberer** (spec. a bad farmer) and **spalpeen** (fr. the Irish word meaning a low or mean fellow, and originally a casual farm labourer). A **wrong 'un** was originally a horse that had been deliberately pulled up during a race while a **torril** referred equally negatively to horseflesh or womankind; **sweep** is an abbreviation of chimney sweep (although in some contexts – notably weddings – sweeps were seen as good luck rather than as bad people) and a **moocher** meant one who mooches or hangs around.

Hard-edged as ever, the 20C scatters its insults with abandon. **Motherfucker**, probably the ultimate in obscenities gives a wide range of synonyms, ostensibly euphemistic but quite transparent: **granny-jazzer, mammy-jammer, mammy-rammer, mammyhugger, mammy-tapper, m.f., mollyfock, momma-hopper, mother-fouler, mother-flunker, mother-raper, mother, mother-grabber, mother-hugger, mother-jiver, motherjumper, triple clutcher** and **poppa-lopper**. No less direct are **cunt-lapper, scumsucker** (cf. **cocksucker**), **dickhead, dork, prick** and **putz** (all based on terms meaning penis), **knucklehead (originally Aus.), douchebag, dumb cluck, dumb fuck** and **dum-dum, four-letter man** (c-u-n-t) and **twat*** or **twot, fuckwit, ponce*, shit, shit on a stick** (AA), **shit-for-brains, shitbird, shithead** and **shitheel** and such characterisations as **you piece of crap, you lump of shit**, etc.

The animal kingdom is represented by **ape** and **baboon** (both tending to violence), **peck** or **peckerwood** (see RACE RELATIONS), **dog** (which often means an unattractive woman, but can be used more generally to describe the second-rate or unappealing in many areas; one theory suggests that **dog** as a prefix implies useless), **horse's arse** or **horse's ass, rat** (originally a 17C term meaning a drunken person who has been arrested; cf. **rat-arsed***: drunk), **rat arse, rat bastard, rat prick** and **ratbag** (Aus.); a **turkey** has signified a theatrical or other commercial disaster since the 1940s, its human dimension appeared in 1951; the 19C **Turk** was also a pejorative, describing Irish immigrants to the US; **alley cat** or **alley rat**, the punning **pheasant plucker** (a play on 'pleasant fucker') and **pug** or **puggy** (the first of which refers to a breed of dog, but properly means a fighter). **Basket** and **bar steward** both mean bastard, as does the Yiddish **momser** and the backslang **dratsab**; Yiddish also gives **schmo*, schlemiel*** and other terms meaning primarily fool (qv) as well as **shtarka*** (a tough guy). Black America has **beige** and **butterhead, out and**

out (cf. **out-and-outer***) and **poopbutt** (fr. **poop**: arse and **butt**: arse). A **ball-buster**, **ball-tearer** or **ball-breaker** is a nag, a **chippy-chaser** pursues prostitutes (cf. **chippy***), a **naus** is rhy. sl. **noah's**, from **noah's ark**: **nark**: informer.

   Nellie, with its implications of effeminacy, is ostensibly an abbrev. of the name Eleanor, but may also come from the rhy. sl. **nellie duff**: **puff***: homosexual; but the term is originally US and the rhy. sl. is a UK coinage. **Nerd**, possibly a euphemism for the equally insulting **turd**, is certainly an American coinage, albeit a mysterious one. The *OED* suggests a rhyme in 'If I Ran a Zoo' (1950) by the children's author Dr. Seuss (Theodore Seuss Geisel, [1904-]) in which he writes, 'And then, just to show them, / I'll sail to Ka-Troo / And Bring Back an It-Kutch, a Preep and a Proo, / a Nerkle, a Nerd, and a Seersucker, too!'. **Cloth-ears** (fr. a hat which has ear-flaps, blocking sound as well as the cold), **face-ache**, **pudding head** and **heel** (fr. **shitheel**) all represent the body; an **oik** began life in Britain's public schools c.1925. The term is linked to *hoick* and *oick*, both meaning spit; it is also an abbrev. of *oickman*: a labourer or shopkeeper and may also refer to the 'common' habit of shouting 'Oi!' to attract someone's attention. **Crud** (fr. **crut**: excrement) means anything or anyone distasteful, a **dub** is complete failure while the rhy. sl. **J. Arthur** means **wanker*** (see MASTURBATION), itself a term of abuse as well as a masturbator. A **kiss of death** (fr. the kiss Judas Iscariot gave Christ) is a person to be avoided, **slag*** dates from the 18C, when it meant a coward, but by the 20C meant a generally unacceptable person, a **smartiepants** is a **knowall***, a **so-and-so** a euphemism for **sonofabitch** and a **weathercock** vacillates. **Freak** (fr. 19C SE: a monstrosity) echoed its SE meaning, but had a brief period, c.1970, of use by the hippies as a term of self-celebration and a deliberate challenge to the conventional, world. Finally **raas** or **raasclat** ('arse cloth') are West Indian terms meaning menstrual towel.

THUGS

The terms listed above are on the whole general insults; this group adds violence to unpleasantness and gives the thug.

The **barker**, more usually defined as a fairground tout, appears in 1483; perhaps he 'barks' his threats; the following century gives **Captain Hackum**, a **rush buckler** (fr **rush**: to force violently and **buckler**: shield; cf. **swashbuckler**) and **tearer**, **tearcat** and **Timothy Tearcat** (fr. **tearcat**, a possible euphemism for **tear arse**: one who runs about excitedly). The 17C **bouncer** went on to become the 20C's nightclub or dancehall doorman; a **twibill** is based on the SE *twibill*: a two-edged axe, while an **oatmeal** is one whose rowdiness must be attributed to his 'sowing his wild oats'. A **roarer**, a **roaring boy** or **roaring girl** all come from **roar**: to riot, and are best seen in the title of the Middleton & Dekker play: *The Roaring Girle* based on the life of Moll Cut-purse (1611); **moll**★ and **cut-purse**★ are, of course, cant terms in themselves. Perhaps the strangest 17C term is **tittery-tu** which comes from the first words of Virgil's first eclogue, '*Tityre, tu patulae recubans sub tegmine fagi*' and which referred to a gang of well-to-do roughs who infested the London streets. The Latin tag implied that these privileged rogues were men of leisure and fortune, who 'lay at ease under their patrimonial beech trees'. Such wealthy scoundrels predated such gangs as the 18C Mohawks and the less highly-born but even more pugnacious Dead Rabbits and Plug Uglies, who assailed the law-abiding citizens of New York a century later. Another brand of street thug was the **scourer** or **scowrer**, whose enjoyments included terrorising passing citizens, beating up night watchmen, smashing windows and similar pursuits.

This period also introduces **tory**, now the shorthand for Britain's Conservative party. The original use, while still political, was somewhat fifferent. It comes from the anglicized spelling of the Irish *tóraidhe*: pursuer, although some sources define a **tory** as the one pursued, and therefore an outlaw. The term was used to describe those of the dispossessed Irish who in the 17C became outlaws, subsisting by plundering and killing the English settlers and soldiers. In time **tory** meant any form of outlaw, including Rajput marauders and Highland rebels. **Tory** with a capital T enters the language c.1679 when it was the nickname given to those who opposed the exclusion of James, Duke of York (a Roman Catholic) from the succession to the British Crown. According to Roger

North writing in *Examen* (1740), The Bill of Exclusion 'led to a common Use of slighting and opprobrious Words; such as Yorkist. That did not scandalise or reflect enough. Then they came to Tantivy, which implied Riding Post to Rome... Then, observing that the Duke favoured Irish Men, all his Friends, or those accounted such by appearing against the Exclusion, were straight become Irish, and so wild Irish, thence Bogtrotters, and in the Copia of the factious Language, the Word Tory was entertained, which signified the most despicable Savages among the Wild Irish.' The 18C brings the **sockie**, **sockhead** and **socker** (fr. **sock**: to hit hard), and the **yahoo**, a philistine, lout or hooligan, invented by Jonathan Swift in *Gulliver's Travels* (1726), who described them thus: 'The Fore-feet of the Yahoo differed from my Hands in nothing else, but the Length of the Nails, the Coarseness and Brownness of the Palms, and the Hairiness on the Backs.'

Thugs of the next century include the **basher**, the **slasher**, the **ramper** (fr. **ramp**: robbery with violence), the **rough**, the **rowdy**, the **bruiser** (which like **basher** originally meant a prize-fighter), the **hood** or **hoodlum** (see above), the **sawney** and **sonky** (also meaning a clumsy person; cf. **lummox**, **lug**) and **ugly customer**★. **Bloodtub** also referred to the lowest form of 'blood and thunder' entertainment the Victorian theatre could offer while a **boy of the Holy Ground** was a member of a gang who lived near the St Giles **rookery** (18C: a slum, largely populated by criminals; the site of this notorious area, once visited by Dickens with a police escort, is now that of London's Centre Point high rise), otherwise known as the **Holy Land**. The **ragster** came from 19C **rag**: tongue and its verb form to **rag**: to tease; **bucko** was originally nautical slang and is usually found in the combination **bucko mate**: a tough and violent ship's officer; **bucko** itself comes from the 18C **buck**: a roisterer or blood. **Hector** was based on the Trojan hero, thus *hectoring*: aggressive verbal bullying; **jibone** or **jabone** originally described newly arrived Italian immigrants to the US.

The language of those same immigrants gives one of the most celebrated terms in 20C criminal slang: **goombah**, translated as godfather and as such a Mafia chieftain; the term is the anglicized pronunciation of the Italian *compare*: a companion or specifically a

godfather. Another widely recognised term is **goon**, which originally meant labour enforcer, but expanded to mean any thug. The
word may come from a cartoon character, Alice the Goon from
the comic *Thimble Theatre* (1919) by E. C. Segar (1894–1938); given
the miminal intelligence of such men, it may also come from from
gooney: a fool, which in turn stems from the Old English *ganian*:
to gape. The remaining 20C terms require no etymology, they
declare themselves unequivocally: **ass-kicker**, **gorilla**, **hatchet
man**, **heavy**, **husky**, **muscle**, **punch-out artist**, **SAN** (stop-at-
nothing) **man**, **tough guy** or **tough nut** and **torpedo**.

SWEARING AND OATHS

The vocabulary of swearing, foul language, oaths or profanity falls
into two basic categories: the religious and the physical. The former,
while still in common use, has lost much of the resonance that it
held in an age when spirituality carried greater weight, the latter
remains capable of shock, albeit much diminished today. This
vocabulary can therefore be divided into a number of sections: God,
Jesus and Christ, Lord, the Devil and Hell, Heaven, Damn and
Damned, Bodily Functions, Fuck, Bloody, and a variety of Miscellaneous areas, a list based on that suggested by Professor Geoffrey
Hughes' *Swearing* (1992), in which he analyses the sociology as well
as the terminology of oaths in far greater detail that is possible here.

GOD

Unlike Judaism, where the tetragrammaton *JHVH*, the unspeak-
able name of God, is a primary taboo, and is usually replaced by
such constructs as *adonai* (the Lord), it is no way incumbent upon
Christianity to avoid speaking the word 'God'. Nonetheless euphemisms for the Deity abound, especially as generated by swearing,
and may be seen as among the very earliest of slang terminology.
Thus the 14C has **gog**, **cock** and its variation **cokk**; **cock** appears

in Chaucer (1386), but perhaps its optimum appearance is in Shakespeare's punning euphemism: 'Young men will do't , if they come to't, By cock, they are to blame' (*Hamlet* IV v. [1602]) in which the Deity and the penis are briefly united. God and the genitalia meet again (albeit quite coincidentally) in the 16C **cod**; the 16C also has **gar** and **Jove** (the Latinised form of the Greek Zeus). The century also introduces a number of elisions, notably **'sblood**, **'slid**, **'slight** and **'snails** meaning respectively God's blood, God's eyelid, God's light and God's nails. Elision continues into the 17C, where one finds **zounds** and **godsookers** (God's wounds), **'sbody** (God's body) and **gods bodykins** (God's little body, from the diminutive suffix -*kin*), **'sfoot** (God's foot) and **gadzooks** (God's hooks; the relevance of hook is debatable: Partridge suggests *hocks* or *houghs*: bones; *hook* or *huck*, meaning hip-bones is also a candidate; in either case it must thus mean simply God's bones). Other contemporary coinages include **od**, **odso**, **dod**, **adad**, **adod**, **gad**, **odsbobs** (cf. **odsbodikins**) and **egad**.

Ounds (cf. **zounds**) and **odsbodikins** (God's little body, cf. **Gods bodikins**) appear during the 18C, as do **agad**, **gosh** (giving the later combinations **gosh-almighty** and **gosh-darn!**), **ecod**, **goles**, **golly** (an AA creation), **odrabbit it** and **odd rat it** (God rot it; cf. **drat**), **gracious**, **gosse** and **bedad** (Irish), **begad**, **begar** and **egad**, all of which mean by God! The 19C errs to paganism with **ye gods** and its peer **ye gods and little fishes**, and uses a variety of proper names as substitutes for God's own: **by George**, **Great Scott**, **great Caesar's ghost** (and **great snakes**, possibly great Satan?) and **Bob**, as in **s'elpe me** (so help me) **Bob**. The American West produces **doggone** which is generally assumed to be a deformation of the profane God damn (cf. **dang**, **darn**, **goldarn**, etc.); some, however, think the original phrase was quite literally **dog on it**, a similar construction to the secular **pox on it! Goddam** (coined in the 15C) became so prevalent an oath that the French began calling Britons *les goddams* (the 20C equivalent is *les fuckoffs*). Variations include **consarned**, **goldarn**, **gosh-damned**, **gosh-danged**, **gosh-dern**, **God-blasted**, **dad-blasted**, **dad-gasted**, **dad-gummed**, **dad-binged**, **dad-snatched**, **dad-rotted**, **dad-goned** and **dad-fetched**.

Britain's North has **gom** and **gum**, typically in the oath **by gum!**, a staple of 'Lancashire' characters; **gum** is either a simple play on God, or possibly an abbreviation of God almighty. Other euphemisms for by God! included **by golly!**, **by gosh!**, **by gorry!**, **by jimminy!**, **by jove!** and **by the great horn spoon!** (US). By **jingo** was another variation, and one that carried more etymological baggage than most. It appears first c.1670 as a piece of conjuror's gibberish, usually as *hey* or *high jingo!* and is pronounced when the trick required something to appear (it is thus the opposite of *hey presto!* uttered when an object disappears), and again in Motteux's translation of Rabelais (1694) where it is a translation of the French *par Dieu* thus underlining its position among the euphemisms. *Jings* has a lengthy pedigree in Scotland, while some sources equate **jingo** with the Basque *Jinko* or *Jainko*: God. The expression **by Jingo!** gained its widest publicity from the music-hall song of 1878, celebrating Britain's involvement in the 'Russo-Turkish War whence Lord Beaconsfield despatched a British fleet to help the Turks, engendering G. W. Hunt's lyric: 'We don't want to fight, but by Jingo if we do / We've got the ships, we've got the men, and got the money too...' **Jingo** or jingoist soon came to mean a blustering hyper-patriot, the homegrown equivalent of the French chauvinist.

Drat and **od rot it** extend the 18C's **odd rat it**. The 20C has **good grief** and **by Godfrey** and **cor** (God), best seen in the phrase **cor blimey** or **gorblimey**: God blind me! A 'gorblimey' was the common term for a floppy, field-service cap worn by a certain type of subaltern in defiance of Regulations during World War I. A popular song ran 'He wears gorblimey trousers And a little gorblimey 'at.' Gorblimey trousers reappeared in Fifties' hit: 'My Old Man's A Dustman'. Another elision, **'strewth** (19C), meant God's truth, while **Gordon Bennett!** referred either to James Gordon Bennet (1795-1892) the founding editor of the New York *Herald* or to his similarly named son.

JESUS AND CHRIST

Swearing oaths by Christ's name, whether Jesus or Christ itself, is a venerable institution. Nearly all such terms are euphemistic, doing no more than lightly disguise Christ's names. **Gis** and **Jis** are both 16C, **Gemini** is 17C and **Jiminy, Jiminy Crickets, gee whillikins, gee whillikers,** and **gee whiz** all 19C. The 20C adds **Jeez, gee, Jeepers,** Jesus wept, **sweet Jesus** or **sweet bleeding Jesus, Judas Priest, Jesus H. Christ** and **Jeepers Creepers**. Plain **Jesus!** is of course equally common. **Bejazus!** means by Jesus (it can also appear as a noun, e.g. **kick the bejazus out of**), while **begorra!** and **bejabers!** those other staples of the world's stage Irishmen mean by God. **Jumping Jehosaphat!** or plain **Jehosaphat** comes from Jehosaphat, King of Judah c.873-849BC. Terms for Christ include the 17C **criminy** (presumably from Christ, but possibly from the Latin *crimen meum*: my fault) and the 19C **crickey, crikey, cripes** and **Christmas**. The 20C exclamation **for crying out loud** is a further euphemism. Like **Jesus! Christ!** itself is common, as are such phrases as **Christ Almighty!, Christ on a crutch!, Christopher Columbus!, cracky!** and the dated and schoolboyish **crumbs!**. While the Mariolatry of many Roman Catholic countries means that Mary plays a central role in their profane lexicons, Christ's mother has hardly a look-in in Protestant Britain and America. Thus the single word **Mary!** is virtually all one finds, although Irish immigrants offer **Holy Mary Mother of God** and similar phraseology.

HEAVEN AND HELL

Lord is synonymous, given the context, with either God or Jesus, but is productive of far fewer terms. Such as do exist include **lud** and **lawks** (18C), **lor!, law sakes!, landsakes** (US), **lor-a-mussy!** or **lawks-a-mussy** (or **mercy**), **lawdy!** and **lumme** (Lord love me!), all of which emerged during the 19C and tend, in fiction at least, to end up in the mouths of female members of the servants' hall. Thus too the 20C **Lord love a duck!, Lord love us!** or **Lord love you!** and a number of terms based on **bless me!**: typically **bless my heart!** and **bless my soul!** (all of which refer in turn to the 17C phrase to **bless oneself**: meaning ironically to swear). **Mercy!** and **Glory!** (plus **Glory be!**) are both the mildest of expletives, while neither **holy cats!**, nor **holy cow!, holy cripes!,**

holy mackerel!, **holy Moses!** nor **holy smoke!** are any of them likely to raise even the most puritan eyebrow. **Heavens to Betsy!** and **heavens to Murgatroyd** are equally anodyne.

Slang terms for the devil are many and various; among them are **old hornie**, **little quid**, **old Bendy**, **old Blazes**, **old driver**, **old Harry**, **old gooseberry**, the **old one**, **old splitfoot**, **old roger**, **old toast**, **old ruffian** and **old toot** (thus **on a toot**: on a spree). That said only **deuce** (17C, plus 18C deuced), and **deuced** (often spelt **dooce** to indicate a splenetic, high Tory speaker) can be cited as specific oaths, although a number of terms are found with reference to his kingdom: hell. **Hell!** itself is very popular, as are the euphemisms **Sam Hill** and **heck** (18C, both often found prefixed by 'what the...'), Other hell-bound terms include **hell-fired** (18C), **hell's bells!**, **the hell with it!**, **to hell with it!** and **what the hell!**. **To hell with you**, **go to hell** and **go to blazes** remain popular curses, although **go to Hong Kong**, **go to Jerusalem**, **go to Putney on a pig** (19C), **go to hell and help your mother make bitch-pie** (18C), and **go to hell, Hull and Halifax** (17C) have all vanished. The latter, also found in the prayer 'from hell, Hull and Halifax, Good Lord deliver us', refers to the Halifax Gibbet Law, under which a prisoner was executed first and his guilt or innocence ascertained afterwards.

DAMN AND DAMNED

Those consigned to hell are, in the eyes of believers, damned, and the use of **damn** as an oath began as an unalloyed religious term. Based on the Latin *damnare* or *dampnare*: to inflict damage or loss upon, it came to mean to condemn, or to doom to punishment and was used as such both in law and in the theological sense, in which case one's condemnation was to the infernal regions. By the 17C the theological aspects, while still at the heart of the term, had softened somewhat, an easing that may be seen in the alternative spellings **demn** and **dem**. Thus Dickens uses **demnition** (fr. 18C **damnation**) in *Nicholas Nickleby* (1838) and across the Atlantic the bowdlerization proceded even further with the introduction of **darn** and **dern** and **dang**. Even milder are **blowed** and **blow it!**,

dashed, dash!, dash it! or **dash it all!**, all witnesses to the increasing use by editors of dashes to indicate unacceptable language; both the practice and the terminology continue with **blankety** and **blank** (19C), each of which indicates white space. Less reticent are **damnit!** or **dammit!, dammit to hell (and back), damn my stars** and **damn my sakes. Tarnation** (fr. **damnation**) is late 18C US, based in part on **tarnal**, an abbreviation of SE *eternal* and used as such in a swearing context.

FUCK

Given its position as the most extreme of obscenities it is hardly surprising that **fuck** (see SEXUAL INTERCOURSE for etymology) has featured for several centuries amongst the vocabulary of cursing. The 16C **foutre** and **foutra** (fr. the equally obscene French *foutre*) are followed by the 17C **foot** and **sfoot** (both from *foutre* again) and the 18C **footer, footy, frig** and **frigging** (which has a parellel meaning of masturbation). **Fucking** itself does not appear until c.1840. The 19C also retreats into euphemism with **fizzing** (a synonym for **fuck** but also used to mean excellent or first rate, and as such referring not to sex but to effervescence). The 20C offers **effing, effing** and **blinding, eff** (especially as in the injunction **eff off!**) and the euphemistic **flipping, freaking** and **fudge**. Fuck-related phrases include **fuck a duck!, fuck this for a lark!, fuck this for a game of soldiers!** and **chuck you, Farley!** (a reverse of fuck you charlie and a variation on the popular **fuck you Jack, I'm all right**, predictably censored for the title of the film *I'm All Right Jack* [1959]).

Fuck gains an extra, and for most people an even less acceptable dimension when it appears in what has been termed the 'Oedipal polysyllable': **motherfucker**. While **motherfucker**, often abbreviated to **mother** may go unremarked in certain circles, and amongst US blacks even exist as a term of affection, or as a neutral noun meaning nothing more particular than 'thing', it remains for the most part the most obscene of all obscenities. Unsurprisingly **motherfucker** and its adjectival form **motherfucking** have been surrounded with a wide range of euphemisms. Among them are

mammy-jamming, **mammy-ramming**, **mammy-tapping**, **molly-focking**, **mother-flunking**, **motherfouling**, **mother-grabbing**, **motherhugging**, **mother-jiving**, **mother-jumping**, **motherless**, **motherloving** and **mother-raping**.

BLOODY

The impact of the so-called obscenities varies as to context and none more so than **bloody**, which is barely acceptable in the UK, the essence (albeit embarrassingly so) of the national vocabulary in Australia, and of virtually no importance whatsoever in America. Its use is universal: as an intensifier, meaning very, exceedingly; abominably or desperately. As the *OED* put it in 1887, 'In general colloquial use from the Restoration to c.1750; now constantly in the mouths of the lowest classes, but by respectable people considered 'a horrid word', on a par with obscene or profane language, and usually printed in the newspapers [as] b----y.' The latter proscription has largely vanished – when **bloody** does crop up in the press it tends to be in direct, quoted speech and is printed in full –but the term, in the UK at least, has yet to enter 'polite' society. As to its etymology, the *OED* links it to the preoccupations of the 'bloods' or aristocratic rowdies of the end of the 17C and beginning of the 18C. Thus the phrase 'bloody drunk' meant 'as drunk as a blood'. Its associations with bloodshed and murder (typically a *bloody battle*) 'have recommended it to the rough classes as a word that appeals to their imagination' and the *Dictionary* goes on to compare its late-19C popularity with other 'impressive or graphic intensives, seen in the use of jolly, awfully, terribly, devilish, deuced, damned, ripping, rattling, thumping, stunning, thundering, etc.' As far as origins are concerned, it has no links to theology, nor to the term **'sblood** (God's blood); in addition, declare Farmer and Henley in their definition, 'In passing it may be mentioned that there is no ground for attributing its derivation to "By'r Our Lady"' Indeed all such fancies are studiously dismissed by the experts; Eric Partridge rounds off any speculation, saying that 'There is no need for ingenious etymologies: the idea of blood suffices'. Euphemisms and synonyms for **bloody** include **blooming** (19C), **bally** (19C), **blasted** (18C), **bleeding** (19C) and **blinking** (19C).

Thus **bloody** continues to exist on the margins (in the UK at least) of language that is acceptable if distasteful and that which is downright taboo. It is in Australia, however, that it has pride of place. Frances Grose wrote in 1796 of how popular **bloody** was amongst the contemporary London underworld; there is no doubt that, along with the transported felons of the period, it made its way to the penal colonies of Botany Bay. Fifty years later it was well-established: writing in his book *Travels in New South Wales* (1847) Alexander Marjoribanks noted the prevalence of the word, claiming that he had heard a bullock driver use it twenty-seven times in fifteen minutes; a rate of speech, he then calculated, that over a fifty year period would produce some 18,200,000 repetitions of the 'disgusting word'. The Sydney *Bulletin* called it 'the Australian adjective' in its edition of August 18, 1894, explaining that 'it is more used, and used more exclusively by Australians, than by any other allegedly civilized nation'. The term gained its final sanctification as the 'Great Australian Adjective' when W.T. Goodge used the phrase as the title for one of the poems he included in his *Hits! Skits! and Jingles!* (1899).

BODILY FUNCTIONS

As well as the pure sexuality that underlines the uses of **fuck**, other bodily functions are productive of swear-words. **Shit** (see DEFECATION for etymology) either exists in its own right or in such euphemisms as **shuck**s (19C), **shoot**, **sheet**, **sugar** and **sherbert** (all 20C). **Shit and derision** remains a common exclamation. **Shitten** and **shitting** both go back to the 16C, while **stinking** (whether or not it refers directly to excrement) was coined in the 13C, although like so much of latterday slang, it remained SE for the next six centuries. Generally acknowledged as less palatable are **cocksucking** and **corksacking**, **pissing** and **cunting** (all 20C). **Balls!** meant exclusively testicles until the late 19C, at which point it began meaning nonsense, and became a dismissive exclamation. **Barf!** and **barf me out!** (both from **barf**: to vomit) come from

California's teenagers; **nerts** and **nuts** (cf. **balls**) are earlier examples of Americana. **Bugger!**, **bugger me!** and the adjective **buggering** all emerge in this context during the 19C. Hughes describes **bugger** as 'the most flexible of all obscenities', serving equally well in each of the eight categories he specifies as the areas in which such terms work, ranging from the personal ('You ----!'), to cursing ('---- you!') to verbal usage ('To ---- about'). Even **fuck**, which seems to work in so many different ways, and in so many combinations, is not so prolific.

MISCELLANY

A number of animals have been enlisted into swearing; they include: **suffering cats!**, **pigs!** and **pigshit!**, **rats!** and the adjectival usage, **cowing. Radishes!** is a lone vegetable. More terms meaning cursed include **plaguey** and **botheration!** (18C), **all-fire(d)**, **blame(d)** (US), **blithering** (fr. **blether***) **cussed**, **sodding**, and **shucks** (meaning valueless, useless, and coming from 17C SE *shuck*: a husk). **Hogan's ghost!** is Australian and comes from the Holy Ghost. **Your mother!** is US and is derived from the ritual insults of the Afro-American 'game': the dozens, in which the parties trade insults; the aim is to break the composure of one's rival while keeping one's own temper. The phrase also gives **yomo**, meaning a black person.

Swearing produces a number of phrases, some of which have been listed above. Other prominent examples include **ferchrissakes!**, **for Christ's sake!**, **for crap's sake**, **for cripes' sake**, **for crying out loud!**, **for a mother-fucker!** (AA), **for gosh sake!**, **for God's sake!**, **for heaven's sake!**, **for landsakes!**, **for the love of Mike!**, **for the love of Pete!**, **my (holy) aunt!**, **my sainted aunt**, **my cripes!**, **my eyes!**, **my gosh!**, **my hat!** (an abbrev. of I'll eat my hat), **my stars** (17C) and **my stars and garters** (19C). More terms are based on the promise 'I'll be...': **I'll be a Chinaman!**, **I'll be a Dutchman!**, **I'll be a dirty word!**, **I'll be a monkey's uncle!**, **I'll be a (lowdown) son of a bitch!**, **I'll be jiggered**, **I'll be blowed**, **I'll be consarned!**, **I'll be darned!**, **I'll be jiggered**, **I'll be hanged**, **I'll be shot** and many

more. Finally two exclamations of surprise are **what the fuck!**
and **what the shit!**. Such phrases are more or less (but not
invariably) euphemistic, as are **fiddlesticks** (17C), **fiddledeedee**
(18C) and **thunderation** (19C).

FOOD

GENERAL TERMS

In his supposed 'conversation' between a pair of 16C rogues,
Thomas Harman has one of them demand, 'Maund of this morte
whate bene peck is in her ken', and translates it, 'Ask of this wyfe
what goode meate shee hath in her house.' **Peck**, meaning meat in
general, but more usually food, is perhaps the earliest slang, or more
precisely, cant term for eatables. Based in the pecking of birds, it
gives such combinations as **peck alley**, the throat and **rum peck**,
good food as well as those at meat, below. **Pecker**, meaning appetite
(as well as penis) is based on **peck**, while to be **off one's peck** or
to **take a holiday at Peckham** is to have nothing to eat. If peck
has an image of a beak snapping at crumbs, then **prog** (17C) takes
its meaning from its verb form, meaning to poke about for food or
to scavenge. Its cant meaning is both that of food, and of any
supplies that have been secreted away for later use.

The 17C also has **belly timber**, with its alternatives **belly chere**
or **cheer** and **belly furniture**. Working as a fiddler, in slang at least,
gradually attracted greater rewards: **fiddler's wages** (16C) meant
nothing but thanks, **fiddler's pay** (17C) meant wine and thanks,
while **fiddler's fare** (18C) meant meat drink and money. **Grub**
(17C) is reminiscent of **prog** in its image of 'grubbing around'; it
is also found meaning to eat, to beg for food and to provide with
food. The 19C **grub stake** (US) means sufficient money with
which to eat, while the 20C **grub up!** is a summons to the table.
The 19C **grubbery** or **grubbing-ken** is an eating house. **Scran**
(18C), with its rhyming slang synonym **Tommy O'Rann**, originally meant the reckoning at an inn or tavern; by 1785 it meant

food. **Yam** (18C) is presumably a version of the onomatopoeic **yum-yum** and is the basis of the nautical phrase **get toco for yam**: to be punished, in which **toco** equals a severe blow and 'for' means 'instead of'.

The remaining slang terms for food are of a wide variety. **Chop** (c.1860) comes from W. Africa where colonists and Africans alike used it to describe indigenous food; it was further suggested that originally chop had meant but one dish: **long pig**, or human flesh. **Chow** (and its derivative **chuff**) (c.1870), came from Chinese pidgin, meaning a mixture; thus the popular dish **chow mein** (created in America by Chinese cooks pandering to a Western version of real Chinese food) meant literally mixed food, although once again it had an earlier root: chopped morsels, notably those of dogs, rats and similar exotica. A third import was **scoff** (19C, and possibly **choff**) which came from South Africa, where it was a Cape Dutch (and originally European Dutch) term meaning a quarter of a day, and thus one of the four meals eaten in a the day; scoff in turn came from *schaffen* (both Dutch and German), meaning to provide or procure (food). South Africa also provided a **Kaffir's tightener** (19C, a filling meal). Like **peck chuck** (19C) embraces all sorts of food, especially meat; it can also mean scraps of meat and when it has been used specifically it has meant a type of steak, a measure of sprats, or, to the Royal Navy, a biscuit.

Munga, **mungy**, **munger** or **mungarly** (19C) all come from Parlyaree, which in turn draws on the French *manger* and Italian *mangiare*, both meaning to eat. Combinations include **mungy-wallah** (19C) used in the services for a man who works in the cookhouse, and **mungarly-casa** (19C), a baker's shop. **Manablins** or **manavilins**, which have the air of being much older, are 19C terms, both meaning broken meat, and thus means bits and pieces (cf. **chow**) as does **hash** (more properly 'a mess'). The term was thus adapted by the Navy, where the verb **manarvel** meant to pilfer small stores; in the wider world it was also used for small change. **Stodge** (19C) meant food, but especially 'stiff, farinaceous food'. **Slush** (19C) began life in the Navy, where it described the refuse fat from boiled meat, the selling of which was a perk accorded the **slushy** or ship's cook. The term was adopted by tramps to describe the tea or coffee available in lodging-houses. A **slush-bucket** is an ill-mannered eater. The fatty mode continues with **gorge grease** (19C, fr. **gorge**: the throat, a heavy meal or a glutton).

Tuck (1844) has the secondary meaning of a hearty meal, but **tucker** (19C Aus.) began life as rations and now means simply food. **Tack** was originally another naval term: **hardtack** meant ship's biscuits, **soft tack** meant bread; both terms were allied to, but predate SE **tackle**: food. Links to a ship's *tackle* are feasible, but those to *tack* — to change direction — seem rather desperate. **Feed** (early 19C), **fodder**, **fuel** and **eats** (all 20C) are brusquely to the point; the singular **eat** meant a meal in 11C. **Nosh** (20C) comes from the Yiddish or German *naschen*, to eat secretly or to nibble at; thus **nosher**: one who eats between meals. **Fixings** means food (though usually the ingredients of a given dish, and in the singular, in Aus., means strong drink); **groceries** (19C) is found in Anglo-Irish dialect as 'a decanter of whiskey and a bowl of sugar'.

Bad food is variously **crap**, a **dog's dinner**, **dog vomit**, **garbage**, **glop**, **gunge**, **slop** or **slops**, **shit** or **vom** (fr. vomit); a **burnt offering** is anything burnt, while **junk food** is fast food.

BREAD

As well as the rhyming slang **needle and thread** (19C) and **Uncle Fred** (20C), bread has generated a number of slang terms. Harman (16C) gives **pannam** which comes directly from the Latin *panis*, meaning bread.

Tommy (18C) has a debatable etymology. The *OED* suggests that it is an abbreviation of the British soldier's nickname for his ration of brown bread, generally known as **brown tommy** or **Tommy Brown** and hence, with time, as plain **tommy**. A similar name, **brown George**, had been used for the bread ration in the 17C. **Brown tommy** was the opposite of **soft tommy**, or soft white bread. An alternative source, however, may be in the tradition in Bedford of making a free distribution of bread to the poor on each St Thomas' Day (December 21, commemorating the apostle who refused to believe in the Resurrection, and was subsequently patron saint of architects and the blind). Other terms for bread include **rooti** (19C), used by the British Army who borrowed it from the Hindi *roti*, a flat, unleavened bread. A **dead 'un** (19C) was a half-quartern loaf, while a **vantage loaf** (19C) was the 13th loaf in a baker's dozen; **vantage** in this context means advantage, and therefore extra. A sandwich, supposedly invented c. 1765, is variously a **thumber** (19C), a **butty**, a **sango** (Australia) or a **sarnie**.

MEAT

Many general terms for meat come from the old, but not wholly obsolete British butcher's backslang. Typical are **beemal** (lamb), **feeb** (beef), **kayrop** (pork) and **delok** (any cold meat); frozen meat is also simply **cold**. Town (i.e abbatoir rather than farm or home killed) meat is **teekay** or **TK**, home killed is **HK**. **Elwoff** (while not strictly meat) means poultry.

Earlier terms include **grunter** and **grunting-peck** (16C, pork; cf. **grunting chete***) and **ruff-peck** (16C, bacon, perhaps literally 'rough food'). **Piano** (20C, AA) is spare ribs, while salt pork (US, 19C) was **galena** (fr. Galena, Ill. a centre of the pork rearing and packing industry), not to be confused **galeny***, the 16C term for fowl. **God's mercy** (19C) meant ham or bacon and eggs, from the grace one might say before eating it; regular visitors called it **365**, from its being available on a menu every day of the year. Such numerology predates the number codes central to the jargon of modern US cafes and diners.

To return to meat, salt pork, especially when served at sea, was **junk**, a term that originally described pieces of rope and which was usually qualified as **old**, **salt** or **tough junk**. Salt beef was **old horse** or **salt horse**. In Australia **Harriet Lane** meant tinned meat; the meat in question was chopped up, and a hapless murder victim, Harriet Lane had been chopped up c. 1875 by one Wainwright. Another brutal killing, this time of eight year-old Fanny Adams, at Alton in Hampshire on August 24, 1867, gives **Fanny Adams**: tinned mutton. This murderer, one Frederick Baker, was hanged at Winchester on Christmas Eve; 5,000 people watched the execution. The **mouse** (19C) is a small piece of meat immediately above the knee joint; a **staggering bob** is meat unfit to eat, a term taken from the meat trade jargon: *bob* or *bobby*, especially when describing animals that have died rather than been slaughtered.

The 19C offers a number of terms for specific dishes. The **sergeant major** is a fat loin of mutton, the origin being in the assumed plumpness of pampered sergeant majors and the streaks of fat that, loosely, resemble his stripes. **Snob's duck** is a leg of mutton stuffed with sage and onions; the **snob** in this context is a cobbler, a usage that precedes the social one. A **wabbler** or **wobbler** is a boiled leg of mutton, while a steak is a **four-wheeler**. A **Field-Lane duck** is a baked sheep's head: Field Lane once linked Holborn to Clerkenwell. **Irish turkey** is corned beef and cabbage.

Shit on a shingle or **twice laid** both mean minced meat on toast in the US; the rhyming slang **kate and sidney** means steak and kidney, while **surf and turf**, popular in the 1970s and beyond, means a meal composed of lobster and steak. Terms for stew include the tramp's **Mulligan stew** (an assembly of any available foods); **bonnets so blue** (rhyming slang for Irish stew) and **lobscouse** (18C) a sailor's dish consisting of meat stewed with vegetables and ship's biscuit; the totemic dish of Liverpool, and, as **scouse** or **scousers**, the collective name of the city's population. **Lob**, meaning bubbling or boiling, is also found in the 16C **loblolly**, a thick gruel, found both as a peasant or nautical dish or as a as a simple medicine; as such it also meant the medicines carried by a ship's doctor. Gravy gives the rhyming slang **army and navy**.

Other stews include **daddy funk**, **dead horse**, **dogsbody** (19C, specifically pease pudding), **dough Jehovahs**, **measles** (more usually found as syphilis, qv), **sea pie** and **meat-fosh** (19C, fosh possibly based on the French *farci*). **Lilian Baylis' leg** is the stew served to actors in the canteen of the National Theatre; named for Lilian Baylis, C.H. (1874-1937), theatrical manager and founder of the Old Vic and Sadler's Wells theatres.

Sausages are **bangers** (20C, thus **bangers and red lead**: tinned sausages and tomato sauce), **skintights**, **spotted dogs** or **mysteries**, **snorkers**, **snags** and **swags** (the last three all mainly Australian); **red-hots** (US) are frankfurters with chili and **girl and boy** is rhyming slang for saveloy); **dogs**, **bags of mystery** (19C), **chambers of horrors** (19C), **gut pudding**, **sore leg** (which can also mean plum pudding) and **Sharp's Alley blood worms** (19C, Sharp's Alley was an abbatoir near the great Smithfield meat market in London) all show an instinctive distrust of the ingredients.

FISH

While a kipper is the rhyming **Jack the Ripper**, a **Cornish duck** a pilchard, anchovies on toast a **whale** and oysters **Miltons**, the bulk of fish slang relates to herrings, for many years far and away the most widely eaten fish in the UK.

Such terms, often prefixed by a local name, include the **two-eyed steak** (also a bloater), **searover**, the **gendarme**, the **magistrate**, the **Glasgow magistrate** or **Glasgow baillie**, the **Atlantic ranger**, the **Gourock ham** (Gourock is a Clyde fishing village; such 'hams' were salted) or the **Digby chicken** (Digby is in Nova Scotia; these herrings are usually smoked and occasionally found as **Digby ducks**). A **soldier** means both herring and boiled lobster; **lobster**, in turn, has meant soldier, notably from the red uniforms worn by British soldiers during the American War of Independence. The red herring was a **red**, a **Dunbar wether**, a **Californian**, a **pheasant** or **Billingsgate pheasant**, a **Taunton turkey** or **Yarmouth capon**. A **Crail capon** was a dried, unsplit haddock; Crail is a fishing port in Fife.

VEGETABLES

Vegetables are **veggies** or, if salad, **rabbit food**; a specific prison use gives the rhyming slang **has-beens**: greens. Somewhat in advance of the brand-name for instant mashed potatoes **smash** (18C) meant mashed turnips. Cabbage is **Joe Savage** and **poor man's treacle** is garlic (17C) or onions (19C), **garden violets** are onions, especially the spring onions used in salads. The potato, as a staple, is slang's most popular vegetable. Many of the references, unsurprisingly, are 'Irish', and come mainly from the 19C: **murphs** or **murphies**, **praties**, **Irish apricots** or **lemons**, **bog-oranges**, **donovans** and **Munster plums**. Other terms include **ruggins**, **ronnys** (fr. the dialect *rouny* or *roundy*: a round object), **spuds** (possibly from the similarly named digging instrument), **tunnel-**

grunters, taturs and **navigators** or **navs;** a steam-engine was a **potato-pie** while on some US campuses **bimps** are french fries.

DAIRY PRODUCTS

The earliest terms for cheese are **cassan** (cited in Harman, 1567), **cass** and **caz** (all of which come from the Romany *cas*; cf SE casein: the milk ingredient that is basis of cheese). Other terms include **choke dog, sweaty-toe**, the rhy. sl. **bended knees** and **stand at ease**. In US cafes, **ace** is a grilled cheese sandwich. Harman has **param** or **yarum** (possibly a corruption of yellow or yallow) for milk, while **lap** is buttermilk or whey. Butter is **ointment, grease, cart grease** or the rhyming **stammer and stutter** and **roll-me-in-the-gutter**. Margarine is **marj**.

Terms for egg dishes come primarily from the vocabulary of US short-order chefs. Thus **Adam and Eve** is two eggs, **Adam and Eve on a raft** (two eggs on toast), **Adam and Eve on a raft and wreck 'em** (scrambled eggs on toast); **two looking at you** (two fried eggs), **sunny side up** (eggs fried on one side only), **two down, two with their eyes closed** or **over easy** (eggs turned over) and **two on a slice of squeal** (two eggs on fried ham).

OTHER FOODS

Cake offers the rhyming slang **Joe Blake** (which can also mean steak or indeed a snake, while the **Joe Blakes★** are the **shakes**, i.e. *delirium tremens* and **Joe Blake the Barthelmy** [19C] meant to visit a prostitute) or **Sexton Blake** (the fictitious detective created in 1893 by Hal Meredith, the pseudonym of Harry Blyth). A **sinker** (US) is a doughnut while 19C Britain had the **rector** and **curate**, respectively the bottom and top halves of a teacake or muffin – the rector, the senior figure, was given more butter; the terms were also used for the everyday poker and its fancy variety, brought out, presumably, for 'company'.

Breakfast cereals are **soggies** or the older **burgoo** (18C, an oatmeal porridge; the word is based on the Turkish *burghul* cracked wheat); sugar is **sand**. Pizza is **za** while spaghetti bolognese is **spag bol**. Soup can be **loop-the-loop** (rhyming slang), **glue, rib**

tickler or **stick in the ribs** (all 19C thick soups), **hishee hashee**, **soap** and **bullion** (fr. the French *bouillon*).

A watermelon (a supposed staple of the black community) is an **African golf ball** or a **culture fruit** (fr. *cultural*: pertaining to black culture); **rape** is backsl. for a pear. A plum or currant dumpling was a **spotted dog**, plum pudding was a **spotted donkey** or **leopard** and a suet pudding with currants or raisins is still **spotted dick**; pudding in general was **steaming** (19C). A snack or a drink before breakfast (as used in the countryside) was a **dew bit** or **dew drink** (both 19C); mayonnaise is **mayo** and pickles **Harvey Nichols** (rhy. sl.); ice cream is **scream**, chilli **red**, prison tea **diesel**, an Indian meal **an Indian** and a Chinese one **a Chinese**.

DRINKING AND DRINKS

More even than sex, unless one lumps together the acts and the organs, drink and drinking, and particularly drunkenness, dominates the slang lexicon. One expert has amassed nearly 2,500 terms. Killing the pain of life has been a basic preoccupation for millenia; slang gleaned from the last four hundred years makes it obvious that very little has changed, or is indeed likely to do so.

TO DRINK

It is perhaps some testimony to human appetites for alcohol that among the earliest terms for drinking are those that have survived the longest. **Wet one's whistle** can be found in Chaucer (14C), and is based on **whistle*** meaning throat or mouth; **booze**, certainly 16C, can be found in the *OED* in 1300, but Partridge maintains that in this context the word means the drinking vessel and not the act of drinking. Either way, the word probably comes from the Dutch *buizen* or the German *buzen*, both meaning to drink to excess.

Hard behind them come **tipple** (late 16C), **disguise oneself** (16C, thus **disguised** means drunk) and **crask** or **crush a bottle**

(16C, presumably the ancestor of the 19C **give a bottle a black eye** and 20C **hit the bottle, hit the booze, hit the jug** or **hit the sauce**, as well as the Australian **crack a bottle** or **crack a tube**). **Mug** (17C) comes from the noun meaning cooling drink; its 19C usage means to bribe with drink, or to get another person drunk. The 17C also offers **swig, tip** and **tiff** and **suck the bottle** (thus **suck-bottle**: an alcoholic). **Fuddle** (17C) becomes a drinking bout or drunkenness in the 19C. **Knock about the bub** (1781) is based on **bub** (18C) which comes (like **bevvy***) from the Latin *bibere*: to drink. **Humming bub** means strong beer, while **grub and bub** is food and drink. To **barleybree** or **barleybroth** come from nouns meaning strong beer, and both **beer** and **wine** are simple verb forms of the relevant nouns. **Bend** (18C, thus **bend the elbow** and **crook the elbow**) becomes **bender**, a drinking bout, in 1827. To **go on the burst** (19C) also relates to a binge, from **burst** meaning a hearty meal. So to does **mop up** (19C), which comes from **mop**, a drunkard or drinking bout; and which creates **on the mop** and **all mops and brooms**: drunk.

A number of phrases imply the pouring of liquid down one's throat. They include **irrigate one's tonsils** or **canal** (18C), **lap the gutter** (19C, either from **gutter-alley***:throat or **gatter***: beer), **dip one's beak** (19C, although **dip one's bill** [17C] is to be nearly drunk), **damp one's mug** (mid 19C, fr. **damp** meaning drink, a rare term, found mainly in Dickens' *Pickwick Papers* [1836]), **do a dram, do a wet do a beer, do a bitter**, etc. (mid-19C), **lower a glass** (19C) **moisten** or **soak the chaffer** or **clay** (19C, **chaffer**:throat; 18C **clay** refers to the 'mortal clay') **oil the tonsils**, and **put one back, put a few back** or **put a few down**.

Gross consumption is reflected in **lush it up** or **lush it around** (1810), **swill, guttle** (19C, probably from *glutton*), **guzzle** (fr. 18C **guzzle-guts**: glutton or hard drinker), **liquor up** (19C), **load in** or **load up, slosh** (late 19C), **sluice the bolt, sluice the dominoes, sluice the ivories** or **sluice the gob** (18-19C, all from terms for teeth), **soak** (20C), **swipe** (early 19C, to drink hastily and copiously, cf. **swipes**), **sling a pot** (1870), **gargle, get a load on** (20C, Aus.), **get a snootful** (fr. **snoot**: nose), **get an edge on, get one's nose painted** and **get one going** (all 20C), **hoist one**

(1860), **inhale, knock (one) back, slop (some) down** (20C), **throw one** or **a few down** and **tie one on** (20C). To **drown the shamrock** is to drink on St Patrick's Day while **chug-a-lug** (to drink down in a single draught) comes from an Australian toast of the 1950s. **Look through a glass** and **read the maker's name** (both 19C) imply an upended, emptied container.

A final mixed bag of terms include **blink, budge** (1820, thus Scots **budge kain [ken]**: pub; the term probably comes from **booze** or **bub), go see a man** or **go see a woman, make fun, malt** (1813, from a **shovel of malt**: a pot of porter; to **have malt above the wheat** or **have malt above the water**: to be drunk), **prime oneself** (19C), **pull, rock, save a life, shift** (late 19C), **squiff** (19C, thus **squiffy** and **on the squiff**: drunk and **squiff**: a drunkard [Aus. 1920]), **swizzle** (19C, from **swizzle**: an intoxicating drink), **take the pin out, take a drop in the eye, take in some o-be-joyful** (19C, thus **o-be-joyful house**: pub), **farm, pull** and **shicker** (Yiddish, from the Hebrew *shikor* meaning drunk).

The Royal Navy has provided a number of drink-related terms. The most celebrated of which is **splice the mainbrace**. The mainbrace was notably hard to splice and was sited in a very dangerous place; thus when the hands had completed their task they were rewarded with a double shot of rum. Almost equally famous is **grog** (19C) used as a verb, but more commonly as a noun, to mean rum and water. The term is supposedly short for grogram (a type of cloth), and was (according to Grose) originally applied as a nickname to Admiral Vernon, known as Old Grog, from the fact of his wearing a grogram cloak. The name was transferred to the mixture which in August 1740 he ordered to be served out instead of neat spirit. **Sly grog** (19C, Aus.) is liquor sold without a license, often through a **sly-grog shop. Suck the monkey** or **tap the admiral** (18C) both mean to suck liquor through a straw from the ship's barrel which has been bored with a gimlet.

Other naval terms include **shed a tear** (19C) which as 'shed a tear for Nelson' originally meant to urinate) and **shake a cloth in the wind** (19C) which a century earlier had meant only to be hanged. To **drink at Freeman's Quay**, meaning to drink at another's expense comes from the free drinks distributed at this quay near London Bridge to porters and carmen between 1810-80; the Navy amplified it to **Harry Freemans** (and used it for anything, not merely drink, that was free) while the Army shortened it to **Freemans**.

Other specific terms include **brownbag** (US, to drink from a 'hidden' bottle when public drinking is banned); **fall off the wagon** (to resume drinking after a period of abstinence; the wagon is short for the 'water wagon'); **wet the baby's head** (to celebrate a new birth by drinking).

To **make a pearl on the nail** (17C) meaning to drink, comes from the 16C custom of dropping the remaining moisture at bottom of glass onto one's nail; the custom was also known as **supernaculum** or **supernagulum**, literally 'over the nail', and meant to drink to the last drop, which one then pours onto one's left thumbnail. To **stab oneself and pass the dagger** (19C) was a theatrical term meaning to take a glassful then circulate the bottle; the verb **stab** (to drink) presumably comes from this source. To buy for the whole bar is to **charter the bar** or **shout oneself hoarse**.

INVITATIONS TO DRINK

The apparent inability of one drinker to ask another, 'What would you like to drink?' means that invitations to drink are often couched in slang terms. Among them are **what will you have?**, **name your poison** or **nominate your poison** (mid 19C), **will you irrigate?**, **will you tod?** (fr. toddy), **how will you have it?**, **what's your medicine?**, **let's drive another nail** (fr. **coffin nail**: a drink), **try a little Indian**, **will you try a smile?**, **let's go and see the baby**, **come and see your pa**. There are many others, to be gleaned from the nation's saloon bars. Responses are equally varied; among their numbers are **here's into your face**, **here's how**, **don't mind if I do**. To **hob and nob** or to **hob nob** is to invite to drink, and then to clink glasses.

A DRINK

The noun drink offers a wide range of terms, most simply considered chronologically. The oldest is **lap** (mid-16C), from the SE action of lapping water or any liquid; it describes any form of drink. **Crater** or **cratur** (16C, both from SE *creature*) were similarly applied to any drink, but have specifically meant whiskey since 19C. **Go-down** (mid-17C) refers to the liquid passing down the throat, as does the later **common sewer** (c.1860; which means variously the throat, a tippler and a whore). A **flash** and a **bit of tape** (both 18C), general in theory, usually meant gin (qv) in practice, while **lush** moves from its 18C meaning of strong drink to the mid-19C drinking party to the late-19C drunkard. **Tift** (17C) is a variation of the verb **tiff**: to drink.

The 19C is especially fruitful in drinking terms. Drink can be **nectar** or **poison**, if unpleasant it can be **slumgullion**, defined as any cheap, nasty, washy beverage or, specifically, fish offal or the watery refuse, mixed with blood and oil, which drains from blubber. **Breaky-leg** (1860) mutated from meaning any strong drink to whiskey only, while **neck oil** reflects the verb **neck**: to swallow, as well as the adjective **oiled**: tipsy. Other terms dependent on parts of the body include a **shove in the mouth** (1811), **titty** (fr. **tit**: breast, which offers 'milk') and a **smile** or **fancy smile**, generally used for whiskey. **Cry** and **shout** are cognate with 'My shout!', an offer to buy a round of drinks; they are both found as verbs.

The liqidity of alcohol provides **damp**, **wet** (19C, from **light wet** or **heavy wet**: respectively gin or beer) **something damp** and a **drain** (1835). Less classifiable are **Timothy** (Scots, possibly from the name of a real brewer), **willy wacht** (fr. Scots: *Willy Arnot* [a distiller?]: good whiskey plus **wacht/waught**: to drink deeply), a **one, a two, a three** (as said prior to tossing off a glassful), a **bender** (1827, originally US then UK from the meaning 'drinking spree'), **old crow**, **tiddly**, (usually as an adjective meaning tipsy), and a **leaf of the old author** (who presumably is God). Further terms include a **ball**, a **bead**, a **bosom friend** (more usually a louse) a **chitchat**, a **dannie**, a **doch-an-dorrach** (fr. the Scots toast and often anglicised as **jock and doris**) a **fip**, a **nut** (thus **off one's nut** meaning drunk, prior to its 20C meaning of insane).

The 20C is less fruitful, although many earlier terms remain in common use. New coinages include **waxer** (Merchant Navy), and three Australianisms: **nobbler**, **rosiner** (1930) and **turps** (1930).

Some specific terms include **jigger stuff** (1820) meaning a secret still; the term comes from **jigger** meaning a key, which locks up the still; thus **jig-water** or **jigger** mean bootleg liquor. A **leg opener** is drink when it is used for seduction; **one for the ditch** or **one for the road** is a farewell drink; the best- known hangover cure is a **hair of the dog**, coined as early as 1546 and based on the belief that the burnt hair of a dog is an antidote to its bite.

A number of terms equate alcohol with medicine. They include **medicine** itself, **bracer** (19C), **gargle** (mid-19C), **tonic** (late 19C), and **lotion** (1876). **Tincture**, much beloved of *Private Eye's* 'Dear Bill' correspondence is a 1960s coinage. Other terms are **pickmeup** (1867) **reviver**, (late 19C, also used as a verb; with the combination **corpse reviver**: a hangover cure), **rince** (also a verb), a **cheerer** (late 18C), an **invigorator**, a **quencher** (19C), a **soother** and a **refresher** (1841). **Pill** (late 19C) has some medicinal qualities, but it also means a means cannon ball or bullet, and thus relates equally to **slug** or **pistol-shot**, below. A **settler** (mid 18C) is a parting drink, 'one for the road', which supposedly settles the stomach after an evening's indulgence.

Many terms for drink echo the short, sharp shock one receives on knocking back a glass of neat spirits. These terms offer **hit** and **jag** (both taken from 20C drug use, although to be **out on a jag** or **have a jag on** – both meaning out on a drinking spree – date to 17C), a **jolt** (1900, originally Canadian and latterly Aus.; both particularly used of brandy), a **shot** (US early 20C), and a **slug** (18C, any kind of strong liquor). Similar are a **go** (18C), which originally meant a three-halfpenny bowl of gin and water, especially that sold at the well-known Go Shop; by 1800 it meant drink in general, a **taste** or **drop** (**of the creature**), a **gasp** (1880), **sniffler** (1880) and a **snort** (1920), all of which stem from the physical reactions that follows a hit of strong drink), a **squirt** (late 19C, otherwise champagne) a **snifter** (US mid-19C and latterly UK), a **sneezer** (1820, also used as a verb: to sneeze), a **dash** (usually as 'a dash of...' although in 1660 a **dash** was a tavern waiter, possibly from his dashing about), a **nip, nipper** or **nipperkin** (cf: **nipitate***; the verb to nip means to catch or take smartly), an **invigorator**, a **pistol shot** (19C, cf. **slug**), a **toothful** (1920) and a **warmer**.

Time also influences one's drinking, as these terms bear out. **Eye-opener**, **rouser**, **livener** (all 19C) denote the first drink of the day, as does the 20C **phlegm-cutter**. A **forenoon**, **dew bit**, **dewdrop** and **dewdrink** imply drinks before breakfast, especially as taken by farm-workers, whose traditional day was once divided into **dewbit**, **elevenses**, **fourses** and **morn-bit**.

An **appetiser** and an **anti-lunch** precede what may, if unaccompanied by food, be termed a **liquid lunch** (20C). **Whitewash** is a glass of sherry taken as the finale after a meal spent drinking port and claret while a **white-washer** is a glass of white wine taken at end of dinner. A **corker** or **caulker** literally 'puts the head or cork on' and is thus the last drink of the evening – probably a brandy. Finally a **reposer** (1870) is a nightcap.

Many terms for drink are also used to denote a measure of alcohol, or of the glass into which it is placed. Best known is **peg**. Popular etymology suggests that each drink is a 'peg' or 'nail' in one's coffin, but although a **coffin nail** (these days more usually equated with a cigarette) did mean a drink in the 19C (thus **put another nail in one's coffin**: to take another drink), the *OED* lays down that these pegs are 'one of a set of pins fixed at intervals in a drinking vessel as marks to measure the quantity which each drinker was to drink'. **Peg out***: to die, comes from the same divided tankard.

Less well-known measures-as-drinks are **flicker** (19C, a glass), **muzzler** (19C, from **muzzle**: mouth), **jorum** or **joram** (a drinking bowl), **shant** (a quart or pint pot; thus **shanting** means drinking and a **shant of gatter**, a pot of beer), a **sneaker** (1710: large covered cup/saucer) and a **dandy** (19C, a small tumbler), both of which were used for punch. A **dodger** (1824), an **out** (19C) and a **facer** held a dram of spirits while a **Johnny** (1860, from Johnny Walker, the famous brand, known in the 20C as **Johnny Red** from the label) was a half glass of whiskey. In Ayrshire a glass of spirits was a **bucket**. A **bumper** (1660) is a full glass, a term much beloved of bodice-ripping novelists. A **pony** (19C, originally US) is a small glass of beer, while a **sleeve button** is a long drink, probably allied to the better known **sleever**, a long beer glass, usually referred to in pubs as a 'straight' glass, as opposed to the shorter, dimpled glasses.

Lounce (19C naut.) comes from SE 'allowance' and is also used to mean a ration of food). A **heeltap** or a **snuff** refers to the liquor left at the bottom of a glass; thus creating the cry: 'No heeltaps': 'Drain your glasses'. A **modicum**, a **modest quencher** (19C) and a **quantum** (1840, from the Latin: 'enough') all denote a small measure. A **slight sensation** (1859, Aus: a half glass of sherry, UK: a quartern of gin) continue the theme of relative self-denial. A **nick** is a short measure, a term based on the 'nick' or bump in the bottom of tankard; **nick** also means a publican (as does **nickum**).

TYPES OF DRINKS

Apart from beer, whiskey, gin and brandy, which are sufficiently well-represented to earn their own sections below, slang has thrown up a number of terms for the wide varieties of drinks on offer. Any adulterated wine or mixed drink was categorised as **balderdash**, drinks mixed with water were **baptised** or **christened**. Those left untouched were **primitive**. **Upstairs** meant spirits, which were usually kept on a special high shelf in the pub, while **suit and cloak** (rhy. sl., presumably from soak) meant any drink, although usually brandy. **Sick wine** was off, while **Gladstone** was cheap claret (a reference to the Prime Minister Gladstone's reduction, in 1860, of the duty on French wine) and a mix of claret with lemonade was a **spider. Peter See Me** was a Spanish wine, properly named *Pedra Ximenes* and named for the famous Cardinal. Port was **bullock's eye** or **kill-priest** (fr. the alleged clerical consumption thereof) or, if second-rate, **treacle**; sherry was **white wash** or **white fustian**, while port or claret was **red fustian** (fustian in both cases being originally in SE a coarse cloth and possibly used in contrast to gin's 'smooth' **satin***). Other terms for champagne include **bub, fizz, dry, bitches' wine** (cf: **cat's water***), **cham, chammy, sham, shammy** and **simpkin. Boy**, also champagne, comes from King Edward VII's habit during a shoot of having a page near at hand with an open bottle; when he required a drink he would merely call, 'Boy' and his glass would be promptly refilled. **Smash** was iced brandy and water and **rob-davy** or **roberdavy** was metheglin or spiced mead; the word comes from the Welsh *meddyglyn*, a combination of *meddyg* healing or medicinal and *llyn*: liquor. **Davy** was presumably a reference to the Welsh name, usually found as Taffy. A **cinder** (mid-19C) is any strong drink that has been mixed with water, tea or lemonade, while a **cooler** (19C), refers to ale, stout or porter taken after spirits.

HOT DRINKS

Hot alcoholic drinks abounded in the 18C and 19C, although their numbers are drastically reduced today. Almost the sole survivor is **toddy** (also used as a verb), although there are, of course, many cocktails (albeit cold), each bearing its own name.

Such hot concoctions included **hot flannel** (heated gin and beer with nutmeg, sugar and spices), **hot tiger** (spiced ale and sherry), **hot pot** (ale and brandy), **huckle my butt** or **huckle my buff** (egg and brandy heated), **humpty-dumpty** (ale and brandy boiled), **lamb's wool** (hot ale, spiced, sweetened and mixed with the pulp of roast apples), **locomotive** (Burgundy, curacao, egg yolks, honey and cloves all heated together), **meat and drink** (strong drink in general, but specifically liquor thickened with egg yolks), **merry-go-down** (hot strong ale), **stone fence** (brandy and ale), **purl** (beer warmed nearly to boiling, mixed with gin or wormwood, sugar and ginger), **samson** (brandy, cider, sugar and water), **soap suds** (hot gin and water, with lemon and lump sugar), **flip** (1690, hot small beer and brandy, sweetened), a **bishop** (warm wine and sugar with either oranges or lemons) and **larkin** (a very strong spiced punch, created in the Raj).

GIN

'No Gin, No King!' declared the London mob, protesting a proposed increase in the tax on their favourite tipple in 1736, and few drinks have played so central a part in a culture. 'Liquid madness', Thomas Carlyle called it in 1839, and a century earlier Alexander Pope welcomed the legislation to curb consumption of the 'spirituous liquor, the exorbitant use of which had almost destroyed the lowest rank of the People'. The People, as ever, simply paid the added cost, and gin remained a vital ingredient of 18C and 19C life. Naturally, it generated a good deal of slang, much of it testament to the spirit's raw power.

One of the earliest of such terms was **daffy** or **Daffy's elixir** (18C) which in 1709 appears as the proprietary name of a popular remedy known as the 'soothing syrup'. Such comforts were at the heart of gin drinking; the transference was simple. The term persisted into the late 19C, although by then it meant tincture of senna. Other 18C terms include **bob** (also used to mean a large beer jug, holding a gallon), **diddle** (1720), **jackey** (1799), **max** (the best quality and like today's **max out** and **to the max** from SE *maximum*), the twin **flash of lightning** and **clap of thunder**, **royal poverty** and **royal bob**, **lap** (although this could applied to any drink) as could **wibble** to any weak drink, and **tittery** (fr. its affect on the drinker, and as such like the 20C **giggle-juice**).

Into the new century and one finds **Lady Dacre's wine** (cited in the *Lexicon Balatronicum* of 1811 but without, alas, further specification of the lady in question), **light wet** (1820, while **heavy wet** meant porter or stout; calls for 'a pint of heavy' are still regularly heard in Scottish pubs), **mother's milk** (1820), which antedates the more recent **mother's ruin** (20C); **mother's blessing**, also 19C, is laudanum, a mix of brandy and tincture of opium, often used to keep the children quiet. Gin could also be the **right sort** (1820), the rhyming slang **Brian O'Lynn** or **Brian O'Flynn**, the **cream of the valley** (mid 19C, paralleling **mountain dew** meaning whiskey), **stark-naked** and **strip-me-naked** (both raw gin). **Dead-eye** and **deady** (1819) referred to a well-known of distiller, as did **Old Tom**. This particularly potent gin was named, according to Brewer, for one Thomas Norris, who was employed at Hodges' distillery and who opened a gin palace in Great Russell Street, Covent Garden. The drink in which he specialised was concocted by another Hodges' employee, Thomas Chamberlain, who christened his brand in honour of Mr Norris. Taking 'Tom' in its feline sense gives **cat's water**, a cousin of **bitch's wine** (champagne) and presumably of the modern **cat's pee** or **piss**, although this means weak, rather than potent drink.

Other terms include **satin**, **ribbon** and **tape**, the latter pair stemming from the former term, itself presumably indicative of the smoothness of good gin. All three terms are responsible for such combinations as **sky-blue**, **light blue**, **blue tape** and **blue ribbon** (all 19C) plus **white tape**, **white satin** (still a proprietary name for a brand of gin), **white lace**, **white ribbon**, **white wine**, (all 19C, bar **white tape** which is 18C); **blue ruin** is an extension.

Other 19C terms include **eye water** (c.1820, which is what strong gin produces), **frog's wine** (mid 19C, fr. **froglander** meaning not French but Dutchman), **misery** (1820), **juniper** (19C, from its primary constituent), **Fuller's Earth** (early 19C, from its property as a scourer and 'cleaner out'), **snopsy** (US, fr. *schnapps*) and **squareface** (fr. the shape of the bottle, although Germans were known as **squareheads** and schnapps was a German drink), **tangle-leg** (19C, from its effect, cf. **tangle-foot**: whiskey), **unsweetened and twankey** (1890s, **twankey**, in the jargon of the tea trade meant green tea).

BEER

For all its popular image as a staple of British culture, beer offers fewer slang terms than gin; perhaps the relative wholesomeness of the former, as is often the case in slang, naturally creates less synonyms than the latter, with its 'glamourous' if negative image.

Early terms for beer include **John Barleycorn** (17C), **stingo** (17C, from its powerful 'sting'), **barley broth** and **oil of barley** (18C, both strong), **act of parliament** (18C, from the weak 'small beer' supplied free to the British army), **English burgundy** (18C, predating 19C **British champagne**), **half and half**, (18C, a mix of ale and beer). **Single broth** and **swipes** (18C) meant small beer as did the 19C **down** (**up** was bottled ale). **Nippitato**, **nippitate** or **nippitatum** meant strong drink in general, while other strong beers include **stride-wide**, **swell-nose**, **pharoah**, **huff** (which makes one **huffy**; it is also used as a verb), **stitch-back** and **humming ale**, while **upsee-Dutch**, **upsee-English** and **upsee-Freese** were all strong enough to knock one over; but **upsee**, while apparently cognate with 'upsy-daisy', is in fact derived from the Dutch *op-zee* and means 'overseas', and thus imported. **Lull** is simply ale while **october** is ale (or cider) brewed in October. 19C terms include **artesian** (as brewed in Australia), **bevy** and **bevvy** (either from Parlyaree or simply an abbreviation of beverage; the root in either case is the Latin *bibere*: to drink; **bevvy** also means a public house; a **bevvy merchant** is a heavy drinker), **bungjuice**, (fr. SE *bung*, the stopper of a barrel), **bunker** (either from a coal bunker at which one fuels up or from Lingua Franca *bona acqua*: good water), **gatter** (possibly from a mix of *acqua* and water?), **heavy wet** (cf. **light wet**) was porter as was **thick**, **knock (me) down**, **pong**, **pongelow** or **ponjello** (all used in the Indian Army; thus **pong**: to drink). The backslang **reeb** means beer, thus **top of reeb**: a pot of beer.

Beer was also **rosin** (18C), a term based on the SE *rosin*: to supply oneself with drink, and underpinning Henry Fielding's punning riddle in *The Pleasures of the Town* (1729) 'A fiddlestick is a drunkard: Why? Because it loves ros'ning.' It could also be **whistle** (usually the throat; the **whistling shop** was a room in the King's Bench prison where one could buy drink illicitly). **Tipper** was a unique ale named for the Brighton brewer Thomas Tipper; it was brewed from notably brackish water which came from one specific well.

Swankey or **swankey swipes** (19C) meant the best beer: fr. **swanky**: pretentious and **swipes**: beer, as did **benbouse** (literally 'good drink'). Bad beer, whether sour, inferior or simply weak, was variously **rotgut** (16C), **belch** and **belly-vengeance** (both 19C), **stinkibus** (18C), **bum clink** (19C, from Midlands dial.), **purge** (19C), **bilgewater**, **whip belly** ('thin as a whip') and **skin disease** (spec. fourpenny ale). Other weak brews included **swish-swash** **water-bewitched**, **slops**, and **taplash** (specifically the dregs).

BRANDY

Brandy, a less populist liquor, has relatively few terms. They include **nantz** and **cold nantz** (both from Nantes in France, a centre of Cognac production), **French elixir**, **French cream**, **French article** and **French lace** (all 19C but the 18C **cream**), **cold tea** (17C), **bingo** (18C, on the model of **stingo**★ or possibly from SE *binge*), **ball of fire** (19C, which with its image of a cannonball relates to the military to **fire a slug**, meaning drink a dram) and

red tape (18C, on the model of **blue tape** or **white tape,** both meaning gin).

WHISKEY

Whiskey rules as Scotland's national drink, although some slang synonyms – **breaky-leg**, the **curse of Scotland** and **family disturbance** –seem to point up its pitfalls rather than its pleasures. Less minatory terms include **barley bree**, **caper juice**, **corn juice**, **cappie** and **farintosh**.

The **hard stuff** (late 19C), **forty rod lightning** (19C, cheap and strong whiskey) and **white lightning** all attest to whiskey's power, while **shine** (US 19C) and **moonshine** (UK 18C) both refer to contraband or illicitly distilled whiskey. **Moonshine** had different meanings according to the county: in Sussex and Kent it referred to white brandy, in Yorkshire to gin. **Mountain dew** (US) began life in 1816 as whiskey; the image of contraband emerges in 1823.

Rough whiskey can be **redeye** (19C, it makes the eyes go red) or **white eye** (19C, one's eyes apparently roll up in their sockets, exposing the whites). **Screech** (fr. its affect on women) and **kill the beggar** are equally unpalatable, if effective. **Simon pure** (19C) and **the real thing** (used usually of people, but here of a spirit) imply the finest quality Scotch. Other terms include **old man's milk** (mid 19C, cf. **mother's milk**), **railroad**, **sit on a rock**, **a glister of fish-hooks** (a glass of Irish whiskey), **grapple the rails** (18C, from its effects: one had to hang on to keep standing up) and the 19C rhy. sl. **gay and frisky**. Australians drank **stringy-bark**, normally the name of a tree.

GLASSES, MEASURES, ETC.

Miscellaneous terms mainly focused on the size of of glass include **chicken** (a pint pot), **flicker** (a glass), **gage** (a quart pot), **rouse** (a large glass), **Salisbury** (17C, a gallon pot of wine with a tap), **size** (a half pint, from the 16C term for the portion of bread and beer allowed to undergraduates in Cambridge colleges), a **small cheque** (1880, a dram; thus to **knock down a cheque**: to spend all one's money on alcohol), a **toothful** (1920, a dram, fr. the

Scottish **toothful**: to tipple), a **snake in the grass** (19C rhy. sl. for both looking and drinking glass, either of which might prove a treacherous friend), **sneaker** (early 18C, a small bowl or a large glass jug used for of punch), a **tall boy** (a large wine glass, or two-quart pot filled with wine). **Tears of the tankard** (17C) were drink stains on one's clothes and a **Tom and Jerry shop** (c.1835), was a cheap tavern. Tom and Jerry, two fictional men about town created by Pierce Egan in his book *Life in London, or Days and Nights of Jerry Hawthorne and his elegant friend Corinthian Tom* (1821) lent their name both to this low inn (although the plain **jerry shop**, with the same meaning but no bearing on the book, can be found a year earlier), and to a highly spiced punch (which is still being drunk in Damon Runyon's short stories more than a century later).

An empty bottle is variously a **dead soldier, camp candlestick, corpse, dummy, dead marine, dead recruit, fellow commoner**, and a **dead 'un**.

DRUNK

'No man must call a Good-fellow Drunkard...But if at any time they spie that defect in another, they may without any forfeit...say, He is Foxt, He is Flaw'd, He is Fluster'd, He is Suttle, Cupshot, Cut in the Leg or Back, He hath seen the French King, He hath swallowed an Hair or a Tavern-Token, he hath whipt the Cat, he hath been at the scriveners and learned to make Indentures, He hath bit his Grannam, or is it by a Barn Weasel.' Thus the 17C compiler of a wealth of 'tavern terms', codified as *The English Liberal Science: or a new-found Art and order of Drinking*. The pamphlet lists around 150 terms, their number has been in no way diminished over the intervening three centuries.

Before turning to a variety of specific categories, it's worth listing some of the many similes that have been coined to mean intoxicated. The key words are, obviously **drunk** itself, plus **pissed** and **tight**, all of which are effectively interchangeable. Some terms will be found listed with etymology or date below, others seem to have neither rhyme nor reason, other than that they are, or have been, widely used. **Full** tends to preface phrases that originated, at least, in Australia; **lit** terms are mainly American, while **pissed** covers the UK and Australia only: in the US it means primarily angry.

Drunk as a: **bastard**, a **bat**, a **beggar**, a **besom**, a **big owl, boiled owl, brewer's fart**, a **cook**, a **coon**, a **coot** or a **cooter**, a **dog**, a **fiddler**, a **fiddler's bitch**, a **fish**, a **fly**, a **fowl**, a **Gosport fiddler**, a **hog**, a **king, a little red wagon**, a **log**, a **lord**, a **monkey**, a **Perraner**, a **pig**, a **piper**, a **poet**, a **rolling fart**, a **sailor**, a **skunk (in a trunk)**, a **sow**, a **swine**, a **tapster**, a **tick**, a **top**, a **wheelbarrow**, as **Davy's sow**, to the **pulp**. Pissed: as a **fart**, as a **newt** (thus 20C **newted**), as a **rat, to the ears. Stewed** (18C) as a **prune**, to the **eyebrows**, the **gills**.

Full: as a **boot**, a **bull**, an **egg**, a **fairy's phonebook**, a **fiddler**, a **goat, googy egg**, a **lord**, as a **pig's ear**, as a **seaside shithouse on Boxing Day** (in Australia Christmas falls in mid-summer), a **state school hatrack**, the **family po**, a **tick, two race trains**, to the **gills**. Lit: to the **gills**; lit up: **like Broadway, a Christmas tree, Main Street, a store window, Times Square**. Loaded: **to the barrel, the earlobes, the gills, the guards**, the **gunnels, the hat, the muzzle**, the **Plimsoll mark** and **the tailgate**.

CONFUSED

Aside from those terms which, logically enough, refer directly to the drink that one has so foolishly consumed, one of the largest sub-categories of this area of the slang vocabulary is a group essentially meaning 'confused' or 'muddle-headed'.

Taking them in rough chronological order the 17C gives the understated **concerned, foxed** (fr. **fox**: to make drunk) and **having a piece of bread and cheese in the head**. The 18C has **muddled, bemused, dizzy, fuddled** and **muzzy** (either an abbrev. of bemused or possibly from the dialect *mosey*: confused or tipsy). **Awry** means confused but the contemporary phrase 'tread the shoe awry' means to fall from virtue. **Jiggered** too has a parallel meaning: contraband or secret, based on **jigger stuff***, a secret still.

As well as the relatively quotidian terms **moony, muggy, noddy** (one's head nods), **oddish, flummoxed, flustered, foggy, fuzzy, mixed, obfuscated** and **woozy**, the 19C has all at sea, **off one's nut, fluffy** and **fluffed** (fr. the theatrical **fluff**) and a selection of endearing phrases, including **can't see a hole in a ladder** or **can't see through a ladder, can't say Naval Intelligencer, can't find one's arse with both hands, can't hit the ground with one's hat**, plus **having a guest in the attic** and **being queer in the attic**. The period also offers **seeing double** and **seeing pink elephants** (although **elephant's trunk** is simply rhy. sl. for drunk, while to **see the elephant** plain and simple means to see the world. To have been **bang through the elephant** is to have plumbed the depths of dissipation, although **bang up to the Elephant**, meaning excellent, refers to the Elephant and Castle Tavern, one of South London's best-known pubs. Other drunken visions include **the bats** and the **bears**.

Wet (16C), **damp** and **sozzled** (both 19C, the latter either from the dialect term *sozzly* meaning sloppy or wet, or the US *sozzle*: to moisten) and **coming from Liquor Pond Street** (19C) are succeeded by the 20C's **all wet**. Other modern terms include **flying blind, mizzled, schizzed** (fr. schizophrenic; cf. **schitzi★**), **vegetable, globular** (possibly from 'going round in circles'), **goofy, bleary, far gone, gaga★, looped** (fr. loopy: crazy), **not all there** and its semantic relation **out to lunch, out of one's head** and **out of one's mind** (also used in a drug context). **Buzzed** means confused here, although both drink and drugs can offer a **buzz** or sensation. **Wollied**, from the popular 1980s term **wolly★** or **wally**: a fool, implies the foolishness that can accompany too much alcohol. A final coinage is **pixillated**, which began life in the Frank Capra film *Mr Deedes Comes to Town* (1936) and was allegedly an elision of 'pixy-led'. Used initially to mean crazy, it soon gained its secondary, and now more general meaning.

UNSTEADY

From confusion in the head springs unsteadiness on the feet. The weaving drunk **makes indentures with his legs** (17C, from the custom of indenting the top edges of legal documents), is **out of register** (19C, from the printers' jargon for badly set type) or **carries a turkey on his back** (19C, fr. **drive turkeys to market**: to be unable to walk straight). He is **skew-whiff** or **squiffy** (19C, from either *skew-whiff* or from **swipes***: beer), **tweeked** (which has a sense of being moved slightly out of true), **slewed, listing to starboard, rolling, helpless** (19C) or **in difficulty**. **Tostificated** (19C, a mispronunciation of intoxicated and so used, but later also associated with **tossed** or **tost**, and used as meaning tossed about, distracted, perplexed; thus **tussy**: a drunk) and **low in the saddle** his condition is **topsy boozy** or **topsy frizy** (both from the SE topsy-turvey). His **arse on backwards**, he has the **blind staggers**, and **walks on his cap-badge** (upside-down), or **on rocky socks** (both 20C). He can feel **swinny** (19C, from dial. *swinny*: giddy) and **swivelly** (19C, unsteady). **Pushed** (19C, perhaps fr. 'did he fall or was he pushed?'), **lame** and **legless**, he **loses his rudder**, **goes belly up**, is **gravelled** or **gets the gravel rash** (19C) and starts **watching the ant races** and **lapping the gutter** (19C). Collapsed, he lies **below the mahogany** (fr. **mahogany**: bar) or **under the table**.

HIT

Images of violence abound in slang terms for being drunk. Aside from the early **jug-bitten** (17C), **swattled** (17C, fr **swaddle**: beat up, hit) and **going down with barrel fever** (18C, resurrected in 20C Australia to mean the DTs), the hapless sufferer has been variously **basted** (**baste**: SE thrash), **belted, blasted, blitzed, boiled, bombed, fractured, fried, hammered, shellacked, totalled, trashed, twisted, wrecked, sloshed** (19C) **smashed, shattered** (1960s), **croaked, crooked, damaged** (19C), **done over, overshot**, and found **dead-oh** (19C). Similar terms include **floored** (19C), **cupshot** (16C), **pot-shot** and **pot sick** (19C), **scammered** (19C), **chucked** (19C), **clinched, shot** and **shot in the neck** (19C, neck as throat), **clobbered, crocked** and **crocko, swacked** and **swacko, squashed, embalmed, laid out, snockered, wasted** (20C, from **waste***: kill), **wazzocked** and **whazood**

(20C, possibly from **wasted***, but equally likely onomatopoeic). **Spiflicated** or (more rarely) **smifligated**, which seems tailor-made for a school story of the 1950s, is actually an 18C coinage, originally meaning confounded or silenced, thence progressing to mean beat up, thrash or kill.

The 17th and 18th centuries are also responsible for a number of 'violent' phrases: **bitten** or **hit on the head by the tavern bitch**, **hunt a tavern fox**, and **bite one's grannam** (fr. *grannam*: corn) are all 17C; **bitten by a barn-mouse** or **by a weasel** are 18C. To **bite one's name in**: to drink heavily is 19C.

World War I offers three terms: **plastered** (fr. the RFC slang **plaster**: to drop bombs), **gassed** and **stonkered**, used originally to mean put out of action, and rooted in the 18C **stonicker**: a military flogging. The theme of whipping also appears in **stretched** (20C), which may come from from 'have one's breeches stretched' and thus to be beaten.

HIGH

The concept of being 'high' is one that is generally assumed to be a 20C coinage, and as such related to the explosion in recreational drug use of the 1960s, but the idea, if not the word, goes back much further. **Hanced** (17C) is an abbreviation of **enhanced** which gives way in the following century to **elevated** and **exalted** (used by Dryden in *The Bloody Duke* [1690]). Similar terms include **in the half altitudes**, **fired up**, **feeling** and **flying high**, **high (as a kite)**, **in orbit**, and the quintessential drug term: **stoned**, which meant drunk long before it ever meant drugged.

DRINK-RELATED TERMS

Drink, and the act of drinking, as one might imagine, lies behind a number of terms that describe the subsequent effects. Typical are a group prefaced by on: **on the booze**, **the grog**, **the piss**, **the sauce**, **the batter**, **the beer**, **the bend** and **the fuddle**, but there are many more.

Swipey (19C, from **swipes***: thin beer), **nappy** (18C, also meaning strong ale), **winey** (19C), **poggled** (19C, from **poggle**:

rum), **corned** (18C), **malted** and **malty** (18C), **groggy** (which has substantially abandoned its alcoholic origins, but in fact stems from **grog★**), **beery**, **aled up**, **mulled (up)**, (fr. mulled ale?) **ginned (up)** (20C) and **chateaued** (20C, punning on both **shattered★** and on the 'Chateau' found in the names of clarets) all refer to given drinks. Terms standing for drink in general lie behind **pickled** and **salted** (18C), **juiced** (20C), **laced**, (17C, from SE meaning mixed with spirits), **likkered** (liquored), **lushy** (fr. **lush★**), **swizzled** (19C), **alkied** (20C), **all keyhole** (punning on alcohol) and **oiled** and **well oiled** (18C, from **neck oil★** meaning drink; thus the 'oiled oiled story': tipsy maundering).

   Stung (20C Australia) comes from **stingo★**, a strong ale, **pruned** (19C) from **prune-juice**: hard liquor. **Tubed** (20C) is based on the Australian **tube★**: a can of beer, **incog** (19C) is another pun, referring both to **disguised★** (drunk) and **cogue** (a dram) as is **grapeshot** (19C, cf: cupshot). **Mashed** (19C) comes from the brewer's mash; thus **mash-tub**: brewer; the defunct newspaper the *Morning Advertiser* was known as the 'Morning Mashtub' because of its brewery interests. **Pogy** and **podgy** (18C) come either from the Italian *poco acqua*, literally 'a little water', the Romany *pogado*: crooked, thus the way one walks, or **poggle★**.

   The act of drinking creates **crooking the elbow** (19C), **looking through a glass**, **lifting the little finger**, **elbow** or **hand** (18C), **talking to Jamie Moore** (Scots, 19C) and **trying Taylor's best** (fr. Taylor's port). **Get the malt above the wheat** warns of the results of injudicious mixing, while **drink out of the island** (18C) means to drink to the bottom of a wine bottle, with its inverted glass 'island'.

   Boozed, **boozed up** and **bowsered**, **swilled** and **overtaken** (by drink) are all 16C, while the 19C offers a variety of additional terms: **comboozelated**, **swiggled** (fr. swig), **stolled** (fr. **stoll**: to drink, possibly originating in the Norfolk dial *stole*: to drink), **bagged** (fr. **in the bag**; bag was printers jargon for a pot of beer, thus **put one's head in the bag**: to drink), **poddy** and **poted** (fr. **pot★** and SE *potation*), **slopped** (**slopping up**: a drinking bout) **battered** (fr. **batter**: a pub crawl) and **bevvied** (fr. bevvy★); **bubbed** (fr. **bub★**) gives **budgy**, which in turn created **buffy**.

Shaved comes from **shave**: a drink, possibly from the excuse 'I'm just off for a shave.' 20C terms include those based on liquor containers — **bottled**, **jarred** (fr. the container, but also from **jarhead★**: drunkard), **boxed** (although 17C **box**: a small inn), **potted**, **canned** and **tanked** (fr. tankard.) **Corked** refers either to the SE cork or to an abbreviation of **corkscrewed**, which itself is synonymous, as is **pot valiant**, with **Dutch courage★**: liquor-based bravado. A further group rely on alcohol's wetness: **lubricated**, **melted** (also meaning to have spent all one's cash on drink), **saturated**, **sauced**, **soaked**, **get one's soul in soak**, **sodden**, **soused** and **have a skinful**. **Snootered** comes from **snoot★**: nose, and gives **get a snootful**.

Less classifiable terms include **in one's cups** (16-18C, then SE), **Taverned**, **corky** (17C) and **smelling of the cork** (19C), **taking one over the eight** (a World War I coinage, with reference to the 'acceptable' consumption of eight pints of beer), **a peg too low** (19C, from the 16C pegged tankard, with its pins marking each drinker's measure), to **have drunk more than one has bled** and to **have been driving the brewer's horse** (19C), to **swallow a tavern token** (17C), **bosky** (18C, not from the SE *bosky* meaning wooded, but possibly from Spanish *boquiesco*: dry mouthed), **noggy** (fr. *noggin*), **nase** and **nazy** (18C, cf: **nazie cove** or **nazie mort★**) and **black-pot** (16C, from SE *black pot*: a beer mug).

FULL

As well as the group of 'saturated' images above, drunkenness also denotes the sense of being full, and in a number of cognate phrases, of actually overflowing. **Full**, spelt, or at least pronounced as 'fou'' is originally Scottish, and produces such combinations as **bitch-fou**, **greetin' fou** (lit. 'crying drunk'), **piper fou**, **roaring fou** and **pissing fou**. **John Bull** is Aus. rhy. sl. for full. **Faced** (17C) comes from **facer**: a brimming glass) and **flush(ed)** (19C) indicates liquid that is flush with the rim of the glass. **Topped up** (20C), **top heavy** (17C), **having a brick in the hat** (19C) or being **up in one's hat** continue as do **in liquor** and **dipping rather deep**.

The idea of physical excess informs a number of phrases, typically **get one's shoes full** (the inference is not merely of beer, but probably of urine), **have one's back teeth afloat** or **under** (19C), **awash** and **decks-awash, buoyant, needing a reef taken in, getting a full cargo** and **carrying a load** (20C, thus **carry ballast**: to hold one's liquor). **Half seas over** (16C) may continue the naval imagery, but it may also be linked to *op-zee zober*, from the Dutch meaning 'over-seas strong beer' (and thus linked to such names as **upsee-Dutch★** and **upsee-Freeze★**). **Half the bay over** is a later version. More navy terms include **boated, overseas, over the bar** (19C), **oversparred** and **three sheets to the wind** (both 19C, both carrying a further element of top-heaviness). **Getting the yellow fever** (19C) originated in the system at the Greenwich Naval Hospital whereby inmate sailors who were caught drunk had to wear a mainly yellow particoloured coat.

OUT ON A SPREE

For all the dire warnings of physical collapse, drinking can be fun. Thus a selection of terms relating to parties and pleasurable drunkenness. Among them are on a **brannigan** (19C US, **brannigan**: spree), **on a tipple, on the floor, on the fritz, on the loose** (20C, Aus.), **on the ramble, on the rantan, on the reeraw, on the rampage, on the spree, on the muddle, on the skyte** and **on a skate** (20C, Royal Navy use, with **skate** also meaning a trouble-making sailor). **Scooped** (19C) comes from **on the scoop**: on the spree).

 Feeling funny (19C), **feeling good, feeling no pain** (20C) and **feeling right royal** mean just what they say, and optimistic drinkers are further represented in **about right** (19C), **at rest, bright in the eye** (19C), **get a jag on** and **jagged** (18C, **jag**: a drunken spree), **primed, stoked** (20C Aus.), **teed up, geed (up), giffed** (20C from **TGIF**: Thank God It's Friday), **glad, glowing** (19C), **maxed** and **maxed out** (this pair a good century earlier than the Valley Girl/hip-hop usage of the 1980s), **off nicely, roaring,** (19C, meaning exuberant, but cf. the 16C **roaring boy★** and **girl★**), **well away** (20C), **taking it easy** (19C), **chirping**

merry (17C), **electrified, fettled** and **in fine fettle** (19C, both from Northern dialect), **looking lively** (19C) **gay** (19C), **golded, glorious** (18C, a literary coinage by Robert Burns), **happy** (18C) **jolly, hearty** (19C), **heady** (17C) **inspired, mellow** (17C, three centuries ahead of the drug use), **miraculous**, (19C, Scots), **salubrious** (19C), **spiffed** (19C), **snug** (19C) and **spreeish** (19C).

Kisk and **kisky** (19C) are either rhyming slang for whiskey, (although Julian Franklyn's dictionary omits them) or from the Romany *kushto*: feeling good or happy, and as such the root of **cushty**, the much-used epithet of television's Del-Boy Trotter.

ILL

Optimism notwithstanding, drunkenness is not generally seen as an admirable or even desirable state and the negative terminology far outweighs the positive.

Addled, afflicted (18C), **far gone, flawed, polluted** (20C) **putrid, reeking, stinking** (20C), **stinko** (Aus., where it also means wine), **skunked, muckibus** (18C, cf: **stinkibus★**), **paralysed** (19C), **paralytic, palatic** (early 20C), **petrified, ripe** and **rotten** (20C, Australia) are all unequivocal in their condemnation. **Smeekit** (19C, Scots) comes from *smeek*: infect, and the 'patient' is variously **bug-eyed, cock-eyed, cross-eyed, pop-eyed, pie-eyed** (out of focus, i.e. *pied*), **bung-eyed** (18C, from *bung*: the stopper of a barrel; thus **bung one's eye**: to drink heartily) and **blind** (18C, abbrev. of blind drunk), **mortal** or **mortallious** (19C: fr. mortal drunk) and even **dead**, from dead drunk. **Rigid** and **stiff** (20C) continue the image of death. One might also suffer a **thick head, burn with a low blue flame** or **burn one's shoulder**.

Further body-related terms include **arseholed** (mid-20C) from the 19C **pissed as arseholes**, and **shitfaced** (20C), **ratted** and **rat-arsed** (both from the 17C **rat**: a drinker, itself allied to **drunk as a rat, inked** (19C, Aus.) and **iced to the eyebrows** (20C), **ripped (to the tits), skulled** (20C, also meaning crazy), **raddled** (17C), **rammaged** (18C), **hickey** and **hicciusdoccius** (18C, both possibly from hiccupping).

Knocked up, lumpy and **sewed up** (all 19C) all have the parallel meaning of pregnant, while **in the blues, in the shakes** and **in the horrors** infer actual or incipient *delirium tremens*. **Cut**, still in general use, dates to 1650, when it was an abbreviation of **cut in the back** or **in the leg**. One could thus **cut one's leg** or **get a cut leg**. **Half-cut** (19C), implies an earlier stage of drunkenness, as do **half-cocked, half-gone, half-slewed** and **half-shot**. The emotional wear and tear of being **under the influence** (20C, 'of alcohol' is unspoken), can make one **quick tempered** or **snuffy** (19C), but the best-known of such euphemisms is *Private Eye's* **tired and emotional**, an old journalistic cliché, with the cognate **tired, flaked** and **flako** (fr. **flaked out**: exhausted).

GENERAL TERMS

A number of terms defy categorisation, and remain outside the sections above. They include the popular, if somewhat dated **tight** (cf. **screwed**), three examples of rhyming slang — **Brahms and Lizst** and **hit and missed** (20C, both pissed) and **tiddly** (20C, **tiddlywink**: drink, and thus pub) — plus the backslang **kennurd** (drunkard). In addition come **commode-hugging drunk** (20C), in which state one **speaks to the great white telephone** (i.e. vomits into the lavatory), **moppy** and **all mops and brooms** (both from **mop***: drunkard), **ploughed** and **been at a plough-ing match** (19C), **bummed** (20C, possibly related to the drug term **bummer***: a bad 'trip'), **blued** (19C), **shickered** (20C, from Yiddish **shicker***), **clear** (17C, very drunk) **dry, frustrated, out of funds** and **hard-up** (19C), **martin drunk, pepst** (16C), **queered** (19C), **starchy** (19C) **so-so** and **so** (19C), **yaupish, yaupy** and **yappy**, (19C, either from **yap**: talkative, or the Yorks. dial.: an idiot), **what-nosed** and **whistle drunk** (18C, so drunk that speech degenerates into whistling).

Phrases include **in the tank, in the wrapper, over the top** (20C), **under the weather** (mid-19C), **bullet-proofed, polled off** (20C, from **get on the pole**: to become drunk). Among the verbs are to **have a bit on** (19C), **have one's eyes opened, bet one's kettle, go Borneo, go for veg, go to Mexico, hang** or

tie one on, have a buzz on, have a few too many, have a
heat on, have one's pots on, kill one's dog (presumably the
black dog of a hangover; cf. hair of the dog), lay and pepper
'em up (both AA) and show it.

One can also have the sun in one's eyes, get the flavour,
(19C), get one's nuff (ie. have enough), have been barring too
much, making Ms and Ts (punning on 'MT': empty bottles, and
cognate with Moll Thompson's mark [18C], in which 'MT' is
inscribed on empty packages), shaking a cloth in the wind (19C,
with an earlier meaning of being hanged), wearing the barley
cap or the head large (the latter implying a hangover), copping
the brewer, letting the finger ride the thumb (fr. finger and
thumb: rhyming slang for rum? or from supernagulum*), seeing the devil (18C) and taking a shard to shoe the goose
(17C, with an inference of wasting time on a futile project).

THE HANGOVER

Finally comes the drunkard's nemesis: the morning after the
night before, the hangover (itself a slang coinage of c.1910, but
long since absorbed into SE). Terms for alcoholic agonies – whether
a simple hangover or fullscale *delirium tremens* – include a head,
pink spiders and pink elephants (19C), DTs, the shakes or Joe
Blakes (20C, Aus. rhy. sl.), blue devils, black dog (19C, better
known as the name of Winston Churchill's bouts of, possibly
brandy-induced, melancholia), rats, snakes in the boots, hee-
bie-jeebies, jams or jim jams, jerks, jumps, quart-mania,
snakes in the boots, triangles (either from *tremens* or because
the sufferer sees everything 'out of the square'), bottleache, gallon
distemper (19C), barrel-fever, hot coppers (19C, a dry throat),
being stale drunk, trembles, uglies, horrors, hyps, and rams.

To vomit is to shoot (19C) or whip the cat (17C), cast up
accounts (17C), audit one's accounts at the court of Nep-
tune (19C) and sling a cat (19C). The general feeling of illness
underpins having a mouth like the inside of an Arab's
underpants. Taking a drink to recover from, or at least postpone
the hangover is to take a hair of the dog, from the belief that

burning the hair of a dog that has bitten one will ensure one's safety from possible rabies.

MONEY

GENERAL TERMS

Introducing the 1867 edition of his *Slang Dictionary*, John Camden Hotten noted that, '"Money", it has been well remarked, "the bare simple word itself, has a sonorous, significant ring in its sound" and might have sufficed...for all ordinary purposes. But a vulgar or "fast" society has thought differently, and so we have slang synonyms...' He went on to comment on the many terms in a lengthy list 'which for copiousness, I will engage to say, is not equalled by any other vulgar or unauthorised language in Europe.' Along with sex and drink, money remains one of the most productive sources of slang terminology, and if in 1867 'Her Majesty's coin' was 'insulted by no less than 130 distinct slang words' then almost 130 years on, the list has only increased.

Slang terms for money reflect its pivotal role in society. Both the abstract — its needfulness, its underpinning of social and commercial transactions — and the concrete — its colour, shape, weight and even the sound it makes. Unsurprisingly the list reaches back into history, and if the oldest actual term **loor** (and its synonyms **lowrie** and **lurries**) come from the 14th century French *lower* meaning revenue or wages, and the old Romany *lowe* to plunder, other terms echo the coins of the Roman empire. **Bull** (a crown or five shillings [25p]) and **hog** (one shilling [5p]) recall the designs on two small Roman coins. **Dibs** or **dibbs** comes probably from the *diobolus*, a Roman coin worth tuppence halfpenny, although claims have been made for *dibstones*, a Scottish children's gambling game involving sheep bones. Somewhat later come other antiquarian terms: **tester** (6d [2.5p]), also known as a **tizzy** came from *teston*, the French name of a silver coin struck at Milan by Duke Galeazzo Sforza (1468-76). It had his own head on it, as did similar *testons* coined by Louis XII (1498-1515) and his successor François I (1515-47) of France and by Henry VIII (1509-47) of England. A 19C usage was simply the **Queen's pictures**. Likewise **winn** meant a penny to the subjects of Henry's daughter. Elizabeth I. From **winn** comes the mid-19C rhyming slang **nose and chin**. The otherwise daunting **simoleon** is possibly a blend of **simon**, a dollar, and the French *napoleon*, worth 20 francs. **Dimmock** (18C) stems from dime, either in its early (14C) meaning of 'tenth' or 'tithe', or more simply from the US dime (ten cents), first minted in 1785. Most fundamental of all is **peck** coming from the Latin *pecunia*, meaning money (itself derived from *pecus* meaning flock), although it is arguable that this **peck★** reflects the more recent slang for food.

The concept of money as the commodity without which life is impossible, is found in **the actual** (the basis of bearable existence), **the needful, the wherewith, coal** or **cole** (the concrete and metaphorical fuel of daily life), **coliander** (or coriander and thus seed), **corks** and **ballast** (which help you stay 'afloat' and 'on an even keel'), **feathers** (with which one 'feathers one's nest'), and plain **stuff** and **old** (possibly an abbreviation of **old stuff**). **Quid** (1668), meaning first sovereign and latterly pound sterling, comes possibly from the Latin meaning 'what', with 'one needs' as an unspoken suffix. **Scramble, bustle** (1810) and more recently **scratch** (1930) carry the feeling of the struggle for existence. **Rowdy** may perhaps be added to this group; a popular term c.1841, Thackeray used it to create his fictitious bankers: 'Rowdy and Stump', a firm who can also be found in Cuthbert Bede's *Adventures of Mr Verdant Green* in 1853. The more recent **dosh** may come from a mix of dollars and cash, but a more likely root is in **doss★**, a place to sleep, and thus the wherewithal for purchasing it.

More metaphors come with **brads** (1812, probably taken from the name of small rivets/nails used by shoemakers and giving the phrase **tip the brads**: to be generous and thus a gentleman), **rivets** (which 'hold life together') and **horse nails**. Similarly **sugar** sweetens life, and **scad**, an abbreviation of *scads*, means abundance or plenty, as does the biblical **corn in Egypt** (*Genesis* xlii.1). **Bread** the hippie standby (fr. the Yiddish *broyt*), is of course the staff of life, and comes with such synonyms as today's Afro-American **cake** and the older **dough** (with its rhy. sl. cousin **cods** as in **cod's roe**, and the punning **do-re-mi**). **Tack★**, also meaning food, is another variation, as is the Australian **motsa** (presumably from the Hebrew *matze*, a piece of unleavened bread which often comes in a large, circular 'biscuit' and can be seen as resembling a huge coin). While Sigmund Freud would make the money/excrement link, the slang coiners were there already with **muck**, **dust** (although this may have been an abbreviation of gold dust) and the unequivocal **crap**. The negative aspects of money are further underlined in **darby**, from the name of a particularly severe usurer's bond — Father Darby's Bands — which in the 16C effectively bound the borrower to the lender while the debt remained outstanding. Debts also enter the obscure **legem pone**. This term comes from the first two words of the fifth division of *Psalm* cxix, which begins the psalms at Matins on the 25th day of the month; associated with March 25th (the year's first quarter day and thus the first major payday of the calendar), they became used to mean the payment of money, or more peremptorily: cash down.

Passing to the concrete images, as well as the sound, giving the onomatopoeic **chink, jink, chinkers, jingleboy** (a pound) and **crackle** (of notes), the colour of money has created many slang terms. The term **greenback** followed hard on the creation of the dollar bill by President Lincoln, and similar terms include **green**, **greenies**, both **long** and **lean green**, and a number of vegetables such as **kale, lettuce** and **cabbage**, although this latter predates its US use: for 17C London tailors it meant pieces of material filched from a job and sold for a profit. As such it is reminiscent of **bunce** or **bunts**, the coster term for second-rate apples which were sold off cheap or even given away to market boys, who could in turn sell them at a small profit. Similar terms include **pudding** and **jam**, while other trades had their own variations on the theme: **skewings** (gilders), **cabbage** (tailors), **blue pigeon** (plumbers; from the slang for lead), **fluff** (railway clerks, meaning simply 'short change'); station offices also enjoyed **manablins** or **menavelins**, odd money in the daily accounts, which probably came from the nautical *manavel*, meaning to pilfer.

Licit or illicit perks are also implicit in **gravy**, Damon Runyon's 'Guys and Dolls' opt for another vegetable: **potatoes**, while their latterday descendents prefer **moolah**. **Spondulics**, much beloved of 20C fictional gangsters and private eyes, may derive from a vulgarisation of **greenbacks**, although more feasible is a link to the Greek *spondulikos* the adjectival form of *spondulox*. a type of shell used as early 'money' and in turn similar to **wampum**, taken from the Algonquin *wampumpeag*: beads made from quahog shells and used as money. The otherwise unclassifiable **wonga** plus **womba** and **wanga**, monetary buzzwords of the 1980s, may be descendents of **wampum**. Still in the world of nature, **clam** means a dollar bill, while **rhino**, dating from 1688, defies etymology; the idea that it refers to the rhinoceros, then a fabulous creature 'worth its weight in gold', implies a certain lexicographical desperation.

Other generalities include **stumpy** (what one 'stumps up'), **tow** (because, claim some, like tow, one burns it so fast), **moss** (none of which is gathered by a rolling stone, although an earlier use means roof lead, which, when stolen, was worth money), and **wad** (coined in the late 19C and enshrined in contemporary comedian Harry Enfield's character 'Loadsamoney,' with his Thatcherite credo: 'Wad is God'). **Mint**, SE for the 'money factory', was the slangy term for money itself from the 16-19C, and produced such variations as **mint sauce** and, in America **mint drops**. **Ribbin, ribbon**, and **ribband** all carry overtones of the richness of ribbon-bedecked packages, and the phrase 'the ribbin runs thick (or thin)' implies the availability or otherwise of cash.

Ducats (plus **duckies** in America), **shekels**, **dollars**, **guineas** and **coin** (fr. which comes the recent **carn**) all reflect the 'legitimate' coinage of those names, while **deaner** and **dinarly** stem from **dinero** (fr. Parlyaree). Parlyaree also produces **ponte** and **poona** (both from *pondo*: a pound), **caroon** (five shillings or a crown), **madza caroon** (2/6 or half a crown), **dacha-saltee** (10d or *dieci soldi*; in Italy one soldo was worth one-twentieth of a lira), and **cinqua soldi** (fivepence). Rhyming slang produces **oscar** (**Oscar Asche**: cash), **sausage and mash**, **bees and honey** (money), and **whistle and toot** (**loot**) while the rarer backslang has **yennom** (money) and **yennop** (penny).

The criminal aspects of money offer the barefaced **loot**, **soap** and **palm oil** (wherewith palms are greased), and **boodle**, much beloved of the late Leslie Charteris' swashbuckling 'Saint' and coming either from the Dutch *boedel* meaning household effects, and thus one's personal estate; or from the Scottish *bodle*, a small coin worth two Scots pence or one sixth of an English one and as such usually glossed as 'worthless'; it is in the US that the modern meaning, whether of criminal or political graft, has developed. Less criminous is **beans**, which comes from the French *biens*, another term for wordly goods. **Shot**, hence the phrase the 'whole bang shoot', originates in the 15th century as does the contrived **sinews of war**, a term used by Francis Bacon, himself quoting the writer Mucianus, who declared that, 'Moneys are the sinews of war'.

Paper money has been known variously as **flimsy**, **soft money** (still current in America), a **bit of stiff**, the **folding stuff** and **rags**; money orders are still known as **paper**, while a large denomination note was a **long tailed 'un**. The signatures of various secretaries to the Treasury, which appear on the notes, led to eponymous coinages, notably the **Bradbury** (Sir John Bradbury, secretary c.1915; cf. **brads**), and the **Fisher** (Sir Warren Fisher c.1919-1933). Coincident was the more contemporary **Archer**, the disputed sum of £2,000 which formed the basis of the libel case in which the popular writer Jeffrey Archer was involved. The **scrope**, not a note, but a farthing, recognised another secretary, Sir John Scrope, in office from 1724-52. A cheque is a **kite**, especially when it is scheduled to 'bounce' or otherwise 'fly'. A bad cheque is a **stumer**, taken from racing use. In America, during the financial panic of 1837, and later during the Civil War of 1861-5, low denomination coins were withdrawn from circulation: in their place came the **shinplasters**, cheques of between three and fifty cents. Reluctantly accepted, they were rarely redeemed.

But banknotes are a relatively recent invention. Until the 19C coins were the norm, and their colour has created a number of terms. Gold gives **gilt**, **goree** and **Old Mr Gory** (both from Fort Goree, on the Gold Coast), **ochre**, **red 'un**, **redge** and **ridge** (1665), **gingerbread** (1690), **gelt** (Yiddish), **delog** (backslang) and **gold** itself. The golden guinea (replaced in 1813 by the sovereign and passing on to it a number of names) was particularly productive: **yellow hammer**, **yellow boys**, **canaries** and **goldfinch**. **Marigold** covered any golden coin, although it also denotes the specific sum of one million pounds. **Blunt** (1812), possibly comes from the French *blond* meaning yellow, but it make just as well stem from the **blunt** edge of unmilled coins, or from Mr John Blunt, chief architect of the South Sea Bubble scandal. **Glistener**, **shiner**, **harlequin** and **rainbow** all attested to the metal's visual allure. The long-obsolete seven shilling coin was a **spangle**. **Iron** (1780) had faded by 1840, but **brass** has been in use since the 16C.

Silver, in turn, has its derivations: **gent** (fr. *argent*), **tin** and **tinie**, **teaspoons** and **wedge** (meaning silver in 1725 and revived, meaning money in general, by among others *Minder's* 'Arthur Daley'). The **family plate** is self-evident. Copper coins offer the obvious **coppers,** as well as **pewter**. **Brown** means halfpenny and **lolly** stems possibly from the rhy. sl. **lollipop** = cop = copper.

Cash in general, rather than credit, gives the **ready** (17C), or **readies**, along with **ready John**, **ready gilt** and similar combinations, while the Yiddish **mazuma** comes the Hebrew: prepared or ready. Immigrants to London's East End also created **oof** and **ooftish** meaning money and rich; hence P. G. Wodehouse's Drone Alexander 'Oofy' Prosser, with the secondary pun on **prosser**: a cadger or idler; it comes from the German *auf tische* or 'on the table'. The term originated c.1850 and, according to the *Sporting Times* 'the aristocracy of Houndsditch, being in the habit of refusing to play cards, unless the money were "on the table".' Allied terms are **oofless** (poor) and the **feathered oof-bird** (money in plenty). Another foreign coinage is **hoot**, from the Maori *utu*, meaning money. **Ackers** stems from the British Army's World War II travails in North Africa, where the Egyptian word *akka* means one piastre.

SPECIFIC SUMS

As well as the million-pound **marigold** (see above), other large sums have attracted their own name: £100,000 is a **plum** or **plumb**; one thousand, whether dollars or pounds, is a **cow**, a **grand** or **G**, a **gorilla** (a big **monkey**, qv) or, most recently, a **K** (fr. kilo). Five hundred pounds is a **monkey**, one hundred a **century, ton, big one, C, C-note, hun, one bill**, or a **yard**; two hundred pounds a **twoer**; one hundred and fifty dollars a **buck-** or a **yard-and-a-half** and fifty dollars is **half a yard**; twenty-five pounds is a **pony** or, in rhy. sl. a **macaroni**. More recently unspecified, but notably large sums have been termed **big bucks, megabucks, a bundle, a packet, a pile** and **telephone numbers**. Those hoping to impress carry the fraudulent, if gaudy **flash roll** or **California roll**, which, whether in the 18th or 20th century mean the same thing: a high denomination note wrapped ostentatiously around a bundle of far lesser currency. Diminutive sums can be dismissed as **hay, chickenfeed, peanuts** and **razoo**, an Australian term usually found in 'not a brass razoo' and possibly stemming from **rags** (see below).

Twenty dollars is a **double sawbuck** or **double sawski**, while twenty pounds is a **score**; ten pounds is a **double-finnup**, a **long-tailed finnup**, or a **tenner**; rhy. sl. gives a **cock and hen** or **cockle and hen**; ten dollars a **sawbuck** or a **sawski**. Five pounds offers an **Abraham**, from Araham Newland (chief cashier of Bank of England 1778-1807) or a **Marshall** (chief cashier c.1870), a **fin, finnup, finnif** or **pinnif** (all from the Yiddish / German *funf*: five), a **fiver**, a **flimsy**, a **horse**, and a **lil** (fr. the Romany word for book). From rhyming slang come **half a cock** (half a **cock and hen**: half of ten), and **jacks** (**jack's alive**: five). Across the Atlantic five dollars can be a **pound note**, reflecting a more generous exchange rate.

As well as the many references to colour the pound, the sovereign, and before them the golden guinea (£1.1.0) have numerous slang nicknames: **quid, thick 'un** (though this also meant a 5/-), a **bar, oncer, nicker, note, smacker** and **smackeroo** (supposedly from the smack of money hitting a counter or table) and **sov**. Also **bean, bleeder** (a racing use, and presumably referring to the haemor-rhaging of cash on horses), **chip, couter** (fr. the Romany *kotor*: guinea), **foont, funt** (fr. Yiddish: a pound), **gingleboy** (onomato-poeic), **Jimmy** or **Jemmy O'Goblin** (1850, rhy. sl.) and **doonup** (backsl.), **Jack, James, Jane, job, meg** (although **mag**: halfpenny, as well as the tip expected by Scottish servants), and **mousetrap** (c1875, from the supposed resemblance of the coin's engraved crown and shield to a set mousetrap). **Portcullis** referred to the design on the 17C silver halfpenny. The monarch's head gave **ned** (1750), **neddy** and **nob** (all meaning head), **monarch** and **portrait**. Less obvious are a **new hat** (1876, from the cost?), a **remedy** (18C, from SE *remedy*, the permissable variation in coins' weight), **skin** (originally meaning purse), **skiv**, **stranger** (mainly tramps' and referring to the rarity of owning such a sum) and **strike** (originally meaning to borrow). The pictures on the coins also give the **horse sovereign** (1870, a coin decorated with Pistrucci's effigies of St George and the Dragon) and the **dragon**.

Ten shillings, now fifty pence, offers the logical **half bean**, **half couter**, **half Jack**, **James** or **Jane**, **half ned**, **half a bar** and **half a sheet**, **net-gen**, and **smelt**, as well as rhyming slang's **calf** (half), and **cows** (cow's calf: half).

The five piece or crown was either a **bull** or **bull's eye** (17C, see above), a **cartwheel**, **hind coach-wheel**, or **wheel** (fr. its shape and size), **decus** (c.1780), from the Latin motto *decus et tutamen*: 'an ornament and a safeguard', from Virgil *Aenied* V and originally describing a breast-plate, subsequently engraved on coins (where it referred both to the inscription and to its helping prevent their being clipped) and which has reappeared on the English version of the modern pound coin, or an **Oxford** (c.1870, rhy. sl.: **Oxford scholar** = dollar = 5/-); a counterfeit crown was a **case** or **caser** (possibly from the Yiddish *chaserei*: rubbish).

As terms for ten shillings echoed those for a pound or sovereign, so do those for 2/6, the defunct half-crown, follow those of the crown. Thus one finds the **fore coachwheel** (the smaller of the two pairs), the **half case**, **half dollar**, **half Oxford** and the backslang formations **flatch** (1851, half) and **half yenork**. Other terms include the **five-pot piece** (a 19C medical students' term referring to the price of a pot [quart] of half and half), a **George** (fr. the King's head), a **slat** (fr. **slate**: sheet, used by market traders till 1970s), a **posh korona** (fr. the Romany *posh*: half, thus **posh horri**: a halfpenny), and a **tusheroon** or **tosheroon** (1859, both from the Parlyaree *madza caroon*: half crown). This latter is still used by Afro-Americans to mean a dollar bill.

The rhy. sl. **Abraham's willing**, and **rogue and villain** mean shilling, as do **blow**, **bob** (c.1780), **bobstick** (possibly the origin of bob, it certainly means a shilling's worth, but defies further elucidation), **borde** (possibly fr. **bord**: shield), and **breakyleg**. **Touch my nob** rhymes with **bob**. The colour of a shilling gives the **lillywhite groat**, the **beong** (1850, from Parlyaree *bianco* = white = a silver coin), and the **gen** (1851, presumably from *argent*: silver, although some claim an abbreviation of **generalise**, a somewhat tortured backslang formation of *shilling*). Other terms include **grunter** (c.1775) and **hog** (see above), **jogue** (market traders'), **levy** (possibly an abbreviation of eleven), a **Brummagem button** and a **Manchester sovereign** (both implying cheapness and possible counterfeiting), **mejoge** and **midjic** (direct thefts of the Shelta term for shilling), a **oner**, a **peg** (either directly from Scottish dialect meaning shilling or from the Yorkshire word meaning **blow**, itself a slang term for shilling), **teviss** (1859, a backsl. form of the small Dutch coin the *stiver*), a **twelver** and a **thirteener**, **touch-me** (rhy. sl.: **touch me on the nob**: bob), **shigs** and **chips**.

The thin silver sixpence was easily bent, and thus named variously **bandy**, **bender**, **cripple**, **croaker**, **crook** and **crookback**. More popular, and longest lasting until decimalization saw it off was **tanner** (1811), stemming either from the Romany *tawno*, meaning small or from a ponderous Biblical joke about St Peter's supposed banking transaction when he 'lodged with one Simon a tanner'. This same tale offers **simon**. Rhyming slang for tanner has variously **goddess Diana**, **lord of the manor**, **susy** (**Susy Anna**), and **kick** (six), while Parlyaree has **deaner** and **downer** (see above). Other terms include **half borde**, **half hog** and **kye** (although see 1/6 below) and the porcine **grunter**, **hog**, **pig** and **sow's baby**. The number six gives **sice** (six on a dice) and its derivative **syebuck**. The size of the coin creates **sprat** and **fiddle** (1750, from **fiddler's money**, which also meant small change, itself otherwise known as **grocery**). A **tilbury** (1780) represented the fare charged by the trans-Thames ferry from Gravesend to Tilbury Fort.

Rhyming slang gives **abergavenny**: penny, while backslang has **yennop**; with them come **d** (fr. the Roman *denarius*), **George**, **harper** (an Irish brass coin with a harp on it), **saltee** (fr. *soldi*), **win** or **winn** (1567), and **debblish** (fr. South Africa). Counterfeit pennies were known as **pollards**, from the coiner who made them during the reign of Edward I.

The colour of the halfpenny gives **brown** and the rhy. sl. **camden town**; **flatch** (meaning half), **madza saltee** (1850, Parlyaree for half soldi); **magpie, magg** (1781), **make** and **mec** all denote the legitimate coin, while **Maggie Rab** or **Robbie** is Scots for counterfeit. Other terms include **scurrick** (fr. *scuddick*: a tiny sum, which in turn stems from the dialect *scud*: a wisp of straw), **tonic** (which comes from *tanner*, despite its meaning of sixpence), and **rap** (thus giving the phrase 'I don't care a rap').

The long-dead farthing, the smallest of all but once a coin of some real purchasing power, gives **farden**, and thus the rhy. sl. **Covent Garden**; **fadge, fiddle*, gennitraf** (backsl.), **gig, grig, quartereen, jack** (17C), **jigg, mopus** (supposedly from Sir Giles Mompesson, a notoriously corrupt merchant of the reign of King James I) and **rag** (both these later essentially meaning very small sum). **Harrington** comes from Lord Harrington who in 1613 obtained patent for minting them.

Finally come a selection of sums rather than actual denominations of money. Six shillings and sixpence was a **George** (fr. the old mark, worth 6/8); five and three was a **whore's curse** (c.1750), a telling off one received for using it: a gold coin, it was substituted for the pricier half guinea by mean customers who liked to be seen giving the girl gold, but saw no reason to be over-generous. 1/6 or eighteen pence was a **hog and a kye**, although **kye** itself, allegedly stemming from a Yiddish term meaning eighteen, could also serve. A **hangman's wages** was one and one penny-halfpenny, the equivalent of a Scots mark and instituted as the executioner's fee by James I; it was later known as a **loonslatt**, possibly from the combination **loon**, meaning a a worthless or boorish person, and **slat** (2/6). Still north of the border, a **ride**, bearing the image of a man on horseback, was a golden coin issued by James VI, tenpence was a **jumper**, while five pence was a **kid's eye**. Ninepence was a **picture of ill-luck** – for not being the whole shilling – and fourpence (the groat) a **flag**, a **castle rag** (rhy. sl.) or a **joey** (fr. the economist Joseph Hume [1777-1855] and coined by London cabbies). A threepenny bit was **threps** (17C), **threeswins**, **thrums**, **thrumbuskins** (c.1775), **thrummup** and the rhyming **currants and plums**. Twopence was a **deuce**, **duce**, or **dace**.

CLOTHING

GENERAL TERMS

The oldest slang term for clothing is also one of most resilient: **togs** dates back to the 14C *Morte Arthure* (later used as the basis for Malory's epic), where it appears in the line 'Alle with taghte mene and towne in *togers* flle ryche'; by the 16C it is cited by Harman as meaning coat or cloak, albeit in the synonymous form **togman** or **togemans**. All these terms are rooted in the Latin *toga*, which also gives the Etonian **tug**, a scholar, and thus one who wears a gown. Harman also has **dudde** (15C), a coarse cloak, which, as **duds**, is still in regular use, although the phrase to **sweat duds**: to pawn one's clothes, has long since vanished. The 17C brings another stayer, **rags**, which produced a number of combinations: **tag-rag**: villainous and poor, now transposed to **rag-tag (and bobtail)**; **rag-mannered**: very vulgar; **raggery**: women's clothes; the **rag-trade**: tailoring, **rag-stabber**: a tailor and **rag-tacker**: a dressmaker; a **rag-sooker** was thief's custom-built instrument used to hook clothes from washing lines or shop-windows; **rags and jags** are tatters while to **have two shirts and a rag** is to be comfortably off; to **tip one's rags a gallop** is to leave; to **get one's rags out** and the later **lose one's rag** both mean to lose one's temper; to **rag out** is to dress up and to **show the white rag** is to surrender or act in a cowardly manner. The 20C **ragtop** is a convertible motorcar. **Rig** (19C) comes from a ship's rigging, in which it is 'dressed', while the nautical background also informs **dunnage** (19C), in its SE form the matting or brushwood used to pack cargo, and **slops** (19C), which initially referred to a sailor's ready-made clothing, but which could be used in a civilian context too; **clobber**

(19C) comes from Yiddish and **traps** (19C) abbreviates trappings: one's personal effects.

Doodads (20C) is synonymous with the unspecified thingumi-bob; but probably has some links to **duds**; **drapes** began life with the drape jacket, a garment much beloved of the 1950s' Teddy boys. The 1990s' **grunge** (fr. **grungy**: filthy, dirty, unpleasant) reflects a more recent teen style. **Schmutter** comes from Yiddish, which it turn draws on the Polish *szamata*: a piece of cloth; **threads** (originally US) and **wrapping** (especially of women) should make themselves clear. Afro-Americans, who contribute a number of clothing-related terms, have **piece**, especially as in **leather piece** — a leather coat or jacket — and **fronts**, which is possibly linked to the show business jargon **front**: a large diamond tiepin or ring worn by vaudevillians to indicate prosperity. **Clear cut** clothes are stylish while in criminal circles **night-clothes** (punning on the SE use) are dark clothes used for night-time robbery. Stylish outfits are variously one's **best bib and tucker** (fr. 18C Lancs. dial.), **glad rags** (US c.1900, then UK), **go to meeting clothes** and **go to meeting bags** (the 'meeting' is Sunday church, especially of a non-conformist faith) and the Afro-American **silks**. Old clothes are **grubbies** or **tat** (fr. 19C **tat**: a rag; thus **tatter**: a rag-gatherer); second-hand clothes are **Monmouth Street finery** (Monmouth Street was the centre of the 19C old clothes trade; Dickens termed it 'the burial place of fashion') and **hand-me-downs** (passed on from another owner); ready-made clothes are **reach-me-downs** (perhaps from the phrase, 'Reach me down one from the rack'?).

GETTING DRESSED

To dress is to **get togged up**, to **pile into** (one's clothes), to **get dolled up** or to **get dolled up like a barber's cat**. To dress up is to **put on dog** (19C, from **doggy**: stylish), to **dike down** (20C), **look sharp**, **spiff (oneself) up**, **tart (oneself) up**, and **tog (oneself) up**. Those who are thus dressed up can be described as (in their) **best bib and tucker**, **dap** (fr. dapper), **dressed to death** or **dressed to within an inch of one's life** (19C), **dressed to the nines** (fr. the importance of the number nine in numerology),

dressed up to the knocker (fr. 17C **knocker**: one of striking appearance, and thus a knock-out), **dressed up like a dog's dinner** (20C), **dressed up like a pox doctor's clerk** (20C, Aus.), **dressed like Christmas beef** (19C); to be **dressed up like a sore finger** (Aus.) is to be too elaborately dressed. Even greater ostentation is seen in the Aus. **flash as a rat with a gold tooth**.

Dressed up can be **dolled up, dyked down, flossed up** (of a woman), the **full buf** (20C, from beautiful, or beautiful fellow), **in full fig** (19C, possibly from figure), **got up** (19C), **kitted up** (20C), **piss elegant** (20C) and **pooned** or **pooned up** (Aus., fr. ponce? or fr. **poon★**: a fool) both carrying an air of flashiness, **spiffed** or **spiffed up** (19C, fr. **spiff**: well-dressed), and **togged to the bricks**. Afro-American terms (all 20C) include **buttered, choked down, fonked out heavy** and **fonky to the bone** (**to the bone**: more than simply skin-deep), **laid out** and **laid to the bone, mod to the bone** (in the US sense of mod: modern, not the UK Mod: a 1960s' teen cult), **pressed, pimped down, ragged down heavy** and **ragged to the bone** (both from **rag★**), **silked to the bone, suited down** and **tabbed** or **tabbed to the bone** (possibly fr. **tab**: a label). To be smart is to be **clean** or **clean to the bone** (AA), **neat** or **nifty**.

UNDERWEAR

Terms for underwear include **frillery** (19C), **ham-bags** (19C, from SE **hams**: a thigh, and referring to women's drawers; thus the early 20C **ham-frills**: female running shorts). Proper names give **Alan Whickers** (20C, rhy. sl.: knickers; from the broadcaster), the US **BVDs** (fr. the clothiers Bradley, Voorhies & Day, specialists in men's underwear), and the Aus. **Harolds** (rhy. sl.?). More rhy. sl. terms include **east and west** (vest) and **fleas and ants** (pants). **Skivvies** (US) are either vests or pants; **didies** come from **diddy**: little, thus 'smalls'; **UBs** (US 20C) are 'underbodies', **kecks** a Liverpudlian version of **kicksies★** and **snuggies** (US) from SE **snug**: comfortable, warm. **Falsies** are false or padded breasts and the **VPL** is a visible pantie line, as seen through tight trousers or skirts. **Long johns** or **John Ls** commemorate the boxing champion John

L Sullivan who wore heavy tights as part of his old-style boxing gear. Finally **passion killers**, any form of voluminous, heavy female underwear, emerged during World War II when they were coined to describe Army-issue women's knickers; parallel terms included **blackouts**: WAAF winter-weight knickers, which were dark blue and **twilights**, the summer weight, which were light blue. Very tight underpants were **like Edgeware Road** (20C), because 'that's got no ballroom either'; or, in Australia, **like St Paul's** (possibly because 'there's no standing room inside').

TROUSERS

The earliest recorded slang term for trousers, or breeches as such garments would remain until the early 19C (although the word itself appears during the 17C) is **kicks** (17C). Like its 18C successor **kicksies** the term moved, as did the garment, from meaning breeches to trousers during the 19C. Thus an East End tailor (quoted by Mayhew) could advertise himself as a 'Slap-up Tog and out-and-out Kicksies Builder' and offer 'Ready Gilt — Tick being no go' 'Upper Benjamins*, built on a downey plan, a monarch to half a finuff*. Slap up Velveteen togs*, lined with the same...A pair of Kerseymere Kicksies, any colour, built very slap up, with the artful dodge, a canary...Pair of out-and-out fancy Kicksies, cut to drop down on the trotters*, 2 bulls.' Both terms are still used, although another 17C coinage, **farting crackers** has totally disappeared. The 18C introduced **hams** and **ham-cases** (both fr. the Romany *hamyas*: knee breeches), plus the defunct **dittoes** (originally tailors' jargon for a suit of which both jacket and breeches were made of the same material, still a relative rarity at the time.

Stereotypes of supposed Victorian prudery abound, and many disappear under proper inspection, but the apparent terror of naming such intimate items as trousers is certainly born out in slang. Such coy euphemisms include **inexpressibles**, **inexplicables**, **indescribables** and **indispensables** (the first three of which appear in Dickens' *Sketches by Boz* [1836]) plus **unmentionables**, **untalkaboutables**, **mustn't mention 'ems** and **unutterables**. **Continuations** (which 'continue' the waistcoat) paralleled the SE term, which meant gaiters: continuing the knee breeches and similarly spared adult blushes, as did **abridgements** although this latter seems to have achieved but a single nonce appearance, in Bulwer Lytton's play *Money* (1840). Yet for all this linguistic circumspection, the Victorians could be as blunt, even coarse, as anyone. **Arse-rugs**, **bumbags** (used for swimming trunks in the 20C) and **bags** (thus **howling bags**: trousers whose lurid patterns 'howl'), **sit-upons**, **sit-down-upons** and **whistling breeches** (corduroys, from the sound the material makes as one walks) make no compromises. Further 19C terms include **drumstick cases**, **rice bags** (19C, a play on **arse**?), **trolly-wags** (abbreviated to the simple **trollies** in the 20C), **mary walkers** (US, after one Dr Mary Walker, notorious for dressing in Turkish trousers), **rank and riches** (rhy. sl.: breeches), **upper stock** (breeches), and **trucks** (possibly fr. **trolly-wags**). **Skilts** (briefly fashionable at the mid-century) were a mix of a kilt and a prototype Oxford bag: short, reaching only just below the knee, they were quite voluminous, being a fully 18 inches broad at the bottom. **Gallyslopes** were the 19C's development of *galligaskins* (16C), a pair of wide breeches, subsequently leggings or gaiters; the term comes from a corruption of the 16C French *garguesque*, which in turn played on the Italian *grechesco*: Greek; such garments were supposedly 'in the Greek fashion'. Tight trousers were **eel-skins**.

The 20C has the rhyming slang **council houses**, **petrols** (Aus. **petrol bowsers**), and **round the houses**, plus **strides** (originally theatrical, now mainly Aus.) and **trou** (US). Teen fashions have **drainpipes** (1950s, very narrow), **flares** (fr. flared trousers, first fashionable c.1972), **loon pants** or **loons** (extreme flares) and **baggies** (US, shorts worn for surfing); **daks** comes from the proprietary name for a make of clothes, especially men's trousers with a self-supporting waistband, patented by the London clothiers Simpson's in 1933.

COAT OR JACKET

Aside from **togman**, **togeman** or **togmans** (see **togs***) Harman cites **caster** as meaning cloak; while 17C sources give **mish-top-**

per (which goes or 'tops' a **mish★**: a shirt) and **vinegar** (which was to be worn, perhaps, in 'sharp' weather); the 18C **wrap-rascal** applied to red cloaks only. Adopting its non-squeamish mode the 19C has **bum-freezer, bum-shaver, bum-perisher, bum-curtain, bum-cooler, arsehole perisher** and **arsehole shaver**, all of which meant a short jacket. The opposite fashion extreme is found in **immensikof**, a term coined to describe a bulky, fur-lined overcoat by the music hall star Arthur Lloyd, who called himself Immensikoff and appeared on stage in such a coat to sing, c.1868, his hit 'The Shoreditch Toff'. Other coats included the **joseph** (fr. the Biblical 'coat of many colours'), and its equally scriptural successor, the **benjamin, upper benjamin** or **ben**, still extant as the 20C **benny**. The shift, according to John Camden Hotten, was in tribute to the large number of London tailors called Benjamin. Similar was **upper tog** (fr. **togs★**), while a **lily benjamin** was a large white coat and a **little benjamin** a waistcoat. **Isle of fling** might, at a stretch, be rhyming slang for lining, **trusty** implies the wearer's faith in his coat, the **upper shell** and **under shell** were respectively overcoat and waistcoat, a **body-cover** did just that and **capella** was a direct adoption of the Italian. This in turn drew on the Latin *cappella*: little cloak or cape, and comes from the *cappella* or cloak of St. Martin, preserved by the Frankish kings as a sacred relic, carried into battle, and used to give sanctity to oaths; thus the name was applied to the sanctuary in which the relic was preserved under the care of its *cappellani* (chaplains), and thence to any sanctuary containing holy relics and thus to any place used for worship, other than a church, the earlier name for which was *oratorium*: the oratory.

Cover-me-decent (1800) and **cover-me-decently** (1825) meant coat; thus **cover-me-properly** was a smart garment and **cover-me-queerly** a ragged one; the **claw hammer, swallow tail** and **sparrow-tail** all referred to the tailcoat of full evening dress, which their shapes supposedly resembled; the **MB coat** was a long coat worn by clergymen – **MB** meant 'mark of the beast' and referred to Popery; **pygostole** was used by churchmen, the Greek word meant literally rump-stole and another Greek term, **panu-petaston**, served at Oxford University to describe a loose, widesleeved overcoat; **rock-a-low** anglicised the French *roquelaure*: overcoat and a **reliever** was an old coat that could be shared by a group of workmen.

Rhyming slang offers **steam packet** (19C, jacket); **I'm afloat**, **bucket afloat** and **bucket and float** (all 19C, coat), **weasel** (20C, **weasel and stoat**) and **nanny goat** (20C). Other recent terms are **benny** (fr. **benjamin★**), the Afro-American **boolhipper** and **leather piece** (both meaning leather coat), **smother** (possibly from the Yiddish-based **schmutter★**; it also describes the pick-pocket's coat, draped over his arm to mask his movements), **rod**, **pussy** (a fur coat) and a **monkey jacket** (Royal Navy: an officer's reefer coat; the monkey possibly refers to an organ grinder's monkey, bedecked in some miniscule jacket).

BOOTS AND SHOES

The SE *hocks*, referring to a horse's leg, gives **hock-dockies** (18C), an early term for shoes while the farmyard further underpins **carts**, a 19C term that supposedly echoes a labourer's heavy, boot-clad step, although an alternative source may be the Norfolk dial. *cart*: the top half of a crab's shell, which a boot can be seen as resembling. Rhyming slang has **daisy roots** (19C, boots) and **howd'ye dos** (19C, shoes). The **beetle-crusher** (19C) began life meaning simply a foot; by the end of the century it had become the boot that covers it; the 20C has **roach-killer** (fr. US **roach**: cockroach). **Trotter-cases** and **trotter-boxes** (19C) come from **trotter**: a foot; **bankers** (19C) are heavy, while **excruciators** (19C) are very tight and pointed, forerunners of the 20C **winkle-pickers**.

The 20C adds **boppers**, **bovver boots** and **cherry reds** (as worn by skinheads or **bovver boys**) and **Doc Martens** (originally skinhead footwear too, but now a wide-ranging fashion staple), **brothel creepers** and **brothel-stompers** (thick-soled, suede-topped shoes, an essential part of the Teddy Boy/rocker uniform), **reptiles** (anything made of reptile skin) and, echoing the earlier **beetle-crushers, stomps, stompers, shit stompers** and **waffle-stompers** (fr. the pattern on the sole which resembles the criss-crossing of a waffle iron).

A **potato** (19C) is a hole in one's sock while **air hose** is a US term for the wearing of shoes without socks. **Wellies** are wellington boots (thus the exhortation: 'Give it some welly', meaning give it a hefty wellington-clad kick: put in some effort) and a **thousand eyes** (AA) is a heavily perforated leather shoe. Boots and shoes aside, the primary contemporary footwear, especially among the slang-using young, is the running shoe or trainer. The UK has used **daps** to mean gymshoes since the 19C (the original term was used by the army to mean slippers), but all other terms are US. **Chucks** and **cons** both refer to Chuck Taylor's brand of Converse basketball boots; **airs** come from the Nike 'Air Jordan' model that was particularly prized c.1990 and is named for basketball superstar Michael Jordan, while **quick starts** and **felony shoes** refer to any brand of these high-priced, high-fashion trainers. Both terms are implicitly racist, suggesting that the black teenagers who particularly favour such footwear are *de facto* up to no good.

HATS

Living in an era when the hat, other than the ubiquitous, logo-be-decked baseball cap (a **gimme cap** in the US), is essentially invisible as a fashion item, it is perhaps hard to appreciate how essential was such headgear up to a century and less ago.

Nabchet or **nab chete**, literally a head (**nab★**) thing (**cheat** or **chete**) is cited in Harman's *Caveat* while plain **nab**, plus **nap** or **napper** all mean hat as well as head by the 17C. **Shappo**, thus spelt, borrowed from the French *chapeau*: a hat. General 19C terms include **cady** or **kadi** (mid 19C, possibly fr. Romany *stadi*: a hat), **golgotha** (fr. the Greek meaning the place of skulls, and as such central to Christian mythology), a **pantile** (properly a tile shaped in an ogee shape, one curve being larger than the other, but in this context simply a roofing tile), its abbreviation **tile** and the rhy. sl. **battle of the nile**. Rhyming slang also gives **lean and fat** and the 20C **titfer** (**tit-for-tat**: hat). **Pimple-cover** and **upper crust** could both also mean the head, while **truck** referred to the nautical *truck*, mounted on top, or at the head of a mast. **Goss** was an abbreviation for a gossamer hat, fashionable c.1830, and costing four shillings and ninepence, thus giving a **four and nine**.

Low crowned hats included the **smouch**, the **billycock** (with its wide brim; thus the **billycock gang**: the clergy) and the **chummy** (this hat was particularly comfortable and thus seen as chummy, or friendly to the wearer). The **wide-awake**, a soft felt hat with broad brim and low crown, was punningly so named because it lacked a 'nap'. Other hats were the **pill-box** (coined for the late 19C soldier's small round flat cap) and the **muffin-cap** (equally small and round and resembling the foodstuff), the **mudge** and **mushroom** (low-crowned circular hats worn by women) the **digger's delight** (Aus.), and the **Jerry** or **Tom and Jerry** (a hard round hat). The **Muller** was named after one Franz Muller, who was hanged in November 1864 for his murder of Thomas Briggs, chief clerk at a London bank. Muller, the first railway murder, had attempted to avoid detection by cutting an inch off his hat. The subterfuge failed, but for a while the fashion did flourish.

Among those that qualify as high or top hats are the **chimney**, **chimney pot**, **pot** (20C: a bowler), **wee-jee** (originally a chimney pot), or **stove pipe**, the **beaver** and the **castor** (17C, originally of beaver fur), the **bell topper** (UK: worn on horseback; Aus /NZ: any silk hat), a **box hat** (19C, a tall silk hat), **plug-hat** (US: a top hat, Aus. a bowler; in both cases the head 'plugs' in to it), a **topper** and a **penthouse-nab** (18C, a large hat). A **scraper** or **three-cornered scraper** (18C) was a cocked hat, specifically a gold-braided cocked hat as worn in the Royal Navy.

A **calp** or **kelp** (18C) was any had considered exotic, the term came from the Turkish *calpac* a Turkish and Tartar felt cap; a **thrum-cap** was any form of rough headgear; its SE equivalent meant a rugged, rocky headland swept by waves; both terms are based in **thrum**: to beat; the **cock and pinch** was favoured by early 19C dandies: cocked back and front and pinched at the sides, it was made of beaver fur; the **fantail** (19C) was the sou'wester type hat worn by coalheavers and dustmen and **moab** (19C, from *Psalms* 60:8 'Moab is my washpot') was a turban-shaped hat worn by women. A **molocher** (19C) was a renovated hat, ironed and greased back to something resembling its original condition, and a **sleepless hat** was a worn hat which thus had 'no nap' (cf. **wideawake**). The **mitre, washpot** (cf. **Moab**) and **colleger** were all forms of cap worn at the universities. The 20C offers three 'occupational' hats: the **skidlid** (motorcycle helmet), the **boonie hat** (US) a soft military hat for use in the jungle or **boondocks**), and the **steel pot,** a steel helmet), plus **cunt-hat** a felt hat (punning, presumably on 'feel').

THE SHIRT

Other than the 16C **lully** which originally meant wet or drying linen, the earliest term for shirt is **camesa,** stolen directly from the Italian *camisa*: shirt. **Camesa** in turn generates **commission** (17C) and its abbreviation **mish** (17C) and later **smish** and **shimmy** (both 19C). Quite defunct, other than in the market-traders' term **milly,** are **mill-tog, mill-twig, mill-tug** and **mill-tag** (all of which 19C terms come from the Shelta *melthog*: a shirt). Rhyming slang gives **dickey** and **dicky dirt** (19C, **dickey** originally meaning only a worn out shirt), **roll me (in the dirt)** and **Uncle Bert** (20C); **fleshbag, carrioncase** and **intimate** (all 19C) imply the garment's proximity to the body, **gad** adopts a Romany term, **shaker** originally meant a hand and **narp** is Scots dialect. A **sideboard** was a stand-up collar, before taking on its 20C meaning as a sideburn. To have one's shirt out is to **show a flag of distress**. The small loop that may be found sewn below the collar at the back of the shirt is a **fag tag** or **fruit loop** (20C, **fag★** and **fruit★** both meaning homosexual). The assumption is that such a loop can be grasped by one man while sodomising another.

The final shirt-orientated term is **piccadill,** an ornamented collar fashionable in the early 17C. The term comes from the Spanish *picadillo*, the diminutive of *picado* meaning pricked, pierced, punctured, slashed or minced (thus *picada*: a puncture and *picadillo*: minced meat). The piccadill was brought to England either by Robert Baker (*The London Encyclopedia*, 1983) or by 'one Higgins' (*The Atheneum*, 1901); whatever the name the individual in question made a fortune from his import, sufficient to buy land around what is now Piccadilly Circus and to erect, c. 1622 a large mansion which was promptly, and irreverently christened Piccadilly Hall. The surrounding area soon became known as Piccadilly. While this version is that generally accepted, the *OED* cites a source writing in 1656 who claimed that the house was thus named because, being at the furthest edge of the parish of St Martin in the Fields, in which it lay, was therefore serving as a 'collar', or outer edge of the area.

POCKETS

Boung or **bung** (16C, fr. Frisian *pung*: purse) meant purse, and by extension the pocket in which it was kept; so too did **cly** (17C) which added an extra definition: a pickpocket, one who extracts the money from its container; **roger** (17C) originally meant a suitcase. The 19C **skin**, **poke**, **poge** and **pogue** were all synonymous with purse, while **haddock** (19C) otherwise meant money. This term comes from the once popular belief that assigned the dark marks on the shoulders of a haddock to the impression left by St. Peter's finger and thumb, when he took the tribute-money out of the fish's mouth at Capernaum. Thus the 16C proverbial phrase: to **bring haddock to paddock**: to spend or lose everything.

   Kick, usually trousers, could mean a pocket, and has survived as such; **brigh**, possibly from breeks or breeches, gave **brighful**: a pocketful; **peter**, otherwise used as safe or any form of receptacle, naturally included pocket among its definitions. **Hoxter** (19C) was an inside pocket (fr. the Northern dial. *oxter*: the armpit), **pit** (19C) was a breast or fob pocket and **slash** (19C) an outside pocket, fr. *slash*: a slit in a garment that is designed to reveal the colour of its lining. **Sky** (19C, **sky rocket**) is rhy. sl. as is **lucy locket** (20C); **bin** (20C) is something into which one dips.

SUITS

Rhyming slang provides **piccolo and flute** (19C) although the plural **piccolos and flutes** means boots, and **whistle and flute** (20C). **Vine**, totally dated now, was a favoured hipster term for suit in the 1950s, like **intimate**★ it implied the way in which the garment molded itself to the wearer. **Mufti**, meaning an military man's off-duty clothes, is virtually SE today, but it began life as

Indian Army slang. According to *Hobson-Jobson* the term is tied to the religious Mufti, the expounder of Islamic law; thus the word 'was perhaps originally applied to the attire of dressing-gown, smoking-cap, and slippers, which was like the Oriental dress of the Mufti who was familiar in Europe from his appearance in Moliere's *Bourgeois Gentilhomme*'. The definition goes on to note that the French equivalent is *en Pekin*: Peking-style. The military synonym **civvies** (19C) abbreviates SE *civilian clothing*, while **dog-robbers** (20C), the tweed suits a modern officer tends to wear when off-duty, refers to the original definition of **dog-robber**: an officer's servant (who would not be dressed in uniform) who gained his unflattering nickname from his post-mealtime habit of grabbing any edible leftovers from the mess tables before they could be tossed out to the dogs.

Formal dress, a dinner jacket or a tailcoat, is various a **d.j.** (dinner jacket), a **monkey suit**, **soup and fish** (the preferred term in Wodehouse) and **tails**. The US **tux** was named for Tuxedo Park, N.Y., where the short but still formal jacket was first introduced at the local country club in 1886. It was also, if briefly, known as the **Cowes coat** and the **dress sack**.

A waistcoat can be a **charley-prescot** (19C, somewhat strained rhy. sl.), a **ben** or **benjie** (cf. **benjamin***), a **fan** or an **MB waistcoat** (19C, cf. **MB coat***). Braces are either the rhy. sl. **airs and graces** (20C), **stretchers**, **gallows** and **galluses** (US). These last terms all carry the image of a judicial gallows, on which men rather than trousers are hanged.

ACCESSORIES

As in the 20C, when for a period the gay community, at least, used this accessory to create an elaborate code of sexual preference, the handkerchief played a large part in 19C life. Rather than a square of material upon which one merely blew one's nose, the **billy**, or silk handkerchief was a central part of costermonger fashion, often apeing that of the prize-ring, where fancy handkerchiefs were an essential trademark of certain fighters. As Mayhew notes, 'The costermonger...prides himself most of all upon his neckerchief and boots. Men, women, boys and girls all have a passion for these articles. The man who does not wear his silk neckerchief – his "King's-man" as it is called – is known to be in desperate circumstances, the inference being that it has gone to supply the morning's stock money.' The major varieties of **billy** were the **belcher** (blue with white or occasionally yellow spots; named for the boxer Jim Belcher, d 1811, whose preferred type it was; since the 19C a **belcher** can be any spotted handkerchief); the **bird's eye wipe** or **bird's eye fogle** (any colour, with eye-like spots); the **blood-red fancy** (red); the **blue billy** (blue, with white spots); the **cream fancy** (white or cream with any pattern); the **kingsman** (a green base with a yellow pattern; a very gaudy variety is a **kingsman of the rortiest**, fr. **rorty**★: excellent, dashing), the **Randal's man** (green base with white sports, used by boxer Jack Randal), the **water's man** or **waterman** (light or dark blue, from the colours sported by Oxford and Cambridge oarsmen); the **yellow fancy** (yellow with white spots) and the **yellow man** (plain yellow).

Other terms include the **fogle** (fr. the Italian *foglia*: a pocket, although some claims have been made for the German *vogel*: a bird, given the **bird's eye wipe**), **lawn** (fr. the fabric), **bubble duster**, **madam** (because it confers some degree of outward respectability), the rhy. sl. **Charlie Lancaster** ('handkercher') and the well-known **snotrag** with its peers the **snottinger**, **snotter** and **snot-box**. **Snot** itself dates from the 15C and is related to the 12C SE *snite* (to wipe the nose) and possibly to *snout*: the nose. **Wipe** appears in 1700, although **nose-wiper** and **pen-wiper** (also the vagina) are both 19C as are **stook** (probably from the German *stück*: a piece) and **sneezer**. **Muckender** (orig. a swab) is 18C, with its successors **muck-rag** and **mucketer** 19C; **fam-cloth** (literally hand-cloth) is 17C, **clout** (a cotton handkerchief) 18C; **conch-clout** (fr. **conk**: nose and **clout**: cloth), **kent** (any coloured cotton handkerchief), **kent-clout** and **kent-rag** are all 19C.

Gloves are **stick-flams** (17C, **flams** is possibly a misreading of **fams**★, thus giving 'stick-[to]-hands'), **turtle doves** (rhy. sl.) and **mittens** (19C, fr. boxing use); a scarf is a **ropper** (fr. the Scots *roppin*: to wrap, and from SE *wropper*) or a **waterfall** (19C, it can also mean false hair); a tie is a **fourth of July** or a **Peckham Rye** (both rhy.

sl.). Socks are **almond rocks** (rhy. sl.); a certain type of US socks (black with thin vertical lines) are **pimp socks**. Spectacles are **cheaters** (20C, US), **Lancashire lasses** (rhy.sl. glasses), **shades** (20C, dark glasses), **bossers** (19C, from boss-eyed) or **barnacles** (16C) the earliest term, coming from the 14C *barnacle*, a form of bit which cruelly pinched the horse's nose, as did these early spectacles. The cane, once so common, could be a **whangee**, a term which came from the Chinese *huang*, originally meaning bamboo sprouts that were too old for eating. Thus the **whangee** was a cane made from the stem of one or other species of *Phyllostachys*, Chinese and Japanese plants allied to and resembling bamboos. Otherwise it could be a **waddy** (19C, more of a club than a cane) or a **toothpick** (an ironic term that similarly described a heavyweight cane, more shillelagh than bamboo). A particular, crutch-handled cane was the **crutch**, thus giving the term **crutch and toothpick brigade**: a broad group of stage door johnnies and late 19C men-about-town whose sartorial badges were a **crutch** and a toothpick (of the dental variety), earning them a music hall rhymester's mock solicitous enquiry 'What about that toothpick, and don't you like that crutch? / And are those trousers very tight, and do they hurt you much?'

A number of term for pocket, above, also meant wallet or purse, typically **bung, cly** and **poke**, but other, discrete terms exist, notably **dummy** (19C), **leather** (20C) and **poggler** (20C, from **pogue***). A **goitre** (20C), is a large roll of money, commonly kept in the trouser pocket. The pocket watch begins to appear c.1600 – Shakespeare mentions them in several plays – and the earliest slang for watch is **loge** (17C, from the French *horloge*: watch). Subsequent terms include a **warming pan** (17C, large and gold and resembling its nickname) and a **yack** (18C, fr. Welsh *yakengeri*: a thing for the eyes; *yak*: eye; **yak** still has some some use amongst market traders). The 19C has **verge**, **toy** and thus **red toy** (gold), **white toy** (silver), **toy and tackle** (a watch and its chain) and **toy getter** (a watch-snatcher). A **white lot** or **white stuff** is a silver watch while a **white 'un** is a watch and chain; a **white jenny** is made of foreign silver. Like the **warming pan** the **turnip** and the **frying pan** refer to a heavy, old-fashioned watch, in this case made of silver. The 20C

Gordon and Gotch refers not to a watch-maker, but (bizarrely) to a long-established firm of book importers. **Bottle of scotch** (19C) also rhymes with watch, but refers specifically to the cheap Waterbury watches, produced since 1884 in Waterbury, Connecticut. Apart from the various combinations of **red** (gold) and **white** (silver) jewellery could be **bobbles** (19C, fr **baubles**; otherwise meaning testicles), **jim** (possibly from **jimmy o'goblin★**, a sovereign) or **tom** (19C rhy. sl. **tomfoolery**: jewellery); diamonds (or any precious stones) are **glass**, **rocks**, **ice**, **sparklers** and **Simple Simon** (rhy. sl.). **Patacca** (20C) was a direct loan from an Italian slang term, meaning fake, rubbishy jewellery, especially a fake Swiss watch, also known as a **mug's ticker** or a **ramped watch** (fr. **ramp★**: a swindle).

NUDITY

From dress with its varieties to undress with its single preoccupation: nudity. The state of nudity has generated a number of similes, based on **naked as...** Among them are **naked as a stone** (14C), **naked as a needle** (14C), **naked as a shorn sheep** (17C), **naked as a worm** (15C), **naked as a cuckoo** (17C), **naked as the cuckoo in Christmas** (17C), **naked as truth** (17C) and **naked as my nail** (19C) but as Eric Partridge points out, while they may have started life as colloquialisms, they soon became 'SE and proverbial'. Other terms have proved more resilient to absorption into standard speech. Those who are naked have been **in the buff** since the 17C (fr. **buff**: bare skin), while the parallel **in the nuddy** (Aus.), **in the raw** (US) and **in the rude** are all 20C. **Peeled**, based on the 18C verb to **peel**, is 19C; **peel down** and **peel off** (to undress) are 20C. The **birthday suit** (the birthday being that of Adam and Eve) was coined by Smollett in *The Adventures of Ferdinand, Count Fathom* (1753); Smollett obviously liked his invention: it appears again in *Humphrey Clinker* (1771). Similar terms are **birthday gear**, used by Jonathan Swift in 1734 and the much later **birthday attire** (a single use in 1860). The 18C also uses **dishabilly** (fr. French *en deshabillé*: undressed), while the 19C introduces **the altogether**, an abbreviation of 'altogether naked', and **un-**

rigged, from rig: clothes. The 20C, inevitably hard-edged, offers **bareass**, **raw** and **stark bollock naked**, a term that despite its use of **bollock***:testicle, can be equally applied to either sex.

Aside from the variations on **peel**, above, to get undressed is to **drop the duds**, **drop the gear** (Aus.) or **shuck down** (all 20C). The popular teen prank of lowering one's trousers and offering one's revealed, naked buttocks to the public gaze is variously to **drop trou**, **hambone** (Aus.), **moon** or **press ham**. To undress someone else is to **unrig** (19C), **debag** or **pants** (20C). Finally three phrases for inadvertent undress, or rather semi-dress: **charlie's dead** (your slip is showing), **there's a letter in the post-office** (one's shirt tail is out) and **it's one o'clock at the water-works** (one's trouser-fly is undone).

ANIMALS

The animal kingdom is not particularly well-served by slang, other than as regards horses, which prior to the arrival of the internal combustion engine, played a substantial role in everyday life. Cats and dogs, as pets, offer a small vocabulary, but the horse's main contenders for linguistic variation are lice, that member of the animal kingdom that lived in closest proximity to its human cousins. The farmyard — cattle, pigs, poultry — musters a few more terms, but the vast majority of such words are to be found in now-obsolete local dialects, which are ineligible for inclusion here.

THE HORSE

The oldest known term for horse is **nag** (15C, there may be links to the Dutch *neg* or *negge*, but the English use is earlier), followed by **prancer** (Harman) and **dobbin** (16C) an ordinary farm horse, though sometimes a broken-down or old one; one of its earliest appearances is in Shakespeare's *Merchant of Venice* (1596). **Tit** (16C) meant a small horse, often a filly; thus the usage is the basis of tit, meaning woman. **Keffel** (17C) is a translation of the Welsh *ceffyl*;

it often implied the second-rate. **Prad,** for many years the basic slang term for horse, emerged in the 18C; it is linked to the Dutch *paard* (a horse) which in turn has its roots in the Latin *paraveredus,* which gives the SE *palfrey:* a riding horse as opposed to a war-horse. The 18C also offers **daisy-kicker,** with the pejorative variation **daisy-cutter:** a horse that refuses to raise its feet properly when moving. A **star-gazer** (18C) holds head up well when trotting.

General terms for horse in the 19C include **gee** and **gee-gee** (both from the 18C exhortation 'Gee up'!'), the rhy. sl. **Charing Cross** (pronounced *à la* Cockney 'crorss') and **macaroni** (pony), **critter,** (US, originally meaning bull, but soon extended to cover most farm animals), a **trotter** (racehorse) which if high-spirited is a **bit of blood** (fr. bloodstock) or a **high-stepper.** An **undergraduate** a horse in training. The British Army coined **long-faced 'un** and **long-faced chum** or **friend;** thus **long-eared chum** or **bastard** means a mule; both terms draw on the slightly early **long-haired chum:** a girlfriend. **Lunk-head** (now a fool or oaf) is possibly linked to **long-head.** 20C Australia offers **crocodile.**

Second-rate, inferior, old or broken-down horses attracted a number of terms. **Jade** (used by Chaucer c.1386) was an all-purpose put-down of such a beast, it could occasionally be applied to a donkey as well. Its use to mean 'faithless woman' does not appear until the 16C. **Crock,** (19C, broken down, either from Scots meaning old ewe, or from broken pots) **Grogham** (18C) meant simply old. Perhaps the best-known description of a 'bad' horse in the 19C was **screw,** a general term that had originally been applied to a racehorse that had to be 'screwed' (ridden hard and probably whipped) by its jockey. The **ginger** required similar efforts: it seemed a fast and showy horse, but had probably been **figged,** ie. made to look better than it was (fr. *feague:* to beat) prior to the race. The **jib** or **jibber** shirks running or jumping, as does the 20C **dog,** described as 'punting poison' and only racing when it feels like it. The old, exhausted **scrub** (also used for ageing cattle) or **knacker** was fit only for the knacker's yard, as were the broken-winded **roarer, whistler** and **wind-sucker.** A clumsy racehorse was a **muddler,** while a **mount** was dangerous and uncontrollable.

The **ning-nang** was a generally worthless horse; in Northern dialect it referred to humans too, and is linked to the 20C Australian **ning-nong** or **nong**, meaning a fool or worthless person. A **weaver** or **wobbler** was unable to keep to straight line when racing while the **bonesetter** or **bone-shaker** (later used for cars) gave its rider an uncomfortable journey. The donkey or ass is variously a **burro** (fr. the Spanish), a **donk**, a **dickey** (fr. Richard) or a **moke** (19C). This last comes either from the Welsh gypsy *moxio* or *moxia*: donkey, or from the cant word *moak*; like many names for animals **moke** is a diminutive, in this case of *Margaret*, just as donkey itself is short for *Duncan*. Other names include the **Jerusalem pony** (19C, from Christ's entry to Jerusalem), the **Egyptian charger** (possibly from their use by 'Egyptians' or gypsies), and the diminutives **ned** and **neddy** (17C) **Jack** or **Tom**.

DOGS AND CATS

Pets tend to have their own names, given by their human owners, but there are certain generic terms. The cat is a **long-tailed beggar**, **baudrons** (possibly from the Scotch Gaelic *beadrach*: a playful girl), a **masheen** (18C, from Shelta), **puss** (16C), **Thomas** (fr. tomcat), **tib** and **tibby** (18C) and **moggy** or **mog** (19C, from Margaret). The oldest slang term for dog is **bufe**, **bufa** or **buffer** (all 16C) all of which echo its bark; the echoic is also found, as it is in the childish **moo-cow** and **baa-lamb**, in **bow-wow** (18C). Other terms include **goddie** (backslang), **mutt** (20C, possibly from **mutton-head**, an affectionate gibe), **pooch** (19C, possibly from 'Putzi', a German pet name for any lapdog), a **tyke** (18C, from the Yorks. dial., and the term most beloved of Yorkshiremen bent on self-glorification). The rhyming slang **alderman's nail** (19C) means tail, while dog excrement can be **dog**, **doggy-do**, **poo**, **poop** or **hocky** (all 20C).

POULTRY

The chicken has gained a number of slang names, among them the logical **cackler** and **cackling-chete** (16C, literally cackling thing, and thus the 17C **cackling fart**: an egg). Harman's *Caveat* also cites

Margery Prater, who appears in *The Joviall Crew* (1641) by playwright Richard Brome (c.1590-1652/3) amongst a number of farmyard peers: 'Here's Grunter and Bleater, with Tib of the Buttry*, And Margery Prater, all drest without sluttry'. **Prater** comes from her constant clucking or 'prating', while **margery** echoes **margery daw**: jackdaw and **margery howlet**: an owl. **Partlet**, from the French and briefly English proper name Pertelote, was often used to mean hen, particularly as **Dame Partlet**; in 1481 Caxton, in the *Tale of Reynard the Fox*, speaks of 'Chantecler the cock, pertelot wyth alle theyr children'. **Galeny** (18C) meant chicken or guinea fowl, both from the Latin *gallina* meaning cock, while the nursery has provided **chuck-chuck** and **chickabiddy** (19C). **Chook** is the definitive term in Australia.

The duck is a **quacking cheat** (16C), **quack** or **quacker** (19C) and **waddler**; a **lame duck** is a defaulter on the Stock Exchange (and any office-holder, particularly a politician, who is serving out his or her time once a successor has been elected); **waddle out of the alley** (18C) means to default. A goose is **roger** or **tib of the buttery** (both 16C, although **tib** usually means cat) and, while not strictly poultry (albeit eaten elsewhere in Europe) a sparrow is either **philip** or the 19C rhyming slang **bow and arrow** (with a nod, presumably, to the death of Cock Robin).

INSECTS

Other than the generic **creepy-crawly** (19C), **skeeter** (fr. mosquito) and **policeman** (19C) which meant a bluebottle (and was subsequently turned on its head when **bluebottle*** emerged as a slang term for policeman) the bulk of insect-related slang refers to what the 19C termed **flats** and **chits**: bugs and lice. The bug, properly a bedbug, offers **chinch**, the **heavy cavalry**, **dragoons** or **horsemen** (cf. **light cavalry** and **light troops**), the **mahogany flat**, a **Norfolk Howard** (19C, in cruel memoriam of one Joseph Bug who changed his name to Norfolk Howard) and **German ducks** (18C) which were both bed bugs and, in the kitchen, half a sheep's head boiled with onions.

Lice are **chates** or **chats** (18C) according to Grose coming from chattels, meaning moveable property, typically livestock. Thus **livestock** itself (18C), **black cattle** (19C, also meaning a parson), **saddle backs, gold backed 'uns** (19C), **greybacks** and **Hampstead donkeys** all stress the 'cattle' context, while the proximity of lice appears in **bosom friend** (19C), **friends in need** (19C), **gentlemen's companions** or **friends** (18C, also used for fleas) and **familiars** (19C). The veteran **crabs**, abbreviating crab-lice, gives the 20C rhy. sl. **taxi-cabs**. Military associations are found in **light troops** (19C), **light infantry** (19C) and **Scots Greys** (19C); this latter gives the **headquarters of the Scots Greys**: a lousy head, and the **Scots Greys are in full march by the Crown Office**: lice are crawling on one's head. **Active citizens** (19C), **creepers** (17C) and **crawlers** (18C) emphasize the insects' motion, while **crums** or **crumbs** (19C) point up their diminutive size. To be lousy is to be **silver-laced** (19C). The most recent term **cooties** (20C) comes specifically from the Malayan for dog tick, but *kutu* itself is a general term in Polynesia for any kind of louse.

THE FARMYARD

Aside from the many dialect terms for farmyard beasts, a cow is a **router** (Scots 19C, thus **router-putters**: hooves), while a **Romford** or **Essex lion** (17C) is a calf. Harman (16C) has **lowing chete** for calf, and **bleating chete** for lamb. A sheep is a **Cotswold lion** (15C) or, in Scotland, a **Lammermoor lion** (18C), a **quaking cheat** (16C, also occasionally a calf), a **wool bird** (18C), a **havil** (18C, although the SE meaning is a small crab) or a **jimbugg** (19C Aus., fr. **jumbuck**: an Aborigine term meaning white mist, ie. a flock of sheep). **May gathering** (19C) is sheep stealing. The pig is a **grunting chete** (16C), **grunter** or the libellous **patrico's kinchen** (16C, fr. **patrico***: priest and **kinchen***: a child).

OTHER

A final selection includes **Cambridge** or **fen nightingale** (19C, a frog), **lion** or **wat** (15C, a hare; cf **ned, philip** and **thomas**), **snag** or **snagg** (a snail), **and heffalump** (a nursery term for elephant).

LOVERS

THE LOVER

In common with much other early slang, the 16C term for lover or loved one borrows from the farmyard; in this case it is **duck**, used a such by Shakespeare, and slightly predating its 17C equivalent, **pippin**, which can also mean a good thing in general (thus see GOOD for its etymology). The 17C French romantic novel used *flamme* as one of its principal clichés; by the 19C **flame** had arrived in Britain, especially as in the extant **old flame**. Coincidentally (or perhaps pointedly) **flame** could also mean venereal disease. **Sprat** was a further affectionate diminutive, while Scotland provided the **Kilmarnock whittle**: a person of either sex who is engaged to be married (the dial. *whittle* means blanket; thus the term may refer to the practise of *bundling*: the sleeping together, albeit fully dressed, by unmarried couples).

Most 20C terms have their origins, like **flame**, in romantic fiction. **Crush** and **pash** (fr. SE *passion*) refer to an infatuation, the former originating in the US, the latter especially pertinent to the obsessions formed at girls' schools by a younger pupil for a teacher or an older girl; **dreamboat**, **heart-throb**, **honeybunch**, **honey bun**, **sweetie** and **sweetie-pie** (cf. **sweetmeat★**) are staples of the most glutinous of love stories. A couple can be an **item** or a **shack job** (fr. **shack up**: live together); a former lover is an **ex** while a new one is **fresh hide** (AA); a casual partner is **it**, a **one-night stand** (punning on the theatrical jargon), a **pick-up** or a **trick** (see PROSTITUTION for etymology). A flirt or teaser is a **gill-flirt** or **jilt** (19C), a **cock-teaser** or **prick-teaser** (both terms mean penis) or if a man, somewhat contrivedly, a **cunt-teaser**.

BOYFRIENDS AND GIRLFRIENDS

The boyfriend can be **Mr Right**, or even more optimistically **Lord Right** (both figures tend to be dreams rather than reality), one's **old man** (equally common as husband; in either sense the over-

riding feeling is of comfort) and **daddy one** or **sweet daddy** (AA).
A girlfriend, as invariably dismissive as are all such terms that depict
women through masculine eyes, can be a **chick**, **dolly**, **frail**,
honey, **sweet patootie**, **toots** or **tootsie** (the etymologies of all
of which can be found at WOMAN). **Miss Right** and **Lady Right**
parallel their male equivalents, while Afro-Americans offer the
unashamedly forthright **main bitch**, **ordinary** or **mat**. **Main
squeeze** (20C) is marginally more affectionate while **old lady**
(which moved from Cockney domesticity to the term of hippie
choice during the late 1960s) is neutral, even amicable. **Mum**,
normally mother, offers the same feelings of continuity as does
steady. Rhy. sl. gives **jam tart** (19C) and **Richard (Richard the
Third: bird★)**. The unflattering **monotony** puns on monogamy,
sweetpea (20C) is ostensibly affectionate, although 19C rhy. sl. uses
of the term include whiskey, tea or **pee★** (urine).

THE MISTRESS

As far as slang is concerned the line between a mistress and a
prostitute is in many cases all but invisible, and there are many
crossovers. Those listed here are on the whole mistresses only.
Loteby (fr. SE *lote*: to skulk or hide) and the related **ludby** are both
14C, where they mean paramour; they give the 17C **ligby** (perhaps
fr. dial. *lig*: a bed). A **natural**, which could be found meaning whore,
was equally common as mistress: in both cases the idea is of a
woman bound by nature in her relationships, rather than by
sanctified marriage vows; **pure** (17C) is heavily ironic as is **miss**
(17C); a **wife in watercolours** (18C, see PROSTITUTION for
etymology) predates the **left-handed wife** (19C, anything 'left-
handed' is *de facto* suspect). **Pout** (18C) comes from *pullet*: a young
hen; the later 19C **pouter** means vagina. A **rainbow** (19C) is
dressed in gaudy finery, a **weekender** (19C) is available only at
weekends and while a **jam** (19C) is a mistress, a **lawful jam** is a
wife. A **she-familiar** (19C) has overtones of the occult; SE *familiar*
means a witch's demonic companion, although the other meaning,
intimate, is obviously present. A **smock toy** can be male as well as
female, depending, presumably, on whether the **smock** (a general

term for things female) is the user of the toy or the toy herself. A **bit of spare** (20C) can be found as meaning mistress, although it usually means no more than an available girl, often at a party.

THE ADULTERER

Adultererous males (adulterous women get but rare mentions in slang – synonyms for whore are, yet again, far more convenient) lend themselves to literary euphemism. **Actaeon** (17C) comes from the stag's **horns★** planted by the goddess Diana on his head after he had unwisely boasted that he was a greater hunter than herself. He was duly torn to pieces by his own hounds. **Lothario** also emerged in the 17C; the name comes from Sir William D'Avenant's (1606-68) play *The Cruel Brother* (1627); amongst its cast list is 'Lothario: a frantic young gallant'. Another contemporary term was **buck face**, using **buck** to mean cuckold despite is earlier, and concurrent use to mean dandy or man of spirit and fashion. The 18C **freeman** or **freeman of bucks** extended the use, as well as punning on Bucks: Buckinghamshire. The **gentleman of the back door★** (18C) was a sodomite, but the **back-door man** (19C), who sneaked in by the literal back door, was an adulterer as was the **fancy man** (originally a pimp and still extant). The **freelance** (19C) was an habitual adultress, though not a professional whore, despite the commercial aspects of the term. The 20C equivalent of **fancy man**, or woman, is a **bit★ on the side**. To cuckold is to **give horns**, **hornify**, **shoe-horn** or to **get the bull's feather** (17C), described as 'a new feather made of an old horn'. Finally the 15C **wittol** was a complaisant husband who made no effort to discourage his wife's adventuring; the term comes from the SE *woodwale*: a bird that is often the target of a cuckoo, who palms its own offspring off in the woodwale's nest.

TO SEDUCE

To seduce (all 20C) is variously to **georgia** or **georgy** (AA), **get across**, **get off with**, **get next to** (AA) **get one's leg over**, **go case with** (which also means to live with or have a long-term relationship), **have**, **have it away with**, **have one over**, **make**,

nail, prong, reel in the biscuit and **race off** (Aus.). To fail in one's seduction is to **strike out** (US, from baseball); to ask a girl **are you saving it for the worms?** is an attempt to overcome her resistance. **Been there** (predating today's dismissive **been there, done that**) refers to a previous sexual partner, while comments indicative of sexual distaste include the irredeemably sexist **don't fancy yours, I wouldn't fuck her with your prick, I wouldn't fuck her with a borrowed prick, I wouldn't touch it with yours** and **I wouldn't touch it with a ten-foot barge-pole**. To be sexually excited is to be **begging for it, dripping for it, fruity, horny, hot** or **hot for, hot to trot, randy, sexed up**; 19C terms include **cunny-haunted, cunt-struck, proud** and **prime**.

Caresses include a **bit of slap and tickle, bush patrol, finger pie, groping, lovey-dovey, parking,** (cf. **parallel parking**) PDA (public display of affection), **pecking and necking** (AA), **stink-finger** and **stinky-finger**. To **get to first base** is to make initial sexual contact (fr. baseball, cf. **strike out**). To caress can be to **canoodle, climb all over, cock pluck** (Afro- American), **cop a feel, dry-fuck, feel up, finger- fuck, goose, guzzle, make out** and **make out with, mess about, neck, smooch, smoodge** (Aus.), **snog, watch the submarines**; to **play footsie** is to rub feet beneath a table. To kiss is to **slake** (19C), **chew face, mug, poof, suck face** (19C: to enjoy drinking) and **swap spit**.

SEXUAL INTERCOURSE

FOREPLAY

Prior to intercourse comes foreplay and while compared with the massive numbers of words relating to love-making those describing foreplay are tiny, they should still appear first.

The earliest use of **caterwaul** relates to the howling of rutting cats; unsurprisingly the 16C adopted it for human purposes, quieting the noise, but accentuating the mutual stimulation that leads on to more intimate pleasures. Another 16C term **fumble** might seem more relevant to foreplay, and links easily with the 17C **fiddle**. **Firkytoodle** (17C) in this context also means to play with, but **firk** itself meant beat, a concept so often associated with sex. The **dildo**, as the *OED* has it, 'a word of obscure origin, used in the refrains of ballads' is usually found meaning an artificial phallus and comes from the Italian *diletto* or (ladies') delight (the Italians also called the instrument a *passatempo* or 'pass the time'). In the context of foreplay the male fingers act as the stimulant and act, it might be felt, as an artificial artificial penis.

The 18C has **feel**, or **feel one's way to heaven** while the 19C plays on the term **fish★**, meaning vagina, for **ling grappling** (**ling★**: vagina) and **get a handful of sprats**; the image of unpleasant vaginal odours is carried on in **play stinkfinger**. **Canoodle** and **spoon** (19C, also meaning a fool) convey a kindlier tone, although **mess**, **giddle** (Scots dial.), **nug** (more usually meaning to have sex), **tip the long** or **middle finger** or simply **finger** and **grope** spare few feelings. **Clitorize** is coldly anatomical, **fam** means to handle intimately and **crooky** more usually means to walk arm in arm, from the crook of the linked elbows. The 20C's **finger-fuck** and the cognate noun **finger-pie** have a suitably modern cold-bloodedness.

FUCKING AND SWIVING

'The vivid expressiveness and the vigorous ingenuity of these synonyms bear witness to the fertility of English and to the enthusiastic English participation in the universal fascination of the creative act.' Thus Eric Partridge, in his edition of *Grose*, and there is no single human activity, other than drinking and its effects, that has attracted so wide a slang lexicon.

The most basic of such synonyms, **fuck**, remains for many the ultimate in taboo terms, although it may just be shaded by **cunt★** in any sweepstakes of opprobrium. The term emerges at the start of the 16C, its first *OED* citation is in 1503, in a line from the poetry of William Dunbar (?1456–?1513) and finds its first dictionary listing in John Florio's *Worlde of Wordes* (1598): '*Fottere*, to iape, to sard, to fucke, to swive, to occupy.' Through this period it remained SE, although by c.1690 it was moving fast into taboo where it has stayed, despite efforts of modern and post-modern novelists and of the critic Ken Tynan who remarked in 1967 to much furore that surely no intelligent person could any longer be frightened of the word – how wrong he was. The etymology of **fuck** defeats the *OED*. The logical link is to the German *ficken*, which means exactly the same, but semantically there are no links and temptation must resisted. Eric Partridge, never loathe to take on the toughest of words, was convinced that real link is to the Latin *pungare*: to strike, which seems substantially likely, given the extent of synonymous terms meaning exactly that. One suggestion that can be discounted is the theory noted in Geoffrey Hughes' *Swearing* (1991) that '*Fuck* originated from a royal injunction at the time of the Plague, when it was very necessary to procreate; it was a code word in which the letters stood for "fornicate under command of the King".' Professor Hughes, of course, was not subscribing to the theory.

Given its negative image, fuck has engendered a number of bowdlerisations, all striving to some extent to echo the genuine article. Aside from the rhyming slang **Donald Duck** and **goose and duck**, there are variously **fugle, futz, fulke** (coined by Byron in *Don Juan* [1819-24]), **futter** (coined by Sir Richard Burton, from the French *foutre*), **fug** (in Norman Mailer's *The Naked and the Dead* [1949]) and **fugh** (concocted by Brendan Behan in *Borstal Boy* [1958]). **Fickey-fick, fuckle** and **fucky-fucky**, while hardly euphemistic, do attempt to soften the grosser word.

Two words precede fuck in the copulatory lexicon: **sard** and **swive**. **Sard**, amongst those cited by Florio (the others are all 15-16C), dates back to the 10C when the *Lindisfarne Gospel* uses it in its translation of *Matthew* v. 27. By the 17C it was the basis of 'a Nottingham proverb': Go teach your Grandam to sard, but vanished soon afterwards. **Swive**, which can still be found occasionally in self-consciously 'literary' contexts, dates to c.1440, and lasted as SE until 1700, when it, like **fuck**, entered the realms of the taboo. Its origin is in the OE. *swīfan*, meaning to move in a course, sweep and the Old Norse *svífa* to rove, ramble or drift. A third term **mell**, while 14C and meaning in SE *to blend* or *mix*, is more a euphemism than a proper slang term.

TO HIT, STRIKE OR BEAT

Of all the many terms for copulation, no group is so wide-ranging as those which, if given a single, unifying label, essentially mean to hit, beat, strike, shake or otherwise assault. As noted above, **fuck** itself may well stem from such a term, and term follows term thereafter, all the way through to today's **bonk**.

The first such term is **foin** (14C) which in SE meant to make a thrust with pointed weapon; two centuries on and one finds **labour** or **stretch leather** (**leather**★: vagina), **job** (job, from jab means to **prod**, itself a term for intercourse), **knock** (which stems both from the 'assault' and from **nock**★ or **notch**★ meaning vagina; thus the later knocked up: pregnant), **shake** (cf. **shag**), **shake the sheets** and **swinge** (SE *swinge*: castigate). Swinge leads on to the 17C **switch** (also meaning beat), **lap clap** (**clap**: beat), **thrum** (meaning thrash), **scour**, **invade** (a literary euphemism), **nodge** or **nudge**, **prig** (cf. **prick**) and **shake a skin-coat** (**skin-coat**: vagina). The 18C has **screw** (perhaps the first, and certainly the longest-lasting of what one might term sex as a do-it-yourself task, typified in its much later combination, the **carpenter's dream**: 'flat as a board and easy to screw'). Other 18C terms include **nub** (in which nub either implies the protruding penis, or comes from the dial. term meaning to jog or shake), **snabble** (which also means arrest), **split**, **bumbaste** (otherwise to beat), **hump** (18C) **plug**, **drill** (also meaning to 'feel up'), **spit** (and **put four quarters on the spit**) and **prod**. **Punch** means specifically to deflower; the SE *punch*: to pierce) while **shag** dates to the 14C when as SE it too meant shake. One last veteran term emerges from the 18C, although it existed as SE long before: **ride** dates to Middle English, joining its fellow synonyms in language's Private Case by the 18C.

The violent motif continues into the 19C with **bob** (also to strike or slap), **bore** (as in bore a hole), **bounce**, **brush** (hit), **bung** (hit), **club** (cf. **club**: penis), **flimp** (usually knock), **hustle**, **jounce** (to shake), **impale**, **spread** (the woman is spread for sex), **peg** and

perforate and **pluck** (both with the accent on defloration). Country life gives **plough** (**ploughshare**: penis; the 20C has **till**), **plowter** (also meaning to splash about in mire or water; cf. **paddle**) and the US **plow the back forty**, as well as the sporting **shoot**, **shoot in the bush**, **shoot in the tail** (with a secondary meaning of sodomise) or **stab in the thigh** (Shakespeare already used **stab in 16C**). More aggression can be found in **poke**, **pound**, **rake**, **rasp**, **rummage**, **stick**, **strike**, **towze**, **touzle**, **muddle**, **muss**, **tumble** and **give a tumble**, **trounce** (SE thrash) **stuff**, **serve** (usually meaning treat roughly) **get into**, **go through**, **grind** (also **have a grind**, **do a grind**) and **sharge** (a dialect term possibly related to *sharg*[*e*], meaning to grind).

The 20C's monosyllabic **biff**, **bang**, **bonk**, **tonk**, **lay** (though **lie with** and **lie on** are both Shakespearian), **make**, **off** (Sixties' radical slang for to kill), **plank**, **plonk**, **pogue** (fr. **poke**), **pork** (cf. **pork sword***: penis), **root** (Aus.; the all-purpose equivalent to **fuck**, as popular in such phrases as **get rooted** as in describing intercourse; in parallel is **Wellington**: rhy. sl. **Wellington boot**), **rout** (SE: defeat or bore into) have all the subtlety of a Tom and Jerry cartoon, but contemporary coinages can be slightly more inventive. Australia offers **spear the bearded clam**, while Black America has **bust some booty** (**booty***: vagina), **hit skins** (a descendant, surely of 18C **wriggle navels** and a cousin of the modern **rub offal**), **mash the fat** and **pile**. **Cut a side** is the Afro-American equivalent of **cut a slice off the joint**, as is **knock it out** parallel to **knock it off** or **knock off a piece** (and the synonymous **tear off a piece**) **Knock off** has the added inference of seduction. Other terms include **throw**, **scrape** (cf. **rasp**), **schtup** (fr. the Yid. / Ger. *stupsen*: push) and most unashamedly of all: **hop on a babe**.

ANIMALS

Less common in the modern industrial world, but widely used in a society still rooted in the rural life, are those terms that seek their inspiration in animal life. The oldest example is **tup** (16C), nominally a young bullock; its anthropomorphic role comes in Shakespeare's *Othello* (1604), when Iago informs Brabantio that, 'An old blacke Ram Is tupping your white Ewe.' The 16C also has **clicket** (which in animal terms applied to foxes) and **mount**, which described any animal coupling. **Cover** (17C), **service** and **tread** (and 19C **chuck a tread**) are similarly general terms. **Rifle** (17C) described the hawk treading the hen, **tom** (19C) came from the male or tom-cat, **caulk** (19C) came either from caulking or stuffing, or from another term used for a male bird treading the female. **Hog** (19C), **horse** (17C) and **dog** all acknowledged the animal kingdom, although bitch related more directly to the 15C term for whore (although that, of course, had its canine origins). The modern **dogging**, probably coincidentally, refers to the practice of spying on others having sex in parked cars. **Roger** (18C), came from the popular name for a bull, while to **play the goat** was to copulate energetically. The relation of the 19C **ferret** to the 20C **exercise the ferret** is probably no more than chance. **Tether one's nags on** (17C) plays on **nag**: horse or penis.

USING THE GENITALS

The elaborate strategems of safe sex notwithstanding, sexual intercourse remains dependent on genital contact and this being so a number of slang terms are based on the genitals. Those meaning penis are **cock★** (19C), **prick★**, **dibble** and **diddle★** (19C), **jock** (17C, from **jockum★**), **pestle★** and **pizzle★**(19C, the latter also meaning an animal's penis), **pole★** and **shaft★** (both 20C), **spike** and **mow** (16C, from the Scots / Northern dialect **mowdiwarp★** = mole = penis). **Stitch** (and **go on the stitch**), while not meaning penis, implies the in-out 'stitching' motion of copulation, with the penis as a needle; the 19C **sew** has similar roots, while **sew up** means to impregnate. Terms relating to the vagina are **hole★** (19C, also as **get one's hole**), **quiff★** (18C, although **quiff** as vagina is apparently 20C), **quim★** (17C), **tail★** (18C) and **trim★**. Relevant phrases include **lay some pipe** (20C, **pipe**: vagina, **lay**: to copulate), **skin the cat** (cf. **skin the pizzle**), **take Nebuchadnezzar out to grass** (19C, the Biblical monarch ate grass and thus 'liked his **greens★**'; thus **Nebuchadnezzar**: penis), **join paunches**, **join giblets** and **have a bit of giblet pie** (all 18C), **nail two wames**

(Scots dial.: bellies) **together, rub offal** (20C), **slip her a length** and **slip it to her** (both 19C), the Scots **slip in Daintie Davie** or **Willie Wallace**, and **slip her a quick crippler** (20C, with overtones of hostility). Other terms include **put it in and break it, peel one's best end in, strop one's beak** and **strip one's tarse** (all 19C). Typical of the 19C's often ponderous puns is **make a settlement in tail**, doubtless amusing the legal profession with its references to entail and thus both **tail**, meaning vagina, and the French *taille* meaning assessment.

WHORING

A few terms accentuate the world of prostitution, especially that of the brothel. They include **occupy** (16C) from **occupying house★**, **vault** (17C) meaning leap or jump but also from **vaulting house★**, **nug** (17C), from **nug** meaning nudge and from **nugging house★** and **accomodate** (19C) from **accomodation house★**. To **bitch** (19C) is to go whoring, from **bitch** (15C) meaning whore; **buttock** (18C) and **flap** (17C) both mean whore as does **split-arse mechanic** in the 19C verb **to take on a split arse-mechanic**.

THE SIXTEENTH CENTURY

The 16C offers two of the most basic of terms: **do** and **have**. 'I have done thy mother' writes Shakespeare in *Titus Andronicus* (?1590), while 'I'll have her – but I will not keep her long' can be found in *Richard III* (1591). Shakespeare also has **line**, as in line or fill a cupboard: 'Winter garments must be lined, so must slender Rosalind' (*As You Like It* [1599]), **grope for trout in a peculiar river** (*Measure for Measure* [1604]) and **make the beast with two backs** (*Othello* [1604]). **Jape**, one of those terms listed by Florio in 1598, dates to the 14C, when as SE it meant to trick and thus to seduce a woman; consigned to taboo by 1600, it soon vanished, although it re-emerged in the late 19C to mean schoolboy pranks, especially as found in turn-of-the-century school stories. Thomas Harman cites **tonygle** ('to niggle') in his *Caveat* (1567), while Florio further includes **ginicomtwig**, a word of the 'thingumibob' family and as such a euphemism. Other early terms include **feeze** or **pheeze** (also to beat), **flesh** or **flesh it** and **jumble**. **Dock** means specifically to deflower, and comes either from the punning farmyard image of docking a **tail*** or from the Romany *dukker:* to ravish. Finally comes **wap** (also in Harman) and a **wapping mort** or whore: 'wapping Dell that niggles well...' appears in Dekker's 'Bing out, bien Morts' (1612).

THE SEVENTEENTH AND EIGHTEENTH CENTURIES

Many 16C terms continued on into the next century, where they were joined by **jumm** (coined by Thomas Urquhart for his translation of Rabelais), **play at pickle-me-tickle-me**, **bumfid-dle** (usually a noun meaning buttocks), **poop** (also meaning buttocks, and as **poop-noddy**: sexual intercourse), **cavault** (fr. Latin *cavolta*: riding), **leap**, **jump** and **jump up and down** (source of the later **give one a jump**), **smoke** and **twang**. **Lerricom-poop**, otherwise unknown, probably played on **lerricomtwang**, a fool. To **ride a St George** was for the woman to straddle the man; such a position was apparently that recommended for couples desirous of conceiving a future bishop. To **blow the groundsels** punned on 'ground', where one might lie, and to **go on Hobbes' voyage** referred to the last words of the political philosopher Thomas Hobbes (1588-1679), who stated, 'I am about to take my last voyage: a great leap in the dark.'

The 18C gives **palliardise** (fr. the **palliard***, the itinerant beggar who slept on straw [*paille* in French]), **huddle** (also meaning hug), **do it**, **go facemaking** (the face was that of an as yet unborn child), **chuck**, **cross**, **rig** (fr. **rig**: a prank, thus to play) and **nick**. In SE **tump** meant to pile a mound of earth round a root. **Ease** meant particularly to deflower, and added an inference of ease, as used in 'relieving oneself' in the lavatory. The 20C **drop one's load** and **empty one's trash** (both AA) have the same feel, as does **lift a leg on**, although this may be better related to **get one's leg over**. **Huffle** (cited by Grose in his first edition, but dropped thereafter) is an early equivalent of the 20C **bagpipe**, coyly defined as '*coitus in axilla*', in other words rubbing the penis against the partner's armpit.' To **engage in three to one (and bound to lose)** suggests a conflict between the penis and two testicles and the vagina. To **Adam and Eve it** refers to the Garden of Eden and the Fall therefrom, while **wind up the clock** may have its origins in a mildy coarse scene in the novel *Tristram Shandy*.

THE NINETEENTH CENTURY

Aside from the many combinations with do, have, etc. the 19C, always a forcing ground for new slang, provides a number of fresh terms. **Greens**, as in **get one's greens**, emerges as a term for sexual intercourse; variations include the **green-grove** (pubic hair), **to be after one's greens** (of a man), **to be on for greens** (of a woman) and **to give a green gown** (sex on the grass, possibly with the loss of virginity). **Chauver**, pronounced and often spelt **charver** and surviving today, came from the Parylaree *charva* which in turn was based on the French *chauffer*: to heat or the Romany *charvo*: to touch or meddle with. The food motif continues with **strain one's greens**, **relish**, **nibble** and **taste**. **Pleasure** has a slightly romantic air, along with its variations **pleasure boat**, **garden**, **ground** and the **palace of pleasure**, all meaning vagina, and the **pleasure garden padlock**: a menstrual cloth. Less fanciful are **bellybump**, **rump**, **block**, **frisk**, **fiddle**, **whack it up**, **wallop it in**, **do ill to**, **paddle** (coming either from the SE: to spank, or possibly from the wetness of vaginal emissions), **do over** and **have a bit of bum**. **Come about** and **come aloft** smack of the sea, and the latter also means to have an erection. **Qualify**, **perform on**, **get one's end away**, **see** and the 20C **give a seeing-to** are equally unromantic, though to **see the stars lying on one's back** has a pleasantly al fresco air.

Adamize has a Biblical tone, although at the Sandhurst military school to **Adamize** a cadet was to lower him naked onto the parade ground, his only chance of re-entering his quarters was by presenting himself to the guard. **Flourish** also meant to expose oneself, while **flutter** drew on the noun meaning any form of sexual experience; **jiggle** came from **jiggling bone***: the penis, and **jig-a-jig** or **jig-jig** were essentially echoic, cf. the various combinations at **dance***. **Jiggy-jig**, while apparently similar, was a specifically Indian Army term, apparently an 'exclamation of delight used by Indian women during sexual intercourse.'

Frig, originally meaning masturbate, takes on what has become its more permanent meaning; **dip it** and **dip one's wick** (fr. rhy. sl. **Hampton wick***: **prick***) predate the 20C Afro-American **dip the fly**, as **stroke** leads similarly to today's **take a stroke**. **Have it**, **have it in** and **have it up** develop the 16C's plain **have**; **man** and **go with** are bald, if ultimately euphemistic. **Getting one's hair cut** and **seeing a sick friend** are both excuses offered by a man slipping out of the house to find alternative pleasures.

Jink means rattle (itself a 20C term) though usually money, **jack** and **jack up** are possibly linked to **jack** (as in **jill**), 'a male sweetheart'; **snib** originates in the Scots *snibbet* meaning intercourse; **turn up** infers, perhaps, the 'turning up' of the woman's buttocks. Perhaps the least likely 19C term is **jazz**, which by the 1920s was established worldwide in the context of the latest thing in music. But as the magazine *Étude* put it in 1924, 'If the truth were known about the origin of the word "Jazz" it would never be mentioned in polite society.' and three years later America's *Journal of Abnormal & Social Psychology* declared that 'the word jazz...used both as a verb and as a noun to denote the sex act...has long been common vulgarity among Negroes in the South'.

Longer phrases include **feed the dummy** or **feed the dumb glutton**, **put the devil into hell**, **get jack in the orchard**, **fire in the air** and **do a bit of front-door work**, **play a tune on the one-holed flute** (and equally 'musical' **strum**); both **dive into the dark** and **take a turn on shooter's hill** survive in today's Afro-American culture. Finally the 19C, as one might expect, offers a number of euphemisms: **caress, compress, embrace, fondle, handle, kiss, know** (in the Biblical sense), **please, solace** and **oblige**.

THE TWENTIETH CENTURY

The occasional romanticism of the 19C fades with the progression of its successor. **Ball** (US), **snag** (fr. SE *snag*: to catch), **gee** (fr. *gee* *up*: to encourage), **mess around, meddle with** and **stoop** are strictly practical. **Score between the posts** (Aus.), **be on the job, lay the leg, lift arse on, make it with,** and selection of Afro-Americanisms: **do the do, do the nasty, do the natural thing, do the pussy, fill one up** and **skeet** are equally uncompromising. **Love up** and **do a kindness** are euphemistic and thus softer, while **play fathers and mothers** or **play mummies and daddies** presumably appeal to those who enjoy lovers' baby-talk and **play night baseball** (cf. ball) is for the sports, as, on another level, is to **play hide the salami**. **Honeyfuck** and **honeyfuggle**, meaning both stimulate as well as copulate, have slightly paedophiliac overtones – a **honey** tends to mean a younger girl. **Feature with** is an Australian euphemism while **drop 'em**, 'em' being panties, refers strictly to women.

A selection of specific terms include **roof it** (to have sex on the roof), to **talk fuck** (to talk obscenely during intercourse) and to **come across** (to allow seduction). To copulate enthusiastically is to **bang like the shithouse door in a gale** (Aus.), to **go in and out like a fiddler's elbow,** to **go up her like a rat up a drain** (Aus.), to **rip her guts down** (AA), to **screw the arse off,** and to **shag like a rattlesnake** (usually said of a woman). An enthusiastic lover is **good at the game** or **nimble hipped**. To **draw one's fireworks** (19C) is to cool one's ardour by coition.

✶✶✶✶✶✶

Aside from those already listed, slang has created dozens of phrases that draw on terms for the genitals or for intercourse which are rendered verbs by the addition of some otherwise neutral verb of action, ie. **dance, go, do, have** and so on. These terms are listed below. Further details (etymologies, etc.) may be found under the relevant entry, typically at PENIS, VAGINA etc.

To Dance

The blanket hornpipe, the buttock jig, the goat's jig, on the mattress or **the mattress jig, the married man's cotillion, the matrimonial polka, the miller's reel, the reels o' Bogie, the**

reels of Stumpie (Scots dial.; the nouns perhaps both meaning penis), to the tune of shaking the sheets (without music), with your arse to the ceiling the kipples (Scots dial.: couple), Sallinger's round (17C, Sallinger being St Leger and the dance a popular ballad).

TO GO

Ballocking, beard-splitting, bed-pressing, belly-bumping, bitching, bum fighting, bum-working, bum-tickling, bum-faking (fake: to make), bush ranging, buttock-stirring, birds-nesting, buttocking, cockfighting, cunny catching (punning on 16C cant coney-catching*), doddling, drabbing, fleshing it, fleshmongering, goosing, to Hairyfordshire, hunting, jottling, jumming, leather-stretching, on the loose, motting, molrowing, pile driving, prick scouring, quim sticking, rumping, rump splitting, strumming, twatting, twat faking, vaulting, wenching, womanizing, working the dumb, double or hairy oracle, twat raking, tromboning (cf bagpiping), tummy tickling, quim wedging, tail twitching, bottom hole working, under petticoating and all the way.

TO HAVE OR DO A BIT OF

Beef, business, bum dancing, cauliflower (18C, from cauliflower: a large white wig, 'such as is worn by the dignified clergy'; it came to mean vagina, according to Grose after a woman used the term in court and was duly reproved by a the Judge, 'saying she might as well call it artichoke. Not so, my lord, replied she; for an artichoke has a bottom, but a **** and a cauliflower have none.'), cock, cock-fighting, cunt, curly greens, fish, fish on a fork, fun, off the chump end, flat, front door work, giblet pie, gut stick, cream stick, sugar stick, jam, keifer (fr. khyfe: a woman as sex object; poss. from the Arabic keyif: 'the amiable beauty of a fair woman'), ladies' tailoring (cf. needlework, sew), meat, mutton, pork, quimsy, rough, sharp and blunt (rhy. sl.), stuff, split mutton (cf. mutton), skirt and summer cabbage.

TO HAVE OR DO OR PERFORM

A **ballocking**, a **bit**, a **lassie's by-job**, a **bedward bit**, a **beanfeast in bed**, a **belly warmer**, a **blindfold bit**, a **bottom wetter**, a **bout**, a **brush with the cue**, a **dive in the dark**, a **drop in**, a **double fight**, a **four legged frolic**, a **fuck**, a **futter**, a **game in the cock loft**, a **goose and duck** (rhy. sl.), a **grind**, a **hoist-in**, a **jottle**, a **jumble giblets**, a **jumble up**, an **inside worry**, a **leap (up the ladder)**, a **little of one with the other**, a **mount**, a **mow**, a **nibble**, a **plaster of warm guts** (18C), a **poke**, a **put**, a **rasp**, a **ride**, a **roger**, a **rootle**, a **rush up the straight**, a **shot at the bull's eye**, a **slide up the board**, a **squirt and a squeeze**, a **touch off**, a **tumble in**, a **wet 'un**, a **wipe at the place**, a **wallop in**, a **back scuttle**, a **buttered bun** (17C), a **dog's marriage**, a **knee trembler**, a **St George**, a **bit of rabbit-pie**, a **cut or slice off the joint**, a **dash in the bloomers**, a **dash up the Channel**, a **shag**, a **tumble**, **one's greens**, **one's oats**, to **have it away (with)** and to **have been there** (20C, a dismissive remark probably referring to a passing girl).

TO GET OR GIVE

To get: **a shot of leg** (AA), **into one's pants**, (20C), **on top of**, **get one's ashes hauled**, **get one's cookies**, **one's jollies**, **one's leg over**, **one's oats** (20C, from wild oats, thus the sex is probably adulterous), **get one's rocks off** (20C, **rocks**: testicles, cf. 12C **stones**), **get some big leg** (20C), **get some cock**, **some pussy**, **some tail**, **get some** (20C). Verbs with give are **give her a length**, **give her one**, **give some body** and **give the dog a bone**.

TO PLAY AT

All fours, **Adam and Eve**, **belly-to-belly**, **brangle** (SE: shake, dance), **buttock**, **buttock and leave her**, **cherry pit**, **couple** or **wriggle your navels**, **cuddle my cuddie**, **Hey Gammer Cook** (possibly from **gammocks**: wild play?), **fathers and mothers**, **the first game ever played**, **Handie Dandie** (16C, Scots), **Hooper's Hide**, **cock in cover**, **houghmagandie** (16C, from *hough* = hock = back of the knee, plus 18C *canty*: cheerful, active), **in and in** (17C), **in and out, Irish whist,** (cf. **Irish toothache**) **where the Jack takes Ace, level-coil** (17C, from the similarly named rough game), **mumble-peg, prick the garter** (fr. a fraudulent game based on pricking the loop of a belt with a bodkin), **pully-hauly** (18C, SE rough and tumble), **push-pin** (17C), **itch-buttocks** (17C), **put in all, stable my naggie** (19C, cf. horse), **thread the needle** (cf. stitch), **tops and bottoms, top sawyer, two handed put** (put = *putain* = whore) and **up tails all** (17C, from the name of a song).

TO TAKE A TURN

All but two of these terms refer to the genitals or pubic hair: **in Cock Alley, Bushey Park, Cock Lane, Cupid's Alley, Cupid's Corner** and **Hair Court; on Shooter's Hill, Love Lane** and **Mount Pleasant, through the stubble, among the cabbages, up her petticoats, among her frills** and **among the parsley**.

WOMEN ONLY

As must be apparent, particularly from the predominant air of violence amongst them, the bulk of these terms presume a masculine point of view on love-making. Certain terms, however, relate only to women.

This vocabulary includes to **do the naughty, turn up one's tail, lift one's leg, open up, take Nebuchadnezzar out to grass, look at the ceiling, play one's ace** (ace: the pudendum), **take in and do for, give standing room for one only, get hulled between wind and water, take one's medicine** (also used for becoming drunk) and **go star-gazing**. The exhaustion of the post-coital male is seen in **draw a cork** and **take the starch out of**, while the links between food and sex are underlined by **suck the sugar stick, take in beef, catch an oyster** (19C, **oyster** meaning semen, although it can also mean vagina) and **take in cream, skin the live rabbit, feed one's pussy, get a bellyful of marrow pudding** and **have a hot pudding** or **a live sausage for supper**. A further group includes give **mutton for beef, give**

juice for jelly, and the cognate, if not food-based **give soft for hard** and **give a hot poultice for the Irish toothache**.

As in the larger vocabulary, there are several verb combinations: verbs with **do** are **do a spread, a tumble, a back fall, what mother did before me** or **what Eve did with Adam**; those with **get** are **get outside it, stabbed in the thigh, a bit of goose's neck** (cf. **turkey neck★**), **a go at the creamstick, a handle for the broom, shot in the tail, a shove in one's blind eye, a wet bottom, what Harry gave Dolly, a green gown, one's leg lifted, one's kettle mended, one's chimney swept (out), one's leather stretched**, and **get an arselins coup** (fr. **arselin[g]s** meaning backward plus **coup** meaning blow or fall).

SEXUAL INTERCOURSE

Although the preceding sections should have covered the bulk of terms meaning sexual intercourse, albeit usually in a verb form, herewith a concluding section in which it is hoped any escapees may be rounded up and itemised. All these are nouns, although it should be apparent that many of the verbs listed above can similarly be used as nouns, e.g. **lay, legover, bonk** and many others.

The 17C has the **business** while the 18C offers **Hooper's hide** (fr. hide and seek, cf. **hide the salami★**) and the Biblical euphemism **the fruit that made man wise** (cf. **Adam and Eve it**). The 19C brings **four legged frolic, shift work** or **shift service** (shift: movement), **matrimonial** (specifically the missionary position), **sport** and **sport of Venus** (a literary euphemism), **perpendicular** (intercourse while standing up, cf. **horry, horizontal** and **knee-trembler**), **naughties** (Aus.) and **nookie** (fr. **nug★**).

Modern coinages include **a bit of the other** and **a bit of how's-yer-father** (originally a World War I music hall catchphrase, meaning thingummy; cf. **ginicomtwig**) and **you know what**; a **bunk-up**, a **bush patrol, fratting** (fr. SE *fraternizing*), **ground rations, horizontal jogging**, a **horizontal rumble** (rumble: a fight) and a **horry** (Aus.). **Indoor sledging, interior decorating**, and **parallel parking** carry on the puns. Afro-American terms include a **dead shot**, a **jack in the box**, a **thrill and chill** and a

hot fling (possibly related to the 16C **fling**: to wriggle the buttocks during intercourse). Other terms include **nasty, nobbing** (fr. **nob★**: penis), **oats**, a **roll in the hay, rubadub** and **turking** (fr. **turkey neck★**). Perhaps the most celebrated modern coinage, at least in the UK, is **Ugandan discussions** or **talking about Uganda**, terms first used in the satirical magazine *Private Eye*. It was popularly thought to have been derived from the alleged discovery, *in flagrante delicto*, of Uganda's female Minister of Foreign Affairs in an airport lavatory, and was so underwritten by the magazine; this theory was latterly repudiated by the writer Corinna Adam, whose letter to *The Times* (Sept 1983) claimed that in 1971 a passionate (male) literary critic was the first to offer this excuse.

Other terms include **straight shot** (intercourse without contraception) and a **dog's match** (sex in the bushes or by the wayside). Spontaneous intercourse: is variously **bip-bam-thank-you mam**, a **bump**, a **fast-fuck**, a **quickie**, and **wham bam thank-you mam**. Lunchtime intercourse is an **afternoon delight**, **funch** (fuck plus lunch) or a **nooner**; the **killing floor** (AA) is where one has sex. Coitus interuptus can be **getting off at Redfern** (Aus.: the station before Sydney Central), **at Gateshead** or **at Edge Hill** (the stops respectively before Newcastle on Tyne and Liverpool Lime Street), **getting off at Hillgate** (with references to hill: the *mons veneris* and a gate, which can be closed) and **leaving before the gospel**.

Sex without ejaculation is a **flash in the pan** or a **dry bob**; an impotent man is **free of Fumbler's Hall★**, a **fumbler** or a **mugwump**. Two fat people making love makes for **melting moments** while **warming one's husband's supper** is to sit in front of fire with lifted skirts.

Orgasm

The orgasm, the climax of intercourse, is the **big O, come** or **cum**. 20C terms for achieving one's orgasm include to **come** or **cum**, to **cheese, get one's gun off, get one's rocks off, light off, pop one's nuts, shoot** or **shoot off, shoot one's load, shoot one's wad, come one's cocoa, come one's fat, cream, pop one's**

cork; to **have a double shot** is to ejaculate twice. Their 19C predecessors are to **give one's gravy** or to **get home**; to give one's partner an orgasm is to **ring one's bell** or **ring one's chimes**.

HOMOSEXUALITY

EARLY TERMS

Given the age-old existence of male homosexuality, the slang vocabulary, while extensive, is notably reticent until the late 19C. Doubtless this reflects the public abhorrence of this aspect of human sexuality, but certainly, those words that precede the 20C are few and far between.

Earliest among them are the 16C **sellary** (fr. the Latin *sellarius*, one who sits upon a *sella*, a couch) and **spintry** (fr. Latin *spintria*), both of which meant a male whore. The latter, a century later, had become a meeting place for homosexuals, the modern **cottage**. **Ganymede** (the cupbearer to Zeus) and **bardache** (16C, from SE *bardash*) both mean catamite as does **angelina** (an **angel** is the older man). A further 16C term was **Jesuit** (1630) product of a general loathing of Jesuits, whose name was used in a variety of negative contexts, not always sexual. The 18C coined **molly**, **Miss Molly** and **moll**, plus **moll-house** meaning gay meeting-house, all of which equated effeminacy with a word that in other contexts meant a whore, while **madge-cull** (**madge-cove** in the 19C) was a variation on **mag**, meaning a sodomite and possibly taken from **maggie**, usually meaning a girl. **Gentleman of the back door** and **backgammon player** are both puns on anal intercourse.

Sod (19C) is an abbreviation of sodomite, while **mary ann**, **nancy**, **nan-boy**, **Miss Nancy** and **margery** are all girls' names; **gussie**, from Augustus, is an Australian parallel. **Faddle** originally meant a trifler, **cissie** and **sissy** (late 19C) both come from SE *sister*, while **renter** precedes the modern **rent boy**. More complex is **cockquean** (1830) a pun on *cotquean* (a peasant housewife) and thus, in this slang form, a man who 'acts the housewife'. Finally come **smockface** (**smock** is a generic term for woman), **soft**, **white liver** (originally a coward), **pap-mouth** and the Irish **bud sullogh**. All are cited in Farmer and Henley but do not appear to have any other sources. The adjective **baker-kneed** (17C) meant originally knock-kneed; its use in the gay context either implies that all homosexuals are knock-kneed, or that women's legs are never straight. A **green and yellow fellow** is more allusive than slangy, and comes from the late 19C *greenery-yallery*: of, pertaining to, or affecting the colours green and yellow, in accordance with the style or fashion of the contemporary 'aesthetic' movement and thus, in short, affected. W S Gilbert used it in Patience (1880) when he derided a 'greenery-yallery, Grosvenor Gallery,/Foot-in-the-grave young man.

CENTRAL TERMINOLOGY

As in most areas of slang, there emerge a number of key terms that stand above the mass of synonymous material. In the case of homosexuality, these terms are **gay**, **fag**, **fairy**, **queen** or **quean**, **queer**, **poof**, and **bugger**. Before moving on to the wider vocabulary, they should be considered first.

Gay (20C) dates back to the late 18C, when, often allied to 'woman' or 'girl' it meant a promiscuous woman, even a prostitute. Thus a **gay house** was a brothel, **to be gay** was to be promiscuous, **gay in the legs, groin** or **arse** meant promiscuity, the **gaying instrument** was a penis and **gaying it** meant copulation. The use of the term as a self-description by homosexuals originated during World War II, when it was probably an abbreviation of the old US tramps' slang **geycat**, meaning the young homosexual companion of an older tramp, also known as a **gonsel**, but the wider use in the heterosexual world did not begin until c.1970, with the emergence of the Gay Liberation Front, first in America and subsequently in the UK. The subsequent **three-letter man** is presumably g-a-y. **Gonsel** itself, most famously personified in Elmer, the young, inadequate hoodlum of Dashiell Hammett's *The Maltese Falcon* (1930, film 1941) is often mistranslated as gunman, while the 20C

punk and **punce** are also catamites. Synonymous with gunsel is **jocker** or **jockey** (20C US, from 16C **jockum★**: penis).

Fag, farg, faggot or **fagola**, these days almost invariably seen as US coinages, have an older, if debatable UK etymology. One, somewhat fanciful version, suggests that a faggot was used in the burning heretics, and thus became transferred to the name of an embroidered patch (like the pink triangles of the Nazi concentration camps) worn by unburnt heretics; homosexuals are certainly heretics, therefore faggot means homosexual. More feasible is the descent from the 18C use of **faggot** as woman (thus playing on homosexual effeminacy), especially in the derogatory form of a **baggage**, which does stem from the faggots that one had to haul to the fire. A link with the British public school **fag** – a junior boy performing menial tasks – is also feasible. Finally there is the Yiddish *faygele* meaning little bird (thus the synonym **birdie**), and thence homosexual. Pig Latin plays on fag to add **afgay** and **agfay**.

The **fairy** (late 19C) started life in the UK meaning, with heavy irony, a drunken old hag; the link with homosexuality seems to stem from a piece, however implausible, that was published in 1895 in vol. VII of the *American Journal of Psychology*. It talked of 'the peculiar societies of inverts. Coffee-clatches, where the members dress themselves with aprons, etc., and knit, gossip and crotchet; balls, where men adopt the ladies' evening dress, are well known in Europe. "The Fairies" of New York are said to be a similar secret organization.' The later **pixie** is an obvious synonym.

Poof, poofta and **poofter** (both Aus.), **poove** and **powder puff** (notoriously used to attack the silent movie god Rudolph Valentino) all stem from **puff**, although the *OED* has an 1850 citation for **poof**, whereas **puff** only appears in 1902 (although the *Dictionary* still sees **poof** as a synonym for **puff**). The inference, as in **faddle★** and the similar **mince** (from mincing steps) and **chichi** or **ki-ki**) is of unmanly fussiness. Allied terms are the rhy. sl. **jam duff** (puff), **horse's hoof** and **iron** (fr. **iron hoof**: poof; its most celebrated use was in The Scaffold's reference, in 'Thank You Very Much' to the 'Aintree iron', the late Brian Epstein, theirs and the Beatles' gay manager). **Foop** and **fooper** are backslang.

In the 17C **queer** was a staple of the cant lexicon; the opposite of **rum***, meaning good, it meant bad and was found in numerous combinations, typically **queer bird** (habitual criminal), **queer cole** (counterfeit money) and **queer doxy** (slattern). The use as a derogatory description of homosexuals did not begin until the 1920s, originating in the US and moving to the UK by the 1930s. Such combinations as **queer as a nine-bob note** or **a three-dollar bill** and **queer as a clockwork orange** (Royal Navy, then gaining greater recognition with Anthony Burgess' novel *Clockwork Orange* [1962, film 1971]) followed in the 1950s. As well as the pig Latin **eer-quay**, **queer** has generated several examples of rhyming slang: **shandy** (**chandelier**: queer), **Brighton pier, ginger (beer)**, **King Lear**, and **jere** (which rhymes with **queer**, but which, in the 17C, also meant both buttocks and a turd, and is thus allied to the various terms at buttocks and **brown** below.) **Q** stands for queer and **K** for the illiterate kweer. Of all the terms for homosexual, **queer** has generally been seen as the most abusive, although, in the same way that young blacks have started calling themselves 'nigger', turning a racist epithet back on itself, so have a number of militant homosexuals chosen to 'recapture' queer, notably in the US movement called Queer Nation, for their own uses.

Quean originally meant a woman; the term dates to the 11C, and soon afterwards became a term of abuse; by the 16C it most often meant strumpet or even whore. The spelling **queen**, and the link to homosexuality emerged in the early 20C; since then **quean** has almost entirely vanished, while **queen** is reserved for older, ostentatiously effeminate gay men – the antithesis of the tough, unabashed image of homosexuality that has been promoted since the rise of the GLF in the early 1970s. Synonymous terms are **grand duchess** and the Australian rhy. sl. **haricot (haricot bean**: queen). A **closet queen** or **queer** is a homosexual who, due to a persistent, allbeit marginally diminished atmosphere of hostility to homosexuality, prefers not to admit to his sexual preference. To **come out of the closet**, or more usually to **come out**, is to abandon such reticence.

A variety of terms based on **fruit** – **fruitcake, fruiter, fruit-fly, fruit-plate, tooti-frooti** (AA) and possibly **frit** – all stem from the earlier meaning of the term: a woman of easy virtue. Such a woman was seen as 'easy picking'. The use of such terms as pejoratives for homosexuality was a simple transference given the necessary homophobia.

Bugger, the accepted SE term for sodomite since the 16C, is not strictly slang, although its use in a number of combinations is. **Bug** (18C and incontrovertibly slangy) is defined as one who incites others to sodomy. **Bugger** itself (1555) comes from the French *bougre* (1340), which in turn originates in the Latin *Bulgarus*, a Bulgarian, a name given to a sect of heretics who came from Bulgaria in the 11C. The term was transferred to the Albigensian heretics, who it was believed were largely homosexual. The term has also been applied to to usurers, while in 19C UK it meant a stealer of breast-pins (**bugs**) from drunks. Terms allied to bugger, and meaning homosexual, include **bunker**, **burglar**, and **budli-budli** (which in 20C India means sodomy). It also remains common as a general term for a man, especially in such combinations as **silly bugger**, **daft bugger** and the like.

EFFEMINACY

Despite 25 years of gay activism, the predominant image of homosexuality remains one of effeminacy, and the majority of the slang underlines this assumption.

So, one of those or **that way** are or were well-established euphemisms, while **nance**, **nancy-boy**, **nellie** or **nelly**, **jessie**, **belle**, **mary**, **ethel** (fr. Ethel Merman?), **daisy**, and **betty** are all quite obvious: they are girls' names, as are the 'flowers' **lily**, **pansy** and **buttercup**. **Flower** itself means homosexual, as does **girl**. **Femme**, **foxy lady**, **bitch**, **butch**, (US 1930s, UK 1950s, also applied to 'masculine' lesbians), **auntie**, **doll**, **femme**, **mother**, **daughter** and **sister** are all 'women', albeit of various ages and degrees of outrageousness. **Swish**, **shim** (fr. *shimmy*:to wriggle, or from **she-him**), **broken wrist**, **limp wrist**, **lightfoot**, **yoo-hoo boy**, **fancy-pants** and **flit** all refer to the exaggerated mannerisms of many queens. **Bananas** implies softness (and perhaps phallicity) as do **quince** and **twiddlepoop**. The stage offers **Dorothy's**

friends (the Dorothy in question being she of *The Wizard of Oz*, played by Judy Garland, a major gay icon), and **omee-polone** (fr. Parlyaree, and literally meaning 'man/woman'). Similar are **he-she**, **hesh**, **himmer** (him-her) and **she-man**. Others terms include **sweet** (AA) and **sweetie**, **three legged beaver** (a combination of **third leg**★: penis and **beaver**★: vagina) and **lavender** or **lavender boy**; lavender has long been considered an 'effeminate' colour, although the word originally meant a pawnbroker who 'laid things up in lavender'. To act effeminately is to **camp**, **camp about** or **camp it up**, to **foop**, **poof about**, **ruin**, **swish** or **wreck**; effeminate is **la-di-dah**.

THE BUTTOCKS

Progressing from theory, as it were, to action, a number of terms are based unequivocally in sodomy, presumed to be the primary gay sexual activity. The somewhat ponderous **inspector of man-holes** (20C, based on 19C **inspector of pavements**: a person in the pillory) is accompanied by the infinitely brisker **arse bandit**, **arse-king** and the punning **aspro** (**ass-pro**), **battyman** (West Indian, fr. **batti**: buttocks), **boy-ass**, **bufu** and **buttfucker**, **ri-madona** (punning on both prima-donna and on **ream**, meaning sodomise) **bum-boy**, **chutney ferret**, **dung-puncher**, **tan tracker**, **turd-burglar**, **turd-packer**, **hitchhiker on the Hershey highway** (fr. the US Hershey chocolate bars), **shirt-lifter** (Australian), **wind-jammer**, **fart-catcher**, **dirt tamper**, **pillow-biter** and **Turk** (fr. the alleged national propensity for sodomy).

A small group of terms use the national stereotype of the classical Greeks, where homosexuality did not suffer the taboos of modern, Christian Europe. These terms include **Greek culture** (anal intercourse, usually in homosexual advertisement; **Greek** as used on a heterosexual prostitute's 'bill of sale' means the same thing), **to Greek** (to engage in pederasty), **Greek love** or the **Greek way** (pederasty), the **Greek side** (gay use) the buttocks, **Irish by birth but Greek by injection** a male homosexual; **low Greek** is heterosexual intercourse; 'high' Greek uses the anus – the vagina is 'lower' down the body).

The anus is further featured in a number of terms based on brown, ie., **brown artist**, **brown family** (1910), **browning family**, **browning sisters**, **brown hatter** (and **hat**) and **brownie**. **Dead-eye dick** and **eye doctor** see the anus as an eye. Finally, still based on sexual practice, though on fellatio rather than sodomy, come **cocksucker**, **blow-boy**, **lapper**, **skin-diver**, **catch** and **receiver** (both punning on baseball terminology; logically the **pitcher** takes the opposite role), **gobbler** and **dicky-licker** (fr. **dick***: penis). The **meathound** and **cannibal** also 'eat meat' while the **mouser** and **muzzler** (fr. **muzzle***: mouth) nibble the penis, like a mouse at cheese. **Larro** is backslang for oral (sex).

GENERAL TERMS

The word homosexual gives **homo**, **homie** (as opposed to **homey** meaning **homeboy***), **four-letter man** (usuually s-h-i-t; here h-o-m-o, cf. **five letter woman**: b-i-t-c-h). The view of homosexuality as perversion is implicit in **bent**, **freak**, **kinky**, **gender-bender** (1980s, exemplified by the Culture Club singer Boy George, for whom the term was coined), **off-colour**, **secko** (Aus., also a heterosexual child molester), **third sexer**, and **funny man** (AA). A **boy**, **baby**, **capon** or **chicken** all imply a young man, whether or not an actual prostitute, while **wolf**, **twank**, **twink**, and **tonk** refer to his older counterpart. **Jock and boxer** (punning on the two kinds of underwear) describes the young man and his older friend. **Midnight cowboy**, from the film of 1969, is a male whore, although the cowboy in question specialized in women. A **trick** is a prostitute's client, as he is in the heterosexual world. **Gear** or **gearbox** refers to one's genitals, while **orchestra** (which also means testicles) and **flute** or **fluter** (both meaning penis) add a 'musical' touch; the former will allegedly perform 'anything with anyone'. **Hock**, otherwise confusing, may be rhy. sl. for **cock***. **Dyna** is short for dynamite and thus rhymes with catamite. **Oscar** comes from Oscar Wilde (1854-1900). **Skippy** (AA) may be a twist on **skibby**, used by US forces to describe Oriental prostitutes.

Further terms include **waffle, angel, bag, buzzer** (US), **con** (US), **flyball** (US), **joyboy, kisser, mintie, mo, mola** and **nola, nic nac, pato** (Spanish), **undercover man** and **willie**.

SPECIFIC TERMS

There are a wide selection of specific homosexual types, all of whom have gained their own particular title. They include **auntie, chickenhawk, chicken queen, dirty dowager, grand duchess, john, mother, mother ga-ga, Mother Superior, your mother** (older men); **belle, bronco, butterbox, chicken, cornflakes, daughter, debutante, ga-ga, lamb, pogue, poggler, tender box, tail,** (novice or youngster); **husband, pitcher** ('masculine' homosexual); **bitch, wife, catcher** ('feminine' homosexual); **peek freak, peer queer, watch queen** (voyeur); **cousin, gazooney, possesh** (older man's young lover), **show stopper** (a particularly attractive boy); **body lover** (homosexual frotteur), **rim queen** (one who practices anilingus); **top man, bottom man** (the dominant and passive partners in a sado-masochistic couple), **privy queen, tearoom queen** (one who solicits in lavatories): **body queen** (one who prefers body-builders); **ill piece** (an unattractive man).

Brilliant (an ostentatious queen); **drag-queen** (one who dresses as a woman), **oncer** (promiscuous male, never repeating a partner); **uniforms** (members of the armed or uniformed services); **sea food** (sailors); **rough trade** (genuine or fantasising 'proletarian' sexual partners); **size queen** (one who prefers large penises); **golden shower queen** (one who enjoys urolagnia); **toe queen** (foot fetishist), **felch queen** (scatophiliac); **angel with a dirty face** (one who dare not reveal his homsexuality); **breeders** (married homosexuals who father children); **kid simple, pee-pee lover** (one who prefers very young boys); **jam fag** (one who is devoted only to sex); **sister-act** (a homosexual couple, or a homsexual man copulating with a heterosexual woman); **payoff queen** (one who prefers to pay for sex); **jam** and **straight** (a non-homosexual male); **pretender to the throne** (one who poses as homosexual for his own purposes).

GAY SEXUALITY

Aside from the many terms that simply mean homosexual, or which specify one's preferred activities, slang offers a number of words dealing phrases with varieties of gay sexuality. The majority come from the American gay sub-culture that existed pre-GLF.

These include **debut** (one's first gay experience); **mother-love** (a gay man's relationship with a heterosexual woman); the **bambi effect** (for a young gay male to turn to heterosexuality); **squelching** (sex without affection). To hide one's homosexuality is to **pass**, to **stay in the closet**, or to **wear a mourning veil**. To **wear a cut-glass veil** is to fail to hide one's homosexuality. To **lose one's gender** is to abandon homo- for heterosexuality.

To become homosexual is to **turn the corner** while to reveal one's homosexuality is to **come out**, to **discover one's gender**, **drop one's beads**, **drop one's hairpins**, **lay it out**, **learn a new way**, **wear one's badge**; to be **brought out** is to be initiated into the gay life, while to **out** is to reveal another person's homosexuality, especially if that person does not wish it. Decades of persecution underpin **turn the tables**: for a homosexual to blackmail a heterosexual. A more literal self-revelation, that of the genitals, is to **take one's meat out of the basket**.

VENEREAL DISEASES

GONORRHOEA

For three and a half centuries, from its coinage in the 16C to the onset of Victorian verbal prudery in the mid-19C **clap**, meaning venereal disease in general, but gonorrhoea in particular, was SE. Henceforth it entered the realms of the taboo, where it has remained. Of uncertain origin, **clap** is believed to have come from the Old French *clapoir*, meaning bubo, and thus **clapoire** or **clapier**: a place of debauchery and the illness one can contract there. It remains the most widely used of all VD-related terms.

Other include **cold in the dong** (20C, possibly punning on 'cold in de dose'), and the rhy. sl. **horse** (19C, **horse and trap**, although **horse** can also mean **crap**★: excrement). Other general terms include **noli-me-tangere**, (Scotland 17C, from the Latin: 'don't touch me'), the 18C **haddums**, an abbreviation of the punning phrase 'been at had 'em and come home by Clapham' (18C), **Venus' curse**, (19C), the **whites** (a vaginal discharge), **nine day blues** (20C, incubation period for gonorrhoea) and **blueballs** (testicular swelling, usually attributed to sexual frustration, but here as disease). A case of gonorrhoea is a **dose** or a **load** (both 19C).

The primary symptom of gonorrhoea in men is the pus-like discharge. **Gleet**, redolent of almost onomatopoeic imagery, has existed as its slang description since the 18C. Like **clap**, it comes from Old French, in this case *glette*, meaning slime, filth, purulent matter; according to John Palsgrave (d. 1535) in his *L'Esclarcissment de la Langue Francoyse* (1530) the 'frothe of an egge' or 'gelly of any thyng that congeleth'. Similar terms include **the drip**, **dripsy** or **dripper** (17C) **the stick**, (1880, either from the stickiness of the discharge or **stick**★: the penis).

Aside from the discharge, gonorrhoea hurts. This pain, or aching, has created a number of other terms: the **Barnwell ague**, (17C), **winter coals**, (19C, which keep one 'hot' even on a cold day)', **Covent Garden** and **Drury Lane ague** (17C) and (**Covent**) **Garden gout** (19C). **Crinkum** and **crinkums** (1618, also found as **grincombe**) come from the SE term for anything full of twists and turns; 18C slang also has **crinkum-crankum** as the vagina. Pain is also underlined in **fire** and **flame** (19C), as well as the **glimmer** and the **glim** (19C, both from the old cant **glim**: fire); finally **goodyear** (17C) possibly comes from *gouge*: a soldier's drab.

SYPHILIS

Although it is commonly used to denote any form of venereal disease, **pox** (16C) should properly be applied only to syphilis, a disease characterized by 'pocks' or eruptive pustules on the skin. Like clap it survived as SE until the onset of verbal prudery, in **pox's** case somewhat earlier, in the 18C, since when it has been off-limits in 'polite' speech and writing. Nonetheless like **clap** once again, it has lasted the linguistic and historical course, engendering on its way a variety of combinations such as **pox doctor** (20C, venere-alogist), **poxed** (17C, diseased), **poxy** (20C, in which the disease element is lost to a more general perjorative); **got up like a pox-doctor's clerk** (20C) means dressed nattily but in poor taste. The exclamations **Pox on't!** and **Pox take you!** can be found in Shakespeare; they too joined the world of taboo by the mid-18C.

The pox, perhaps due to its virulence and the concomitant need to blame it on some external agency, threw up a number of national names. First come the 16C **Spanish needle**, **Spanish pox**, **Spanish gout**, reflecting the role of Spain as the current national enemy; by the 18C Spain had been replaced by France, thus generating such terms as **Frenchman**, **French crown**, **French goods**, **French gout**, **malady of France**, **French pox**, **French disease** and **French pig** (a bubo). **Frenchified** (17C) meant diseased, and **knocked with a French faggot** described one whose nose had been lost through the disease. The **Naples canker** gives the nod to Italy, never an enemy but, like France, envisaged as an exotic – hence 'dirty' – land. Only the **Scotch fiddle** (17C) remains something of an anomaly. **Pox** has created three examples of rhyming slang: **band in the box** (20C), **Nervo and Knox** (two members of Crazy Gang, music hall stars of the 1930s and 1940s), and **jack** (Aus., fr. **jack-in-the-box**).

Other terms for syphilis include **scabbado** (17C, an Spanish-ised version of SE *scab*), **measles** (20C), **the pip** (16C, Philip Stubbes, the Puritan pamphleteer warned in his *Anatamy of Abuses* [1583] 'Beware the Spanish pip'), **syph**, **sypho** (Aus.). A case of both syphilis and gonorrhoea is a **full house** or a **double event**.

The pox or pocks themselves, the venereal bubos, have their own lexicon. Terms include the **marbles**, (19C, possibly from the French *morbilles*: small blisters), the **French pig**, the **Winchester goose** (16C, the popular brothels of Southwark came under the jurisdiction of the Bishop of Winchester), **scalder**, **shanker** (chan-cre), **blue boar**, (18C, possibly from the Blue Boar Tavern, sited in London's red light district) and **blue boy** (18C).

To BE INFECTED

Terms for having contracted VD include **jacked up** (20C Aus. from **jack in the box**), to be **one of the knights** (20C, gay use), to **cop a dose** or get **dosed up** (20C), to **piss broken glass**, to **ride the silver steed** and to **take the bayonet course** (all 20C), all of which imply the pain involved, as do the 19C to be **burned**, to **pass through the fire**, to be **hot**, to **burn one's poker** and to be **in for the plate and win the heat**. A **fireship** (17C) is a diseased whore, while a **fireplug** (19C) is an afflicted young man.

To give someone else the disease is to **tip the token** (18C, *token* meaning a sign of disease, *tokens* being SE for plague) and to **burn** (16C). Those who suffered took a cure of **blue butter** (mercurial ointment) at the **powdering tub** or at **Mother Cornelius' tub**. This name of this tub, literally the tub in which the flesh of dead animals was pickled or 'powdered', was extended to the sweating tub used in the 16C for the cure of venereal disease.

MASTURBATION

'The good thing about masturbation', the writer Truman Capote once observed, 'is that you don't have to dress up for it.' And however strident and minatory the threats against what was once dismissed as 'self-pollution', it remains a primary human sexual activity. And as in the case of all such activities, the slang terminology is legion. It also, as in so many sexual activities, appears linguistically as an almost unreservedly male activity. This is surely speciousbut slang, echoing Queen Victoria's alleged refusal to acknowledge the existence of lesbians, persists in its blinkered ways.

MASTURBATION

Aside from the present participle forms such as **jerking off**, **tossing off** and many others – the relevant verbs can found below – there are a number nouns for masturbation.

The baldest is probably **hand job** (20C), although, like **finger-fucking** and **touching up** (when the object is a woman) the implication is of a second person, administering the relevant stimulation. The verbs to **milk** and to **fetch mettle** (both 17C, fr. **mettle**: semen, 'the mettle of generation') have the same image of mutual, rather than solitary pleasure. **Hand shandy** and **hand-gallop**, however, are more personal, as are **jerking the gherkin** (one of a number of variations on **jerk off**, q.v.) and the **j/o** (fr. **jerk off**) **scene**. The **lonely art** (20C) and the **soldier's joy** (19C, otherwise describing, in the Royal Navy, pease pudding) underline the assumption that most masturbation is a solitary pleasure. Solo performance further points up the **one-legged race**, **one off the wrist** and **one-stick drum improvisation**, while there is a certain literary tone to **Onan's Olympics**, based on the story of Onan, who 'cast his seed upon the ground' (*Genesis* xxxviii.9). **Pocket pool** is sporting, and as such linked with variations on **play with oneself***, while **slaking the bacon** and **whizzing the jizzum** (fr. **jizzum**: semen) are unashamedly auto-erotic. **Paw-paw tricks** (which one 'plays') come from the 19C **paw-paw** meaning naughty (with its image of pawing the sought-after person), while the racial stereotype of mean-ness gives the **Dutch husband** or **Dutch wife**.

Rhyming slang offers four popular terms: **J. Arthur** (fr. J Arthur Rank [1888-1972], the flour magnate turned movie mogul), **Levy** (fr. Levy and Franks, the firm of restaurant and pub proprietors), **Jodrell** (Jodrell Bank) and **Barclay's** (Barclay's Bank). All rhyme with what, in the UK at least, is the best known term for masturbation: **wank**, originally spelt **whank** and dating to c.1870. Its etymology remains frustratingly mysterious: the best guess would appear to be echoic. Finally the hand, usually essential to the activity, is personified as **Five-Finger Mary**, the **five-fingered** or **dry-mouthed widow**, **four sisters on Thumb Street**, **Lady Five Fingers**, **mother fist and her five daughters**, **Mrs. Palm and her five daughters**, **Rosy Palm and her five little sisters** and **Miss Fist**. The only exception to this feminine parade is a **corporal and four** (19C, the thumb and four fingers, which one 'mounts', as in mounting a guard).

Finally mutual masturbation is either a **circle jerk** or **playing chopsticks**.

To Masturbate

The essence of masturbation is rubbing, and it is logical that the earliest slang for the verb to masturbate is **frig** (16C, from the Latin *fricare*: to rub). **Friggle** is a defunct 19C version; **frig** itself has survived but almost invariably as a euphemism for **fuck***, thus frigging around, etc. **Rub up**, (19C) is a direct descendent, while **diddle** (19C) is cognate with **fiddle**.

Given the supposedly pleasurable, but for many years vilified outcome of masturbation, one can but assume that deep-rooted guilt lies behind the violence of so many of the images that are conferred upon its slang synonyms. **Bob**, (19C) has roots in a variety of dialect terms meaning variously to hit or strike lightly; to poke or push through or, in the sort of pun that emerges so regularly in 19C slang, to toss. **Claw** (19C) usually means to beat while **shag** (19C, now meaning only to copulate) means shake and the 'dash' in **dash one's doodle** (19C, thus **doodle-dasher**: masturbator) is the same 13C SE term that means to smash violently or to break in pieces.

There are whole groups of violent combinations, all banging, flogging, pounding, pulling and the like. Among them are **bang the bishop** (19C, Partridge suggests from the resemblance of the penis to a mitre, or to the eponymous chess piece), **beat one's little brother**, **belt one's hog**, **flog one's mutton**, **flog the dolphin**, **flog the bishop**, **flog the dog**, **flog the log**, **hack one's mack**, **beat off**, **beat one's dummy**, **beat one's hog**, **beat one's meat**, **slam one's hammer**, **slam one's Spam**, **slap one's wapper**, **spank the monkey**, **spank the salami**, **whip it**, **whip one's dripper** and **whip one's wire**. Equally aggressive are **choke the chicken** or **choke the chook** (both 20C Aus.), **pound one's pork**, **pound one's pud**, **pound one's flounder**, **pull one's joint**, **pull one's pud** or **pudding**, **pull one's taffy**, **pull one's wire**, **pull about** (all 19C), **pull the pope**, **thump one's pumper**, **wonk one's conker**, **yang one's wang**, **yank**

the yam and **yank one's crank.** Best-known of all, coined in the 18C and now the US equivalent of the British **wank,** is **jerk** or **jerk off,** with such combinations as **jerk one's jelly** or **jerk one's juice** (18C), **jerk one's mutton** and **jerk one's turkey** (19C) and the 20C **consult Dr. Jerkoff.**

The assonance that permeates a number of those terms is found again in the less violent **crank one's shank, dinky one's slinky, file one's fun-rod, fist one's mister, flex one's sex, flick one's bic** (AA), **hump one's hose, please one's pisser, prompt one's porpoise** (and **wax one's dolphin**), **prime one's pump, tickle one's pickle** and **feel in one's pocket for one's big hairy rocket.** The well-known **toss oneself off** (18C) gives a number of similar 'off' phrases: **work oneself off** (16C), and various 19C coinages: **get one's nuts off, jack off, jerk off, do oneself off, play off, rub off, whip off, whack off, flip oneself off** (Aus., thus **flipwreck**: one who supposedly masturbates to insanity), **pump off** or **work off. Bring up** or **bring off by hand** are both 16C, possibly only in a transitive sense, i.e. exciting a partner.

The auto-erotic aspects of masturbation, all of which are essentially developments of **play off** (18C) and its descendent **play with oneself** (19C), give a wide range of images. Playing gives **play pocket billiards** or **pocket pool, play the male organ** and **play a flute solo on one's meat whistle. Lark** (19C) is a slang synonym for **play,** just as it is an SE one. Among the wide range of synonyms are **clean one's rifle, grease one's pipe, unclog the pipes, polish one's sword, shine one's pole, run one's hand up the flagpole, varnish one's pole, do a dry waltz with oneself, haul one's own ashes** (fr. 20C **get one's ashes hauled,** to have sex; ashes is presumably fr. **ass★**), **milk the chicken** (cf. **choke the chook**), **paint one's ceiling, fight one's turkey** (cf. **turkey neck★**: penis), **fuck one's fist** and **fist-fuck** (cf. the 20C gay use), **mess about** (19C, usually as take liberties with), **sling one's jelly** or **sling one's juice** (19C), **burp the worm, butter one's corn, strike the pink match, prompt one's porpoise, prime one's pump, prune the fifth limb, point one's social finger, shoot the tadpoles** (fr. the tadpole-like sperms), **stir one's stew, stroke one's beef, stroke one's**

poker, stroke the dog, twang one's wire and **tweak one's twinkie**.

Less personal are **box the Jesuit and get cockroaches** or **eat cockroaches** (16C, mixing a pun on **cock***: penis with a general loathing of Jesuits), **shake hands with the wife's best friend, sew** (20C AA, cf. 18C **needle*** meaning penis), **shake hands with the guy who stood up when I got married, handle** (19C), **keep down the census** (19C, also meaning abort) **walk the dog** and **watch the eyelid movies** (fr. one's masturbation fantasies).

As suggested above, slang barely acknowledges female masturbation, but there is a small lexicon. Once again, violence underpins many of the terms. The 19C has **digitate** (19C, cf. **finger-fuck**) and **tickle one's crack** (19C). Contemporary terms include **beat the beaver (beaver***: vagina), **buttonhole, clap one's clit, cook cucumbers, grease the gash, hide the hot dog** (cf. **hide the salami***: copulation), **hit the slit (slit***: vagina), **hose one's hole, make waves, pet the poodle, slam the clam** and **stump-jump**. To **catch a buzz** is to masturbate with a vibrator.

PROSTITUTION

Neither *prostitute* (fr. the Latin *prostituere*: to place before, expose publicly, offer for sale) nor *whore* (fr. a variety of north European languages in which the cognate terms mean adulterer, and before that from an Indo-European root *qar-* which can also be found in the Latin *carus*: dear, the Old Irish *cara*: friend and the Lettish *kars*: lascivious) were ever slang. But the 'oldest profession' (coined by Kipling as 'the most ancient' profession in 1888) has accrued a wide slang vocabulary over the years and given its near-taboo status, virtually every other word allied to the job is.

THE SIXTEENTH CENTURY

The first use of **bitch** (a female dog since 1000) as a derogatory term appears c.1400 and as such it was swiftly extended to meaning a whore; that meaning clung for two centuries, returning to a merely generalised slur c.1600. Only in the US pimp culture does it still mean whore. **Baggage**, first used in this context by Shakespeare in *The Taming of the Shrew* (1596) followed a similar course; twenty years later, in Middleton's play *A Chaste Maid in Cheapside* it meant merely a saucy young women. Another Shakespearian term was **filth** (the 17C has **fen**, with similarly rank overtones), and equally antagonistic synonyms included **puttock** (SE: a bird of prey, the kite or buzzard; the 18C offers the similar **carrion**), the **barber's chair** (fr. the phrase 'common as a barber's chair', and an antecedent of the modern **town bike**), a **barrack hack** (available to anyone who wishes to 'ride') a precursor of the 19C **garrison hack** (although this also meant no more than a regular attender at military balls), a **hobby horse** (which is 'ridden') and the coldly disinterested **commodity** (which prefigures the 19C **article**). A **hilding** came from the SE meaning a contemptible, worthless person of either sex; a good-for-nothing.

Other general terms include **hedge-creeper** (a low whore, from **hedge**: a generic term for inferior, dirty), **jay**, **kat** or **kate** (Scots dial.), **ladybird** (**bird** as whore resurfaced briefly in the late 19C but only the general meaning, woman, has lasted, especially as revived in the 1960s). A **mermaid** referred to the sirens of Greek myth, beckoning men to their doom, **Maid Marian** came from the Morris dancing tradition of having that character played by a local strumpet, and an **occupant** worked in an **occupying house*** or brothel. The use of **punk** as whore is the first ever use of the word in English; it appears in 1596, in *Wits Miserie and the Worlds Madnesse: Discovering the Devils Incarnat of this Age* by Thomas Lodge (1558-1625). Staunchly defiant of any etymology is **skainsmate**. Used in *Romeo and Juliet*: 'Scurvie knave I am none of his flurt-gils I am none of his skaines mates' the context seems to indicate a prostitute, but the cautious *OED* admits only 'origin and exact meaning uncertain.' One interpretation might be **skain** means *skein*, as in skein of thread or wool, and thus relates to the 'sewing' imagery of intercourse (cf. **needle woman***).

The close relations between criminal vagabonds and the whores who accompanied them gives a number of terms: the **autem mort** accompanied a **ruffler*** or an **upright man***; from **autem***: church and thus, if only in name, a 'married' woman), **doxy** probably came from the Dutch *docke*: a doll, a **bawdy basket** doubled as a hawker of obscene literature, a **trull** (fr. the synonymous Ger. *trulle*) almost immediately entered SE. **Mort** or **mot** meant both woman in general and whore; it came either from the Dutch *mot-huys*: a brothel (lit. woman house), but later claims associate it with the French *amourette*: little girlfriend; a **walking mort** was a tramp's companion who often worked as a whore.

Mutton (which gained the additional meaning of copulation and of the female genitals) and **laced mutton** both meant whore, leading to the 18C **old ewe dressed as lamb** and the 19C **mutton dressed as lamb**; the **mutton walk** was the junction of Coventry Street and Windmill Street in the West End of London — a crossroads well-known for its whores; a **twigger**, from SE meaning a vigorous and prolific breeder, a term originally used of a ewe. A young or even virgin whore was a **dell** (who became a **doxy** once she had been broken in, often by her first lover and exploiter, the **upright man***), while the **green goose** was young and innocent and the **puzzle** came from the French *pucelle*: a virgin. A **guineahen** punned on the girl's price as did **hackney** from the 14C hackney horse which, like its namesake, was available for hire. Other terms originated in clothes: a **stammel** or **strammel** was defined as a lusty strapping wench, especially one who wore a stammel: a coarse woolen petticoat, **white apron** referred to the garment that for a while was a 16C whore's 'uniform' (the 17C had the similar **waistcoateer**) and **tiffity-taffety** to tiffany and taffeta, transparent silks used for dresses. A **loose bodied gown** referred both to the garment and to the **loose coat game**: copulation.

Finally come terms which while in context mean whore, may also, with that prejudice which, far from abated, still confuses the self-determined woman with a tart, simply mean an independent woman: **lioness, polecat** (referring both to the notoriously aggressive animal and to **pole***: the penis), a **ramp** or **rampager** (fr. **rampant**: exhibiting fierceness or high spirits), **randy-dandy** or **ranty-tanty** (fr. **rant**: a spree and thus giving **on the ran-dan**: out on a spree and **randy**: sexually excited), a **rude girl** (where rude means boisterous; some four centuries before its modern, Black use) and a **Shoreditch fury** (fr. a tough area of London).

THE SEVENTEENTH CENTURY

If Shoreditch was London's centre for whoring in the 16C, then Bankside in Southwark had joined it by the 17th and a **Bankside lady** was now a prostitute. Indeed its reputation went back much further, as Weinreb and Hibbert characterise it in their *London Encyclopedia* (1983) 'with its numerous brothels and bear-baiting, the area...was for long one of medieval London's main centres of dissipation.' Also known as Stew's Bank (fr. **stew★**: a brothel) it contained an unconsecrated graveyard where the corpses of the hapless whores were unceremoniously deposited. Under the jurisdiction of the Bishops of Winchester (thus **Winchester goose★**: venereal disease), Bankside was, but for a brief period of morality and temporary closure under Henry VIII c.1546, London's leading 'red-light area'. It lasted as such until the 18C when the game moved to Covent Garden and the 19th when the Haymarket became whoring's HQ. Another geographical label is **Whetstone Park deer** or **Whetstone Park mutton**; the term comes from Whetstones Lane which ran between Holborn and Lincoln's Inn Fields and was 'famed for a nest of wenches'. The whore, or at least the promiscuous young woman as a **deer** persists into the 19C when it can be found in *The Adventures of Mr Verdant Green* (1853). Another animal is the **bat**, giving the 19C **on the batter**: working as a prostitute, and derived from the image of whores plying for trade like bats fluttering in the twilight. A **Spital whore** referred both to Spitalfields, another tough East End area, and to SE *spital*: a hospital, thus underlining the physical perils of whoring. A **Scotch warming pan** was an obliging chambermaid.

17C terms are many and varied. **Buttock**, a prostitute, gives a number of combinations: the **buttock and twang** or **buttock and file** (a whore and pickpocket team), the **buttock broker**: a brothel keeper, and **going buttocking** or **buttock-banqueting** is working as a whore; a **buttock and tongue** is a shrewish woman and a **buttock-ball** is either a dance attended by whores or sexual intercourse. **Blowze** and **bloss** both began as meaning a beggar's companion, and generate the 18C **blouzalinda** and **blouzabella**; **blowen** comes from the Romany *beluñi*: a sister in debauchery, while **blower**, with similar roots and equally derogatory, is the specific opposite of the complimentary **jomer**: a girlfriend (either from Romany or Parlyaree). More foreign origins can be found in **bona** and **bona roba** (fr. the Ital: a fine dress), a **Dutch widow** (17C), a **vroe** or **vrow**, which becomes **froe** in the 18C (all from the Dutch *vrouw*: a woman), a **case vrow** (either fr. **pintle-case***: vagina or **casa**: house, thus giving the phrase **go case with**: to have a relationship), the euphemistic **quaedam** (Latin: a certain woman) and **quicumque vult** (Latin: whomsoever wants) and the **scolopendra** or its anglicised peer the **stingtail**; both terms originating in the sting in a scorpion's tail; as defined in the *OED's* 17C citation the scolopendra was 'A fabulous sea-fish which feeling himselfe taken with a hooke casteth out his bowels vntill hee hath vnloosed the hooke and then swalloweth them vp againe'. The 18C **cockatrice** continues the association; the mythical cockatrice (first used in the 14C) being a serpent identified with the basilisk and said to kill by its mere glance and to be hatched from a cock's egg. The possibility of such a 'sting' was underlined in **fireship** (a diseased whore) although **brimstone** simply meant 'hot stuff'.

Further synonyms include **dolly**, a development of the 16C **doll**, and a forerunner of the 19C **dollymop** (an 'amateur', often a milliner or 'governess') and the 20C **dolly** or **dollybird** (to neither of whom prostitution was imputed); **rig**, **rig-mutton** and **rigsby**, **gamester** and **wench of the game** (thus the 19C **on the game**, which can also mean thieving), **bobtail**, **brown Bessie** (later, perhaps by association, a musket, otherwise known as the 'soldier's best friend'), **bulker** (a low harlot who sleeps on a heap or **bulk**) **buss beggar** (fr. **buss**: kiss), **carry knave**, **light lady**, **light frigate** (punning on **frig**: to copulate), **pinnace** (fr. SE: a light vessel in attendance on a larger one) and **land carrack** (fr. SE *carrack*: a large ship), **flesh broker** and **flesh peddler** (the terms also meant marriage broker; thus the **spiritual flesh-broker**: a parson) and a **she-napper**. Proper names give **nanny** (a popular name), **florence** (fr. Northants. dial: one who dresses untidily), **Madame**

Van (perhaps an actual madame or brothel-owner), **maux** or **mawkes**, both of which derive from **malkin**, itself a variation on Matilda, the ironic **Puritan** or **pure** (the 18C has **impure**), a **common Jack** or **common sewer**, and **flirt-gill** or **gill-flirt** (fr. **gill**: a wanton wench), and the 19C **Flirtina Cop-all**. **Placket-lady** refers to **placket★**: vagina, thus giving **placket-stung**: venereally diseased; an **open-arse** was originally a medlar, **trillbye** comes from **trill**: the anus and **treddle** from tread: to have intercourse; **niggler** is based in **niggle**, also meaning to copulate.

The earlier **commodity** is echoed in **convenient**, **natural** and its converse **peculiar**; **crack** refers to the vagina and **tit** or **willing tit** to the breasts; **prugge** is possibly based on **prig**, in its meaning of haggling over a price. A **fling-dust** is a street walker as is a **girl about town**; a **suburban** or **suburban wench** plies the **suburb trade** (see Brothel for further combinations); **light o'love** was euphemistic, **miss** verged on SE, **mob** came from the 16C SE *mab*: a slattern, **moll**, **molly** and **mollisher** prefigure the 20C US **gangster's moll** (although whoring was no longer directly implied); **pug** is possibly a development of **punk★**, **soss-brangle** comes fr. **soss**: a slut, **tweak** is from the SE to twitch, and **trug** and **trugmoldy** are linked to **trugging house**: a brothel.

THE EIGHTEENTH CENTURY

Whoredom had shifted its focus by the 18C, moving north across the river from Bankside and centring on Covent Garden and adjacent areas of the City and West End. Thus the **Covent Garden nun** and the 19C **Covent Garden lady**, the **market dame** (referring both to her 'wares'; and presumably to her pitch at Covent Garden market), a **Drury Lane vestal**, a **Fleet Street dove** or **Fleet Street houri**, a **Fulham virgin** and, as a general term, **Haymarket ware**. The 19C added **St John's Wood vestal**, referring to the north London suburb where so many gentlemen established their mistresses. **Tail**, meaning the vagina (although it could also mean the penis and the buttocks) which has already been found in **bobtail**, reappears in **bangtail** (still current among US Blacks), **tickletail**, **wagtail** and **flashtail** and the 19C **cocktail**; a

squirrel was so-called because, according to Grose 'like that animal she covers her back with her tail' and nature also appears in **tib** (also a generic term for women, the opposite of the male **Tom** and as **tib of the buttery★**: a goose; cf. **green goose★**), the game birds (possibly an unconscious pun on the game: prostitution) a **partridge**, a **plover**, a **pheasant** and a **quail**; plus a **canary** or **canary-bird**; a **game pullet** was a young whore, although the contemporary 'Game Chicken' was the prizefighter Harry Pearce, the **lady of the lake** or **laker lady** appears 'natural' but in fact reflects the theatrical slang **lake**: to play amorously (probably from **lark**); a **star gazer** like a **hedge whore★** lay on her back in the open air; a **dragon** referred to St George's vanquished opponent, although it also punned on **ride a St George**: for the woman to mount the man, as does **rantipole**, which echoes the phrase **ride a rantipole**, meaning the same thing.

An **abbess** and **presbyteress** both ran brothels, while a **nun** worked there; although **nunnery** is used in *Hamlet*, two centuries earlier and the term may thus possess a far older, if undocumented pedigree. An **academician** also worked in a brothel or **academy**; a term later extended to mean a thieves' kitchen. Other 18C terms include the **demi-rep** or the 19C **demi-mondaine**, a relatively classy whore, and a figure defined by Henry Fielding in *Tom Jones* (1749) as one 'whom everybody knows to be what nobody calls her'; **rep** itself was an abbreviation (as it is today in street gang usage) of *reputation*, although some have suggested the word thus shortened is *reprobate*.

Drap comes from the SE *drab*: a slattern; the term is linked to the synonymous Irish *drabog* or Gaelic *drabag* but there is no hard evidence as to which influenced which; it may also be linked to Low German *drabbe*: dirt. Dirtiness also underpins **bunter**, originally a woman who scavenged for rags in the street; and latterly used as a general term of contempt. A **jack-whore** was big and tough while a **piece** (still extant although with no obvious inference of whoring) gives the doubly punning toast: 'May we never have a peace that will injure the Constitution'. A **rainbow** dressed in brightly variegated colours, a **dasher** was a flashy whore while a **wife in water colours** derived either from the image of colours fading as do the passions of the newly married or from the idea that the loving (if hired) whore was less strident than an intolerant harridan of a wife. A **dopey** was a contemporary version of the beggar's **trull★**, the **piper's wife** was Scottish while the **public ledger** was 'open to all parties', a **strum** either abbreviated strumpet or referred to the strumming of a tune or playing of an 'instrument'; a **woman of all work** was servant who could be seduced, while the **woman of pleasure** or **woman of the town** was a whore pure and simple, as was the **giglot, giggler** or **goglet**, the **good girl** and the **easy virgin** or **easy virtue** (fr. **easy**: compliant). A **wriggler** was linked to the **wriggling pole★**: a penis and the verb to **wriggle navels★**: to have intercourse; **necessary** in the plural meant the genitals while **one of my cousins** and **one of them** (subsequently used to imply homosexuality) were strictly euphemistic.

THE NINETEENTH CENTURY

Classical allusions pervade 19C language, and the slang is no exception. Euphemisms for prostitutes include **Thais, Phrynne** (a 4CBC *hetaera* or courtesan) and Aspasia (19C, the 5CBC mistress of Pericles and a friend of Socrates); **cyprian**, meaning literally belonging to Cyprus, refers to the island's worship of the goddess of love Aphrodite or Venus while **paphian** recalls Paphos, the city in south-western Cyprus, where it is claimed that Aphrodite was born; **dromaky** (Northern dial.) comes from Andromache, wife of the Trojan hero Hector, and referred to the poor reputation of the travelling actresses who played her in Euripedes' eponymous play, while, still in the theatre, the use of **Hector** to mean pimp underlines the image; **Columbine** is Harlequin's mistress. Similarly euphemistic, if not so literary are **laundress**, a **perfect lady** or a **real lady**, a **summer cabbage** (one picks it when it is young; the term also meant umbrella or parasol), a **soiled dove** and an **unfortunate**, a term that may well be based in a misreading of Thomas Hood's poem 'The Bridge of Sighs': 'One more unfortunate/weary of breath/rashly importunate/gone to her death'. A **Pickthatch vestal** recalls the 16C **go to the Manor of Picked**

Hatch or **go to Picket-Hatch Grange**, itself referring to the pickt hatch or a hatch with pikes, commonly used as a brothel-sign. The original such address was a tavern-cum-brothel in Turnmill Street, Clerkenwell. Similar term are to **go to (Saint) Paul's** or to **go to Westminster for a wife**.

Clothing informs such terms as the **dress-lodger** who is dressed in finery by her landlady and repays the favour by walking the streets and turning over her profits; a **cotton top** attempted to present a respectable image despite her actual profession; the term refers to a particular type of stockings of which the lower, visible portion was silk, but the remainder was cheaper cotton; a **bit of muslin**, a **bit of stuff**, a **bit of fluff**, a **bit of fish**, a **bit of calico** and a **bit of skirt** all meant a whore; other clothes-related terms were **flash piece**, **flash mollisher**, **flash girl** and **flash moll** (all meaning a showy dresser), **lift skirts** or **light skirts**, a **needle-woman** (fr. **needle***: penis) and **sempstress**; **smock-servant**, **smock-agent** and **smock-piece** are all based on **smock**, generic for female debauchery; thus **smock-alley**: the vagina.

Military life gives the **ammunition wife** (who was 'hot stuff', as is a **warm 'un**; an **ammunition leg** was a wooden leg), a **brevet wife** (punning on the SE *brevet*: an acting unpaid rank); a **double-barrelled gun** and a **fore and after** prefigured the 20C **two-way girl**: in all cases describing a girl who was agreeable to group sex, involving vaginal (**fore**) and anal (**aft**) intercourse. **Twofer** appears to be similar, possibly 'two for the price of one'. Street walkers numbered among them the **cruiser**, the **hunt-about**, the **sparrow** (who does a 'flutter', cf. **bat**) the **curbstone sailor**, the **flagger** and the **flag-about** (fr. **flag**: pavement); **noffgur** came from the Yiddish *nafka*, which in turn came from an Aramaic term meaning street-walker. Like the **barrack hack** anyone could 'ride' an **omnibus**, while the older **guineahen** had become the **onicker** (fr. the price: one **nicker***: one pound); a **threepenny uprighter** is notably further down the market, a **cab moll** either works literally in cabs and trains or possibly from a cab: a brothel; the **lone duck** or **quiet mouse** is a brothel prostitute, as is a **panel**, **parnel** or **tender parnel** (all from the **panel house***: a brothel where customers are robbed). **Mrs Lukey Props** was either a tramps' companion or a madame, while **hooker**, one of the longest lasting of all such terms, comes from New York City's 19C brothel area, Corlear's Hook. Night-workers include the **flybynight**, **moon-lighter** (a good century prior to its current use, shorn of sexual overtones, but still smacking of illegality), the **nightingale**, **noc-tress**, **nocturne**, **night-bird**, **night-cap**, **night-shade**, **night poacher**, **night-snap**, **night-trader** and **night-walker**; the **owl** comes out at night as does the **evening star**. **Pross** or **prossy** is the most obvious of abbreviations and **rory**, from **Rory O'Moore**: whore; it could also mean a floor.

Terms alluding to the genitals include **pinch-prick**, **pinch bottom**, **pintle-bit**, **pintle fancier**, **pintle maid** and **pintle ranger** (all from **pintle***: prick), **pole-climber** and **prick-climb-er**, **rabbit pie** (fr. **rabbit** or **live rabbit**: the penis; thus the **rabbit-pie shifter**: a policeman), **foreskin hunter**, **receiver general** (punning on the official title of the receiver of public revenues), **rigol** (fr. SE *rigol*: a watercourse or furrow and thus the vagina), **shake** and **shake-bag** (possibly fr. **shag*** and also meaning vagina), **split arse mechanic** (cf. **open-arse**), **split mutton** (cf. **mutton**), **treble cleft** (fr. female physiology), **bum-worker**, **holer** (fr. the 13-15C *holour*: a fornicator or whoremonger and as such applied to men only), **nestcock** and **nestlecock** (fr. **nest**: vagina). **Tail**, **tailist**, **tail-trader**, **tail-worker**, and the punning **tenant in tail** all refer to **tail***. **Merry bit**, **merry-arsed Chris-tian** and **merry legs** take the positive view of whoring as do **pleasure-lady** and **pleasure-merchant** and the nautical **Jack's delight** (fr. Jack Tar: a sailor). **Rump** and **screw** are both from verbs meaning to have intercourse while **scrudge** comes from **scrouge** which in turn means squeeze. **Fuckstress** is maximally basic as is **poke**, while **put** is from the French *putain*: a prostitute.

Upper-class terms included the euphemistic **anonyma**, **incog-nita** and **pretty horse breaker** (punning on rider); an **artichoke** was debauched old woman: spiky on the outside but still tasty within, while a **graduate** was 'a spinster skilled in sexual practise' and a **flapper** (the predecessor of the relatively neutral 20C usage) a very young harlot as was a **kid leather** (fr. **kid**: a child and **leather**: vagina; thus **kid stretcher**: a paedophile). A **shoful-pullet** (fr.

shoful★: counterfeit money) is a fake virgin, much prized in contemporary brothels, and a **virgin pullet** is 'a young women who though often trod has never laid' (cf. **tread**). **Burerk** or **burick** comes either from the Romany *burk*: breast or the Scots *bure*: a loose woman; the latter is presumably linked to **bewer** or **buer** (fr. the Shelta term for a girl) although this term has no implications of prostitution. **Chauvering donna** and **chauvering moll** come either from **charver**: to copulate, itself from the Romany *charvo*: to rub, although claims exist for the French *chauffer*: to heat. **Gay girl** or **gay woman** are examples of the earlier, hetersoexual use of **gay★**.

Some form of relationship underpins **pillow-mate**, **ligby** and **loteby** (fr. **lig**: bed, and thus a bedfellow), **palliasse** (fr. the straw bed upon which one lies), **bed-fagot** (cf. **Scots warming pan**), **bed-presser**, **fancy-fagot** and **straw fagot** (all from **faggot**: woman, cf. **baggage**), **poll** and **polly** (fr. Mary = Moll = Poll; thus to **poll up**: to live together) and **spoffskins** (a whore who pretends to temporary marriage). A **Sunday girl** is a weekend mistress (cf: **Sunday man★**, **weekend ho**). Derogatory terms include **wrong 'un**, **badger** (the badger is nocturnal and carnivorous; thus the **badger game**: robbing or blackmailing a client) and **cow**. The **naughty pack** and the synonymous **naughty dickey-bird** are similarly uncomplimentary. **Jam** is short for **jam-tart** and synonymous with **tart**; **sweetmeat** is synonymous.

More 19C terms include a **fly-girl** (fr. **fly**: artful, cunning and streetwise), a **gook** (possibly from **gowk**: a tramp), **hair** (fr. the generic term for women viewed as sex objects, thus the term **hair to sell**: to be willing to offer sex), **hen** or **hen of the game**, **hiver** (US) from the image of whores 'swarming like bees' to the newly settled Western towns, a **hop-picker** or **hopping wife**, a **left-handed wife** ('left' always meaning dubious or illegal), a **jerker** (fr. **jerk**: accost), **jude** or **judy**, **kittie** and **maggie** (all fr. proper names), **kiddley-wink** (the origin of the non-sexual kiddy-wink) a **nit** (Scots dial), a **particular**, a **purse-finder** and a **shikse**, **shakester** or **shickster** (19C, Yid. all from the Yiddish *shikse*, a gentile girl, itself derived from Heb. *sheques*: a blemish).

THE TWENTIETH CENTURY

With **hooker**, still probably the most common name, already a century old, the 20C has relatively few general terms for whore, although the specifics are legion. **Tart, tartlet** and the backslang **trat**, terms which had previously been primarily affectionate, took on a more pejorative meaning; **hooker** was abbreviated to **hook** (US), while the business side of the sex took pride of place with the euphemistic **working girl, pro** (short for professional woman rather than prostitute), **business girl** and the blunter **ass peddler**. Today's *sex industry worker* is merely PC euphemism, not slang. The decline of the brothel and the vast expansion of girls working from their own flats gave **call-girl**. Older terms included **brass**, which stems from the rhy. sl. **brass nail: tail**★, and is still widely used, and the pre-Sexual Offences Act division of **Edies** (working the cheaper areas of London, notably **the Baze** – Bayswater Road – the East End and the railway stations), and the **Toms**, who concentrated on the carriage trade of Mayfair. **Edie** has vanished, although **tom**, now bereft of any class connotations can be found in the Metropolitan Police jargon: the **tom patrol** (surveying and arresting street prostitutes), known in the US as the **pussy posse**.

Australia has offered a number of indigenous terms: **prosso** (using the -o suffix found throughout the nation's slang), **princess** and **pavement princess, charlie** (fr. the rhy. sl. **Charlie Wheeler** = **sheila** = girl), **chromo** and its abbreviations **cro** or **crow**. all of which come in turn from chromolithograph, a picture printed in colour, and thus referring to the prostitute's supposed penchant for an excess of makeup, **grunter** (fr. her –faked –groans of pleasure), **KP** (common prostitute) and **Mallee root** (rhy sl: prostitute; a mallee is small eucalyptus, also found in such phrases as **fit as a Mallee bull**). Afro-Americans have **ho** (the quintessential Black term for whore, a literal transliteration of the way that word is pronounced), **hoowah, stepper** (fr. stepping out), **stick, open game** and, harking back to an earlier era, **bird**.

Other terms, mainly from the US, include a **ragtime girl** (US), on the same lines as **jazz**: sexual intercourse; **shortheels** and **roundheels** (US, although both are equally likely to mean merely promiscuous), a **troll** (cf. **trull★**), a **cruiser**, a **flatbacker** (who only offers missionary position sex), a **kurve** (Yiddish, and thus from Hebrew: a strange woman who approaches too close), **puta** (fr. Spanish), a **short-time girl** and the heavily humorous **industrial debutante** (who specialises in business conventions).

More specific terms cover the part-time or semi-amateur girl: a **B-girl** (fr. bar-girl), a **sitter** (US, who sits in a bar), a **charity moll** (Aus., who 'gives it away'), a **chippy** (19C, possibly fr. 'cheapie'), a **half-brass**, and a **weekend ho**, a **weekend warrior** and a **summertime ho** (all AA; cf. **Sunday girl**, **summer cabbage**). An ageing prostitute is an **old timer** or a **vet** while a worn-out girl is **fleabag** or an **over the hill ho** (AA). An incompetent, who fails to net her share of clients is a **flaky ho**, a **hold-out** (the inference is she is deliberately not trying), a **mudkicker** (otherwise a racehorse that gets stuck in the mud), a **nag** (usually an old horse) and a **slouch**; an **outlaw** is a girl who works without a pimp). For a US pimp an experienced prostitute is his **bottom woman** (the implication is of solidity and dependability; the term echoes the 18C *bottom*), **main bitch**, **star of the line**, **rose among the thorns**, a **share certificate** (an 'investment'), or, to maintain the racetrack imagery, a **thoroughbred**. A girl who robs her clients or, more foolishly, her pimp is a **ginger** (fr. 20C **ginger**: to rob, used by whores since the 1930s) or a **rip-off artist**. Finally an under-age prostitute is a **baby-pro** or **sweetmeat** (cf. 19C use). More recent terms are **pretties** (new young sex objects whether male or female), **twinkies** (also a US sweet) and **chicken** (children ripe for sexual exploitation) and, most chilling of all, **kleenex**: you use them once and throw them away; to **sparrowhawk** is to pick up homeless youngsters (of either sex) for sexual exploitation, typically runaways who have just arrived at rail or bus stations; it comes from the predatory bird of the same name; a **chicken hawk** is an older gay man who prefers sex with teenage or younger boys.

MALE PROSTITUTES

The majority of terms for almost invariably gay male prostitutes either echo their female peers – **call boy**, **puto** – or incorporate a variety of terms meaning penis with those meaning trader or seller – **dick peddler**, **prick peddler**. While the practise of male prostitution is obviously as old as its female equivalent, the image of homosexuality has been (and in many ways remains) such that even slang has steered clear of making reference to it. The main heterosexual term is **gigolo**, formed c.1920 as a masculine version of the French *gigole*: a tall thin woman and hence a woman of the streets or public dance-halls. Such a man, as the *Woman's Home Companion* put it in 1922 was one 'who lives off women's money...a gigolo, definitely speaking, designated one of those incredible and pathetic male creatures, who for ten francs would dance with any woman wishing to dance in the cafs, hotels, and restaurants of France.' From there he moved on to greater intimacies, and would live, a male version of the mistress, on his new friend's money. The **toy–boy** of the 1980s is his descendant.

Otherwise the terms are universally homosexual. Perhaps the definitive reference to money and transience is **rent** (1930s) and its later development, the **rent boy** (1970s). Both terms spring from the 19C **renter**, although such figures were not whores as such, but preferred a more casual relationship, swapping sexual favours for 'presents', whether in cash or kind. Other 'economic' terms include **ass peddler**, **ass pro** (cf. **pro**), **business boy**, **COD** (the punning 'cock on delivery'), **career boy**, **coin collector**, **commercial queer**, **crack salesman**, **pedlar**, **trade** and **working girl**. Sexually descriptive terms include **bird taker** (**bird**: penis), **buff boy** (**buff**: naked), **cocksman** and **cocktail** (cf. female use), **floater** (19C meaning penis, although it might also come from his 'floating around') and **two-way man**. Ambiguous sexuality is underlined by **broad boy** (**broad**: a woman), **he-whore** and **puto** (fr. Spanish, cf. **puta**). Further terms include **bunny**, with its implications of promiscuity (is it only coincidence that the fictional Raffles, the epicine 'Gentleman Cracksman' has as his intimate male companion, one 'Bunny' Manders?), **come-on boy**, **fag★ boy**, **foot soldier**, **goofer** (its etymology is obscure, but there are possibly, punning connections to the early 20C Royal Navy slang **goofer**: a bumboat), **Hollywood hustler** (underlining Middle America's fascination with Hollywood as a modern Babylon),

party boy, **sport** and **sporting goods** (fr. **sport**, a general term for raffish lowlife) and **trabajado** (fr. Spanish: 'worked over'). To work as a male prostitute is to **hawk one's brown** (fr. **brown**: the anus, cf. **Brown family★**, **Browning Family★** etc.) and **peddle one's arse**. A **hand gig** is a male prostitute who masturbates his client or joins in mutual masturbation (**gig** comes presumably from the modern rock n roll meaning of performance, but may be personal, echoing the 17C **gig**: a wanton, flighty girl).

WORKING AS A PROSTITUTE

Those whose profession is prostitution work the **pussy game** or the **game**, indulge in **fancy work** (19C), or go **on the game** or **on the batter**, **on the battle** (Aus.), **on the bottle**, **trolling** or **stepping** (both AA). To be **on the case** is to be earning steadily from one client, the phrase either comes from **go case**: to have a relationship, or from the police-orientated **be on the case**, with image of getting on with a job. To **work the cuts** is to work on the street rather than in a brothel. The prostitute's invitation to a passing client is **wanna do a thing?** or **wanna go out?**. The act of selling one's body is to **hawk one's fork** (Aus., fr. **fork**: crutch), **hawk one's mutton** (19C, **mutton**: vagina) or **hawk one's pearly** (20C); **hawk one's meat**, however, was merely to display one's body, synonymous with the 19C **air the the dairy**: to expose the breasts. **Hook** is the verb form of **hooker★**, **peddle pussy** is self-evident and **sit on one's stuff** and **step** both Afro-American. **Git-down time** is the start of a working day (one 'gits down' to business) and to **break one's luck** is to meet the first client of the day. To **do the milk route** is to tour bus stations or other such places late at night or very early in the morning looking for trade.

The primary US term is to **turn tricks** and **trick** is a central term in US prostitution. It appears to combine the 17C use of **trick** to mean sexual intercourse, and as such paralleled by the contemporary **prank** and **toy** (all found in Shakespeare), with the 19C US cant term meaning a burglary; the original use of **turn a trick** was to accomplish a successful robbery. **Trick** has created a whole mini-vocabulary of its own. A **trick** is not only the sexual encounter but the client as well, thus the abbreviation **TOS** (trick off the street); a **champagne trick** is a generous client, probably a regular one, a **straight trick** requires no 'extras' beyond normal intercourse while a **freak treak** demands a variety of refinements, some of which may be potentially dangerous. A **trick baby** is a prostitute's client-fathered child, a **trick suit** is a dress that can be removed easily and is thus suitable for business and to **beat a trick** is to rob a client. With the advance of the gay subculture into mainstream metropolitan life during the 1970s, **trick** took on a secondary, overtly gay meaning: a trick was a youthful companion, the equivalent, perhaps, of the 19C **renter**.

Earlier, 19C, terms include to **range** (possibly from **ranger**: the penis), to **tread one's shoe awry** (with its respectable opposite, to **tread one's shoe straight**), to **go sparrow-catching**, to **walk the Piazzas** (of Covent Garden), to **take a stone up in the ear** (fr. **stone**: a testicle), to **go on the town** and to **get up to tricks** (tricks used here euphemistically, rather than in the US sense). To **pick up a flat** (fr. **flattie**: a dupe) is to meet a client; to **do a bit of flat** is to have sex. The quasi-amateur status of some 19C whores, typically the **dollymop***, gives the phrase to **work for one's living and do the naughty for one's clothes**. US prostitutes working for a pimp are variously his **flock**, **nest** or **stable**.

PIMPING

THE PIMP

While **pimp** has been SE for probably three centuries now, it started off as a slang term, probably based on the French *pimpreneau*: a scoundrel. Other influential 16C French terms were *pimpant*: alluring or seducing in outward appearance or dress and *pimpesouée*: a pretentious woman. Pimp, however, was soon absorbed into the mainstream language and a wider slang vocabulary took over. **Knight** and **squire**, both of which can be found in a variety of combinations – in all of which they mean simply devotee or practitioner – give **apron-knight**, **apron-squire**, **apple-squire** and **squire of the body**. **Apron**, like **smock**★ means simply woman, albeit with an inference of promiscuity, while **apple**, although debatable, very possibly refers to the female breast. **Monger**, another term implying expertise or at least interest in, gives **apple monger** and **mutton monger** (**mutton**★ meaning vagina). The similar **tug-mutton** can also be found as the root of the Etonian **tug**, meaning colleger or scholar, and comes from the tough meat which was apparently the constant diet of such pupils.

The 17C gives **bully**, a term that for the next two centuries rivalled, if not actually replaced pimp and its peer **ponce** as a term for what SE defined as a *pander*. Its etymology is obscure: possibly coming from the Dutch *boel* meaning a lover (of either sex); the term can also mean brother. There may also be a connection with the German *buhle:* a lover, which can also mean a friend or kinsman. Writing in 1721 the lexicographer Bailey defines **boolie** as beloved, and calls it 'an old word'. While **bully** no longer means pimp, the man's role as the ' heavy' in a brothel is undoubtedly linked to the modern **bouncer** or **bruiser**. Other 17C terms include **brother of the gusset** (**gusset**: vagina), a **led captain** (who could also be a sponger or toady), or a **cock-bawd** (literally a male whore). The 18C adds **captain**, **flash man** (**flash** being a general purpose description used for the criminal underworld) and **pimp whiskin** or **whisking**, meaning a first-rate pimp, although **whisk** usually meant the derogatory whipper snapper).

Of the many abiding myths to be created in modern assessments of the 19C the idea of the paterfamilias at home and the whoremonger abroad remains one of the most potent. Certainly the easy availability of female flesh made 'pay as you play' one of the truest 'Victorian values'. And if prostitutes abounded, so did their pimps.

Pensioner, **cunt-pensioner** and **petticoat pensioner** all came from the French *pensionaire*, meaning lodger. The terms have long vanished, but with another defunct pair, the **pouncey** or **pounceshicer**, they lead on to the far more common, and still extant **ponce**, which would appear to come from the pronunciation of *pensionaire*. **Pounceys** flourished at the mid-century, Henry Mayhew talked of 'The "pounceys", (the class I have alluded to as fancy-men,' in his *London Labour and the London Poor*, vol III. (1861), while **ponce** appeared perhaps a decade later. It promptly created a pair of rhyming slang terms: **Alphonse** (a nod to French stereotyping, although the French also used the term, in their case taking it from the Spanish *Alphonso*) and **Charlie Ronce**. There are many synonyms. **Fancy man, fancy cove** and **fancy Joseph** come either from the French *fiancé*, or from the **Fancy**, the generic term for the contemporary sporting fraternity. **Kiddy**, a small-time pimp, came from the same 'fast', semi-criminal world. **Mackeral** (fr. the French *maquereau*, which came in turn from the Dutch *makelaar*, both of which words meant pander) had meant pimp since the 15C. Abbreviated to **mack** in the late 19C, it had crossed the Atlantic, and flourished there, especially amongst the Black community. It survives today, alongside **mack man** and **macaroni** (both AA), although the link with the 18C use of **macaroni** (refering to the Italian foodstuff rather than the French ponce) to mean dandy is purely coincidental, if nonetheless pleasing, given the pimp's abiding taste for extravagant adornment.

More blatant descriptions included **fucker, rumper, holer** and **holemonger, meat merchant, gamester** (also the whore), and **ribald**. The all-purpose **smock** (cf. **apron**) gave **smock servant, smock pensioner, smockster, smock-merchant, smell-smock** and **smock tearer**; what had once euphemistically been termed the 'sport of Venus (love-making) gave **sportsman** and **sport, sporting house** (a brothel), and in fiction the celebrated pimp 'Sporting Life'. Other pimps were an **abbot**, an **abbot on the Cross** or a **croziered abbot** (the male version, logically, of the **abbess** or female brothel-keeper, more generally known then and now as a **madam**), **Cupid**, a **faker**, a **twat-faker** or **twat-masher** (fr. **twat**: vagina, and **masher**, fr. the Romany *masher-ava*: to entice), a **flower-fancier**, a **pinch-bottom, pinch-buttock** or **pinch-cunt**, or a **knight of the petticoat**. A **rounder** (US) toured clubs and bars, touting for trade, while **stringer** (fr. **string along**: to deceive) emphasised the duplicity of the operation. Pimping as a noun was **sawneying**, literally soft soaping.

The **Sunday man** was so-called because Sunday, the day she had off, was the only day he was willing to appear in public with his girl, while **Haymarket Hector** and **prosser** both came from names for whores. The former from **Haymarket ware** (working girls had long established London's Haymarket as the centre of their metropolitan activities) and the latter from **pross**, an abbreviation of prostitute, although the Gaiety Theatre's celebrated **Prossers' Avenue**, the bar where the more raffish elements of society were wont to promenade, came from **prosser**: an idler or sponger, although the pimp element must have had some influence. **Hector**, from the Trojan hero, was an all-purpose term for hero, however ironically. The **jack-gagger** (US) was married to his whore, while **kaffir** came from the Arabic *kafir:* infidel. The derogatory description of South African blacks comes from the same root.

The 20C has **stallion** (also the customer) and **town stallion** as well as **town bull** and **town rake**. Rhy. sl. has **Joe Bonce** and **Joe Ronce** as well as the Aus. **silver spoon**, rhyming with **hoon**, the national term for pimp. A further Aus. term is **fence**, a new twist on the UK use of the term as a dealer in stolen goods. A **bit of mess** is a whore's lover: neither a proper pimp nor a client.

Many of America's most successful pimps are, and traditionally have been black. Thus the much of the 20C terminology comes from that community and does not appear in the UK. In that world any pimp is a **player** (used generally as a smart operator in any form of business); a small-time pimp is a **simple pimp**, a **chili chump** or **chili pimp**, a **popcorn pimp** or a **coffeeand pimp** (a description stemming from the US theatrical term a **coffeeand role**: a role which pays so badly that the best the actor can expect is enough money to buy 'coffee and' cakes). Other specialised terms include **boss player** (a superior pimp); **faggotter** (a pimp for male prostitutes, from **faggot***); **gorilla pimp** (a violent pimp); **promoted pimp** (an experienced, senior pimp); **sugar pimp** and **sweet pimp** (a kind or at least non-violent pimp); **macaroni with cheese** (a pimp who has other interests).

ACCESSORIES AND LIFESTYLE

This same world has engendered a wide vocabulary for describing the pimp lifestyle. That world itself is known **the Life** or **mackery** (fr. **mack**). Pimps work from **the Book** (a verbally transmitted 'book of pimping rules'). Anything pertaining to pimping is **mack**.

The **office** is wherever a pimp conducts business; the **fast track** is the centre of whoring in a city, and the cities of America's East Coast in general; the **slow track** is the West Coast cities. **Bonds** are clothes given to his prostitutes; **copping clothes** are the 'best suit' used when enticing a new girl into his stable of **hos**; **kimible** is the noticeable 'pimp walk'; a **pimp's arrest** is the revocation of statutory bail bond the pimp has put up for each girl: if a girl wants to leave the pimp can simply cancel the bond, rendering her liable to instant and punitory arrest; **pimp dust** is cocaine; **pimp fronts** are any pimp-style clothes; a **pimp ride** is the expensive car that proclaims his, or his girls' success; **pimp shades** and **pimp tints** are dark glasses while a **pimp stick** is a homemade whip, made from a straightened wire coat hanger.

To entice prostitutes is to **cast the net**, **cop**, **cop for**, **hit on** or **take an application** while to work as a pimp is to **drive one's hos**, **put (one) on the block**, **put (one) on the corner** or **turn (one) out**. To **cop and blow** is to exploit a prostitute; to **lock** is to ensure a prostitute's fidelity; to **work from a book** is to run call- not street girls (the **book** in this case is a 'little black' version in which the names of regular clients are kept). UK pimps **ponce off** their girls. To discuss pimping is to **run down game** or **talk game**, to **file** is to give instruction to a prostitute); to **rig a jig** is to prepare a sexual con-trick; to **put snow in one's game** is to ensnare a white person for financial gain; to **creep** is to defraud a client and to **drop a lug** is to confront or argue with. In Aus. to **work a ginger** is to rob a client.

BROTHEL

While the word *brothel* is and always has been standard English, it is, if not slang, then something of a misnomer, since *brothel* in its original, 14C usage meant simply a disreputable person, of either sex. A century later the disrepute had overtaken the individual, and *brothel* meant first and foremost a whore; it was not for another century that, as an abbreviation of 'brothel's house' or 'brothel-house', that it replaced the person with the place. Meanwhile there already existed a perfectly good word for brothel: **bordel**, from *bordar* – a feudal term meaning the owner of a hut or cottage, which in turn came from the Latin *bordarius* (cottager) and hence from, *borda* (a cottage or hut). **Bordel** vanished from popular use as brothel took its place, but **bordello** (late 16C), meaning the same thing, is still in use, a conscious mix of the exotic and the archaic.

HOUSE

The euphemistic **house** has stood for brothel, whether as a terse monosyllable, or in a variety of combinations. The American madame Polly Adler entitled her memoirs *A House Is Not A Home*, and both Bob Dylan and the Animals essayed the old folk hit *The House of the Rising Sun*. In neither case did the knowledgeable overlook the reference. **House** emerges in the 19C, often as a 'house of blue light' or a 'house of ill fame'. Its roots, possibly, lie in the French *maison de tolerance*. That said, combinations of house appear much earlier.

The 16C brings **occupying house** (fr. **occupy***: to have intercourse) and **trugging ken**, (**trug**: a low prostitute; in 1703 **trugmolly** meant a whore). The 17C has **vaulting house** (1605), **punch house** (c. 1696; **punch** meant to have intercourse, specifically to deflower a virgin; it is used today as an Afro-American term for a place where pimps and whores meet; **punch** is also found in the modern **bunch-punch**: a gang rape) and **garden house** (see also at suburb below). This last comes either from Covent Garden, a notably louche area – there might actually have been a specific inn named the Garden House – or from **garden** meaning female pubic hair. **House of accomodation** and **house of civil reception** were coined in the 18C, as were **leaping house**, (18C, **leap**: to have intercourse), **coupling house, nugging-house / ken** (**nug**: to copulate) and **kip** (18C, from Danish *kippe*: hut; the use of **kip** to mean sleeping place is 19C).

The 19C, with the fullscale entry of Americanisms into the slang lexicon, introduces yet more 'house' terms: **barrelhouse** (US originally a saloon, literally a house with a barrel), **benny house**, **call house** (fr. **call girls**), **cathouse** (**cat***: whore or vagina), **juke joint** (**juke:** to copulate, in the Southern states), **a bawdy-house**, **bawdy ken** (or **bodikin)** or **smuggling-ken** (**smuggle:** to caress), **touch crib**, **fancy house** and **bed-house**, (although this was more a short-time hotel than a fully-fledged brothel). The old cant word **flash** (denoting crime in general since the 17C) gave **flash drum**, **flash house**, and **flash ken**, (all of which originally meant a criminal lodging house, before becoming a brothel), **hook house** (US, from **hooker***: whore), **mot house** and **mot case** (**mot**, from the earlier **mort**, meant woman, **case**, from the Italian *casa* meant house). Twentieth century terms include a **leaning house** (AA), a **rap parlour** (euphemism for 'massage parlour', itself a euphemism, in many cases, for a brothel, cf. **rap**); **peg house** and **show house** both meant a homosexual brothel.

Specific terms include the **panel-crib** and its synonym the **badger-crib** (19C). Such brothels were home to the fraudulent 'badger game': this entailed the ensnaring of a client by the girl, and his subsequent robbery, either by her or, more often, by her pimp, posing as an 'outraged boyfriend'. The earliest 'badgers' were 'a Crew of desperate Varlets, who rob and kill near any River, and then throw the dead Bodies within' (*New Canting Dictionary*, 1725); by 1889 a **badger** was a pimp or brothel-keeper and subsequently a blackmailer. The 'badger game' was so named in the mid-19C, though it undoubtedly flourished much earlier.

Perhaps the most satisfyingly subversive 'house' euphemism is the 19C **house in the suburbs**. Due, perhaps, to the reputation of the then quintessentially suburban St John's Wood as a place where a man could set up his mistress at a decent distance from his respectable West End family home, 'suburban' had become, as Farmer and Henley put it, 'generic for disorder and loose living'. Allied terms include **suburb trade** (prostitution), **suburb wench** (a prostitute), **suburb garden** or **garden house** (the house where one's mistress was kept, or, to quote Farmer and Henley once more, a 'private fuckery').

Shop

The essentially mercantile aspect of prostitution can be seen in the variety of terms using the suffix **shop**, or some other form of sales place. These include **molly shop**, (c.1900, fr. **molly***: whore), **nanny house** or **shop** (17C), **whore shop** (19C), **hook shop** (US) — in all of which cases the qualifying noun meant a prostitute. Other terms all stem from the commodity on sale, whether intercourse or, crudely, the vagina: **bumshop** (19C), **buttocking shop** or **ken** (early 19C), **cunt-shop** (19C), **grinding shop** (19C), **knocking shop** or (rarely) **knocking house** (19C), **flesh market**, **fish market** and **fish pound** (mid-19C, fr. **fish***: vagina), **green grocery** (mid-19C, from **greens***: intercourse), **meat-fancier's** (19C), **meat-house** (both fr. **meat***: vagina) and **buttonhole factory** (19C); **meat market**, while occasionally signifying a brothel, can also simply mean any form of pickup place, irrespective of whether money enters the sexual equation. Finally comes the **bread and butter warehouse** (18C). This meant specifically Ranelagh Gardens in Chelsea, built as a pleasure garden in 1741. It featured a large roccoco rotunda, a Chinese pavilion, booths for gentlemen to smoke and places for drinking, eating and socialising. At its peak Mozart played there, Canaletto painted it and Edward Gibbon termed it 'the most convenient place for courtships of every kind — the best market we have in England'. It was the last aspect that caused its downfall. Whether the slang nickname came from the Garden's tea rooms, or from the fact that **bread and butter fashion** meant copulation is debatable; probably the one punned on the other, but whatever the etymology, Ranelagh Gardens gradually fell into disrepute. It was demolished in 1803 and is now part of the gardens of Chelsea Hospital.

School

The last and briefest, though generally earliest mass category of brothel terms involves school: **academy** (17C, where worked **academicians**), **finishing academy**, **cavaulting school** (17C, from **cavaulting**: copulation, from the Lingua Franca *cavalta*, riding, itself rooted in the Latin *caballus*: horse), **vaulting school** (17C), **ladies' college** (18C) and **pushing school** (18C).

GENERAL TERMS

General terms for brothel, falling outside the major categories include **case** (from Italian *casa*: house, although **case★** could also mean vagina) and **vrow-case** (fr. the Dutch *vrow*: woman), **hummums** (19C, from the Arabic *hammamm*, a hot or Turkish bath; the original **hummum** was set up in Covent Garden in 1631, it later became a hotel; **hummum** is reminiscent of another SE term for brothel: *bagnio*, also meaning bath), **cab** (19C, probably from cabin), **Corinth** (17C, from the allegedly lurid reputation of the ancient Greek city), **nunnery** (17C, from the *nonariae*, the Roman harlots, and best-known today from Hamlet's command to Ophelia: 'Get thee to a nunnery' [*Hamlet*, III, i]; **nun**, therefore meant a prostitute and both terms somewhat undermine the 19C slang image of incongruity: 'like a nun in a knocking-shop'), **Covent Garden nunnery** (18C, plus **Covent Garden abbess**: a madame or procuress, and **Covent Garden nun**: a whore), **warren** (17C) and **cunny warren** (18C, **cunny**: vagina, plus a pun on SE *bunny*), **fuckery** (19C), **girlery** (19C), **place of sixpenny sinfulness** (19C, a suburban brothel) and **chicken ranch** (US 20C, based on the original Chicken Ranch, a licensed brothel).

Brothel areas include the **stews**, and the 20C **ho stroll** (AA; **ho**: whore), **pitch**, **stroll**. **bricks** (thus 'working on the bricks') and **track**. **Red light area** comes possibly from the late 16C when a **red lattice★** meant a tavern sign and thence if the tavern was thus inclined, a brothel; **red grate** also meant an inn or brothel. *Gropecuntlane*, cited by the *OED* as the earliest printed use of the word **cunt★**, and sited at the heart of London's City stews, presumably left few visitors in doubt as to its primary commodity.

Madames, who ran brothels, include a **Covent Garden abbess** (18C) or plain **abbess**, **Bankside ladies** (17C, who could also be the whores themselves, see PROSTITUTION for Bankside etymology), **mother** (18C, only a whore in 17C), **mother midnight** (18C, which also meant a midwife), **mother damnable** (19C),

mother of the maids (18C), **Mrs Lukey Props** (19C, also a tramp's companion), **wafer-woman** and **house mother** (20C).

RACE RELATIONS

In the world of slang race relations are invariably difficult: at best suspicious, at worst outright hostile and inevitably laden with stereotypes. Terms for certain specific national groups are listed elsewhere; this section deals with the black (and brown)/white divide. The bulk of such terms are of 20C coinage; this is less a tribute to the tolerance of earlier centuries, than testimony to the prior invisibility of blacks within a predominantly white culture.

BLACKS (BY WHITES)

Blacks began appearing in Britain during the 18C, usually as sailors who had decided to make their home in such port cities as Liverpool, or as servants brought home by merchants and explorers, and their existence duly impinges upon contemporary slang. Aside from such heavily 'humorous' terms as **snowball**, **lilywhite** and **chimney chops** (all 18C, the latter pair of which had earlier meant chimney sweep) the first 'modern' term to enter the language is **nigger**, which appears during the late 18C. Taken from the SE *negro* which had appeared (via the Spanish *negro*: black) in the mid-16C, it was used among others by Robert Burns and Lord Byron before crossing the Atlantic and taking its place as what is still the most widely used of such racial epithets. Although primarily attached to that section of the US population imported as slaves and now known as Afro-Americans, **nigger**, especially in the UK, was used for any coloured race, e.g. the Indians encountered by the soldiers of the Raj, Australian Aborigines, various African tribes and so on. Almost contemporaneous is **darkie** or **darky**, another English coinage, which migrated to the US c.1840.

More lasting terms emerged during the 19C, almost all of them US in origin. **Sambo** (c.1800) was taken from the Spanish *zambo*, used to describe those of mixed Negro and Indian or European blood; that the term also described a breed of yellow monkey and may have been the same word as that meaning bandy-legged merely underlines the gut racism that informs such language. The US use, however, may have a different root: the Foulah *sambo*:uncle; the suggestion by Farmer and Henley of a third root, an African tribe the Samboses (for whom they claim an appearance in a text of 1558) has no validity. Like **darky** (which smacks of the music hall) three other terms are redolent with the popular exploitation of blacks as figures of fun. **Rastus**, probably an abbreviation of the name Erastus, can be found in a number of songs (and subsequently Hollywood movies) in which the 'typical' black is seen as subserviently stupid, more of a dog than a human; the name also shares the billing for a series of 'Rastus and Liza' jokes, predicated on the same stereotypes. **Coon** (c.1860) is an abbreviation for raccoon and the 'chocolate coloured coon' (usually a white person in blackface) was for years a staple of mass entertainment, typically as in television's *Black and White Minstrel Show*. Unlike other such terms **coon** had a non-racial meaning: slightly earlier (c.1832) it described any man, especially a sly and shrewd one; a further meaning, c.1840, was of a member of the old US Whig party, which for a while had the raccoon as its emblem. By the late 19C the meaning was unequivocally racist, and used as such in Australia too, where it described not blacks but Aborigines. It also generated three rhy. sl. phrases: **egg and spoon**, **harvest moon** and **silvery spoon**. Finally **Jim Crow**, based on the 'nigger minstrel' song (first performed c.1832 by Thomas D. Rice [1808-60]) with its refrain 'Wheel about and turn about and jump Jim Crow', came by the mid-20C to characterize not simply the individual black, but as **Jim Crowism** the whole apparatus of racist segregation that underpinned the government and society of the Southern states of America. The name **Jim Crow** moved to the UK where it described 'nigger minstrels', who, blacked up like their US counterparts, 'jumped Jim Crow' as part of their regular repertoire. The term **picanniny**, for a black child, comes from the Spanish *pequeño* or the Portuguese *pequeno*, both meaning small; the pejorative phrase a **touch of the tarbrush**, meaning of partially black ancestry, is a UK coinage, although the term originally referred, in the Royal Navy, to an over-zealous officer (fr. his endless ordering of his men to apply tar to various parts of the ship).

The main UK contribution to this dubious lexicon in the 20C is **spade**, from the popular phrase 'black as the ace of spades' and coined in the 1920s. It is echoed in the rhy. sl. **lucozade** and **razor** (**razor blade**). It is, in fairness, perhaps the least overtly racist of any such term. The opposite of **spade** is **jumble** (fr. John Bull) a term supposedly used by London's black community during the late 1950s and early 1960s. It is cited as such by the writer Colin MacInnes (although it is conspicuously absent from Partridge's *DSUE* which does have **spade**) but does not seem to have survived. Other UK phrases are **chocolate** (presumably from the colour, but possibly from rhy. sl. **chocolate frog: wog***), **jungle bunny** and **chungo bunny**, but for the remainder of the racist vocabulary, the palm must go to the US. Terms include **dinge** (fr. the 'dinginess' of black skin), **shine** and **smoke** (all pre-World War II), **jig, jigaboo** and **zigaboo**: terms that may draw on the alternative definition of *jig* as a dance, and thus based on the French *giguer*. to leap, gambol and frolic (the classic 19C black stereotypes) or modeled on *bugaboo*, which in the 13C was the name of a demon, and since the 18C, the fear demons in general. **Boog, boogie** and **oogie** either come from *boogaloo*, thus perpetuating the dance motif, or from *bogey*, which also refers back to *bugaboo*. **Dark meat** tends to imply black girls (thus the equivalent **white meat**) seen in a sexual context, **eight ball** refers to the black eight ball in the game of pool and **groid** is a collegiate abbreviation of negroid. Yiddish supplies **schwartzer** and **schwartze** (fr.. German *schwartz*: black) and **schvug** or **schvugie** (a mix of **shwartzer** and **boogie** and artificial, rather than genuine, i.e. European 'old country' Yiddish). Finally **shadow, smut-butt, spook** and **stove lid** all attest to the perceived 'darkness' of blacks.

Blacks in Africa hadtheir own description, although they too could be **niggers**. **Kaffir** (late 18C) meant literally a member of a South African race which in turn is part of the Bantu family. As such the term has long been used for any Black African. It was also used on the London Stock Exchange as a nickname for South

African mine shares during the late 19C; thus the **Kaffir Circus**: those stockbrokers who specialized in such shares, and the offices in which they worked. Other terms for Africans are the abbreviation **Af** or **Afs**, and **munt**, from the Bantu *umuntu*: a person, or a servant. White Australians too developed their terms for the indigenous population. **Boong** began by meaning Aborigine, although it has spread to mean any coloured person, including Asiatics. **Din** or more recently **gin** (both from the Dharuk *diyin*: woman, although coincidentally an abbrev.. of Aborigine) means a black woman, giving such terms as **gin-burglar**: a white man who has sex with Aborigine women (earlier versions included **gin-masher**, **gin-banger**, **gin-stealer**, **gin-hunter** and **gin-jockey**); their half-caste offspring are **creamies**. Opposed to such miscegenation is the **gin-shepherd**, who seeks to keep the races separate. **Gin's piss** is inferior beer, to be **like a gin at a christening** is to be ill-at-ease. Aside from US imports, which deal impartially with the West Indian, Indian and Pakistani populations, Britain has coined its own term **wog**, which is aimed specifically at Indians and Pakistanis, although it has been extended to cover any 'brown' immigrants, especially Bangladeshis and even the small group of Vietnamese. The term, which emerged during the 1920s, defies any accurate etymology, although F. C. Bowen states in *Sea Slang* (1929) 'Wogs, lower class Babu shipping clerks on the Indian coast', but provides no further detail; popular belief has always chosen the acronym WOG: westernized oriental gentlemen, while Partridge opts for what he sees as the simplest and most obvious root: an abbreviation of golliwog. Certainly this once-popular doll, with its caricatured 'black' features, has long since been marginalised as politically incorrect. As popular as, and something of a successor to **wog** is **Paki** or **Pakki**, an abbreviation of Pakistani but by no means restricted to actual Pakistanis. 20C US has **yom** or **yomo**, abbreviations of the common Black street phrase 'Your mother!'

BLACKS (BY BLACKS)

If white terms for blacks are typified by their hostility, then black terms for themselves are mainly predicated on the need to reinforce the group, followed by a selection of terms which unlike the white vocabulary which is based on the theory that 'they all look the same to me', emphasizes the differences between individuals, especially as regards the degree to which their skin is actually 'black'. That said, these terms are all US and all 20C. Britain's black community has not developed so diversified a lexicon.

General terms include **original** and **all-originals**, **black 360 degrees**, **bleed** and **blood** (fr. *blood brother*) **boot**, **brother** and **the brothers** (coined by the revolutionary black groups of the 1960s), **member**, **skillet**, (early 20C, from the SE *skillet*: a black iron frying pan), **speck** and the most recent coinages: **homeboy**, **homegirl** and their common abbreviation **homey**.

A notably dark-complexioned black is a **black bird**, **black dust**, **inky-dinky**, **midnight**, **smokestack** and a **zombie** (originally a West African or Haitian snake deity, latterly a soulless corpse said to have been revived by witchcraft). Names for a light complexioned person include **bright**, **buckwheat** (the name of the black child in the movie series *Our Gang*), **casper** (fr. the television cartoon *Casper the Friendly Ghost*), **grey** (also used to mean a white man), **suede**, **lemon** (i.e. **yellow** or mulatto), **pinkie** and **pink-toes** (specifically a light skinned black woman). A Mulatto woman is a **high yaller**, **high yellow**, **yellow ass** or **yellow girl**. A rebellious, non-conformist black is variously a **bad nigger** or **bad-ass nigger**, a **bad boy**, a **cut-throat**, a **field nigger** (cf. **yard nigger**) or a **hardhead**, all of which terms play on white stereotypes and indeed terminology (esp. **bad nigger**), reversing the usual balance of 'good' and 'bad' (cf. **wicked**, **bad**). A subservient or middle-class black is an **Uncle Tom**, **Tom**, **Dr. Thomas** or **Mr Thomas** (all from the black slave Uncle Tom, pious hero of Harriet Beecher Stowe's anti-slavery novel *Uncle Tom's Cabin* [1852]), **Aunt Jane** or **Aunt Jemima** (the classic 'mammy' figure for whom a chain of pancake houses was named), a **fade** or **faded boogie** (who has metaphorically 'lost' his colour), **handkerchief head** (as worn by Aunt Jemima, but see **hankiehead**★), a **house nigger**, **HN** or **yard nigger** (all based on the differentiation under slavery between the 'domesticated' blacks who worked as house servants, and those who merely toiled in the plantation fields). A **shuffle** mocks the stereotypical shuffling, foolish darky, **seddity** (fr. SE *absurdity*) is specifically a black who attempts to ape whites and an **oreo**, like the chocolate-covered Oreo cookie, is black outside but white within. Other phrases include **John Henry** (fr. the song), a tough, hard worker despite the odds and **firsts** or **blockbusters**: blacks who are first to move into formerly all-white areas.

WHITES (BY BLACKS)

As one might expect, the whiteness of whites provides some of the basic terms used when blacks are describing their opposite numbers: among such terms are **blanco**, **chalk**, **gray**, **lily**, **paleface**, **pink** and **whitey**. **Cracker** and **Mr. Cracker** are based on the 18C *cracker*, meaning natives of Georgia and Florida, and are synonymous with the phrase **white trash**; similarly **crack-corn** refers to white natives of Kentucky, and has been linked to **cracker**, although it appears some sixty-five years later. Poor whites are similarly apostrophized in **peck** or **peckerwood**, a reference to the red woodpecker, supposedly a symbol of whites, as opposed to the black crow, the emblem of blacks. **Beast** and **devil** testify to the white man as inherently wicked, as does **yacoo**, which comes from *Yacub*: the white devil-figure at the heart of Black Muslim mythology. The widely used **ofay**, with its abbreviations **fey** and **fay**, has generated a number of etymologies. The suggestion that the word is Pig Latin for *foe* is generally discounted as overly simplistic, while H. L. Mencken, writing in *The American Language* (1936), is taking an equally easy, but no more viable route in offering the French *au fait*: in tune with, aware of, as 'signifying mastery'. The *OED* opts for an African language: the question is which one? In 1932 the magazine *Africa* stated that 'The root of the word appears to come from the Ibibio *Afia*, white or light-coloured' while fifty-five years later a contributor to *American Speech* preferred the Yoruba *ofe* 'a charm that lets one jump so high as to disappear', and thus by extension the trouble which causes one to require such vanishing; that a West African tribesman facing the prospect of enslavement saw the white man as such a problem, and thus the essence of trouble, seems feasible. Less common are the

obsolete **kelt** (early 20C, from the SE celt?), **rabbit**, **hay eater** and
the **man with fuzzy balls**. **Honky** or **honkie** comes from
hunkie, a name originally given to the Poles and other immigrant
Slavs who worked in the Chicago stockyards; it was transferred
during the 1960s to any racist white who was seen as opposing
black demands for greater civil rights. A **superhonkie** is an
extreme example of the breed. During the 19C **Mr. Charlie** and
his feminine equivalent **Miss Ann** were the generic terms for the
white master and mistress; the 20C added **Mr Peanut**. In a non-US
context the Rastafarians of Jamaica use **ballhead** (fr. *bald-head*,
which, compared to their flowing dreadlocks, most whites, however hirsute, may be considered to be) to mean white. As well as
the generic **Miss Ann**, white women have also been **Miss Lillian**,
Miss Amy (**Mr. Charlie's** daughter), **Little Eva** and **Lady Snow**.
Alternative terms include **bale of straw** (straw: blonde hair)
pinktoes, **silk**, **snow** and **white meat**.

Other coloured groups have their own terms for whites. Mexicans
offer **gringo** and **gringa**, both from 19C, as well as **anglo**: anyone
of ostensibly Anglo-Saxon appearance and thus a white person.
Aborigines have **gubba**, **gubb**, **gub** or **Mr. Gub**, Asiatics prefer
the descriptive **roundeye** (a term adopted by US troops during
the Vietnam War, especially when referring to white girls). American Indians characterize their fellows who yearn for assimilation as
apples: red on the outside but white under the skin (cf. **oreo**) or
Uncle Tomahawks (cf. **Uncle Tom**). **Banana** (yellow on the
outside and white inside) fulfils the same function for the Chinese.

OTHER GROUPS

Gypsies, rarely popular in the UK, have been variously termed
diddicois or **didekeis** (fr. Romany *didakeis*: halfbreed gypsies),
gyppos, and the **fair gang** (fr. their regular appearances at country
fairs). Farmer and Henley (but no other authority) add **mugger**,
which did exist in the 18C to describe a travelling hawker of
earthenware, who, like many such travellers, might be considered
a potential thief. Orientals are known as **chopsticks**, **dinks**, **gooks**
(a term that in the 19C meant a prostitute, but in the 20C has always

meant a foreigner, whether Filipinos in the 1930s, Koreans in the 1950s or Vietnamese during the 1960s and 1970s), **little people**, **ricers** (fr. their supposed staple diet), **slants**, **slits**, **slopes** or **slopeheads** (all of which refer to the 'slanted' oriental eye) and, generically, as the **yellow peril★**. Arabs, or more precisely Iraqis, became known during the 1991 Gulf War as **towel-heads**, **rag-heads**, **hankie-heads** and **sand niggers**.

COGNATE TERMS

As in any area where race determines the vocabulary, blackness carries with it a cognate vocabulary, in which such terms as **African**, **black** and **nigger** are combined to produce a range of almost invariably pejorative and stereotypical terms. Among them are **African dominoes** and **African golf** (craps dice), **African engineering** (shoddy, second-rate workmanship, cf. **Mexican**), the **African Railroad** (the San Francisco municipal bus line — which is principally used by blacks); the **Black Belt**, **Black Bottom**, **Black Town**, **Nigger Hill** and **Nigger Town** the black area, whether or not a ghetto proper, within any larger town or city. **Blackleg** and **black pencil** are both a black man's penis while **black bagging**, **black jack**, **black joke**, **black meat** (also black women in general), **black mouth** and **black Maria** (which also means black prostitute) all mean a black woman's genitals. A **blacksmith's shop** is a brothel run by a black madame, a **black bezer** is a black person's face (cf. **beezer**) and **blackplate** is soul food (punning on the regular US restaurant dish, the 'blue plate special'). To **let off a little nigger** is to let off steam, to **niggerlip** is to wet the end of a cigarette while smoking it (a term known to the hippies as **bogging**), **nigger bait** is an excessive display of chrome on one's car, **nigger daytime** is night time, **nigger heaven** was synonymous for the theatre's gods, the highest and cheapest tier of seats, and that which is **like a nigger girl's left tit** is neither right nor fair. A **Harlem credit card** is a piece of hose used to syphon petrol from another car into the tank of one's own. A **Harlem sunset** is the heavily bleeding wound caused by a slash from an open razor.

The lowly image of America's Mexican immigrants is reflected in a similarly derogatory range of terms. **Mexican** itself means cheap, second-rate; to **go to Mexico** is to become drunk (for US teenagers brief trips across the border usually implied non-stop excess), a **Mexican breakfast** is a cigarette and a glass of water, i.e. nothing nourishing at all, **Mexican green** is a grade and type of marijuana and to **fly Mexican airlines** is to smoke it, a **Mexican cigarette** is a poorly rolled marijuana cigarette; a **Mexican stand-off** is any situation in which neither party is willing to back down from a stated position but simultaneously neither party has a superior edge; the result is that both parties give in and walk off. The **Mexican credit card** is a synonym for the **Harlem credit card***, a **Mexican Buick** is a Chevrolet (fr. the respective status of the cars, the **Chevvy** being the lesser model), a **Mexican carwash** is washing the car by leaving it out in the rain, a **Mexican muffler** is a home-made silencer made from a tin can stuffed with steel wool which is then attached to the car's exhaust pipe, a **Mexican jeep** is a donkey and **Mexican overdrive** is free wheeling to save petrol (**Jewish overdrive** has the same meaning).

A **Mexican athlete** is an unsuccessful candidate for a college or school sports and a **Mexican nose guard** a jock strap or athletic supporter; a **Mexican dragline** is a shovel or spade, a **Mexican jumping bean** is an amphetamine pill, a **Mexican nightmare** or **Mexican schlock** is third-rate art, especially gaudy ceramic crockery, typical of that sold to tourists in Mexico; a **Mexican promotion** or a **Mexican raise** is a better job but one which brings no increase in salary; **Mexican toothache** and the **Mexican two-step** both mean diahorrea, often contracted on a foreign holiday (cf. **Aztec two-step**, **Montezuma's revenge**, etc.).

THE JEWS

The Jew as a racial stereotype requires greater space than is available here, as do the arguments for or against the inclusion of any such vilifications in this or any other reference work. Anti-semitism boasts too lengthy and dishonourable a pedigree for discussion here: the status of the terms it inspires should be self-evident. As far as slang goes Jew equals money (with a spot of tailoring and an aversion to pork) to his gentile peers (unlike the Scot who may also equal money but is at least inventive and brave as well) and the words below bear this out.

JEWS

Other than the opprobrious **Jew-boy** (19C), which was applied mainly, but not invariably to younger Jews, the core slang term for Jew was and remains **Yid**, with its occasional diminutive **Yiddle**, and the adjective **Yiddish** or **Yiddisher**. Taken from the German *Jude*, meaning Jew, and prior to that from Yehuda or Judah, one of the Biblical Jacob's sons, the term, as the writer Leo Rosten points out, is neutral if pronounced 'yeed' as it would be by Jews speaking the Judaeo-German language Yiddish, but unashamedly offensive if pronounced 'yid'. As is the way of such modifiers, **Yiddish** or **Yiddisher**, as found particularly amongst Cockneys, whose community lived side by side with many Jewish immigrants and their descendants, was and is relatively affectionate. **Yid**, *tout court*, is not. Calling Tottenham Hotspur FC, **the Yids** (fr. their supposedly large numbers of Jewish fans), is not meant as a term of endearment.

Slightly earlier than Yid came **ikey** or **ikey-mo** (c.1835). Both terms come from proper Jewish names: Isaac, and in the combination Moses too. Like a number of 'racial' names (by no means only those for Jews) the term while initially meaning only a member of the relevant race, was used to personify those with 'Jewish' characteristics. Thus **ikey** also describes someone seen as artful, crafty, knowing or 'fly', or one who has too high an opinion of themselves. **Abe**, **abie** and **Abie Kabibble** (all US) are similarly name-based, in this case on another Biblical figure, Abraham. **Abie Kabibble** comes from the phrase 'ish kabibble', meaning who cares, or don't worry, probably based on the Yiddish *nish gefidlt*. Adopted by the vaudeville superstar Fanny Brice the term was picked up by America's 'dean of cartoonists' Harry Hershfield who in 1917 launched a character called *Abie the Agent*, based on one 'Abie Kabibble'. Highly successful, the strip lasted until 1932. The term was further popularized by a swing trumpeter who adopted the name Ish Kabibble, and started performing as a comic.

Moch, mouchey and **mockie** (19C) come from Moses, although they may have some connection to what is probably the oldest if defunct term for Jew: **smoutch, smouse, smouch** or **smous** (all 18C) which derive from the Dutch *smous* and the Yiddish *schmus*, meaning patter or profit. These in turn come from the Hebrew *schmuoss*: news or tales. The **schmoose** was an itinerant Jewish peddlar. The term survives today in Yiddish as *schmooze*: to have an intimate chat, although the noun *schmoozer* implies a flatterer. **Shonk** (19C) comes from the Yiddish *shonnicker*, a small-time trader, and leads to the 20C Cockney **shonk** meaning nose and the Royal navy **shonky**, a miser whose meanness is typified by his like of drinking but his unwillingness to stand his round. A **jew-fencer** (18C) is a street salesman or pedlar, usually of stolen goods, while **Jack the Jew** is a **fence★**, usually of the least valuable goods. A **Jew joint** (US use) is a second hand clothes store, where such fences may operate.

Sheeny began life in Britain c.1816 and progressed to the US sometime during the 19C. On the whole it has become a naturalized US term. Its etymology remains debatable, with Partridge suggesting the overuse of brilliantine on heads of Jewish hair. More likely is his, and Leo Rosten's note of the Yiddish pronunciation of the German *schön* (pretty, beautiful). Rosten also suggests a derivation from the Yiddish phrase a *miesse meshina*, meaning an ugly fate or death, which was in common use.

Last of these popular terms is **kike**, which originated in the US c.1900. It is supposedly based on the suffix *-ki* or *-ky* that was found in so many of the surnames of the Eastern European Jews who were flooding across the Atlantic to the New World.

A number of terms for Jew are based on rhyming slang: **half past two, five to two, quarter to two, four by two, pot** or **box of glue, Sarah Soo, buckle my shoe, fifteen-two**, and **kangaroo**, all meaning Jew; **front-wheel skid, four-wheel** or **three-wheel skid, God forbids** (though far more common as *kids*) and **sauce-**

pan lid, all meaning yid; **eskimo** rhymes with **ikey-mo**, just as **goose** is presumably based on the pronunciation 'joose'. In bingo terminology **dirty old Jew** meant two. Other names include **hooknose** (20C), **hebe** (20C, from Hebrew), **Red Sea pedestrian** (Aus., from the Biblical Exodus myth), and the particularly repellent **oven-dodger** (a British coinage in common, if sniggering currency; the ovens, of course, are those of Auschwitz and Treblinka). Jewish *kashrut* laws give **porker** (19C) while traditional menus have coined **bagel bender** (US) and **lox jock** (US, lox being smoked salmon and jock an aficionado). A **JAP** is a Jewish-American princess, the by-word in spoilt brats.

Finally the racial tension between America's blacks and Jews give **Goldberg** (a generic surname), **fast-talking Charlie** (a smoother version of the usual **Mr Charlie**, a white man), the similarly duplicitous **slick-'em-plenty** and **three balls** (fr. the ghetto pawnbroking shops that are often run by Jews).

STEREOTYPICAL TERMS

In slang **Jew** as a noun and a verb is based on the primary racial stereotype (other than that of 'killing Christ'): that of grasping miserliness and of exorbitant usury. In neither case need the term apply to an actually religious Jew. Thus **a jew** (17C) is a mean person, a skinflint while **to jew** or **jew down** is to cheat financially. It was not until the *OED* produced the second volume of its supplements (*H-N*, 1976) that the note 'These uses are now considered to be offensive' was added, although some campaigners still fought hard to have both terms excluded in their entirety.

The sense of greedy miserliness and an obsession with money underlines a number of terms. Among the earliest is the 16C **worth a Jew's eye**, which denotes great value and is assumed to refer to the medieval torturers who, amongst other measures, put out Jews' eyes to force them to hand over their possessions. **Jew bail** (18C) was insufficient or useless bail while the phrase **thick as two Jews on payday** (19C) means very intimate and a **Jewish compliment** (19C) offers a girl a large penis but no presents. A **Jew sheet** is an account, often imaginary, of money lent to friends. To **take the Jewish airlines** is to walk, another testimony to meanness.

Jewish Oxo (20C) is money (it makes 'gravy') while **Jewish lightning** is deliberate arson in order to gain the insurance on an otherwise unprofitable business. The **Yiddisher** or **Jewish piano** or the **Jew Joanna** (rhyming slang) is a cash register; it was also used c.1907 to describe the the the first taximeters, installed in London cabs by the General Cab Company. The **Jewish typewriter** is also a cash register. **Jewish overdrive** is freewheeling down hills to save petrol (cf. **Mexican overdrive**) while the assumption that even succcessful Jews remain bound by their essential vulgarity informs **Jew's Bentley** or **Jew's Rolls Royce** (1930s), meaning a Jaguar, as does **Jew canoe**, which in the US means a Cadillac. The 'vulgarity' smear further underlines **Jewish Renaissance** or **Jewy Louis**: flashy interior decoration, probably featuring (fake) Louis XV or Louis XVI furniture — over-elaborate and in doubtful taste.

The widespread Jewish involvement in tailoring led to a number of 19C terms, often found in the services. The Royal Navy has **jewing** (tailoring), **jewer** (a rating who for a given wage will make another man's uniform), a **jewing bar** or **jewing bundle** (a bag in which a sailor's of sewing kit is kept) and a **jewing firm** (a group of men who are a self-appointed tailoring 'company' on board ship). A **Jew's harp** (RN) was a shackle shaped like the musical 'harp' that secures the anchor chain to the anchor; **Jew's letters** are tatooing — presumably from the use of a needle, albeit not a tailor's. The Army adds **Jew parade** to describe the cookhouse duties imposed on anyone failing to attend church on Sunday morning, irrespective of their religious beliefs.

Aside from the **Jewish compliment★** the main aspect of Jewish sexuality to influence slang is circumcision. Thus **Jewish corned beef**, a **Jew's lance** and **Jewish National** (the reference is to the Hebrew National brand of kosher salami) all mean a circumcised penis, as does a secondary use of **Jewish compliment**; a **Jewish nightcap** is a foreskin while **Jewish by hospitalization** (gay use) refers to a circumcised gentile. In **Jewish foreplay** the man pleads for sex, while his partner refuses all physical contact.

Geography creates a number of terms. In the US **Jew Town** is the Jewish area of any city, while **Jew York** is New York; Sidney, Australia, is **Yidney** and Johannesburg, South Africa is **Jewburg**. Those areas of London with notable concentrations of Jews include **Yidsbury** (Finsbury), **Abrahamstead** (Hampstead), **Cricklewitch** (Cricklewood), **Goldbergs Green** (Golder's Green); all these appear anti-semitic but according to Partridge, who cites a Jewish informant, are 'self mocking'. Jewish cookery gives **jewbutter** (US, 19C) meaning goose fat and **Jewish penicillin**: chicken soup. **Jew food** is ham. The religious prohibition of pork gives **to go down like a pork chop at a Jewish wedding** (to make a gross social faux pas) and as **useless as a pork chop** or **a slice of bacon at a Jewish wedding** (extremely unpopular).

Among other terms are **Hebrew** (17C) meaning unintelligible, a **Jewish forest**, used in poker for three threes (fr. the pronunciation *t'ree t'rees*) while a **jew's poker** (19C) is a gentile who lights the fires on the Sabbath, a figure known in Yiddish as the *Shabbos goy* (lit. Sabbath gentile). Synonymous with Jew or Jewish is Jerusalem. Such terms include the **Jerusalem cuckoo** (20C British Army) a mule, the **Jerusalem pony** (20C) an ass, a **Jerusalem parrot**, a flea and a **Jerusalem artichoke**, a donkey (rhy. sl. **artichoke**: moke). The actual vegetable is known to grocers as a **Jewboy**. **Jerusalem the Golden** or **Jerusalem-on-Sea** is Brighton, home to many Jews. Finally the Jews themselves differentiate their numbers between **Litvaks** and **Polacks** (immigrants respectively from Lithuania and Poland) and describe their non-Jewish neighbours variously as **goys** or **goyim** (fr. the Hebrew word meaning nation) and **yoks**; a **shikse** is a gentile girl, thus the rhyming slang **flour mixer** and a **shaygets** is a gentile boy.

THE IRISH

In the realm of racial stereotypes, few nations fare worse than do the Irish, branded for at least two centuries as slow-witted, bungling peasants. The bulk of these terms, like the immigrants themselves, arrived during the 19C.

Irish by itself means either whiskey, in which capacity it has served since at least the 17C, or anger (thus, **get your Irish up**). Combinations with Irish, in no special order, include **Irish assurance** (bold, forward behaviour, otherwise known as having been **dipped in the Shannon**), **Irish evidence** (17C, perjury), the **Irish harp** (a long-handled shovel, known elsewhere as a **banjo**, or **Mexican dragline**). The rhyming slang **Irish jig** (20C) is either a wig or cig (arette). An **Irish mile** is synonymous with a country mile, in both cases winding and apparently much longer than the yardstick might indicate. To be **Irish as Paddy's pig** or **straight from the bog** is to be quintessentially Irish.

To maintain the stereotypes, one has a number of terms pertaining to the sea, to violence, and to potatoes. The former include an **Irish hurricane** or **Paddy's hurricane**, both of which mean a flat calm, **Irish pennants**, which are frayed ends of ropes flapping in breeze and an **Irish man o'war** or **Irish battleship** – an unpowered barge. Violence, especially on a domestic level, or as inspired by an excess of drink, offers the **Irish beauty** (a woman with two black eyes), the **Irish wake** which is any boisterous occasion, not necessarily a wake as such and the **Irish wedding** which means variously masturbation, the emptying of a cesspool, or what in the 18C Frances Grose termed any occasion 'where black eyes are given instead of favours'. A **donnybrook**, from the eponymous village, means a a large-scale public brawl. **Irish confetti** is bricks, especially as tossed during such a riot, although it can also be a large emission of semen, while an **Irish hoist** is a kick in the behind.

Potatoes, the supposed national staple, can be **Irish apples**, **apricots**, **grapes** (and **Paddy's grapes**) or **lemons**, while the **Irish mails** are sacks of potatoes, a reference to the substantial 19C Anglo-Irish trade in the commodity. Other food references include **Irish turkey** (US) corned or (UK) salt beef and cabbage and an **Irishman's dinner** meaning a fast.

As **Irish beauty**, above, indicates, Irish women, in slang at least, have a poor reputation for physical charm. This is borne out by **Irish draperies** (pendulous breasts), **Irish fortune** (the vagina),

and **Irish legs** or **arms** (heavy female legs). Nor does Irish
sexuality get much recommendation: **Irish whist** 'where the jack
takes the ace' is sexual intercourse, an **Irish clubhouse** is a refined
house of prostitution, an **Irish dip** sexual intercourse, an **Irish
marathon** an extended session of lovemaking, an **Irish root** or
Irish toothpick the penis and an **Irish toothache** an erection.
An **Irish promotion** or **Irish rise** is either masturbation or the
loss of one's erection; in the non-sexual area it means a loss of wages.
Irish horse is either an impotent penis or, as food, tough, under-
cooked salt beef. The **Irish shave** is an act of defecation.

The Irish as nature's labourers are found in an **Irish buggy** or
Irish local (both US, local usually means a local railway or subway
line) a wheelbarrow and the **Irish screwdriver** meaning a hammer (cf: **Birmingham screwdriver**, **Jewish screwdriver**). One
of the few positive terms is **Irish lace**, a spider's web, although in
US politics an Irish shift is an even a more than routinely hypo-
critical action by a politician. Finally come the **lace-curtain Irish**:
genteel petit-bourgeois Irish-Americans; who adorn their windows with such items and the rhyming slang exclamation **too Irish
stew!** meaning too true!

Paddy, the diminitive of Patrick, is synonymous with Irish and
thus **Paddyland** or **Patland** means Eire. And in a grim finale, a
Fenian or **three cold Irish** was the name given in late 19C
Victorian taverns for the threepenny measures of Irish whiskey and
cold water, sold both in 1867 when the Fenians Allen, Larkin and
O'Brien – The Manchester Martyrs – were hanged for the murder
of Police Sergeant Brett and in 1882 when three more Fenians
were hanged for the Phoenix Park murders in Dublin.

THE DUTCH

In Britain's lexicon of national stereotypes the Dutch are two-faced,
selfish, gluttonous and definitely not a nationality with whom to
do business. A harsh judgement on a country best-known to most

contemporary Britons for its footballers and its liberal drug legislation, but between the 17th and 18th centuries – after the Spanish and prior to the French – the Dutch provided the necessary national enemy. Rivals in trade, as well as on the battlefield, the Dutch were convenient bugbears and much of the slang that has accrued to the word **Dutch** duly reflects that role.

Ironically, given the imminence of the French or **frogs★** as the national bogeymen, the 18C Dutch were known as **froglanders**, possibly from the term **Dutch nightingale**, a frog. Alternatively a Dutchman was a **butterbox. Dutchman**, however, meant a German, a terminology reflected in the phrase *Pennsylvania Dutch*, a German, not Flemish dialect, and based on a mispronunciation of *deutsch*, meaning German.

Dutch as a noun is best known as a Cockney term for wife, almost invariably as **old Dutch**. The precise origins of this remain debatable. Either, as is still the majority belief, the term is an abbreviation of the rhyming slang **Duchess of Fife**, or, according to the 19C music hall star Albert Chevalier, whose signature song was entitled 'My Old Dutch', the term was semantically linked to another piece of slang: **dial★**: face. In Chevalier's version, the original term was 'my old Dutch clock', whose face, ie. **dial**, resembled that of his wife. Partridge, formerly a partisan of the Duchess, claimed to have changed his mind in the later editions of the *DSUE*. The *OED*, however, while citing Chevalier's song in 1893, has a previous citation, dated four years earlier, and states unequivocally that in this context **dutch** is 'an abbrev. of duchess'. A secondary noun form is as beer, a 17C term which is part of a list in which **English** is ale, **Spanish** sack, **Latin** Alicante and so on. A second piece of undoubted rhyming slang is **dutch plate** (20C), meaning mate.

While none of these noun forms has any bearing on racial stereotyping, as a verb **dutch** offers a selection of hostile terms, meaning variously to speak emphatically, to ruin another's business, social standing, enjoyment, etc. with deliberate malice; or to bet in such a way that the bank is broken.

From hereon in, in a variety of more or less pejorative combinations, stereotyping takes over. Perhaps the best-known of these put-downs is **Dutch courage**, cowardice that, fortified by generous quantities of alcohol, becomes (temporary) bravery. Coined during the 18C it has gained a modern successor in **dry Dutch courage**, in which the consumption of narcotics replaces that of the traditional alcohol. Almost equally common is the **Dutch uncle** (19C), whose persona trades on the image of the Dutch as stolid Calvinists. Thus to **talk like a Dutch uncle** is to talk severely and critically, to lay down the law. Thus **Dutch consolation** or **comfort** (18C) is strictly limited; as Grose defined it in 1796, 'Thank God it is no worse'. To **talk double Dutch** or **Dutch fustian** or **High Dutch** was (and in the case of double Dutch remains) to talk any foreign language.

To turn to Anglo-Dutch mercantile rivalry, a **Dutch bargain** (17C) is either a one-sided bargain, or a deal concluded over drinks, and as such also known as a **wet bargain**. A **Dutch auction** (19C) is a mock auction or sale in which the much-touted 'reductions' have no bearing in commercial fact; a **Dutch reckoning** (17C) is bill presented as a lump sum, with no details attached; otherwise it is a bill that if disputed only gets higher (17C) or, amongst sailors, a bad day's work (19C). Flanders, synonymous with Holland, offers a **Flanders fortune** (17C): a very small one, a **Flanders piece** (17C): a painting that looks good from a distance but no so good close-up, and a **Flanders reckoning** or **Flemish account** (17C): a badly prepared account, or books that do not balance.

On a social level the Dutch are much vilified as both mean and greedy. Thus the well-known **Dutch treat** or **Dutch party** (19C) describes an an outing, a visit to a restaurant, or whatever in which the costs are shared equally — i.e. there is no 'treat' at all in the sense of one party being entertained at the other's expense. To indulge in such an outing is known as **eating in Dutch street**, and **going Dutch**, although the latter has also been used for committing suicide, on the lines, presumably, of **doing the Dutch** (19C): to desert or run away. This meanness is underlined in **Dutch fuck** (World War II): the lighting of one cigarette from another — thus saving matches. Still in the world of food a **Dutch red** is a smoked Dutch herring, **Dutch gleek** (17C) is any form of drinks, and a **Dutch feast** (18C) is one where the entertainer gets drunk before his friends, while at a **Dutch concert** or in a **Dutch medley**

(18C) everyone plays a different tune. A **Dutchman's drink** (19C) is one that empties the pot or drains some form of communal drinking vessel, while a **Dutchman's headache** (19C) means drunkenness (cf: **Irish headache**, **Irish toothache**).

Britain's maritime rivalry with Holland inevitably coloured the language. A **Dutchman's anchor** (19C) is anything that has been forgotten or left behind; the term comes supposedly from a Dutch skipper who claimed after suffering a shipwreck that while he had an excellent anchor, he had unfortunately left it at home. To the 17C a **Dutch caper** was a light privateering ship, while in the 19C a **Dutch brig** was the cells on a ship (a term perpetuated, without the Dutch, in the US military), **Dutch pennants** were untidy ropes and a **Dutchman's Cape** imaginary land on the oceanic horizon. More recently a **Dutchman's fart** has become a sea urchin. A **Dutchman's breeches** (19C) are two streaks of blue in an otherwise cloudy sky. A **Dutch pump** (17C) was a naval punishment involving vigorous pumping.

Given the odium the Dutch in general enjoyed, Dutch women, inevitably, were branded as immoral. **Dutch by injection** meant any woman living with foreigner, a **Dutch widow** (17C) was a whore while a **Dutch wife** (19C) was a bolster, otherwise defined as a 'masturbation machine'. More recently **Dutch dumplings** are the buttocks while a **Dutch girl** is a lesbian, punning on the 'dikes' of Holland (cf: **dyke**). A **Dutch kiss** describes any form of sexual intimacy, although not intercourse.

On a personal level a **Dutch cheese** (19C) was a bald person, a **Dutch build** or **Dutch built** (19C) indicated a stocky, thickset individual while a **flanderkin** was a fat man. A **Dutch palate** (17C) was a coarse palate, **Dutch pegs** are rhyming slang for legs (cf: **Scotch pegs**) and **Dutch pink** (19C) is blood. A **Dutch oven** is the mouth, although it can also describe the smell of a bed in which someone has just farted (both early 20C).

Finally **in dutch** (20C) means in trouble or out of favour, to **beat the Dutch** (18C) meant to do something outstanding while in 19C **that beats the Dutch** described something that was otherwise barely credible and in the early 20C **sink the Dutch** was a general exclamation of distaste.

THE FRENCH

Despite the French, or at least the Normans having played a central role in the essential development of what is now seen as the British character, linguistically France has been set firmly among the tribes without the law since the early 18C. With the gradual fading of Holland as a major power, France, with the advent of first the Revolution and then Napoleon's expansionist wars which pitted her directly against Britain, took over as Britain's national enemy. But although the French too lost their bugaboo status – around the end of the 19C – to be replaced, somewhat reluctantly it sometimes appeared, by the Germans, slang did not forget them. They had gained a secondary, and far more pervasive stereotype: that of sexiness, a quality that, from the Protestant point of view, is perhaps even more threatening than military might.

The adjective **French** is still redolent of fantasies of 'gay Paree' and its supposedly sex-crazed denizens. At best they are obsessed with sex, at worst downright pornographic and dirty. Henry Fielding, in *Tom Jones*, refers, with some disapproval, to 'French novels' in 1749; 'French postcards', those prototype pin-ups, appear a century and a half later, along with the equally 'naughty' French prints, although the **French kiss**, no doubt an age-old phenomenon, is, linguistically at least, a 20C development.

GENERAL

What would appear to be the earliest slang use of French is to describe a variety of slang itself: **pedlar's French**, which from the 14C was a synonym for cant or criminal slang. Thus in 1386 Chaucer described one such user, 'And French she spak ful faire and fetishly/After the scole of Stratford atte Bowe/for Frensh of Paris was to hir unknowe'. At the same time **French** or **Frankish fare** meant over elaborate politeness.

By the 17C **the Frenchman** was shorthand for any foreigner, although the term, plus definite article, moved on in the 19C to mean alternatively syphilis or brandy. **Frenchie** (19C) – as in 'those Frenchies seek him everywhere' – meant simply Frenchman.

To have **seen the French King** (17C) meant to be drunk, while **French pie** was Irish stew, **French pigeon** (19C) was a pheasant mistakenly shot in partridge season and a **French 75** (fr. the eponymous World War I era gun) was a Tom Collins (a cocktail made of gin, lime or lemon juice, sugar, and soda water) mixed with champagne. A **French loaf** was £4.00, based on the backslang **roaf**: four; to **French inhale** (20C US) was to blow out smoke through the nose, while in the gay lexicon of the Fifties and Sixties a **French kiss filter** was any filter-tipped cigarette. Another gay term was **French bathe**, meaning to use perfumes as a deodorant in lieu of bathing. In a new, and somewhat unlikely twist on the traditional **Birmingham screwdriver**, the **French screwdriver** is a hammer: the assumption being that the French, like the Brummies, prefer to bash rather than turn their screws. Finally one of the best-known, and older 'French' phrases is **French leave** (18C), meaning to absent oneself from a job or duty without prior permission; the French duly return the compliment with *filer a l'anglaise*, meaning just the same.

SEXUAL

Excuse or **pardon my French** exclaims the genteel euphemism automatically offered after the speaker has sworn in public. There may be a subconscious recognition of the old **pedlar's French** (above) but this linkage of France and the French to everything 'dirty' underpins the remainder of this vocabulary, much of it central to the discourse of pre-Gay Liberation, ie. unashamedly queeny, campy homosexuality.

Francophobia is at its most rampant in those terms relating to sexually transmitted diseases and a variety of such terms can be found at VENEREAL DISEASE. The deep **French kiss**, as noted above, is not gender-linked and nor are a range of terms based on oral sex, notably the act of fellatio. Fellatio itself can be **French tricks**, **French love**, **French head job** or the **French art** or **culture** (cf: **English culture**★, **Greek culture**★ and **Swedish** culture*), while to **french** means simply to fellate (1950s); **French active** is the active (sucking) partner and **French passive** the fellated. Anyone particularly adept at fellatio is **French by injection**, (although **German** or **Dutch by injection** both refer to a woman, living and having sex with any type of foreigner); **French language expert** (gay use) is a fellator, while **French language training** (gay use) means teaching fellatio. To **tell a French joke** (gay use) is oral stimulation of the anus.

A **French letter** or **French safe** (19C) is a contraceptive sheath (the French fight back with *capote anglaise*), although it was for a time used in the RAF to mean a windsock or wind indicator. A **French tickler** is a contraceptive sheath with extra protrusions for added stimulation. A **French article** was a French prostitute (20C) but earlier (18/19C) it could also be synonymous with **French cream, elixir** or **lace** to mean brandy. A **French postcard** (20C, gay use) was an exciting, prospective sexual partner. To **speak French** was to indulge in unconventional sexual play.

French dip (gay use) is vaginal precoital fluid, **French dressing** (gay use) is semen as is **French-fried ice cream**. A **French embassy** (gay use) was a YMCA where homosexual activity ran extensively and unchecked, a **French photographer** (gay use) took gay porn, while **French stuff** (gay use) was either the pictures he captured or simply any out of the ordinary sexual activity. Finally in a camp tribute to a new era, the **French revolution** was the movement for homosexual rights.

THE CHINESE

George Orwell set it out in his essay 'Boys' Weeklies' (1939) when he apostrophised the stereotypes of popular culture: 'Chinese: sinister, treacherous, wears pigtail'. This last differentiated him from the Spaniard, Mexican, Arab, Afghan and the like, who betrayed similarly deficient, i.e., non-English, sensibilities but at least scorned the added insult of an alien hairstyle. Of all the racial stereotypes that have yet fully to vanish, probably only the French and the Jews exercise the same fascination on the British imagination, and on the nation's slang vocabulary, as do the Chinese. And while the first are 'dirty' and the second 'money-grabbing', both at least are white. The **heathen Chinee** (coined 1870 by US writer Bret Harte [1836-1902] in his poem 'Plain Language from Truthful James', better known, from this coinage, as 'The Heathen Chinee'), or the 'yellow peril' (1890s) as these terms bear out, are not just different, but wily, 'inscrutable' and oriental too. Not only that, but the shape of their eyes is not as that of Western eyes. Thus the 'Chinaman' is not to be trusted, and the underlying implication of all these terms is of something slightly out of true, either physically, ethically, or otherwise. Typical of this attitude are the phrases **damned clever, these Chinese**, or **clever chaps these Chinese**, both of which are used when remarking on some particularly ingenious or incomprehensible invention; apparently coined in the Services during World War II and then filtering into 'civvy street', the attribution owes less to the skill of the Chinese than to their supposed wiliness.

The first mainstream appearance of the Far East in slang would appear to date to the mid-19C, when the term **chop-chop**, from Cantonese pidgin, was recorded as being used to mean 'quickly!' or 'hurry up!'. This in turn may well have stemmed from the century-earlier **chop**, meaning to hurry, and presumably imported by sailors involved in the China Sea trade.

It was still geography, rather than racial stereotyping, that created the first slang use of **China** itself in the UK: mid-19C Cockneys used it as a blanket term, meaning anywhere other than England (possibly even than London) or the place rich people went for holidays; a **Chinaman**, logically, was thus anyone not wearing Western dress. The other 19C use of **china** is totally coincident: the rhyming slang **china plate,** to mean mate. Given that even London's Chinatown (Gerrard Street, Soho) was not really established until the 1970s, specifically racial terms are very much a 20C phenomenon. They include **chink, chinky** and the rhyming slang **tiddley-wink; chinky-chonks** (c.1978) means Asians in general, a term reminiscent of the earlier **nig-nogs***, meaning not just

niggers (i.e. West Indians and Africans), but Indians, Pakistanis and Arabs.

Chinaman first appears in SE in the 18C, meaning a trader in porcelain; its purely racial aspect emerges in the 1850s, first used in print by the US writer Ralph Waldo Emerson in 1854. Twenty years later it had crossed the Atlantic, often as 'John Chinaman'. There are various slang terms involving Chinaman: in America a **Chinaman's chance** (or **Chinese chance**) means no chance whatsoever, or no luck; it comes from the gold rush of the 1840s, when the Chinese worked otherwise abandoned claims. **Chinaman**, possibly through the Cockney use of **China★**, meant an Irish immigrant to the UK.

A **Chinaman's** or **Chinese copy** (1920s) is a slavishly precise drawing of a structure or piece of apparatus, based exclusively on its appearance with no other information; the term is presumably based on the alleged – if unproven – copying by the Chinese of things Western, a slur echoed in attitudes to Japanese inventiveness during the 1950s. A **Chinaman's shout** is a synonym for a **Dutch treat★**. Considered politically incorrect today, the one area where **Chinaman** still goes unchallenged is in cricket where it is an off break bowled out of the back or side of the hand by a left-handed bowler, an action that is equivalent to that of the right-hander in bowling a leg break. The term was first used to describe the bowling style of the West Indian player Ellis Achong in 1930s. As his name attests, Achong was of Chinese descent, but the slang refers to the wiliness of the bowler, rather than any real racial origin.

Cricket also provides, this time with slantedness aforethought, the **Chinese cut** (1930s): this is a stroke that sends the ball in quite another direction from that in which the batsman aimed. However such slantedness cannot be solely Chinese, at least in sporting terms: the lucky shot is also known variously as a **Staffordshire**, **Surrey** or **Harrow cut**. Other 'Chinese' terms include **Chinese duckets** (US), complimentary tickets to a theatrical or sporting event (otherwise known as **Chinees**); such tickets were punched with holes like old fashioned Chinese money. The holes are also the source of their alternative name: *Annie Oakleys*, taken from the celebrated markswoman's shooting of the pips from playing cards.

Chinese fire drill (1940s, bedlam, chaos), **chinese brown**, **chinese rocks**, **chinese white** and **chinese number 9** are all forms of heroin; sex **chinese fashion** has the partners lying on their side; the **chinese national anthem**: loud burp; a **chinese ace** (US World War I) lands with 'wun wing lo', as does one making a **chinese landing**; in the same punning refrain **chinese consumption** (Aus. 1930s) denotes a sufferer with smoker's cough or 'wun bung lung' A popular US phrase for extreme difficulty is **harder than chinese arithmetic**. The **chinese screwdriver** (a hammer) is synonymous with the **Birmingham screwdriver**.

Like its nearer East equivalent **an Indian**, **a Chinese** is a Chinese meal, often a takeout; Chinese food is also **Chink chow**. **Chow** itself, a synonym for Chinaman in Australia c. 1880, means any food, especially in an institutional setting. Originally used as such in America c.1856, the term passed onto the Raj, and is recorded as such by Yule and Burnell (*Hobson-Jobson*) in 1886.

Finally the US campus phrase to **get Chinese** is to succumb heavily to a given drug, although usually marijuana; the inference, as ever, is in the stereotype rather than the fact: thus it is the deviousness of the Chinese that underlies the term, not the presence of the quintessential Chinese drug, opium.

POLICE

THE POLICEMAN

In the words of John Farmer and W. E. Henley, writing in their *Slang and its Analogues* (1890-1904), the police are 'a class of men who, perhaps, above all others, have been the recipients of nicknames and epithets, and these, be it noted, not always of a complimentary character.' Indeed, the oldest of such terms, **beak**, seems to bear this out. It dates to 1573 when in Thomas Harman's *Caveat for Common Cursetours* it was defined as 'constable'. The term occurs as part of **harman beck**, **harman** meaning 'the stocks', and the constable might thus be seen – although there is no hard etymological proof—as one who works as the 'beak' of the stocks, plucking up malefactors like a bird with a worm. The parallel meaning of magistrate or justice of the peace emerges later: certainly the JP Sir John Fielding was known c.1750 as 'the Blind Beak'. It remains the primary, if dated, use, but the older meaning lasted until the mid 19C. Dekker uses it in 1609, and the term **budge a beak** or 'run away from the constable' appears a year later. But by 1890, despite its use in Thackeray (1840) **beak** as policeman had been long overtaken by a new term.

Peeler, named for Robert Peel, the Secretary for Ireland (1812-18), first described only the Irish constabulary. As of 1828, when Peel's Metropolitan Police Act set up the embryonic modern police force, the term crossed the Irish Sea. Peel's given name added a second term, **bobby**, although the phrase **Bobby the beadle** had long been in use to describe the guardian of any open space, and Oxford's proctors, responsible for University discipline, were once called **bobbies**. **Peeler** did not survive the 19C in England, although it still persists in Northern Ireland; **bobby**, a neutral, even affectionate nickname, remains common.

Across the Atlantic the word was **cop**, anglicised as **copper**; it emerges around 1840. In either case the term springs from the Latin *capere*, meaning to take or capture. There is some British dialect use of **cop** later in the century. Dialect also produces the Liverpudlian **scuffer**, a derivative of the Scots/Northumbrian **scufter** meaning a busy, hurrying person; another root may lie in Yorkshire's **scuff**: 'a mean sordid fellow, the scum of the people' (Wright) and even from **scurf**, the back of the neck, and thus one who grabs you by it. A further 'occupational' term was the early-19C **forty-pounder**, referring not to weight but to the cash bonus awarded to any policeman who secured a 'Tyburn ticket', i.e. captured a murderer.

Other general terms include **bulky** (Scots dial. 1821), **fry** (fr. pry?), **grog** (fr. his alleged drinking habits) and **mug** (US 1929), a term used originally by US tramps to mean a tough guy and thus foisted on their enemy, the policeman. Hobo slang also produced **shag** and **shagger** (US 1930 both from the noun meaning a chase organized by the police or irate citizenry). **The works** stems possibly from being 'worked over' with the third degree, while **the**

law (1929), and **the man** (1938, especially amongst drug users, who use the same term for their dealer) are self-explanatory.

The specialist Romany language of gypsies and market traders offers three terms, notably **rozzer** (1890) which echoes *roozlo*, meaning strong, although it might be a corruption of 'roast' as in figuratively 'roasting' a villain. **Mork** (1889) and **muskra** both come from *mooshkeroo*: constable. **Mingra** is another market term, but neither from Romany nor any dialect. Instead it has been linked to **minger**: prowler, which in turn stems from **mingy**: deceitful. That said, as a pejorative term it might have links to the Romany *mindj*, popularised as **minge★** and meaning the female genitals.

THE DETECTIVE

London's 'detective policemen' were formed, as the plainclothes branch of the regular force, in 1843; by 1856 term had been reduced to 'detective' and by 1879 villains had abbreviated this to **'tec**. By the turn of the century there were a number of new terms. **Bogey** (1910) was based on the old synonym for the devil; like Satan the police were 'persons much to be dreaded'. The **busy** (1910) was just that; his uniformed colleague might plod steadily along his beat, the detective hustled about. **Dick**, and its abbreviation **D** may well stem from the Romany *dikk*: to look at (derived in turn from the Hindi imperative *dekh-na*: look!) but since its coinage c.1879 it has been primarily an American usage. **Dick** also meant Irish-Catholic in America and as such relates to **shamus★**, the quintessential 'Irish' nickname for members of the force.

Other terms include **hawkshaw** (UK 1863) the name of a detective originally created in Tom Taylor's play *The Ticket of Leave Man*, the first ever melodrama to feature a detective. **Hawkshaw** was revived by Cecil Henry Bullivant in his 'novelization' of the play, which appeared under same name in 1935 and in US cartoonist Gus Mager's strip *Hawkshaw the Detective*. **Pink** (1904, often found as **the Pinks**) is an abbreviation of the Pinkertons, the detective agency founded by Allan Pinkerton (!1819-94) in 1850; the Pinkerton's reputation as strike-breakers gives **fink**, both a company policeman and a police informer. The **fuzz**, a popular term among 1960s youth, and meaning any form of policeman, dates to 1931, although its etymology remains obscure; possibly it comes from 'fuss', since a policeman makes a 'fuss' over criminality.

THE NOVICE

As with new boys (and latterly girls) in the army and the world of sports, the novice policeman is a **rookie**. The origin remains obscure, but the accepted etymology is a corruption of 'recruit'; certainly Kipling used it as such in the *Barrack Room Ballads* (1892). That said, the term is almost exclusively American today. In Britain the popular equivalent is the undoubtedly derogatory **wally** or **wolly**, which enjoyed a brief celebrity in mainstream slang during the early 1980s. Other terms include **butterboy**, in whose mouth butter will not melt, and the foolishly naive **dupey-dupe**. His peers in America are **choirboys** (the title of a Joseph Wambaugh police procedural), innocents who work strictly by the rulebook.

THE UNIFORM

Police uniforms provide, through metonymy, a number of nicknames. Early uniforms, whether American or British, were invariably blue: thus **blue, bluebelly, bluebottle, blueboy, bluecoat** (all 19C) and, more recently, **sky** (US 1980). Similarly one finds **buttons, brass buttons**, and **brassey**; British plainclothesmen describe their colleagues as the **button mob**. Colours other than blue emerge in Australia's names for a parking policeman: the **brown bomber**, and his successor the **grey ghost**. In Toronto a **green hornet** is a motorcycle policeman, named both for his uniform and for the *Marvel Comics* superhero. The briefly popular **blue meanie** was based on colour as well, but derived its real inspiration from the Beatles' cartoon film, *Yellow Submarine* (1967).

The traditional policeman works on foot and walking the beat has produced a number of variations on **flatfoot** (US 1900), including **flat, flat arch, flathead, flatter** and **flattie**; similar are **beat pounder, pavement pounder** and **sidewalk snail. Crusher** (UK 1835), used variously to mean a naval policeman, a member of the Special Branch or of the military police, as well as the everyday constable, refers to the officer's supposedly outsize boots. **Gumshoe** (US 1925), on the other hand, emphasizes the need for silence, and like **gum foot, gum heel, gomes, goms** and **round-heels** means detective. Paradoxically so does **squeaky shoe**.

A **rubber heel** (UK 1935) works either for Britain's political police – the Special Branch – or the various bodies charged with investigating corrupt policemen. The Special Branch are also known as the **heavies**, the **heavy mob**, the **hot lot** and, acknowledging their bureaucratic masters in Whitehall, the **umbrella branch**. Their American cousins, the Federal Bureau of Investigation (FBI) are either **feds, G** (government) **men** (US 1922) or **T** (Treasury) **men** (US 1938).

LINGUISTIC TERMS

Like many slang terms, some of those covering the police have a purely linguistic dimension. Though largely obsolete today, back-slang has produced **slop** (UK 1855), **esclop, namesclop** (police, policeman) and **reppock** (copper). Other terms include **ossifer** and **Richard** (abbrev. of **dick**). Rhyming slang offers **bottle (and) stopper (copper), string and top (cop), club and stick (dick)** and in Australia **Joe Goss** (the boss). The Flying Squad, often known simply as **the Squad**, is the **Sweeney** (fr. Sweeny Todd, once the 'demon barber' of Fleet Street), a name popularised in the eponymous television programme of the 1970s. Rural policemen employed in Operation Countryman, investigating corruption in the Metropolitan force, were punningly known as **the Swedey** (fr. **swede**: peasant). Uniformed officers on that investigation, routinely dismissed as **woodentops** (fr. another, juvenile television show) repaid the compliment by calling the plainclothesmen **bananas**: 'yellow, bent and hanging around in bunches'.

A **bent copper** unsurprisingly, is a corrupt policeman, known to his criminal 'clients' as a **right copper**. There are gradations and the Knapp Commission, investigating corruption in the New York Police Dept. c. 1973 came up with two parallel categories. The **grass-eater**, while still corrupt, remains satisfied with what perks – material and financial – his beat offers; he resists canvassing for extras. His antithesis, the **meat-eater**, is less easily satisfied and actively compels people to offer him a variety of bonuses. Both are pursed by the **shoo-fly**, described either as a plain-clothes policeman on observation duty or an undercover policeman who spies on his colleagues. Both terms originate in the popular song lyric 'Shoo fly! Don't bother me'.

NAMES

Although Britain's police recruitment has no specific ethnic bias, the predominance of Irish immigrants in New York created **shamus** (US c.1925) whether a uniformed policeman or detective (and even more commonly a private detective). It comes from *Seamus*, a common Irish name and is usually pronounced as such, for all that Humphrey Bogart persists in 'sharmus' in the film of Raymond Chandler's *The Big Sleep*. Variations on **shamus** include **chom**, **chomus** and **sham**. **Paddy**, from Patrick, fits the same pattern. Similarly 'Irish' are **shamrock** (the national emblem) and **muldoon** (a common surname). A direct lift from the French gives **gendarme,** which in turn produces **John**, from which come **jack** (UK 1854) or **jacks** (usually meaning detective).

John or **Johnny** appear in a variety of combinations. **Johnny**, **Johnny Darby** (UK 1886 fr. **darbies**: handcuffs), **John Nabs**, **Johnny Gallagher** (UK 1935) and **Johnny Law** (US 1921) all denote a uniformed officer, while **John Elbow** (he grasps you by it) means detective. Aus. rhy. sl. produced **John Hop** (1900, cop), which is often found as **jonnop** (Aus. 1910). **Johnny Tin Plate** is a rural sheriff in America, as are **county mountie** (a CB radio term), **tin can cop** and **town clown**. The 'metallic' references contrast with **gold badge man**, a big city detective. **Oliver** and **Ollie** both mean uniformed policeman, presumably referring to the comedian Oliver Hardy. **Keystone** also derives from Hollywood, recalling the Mack Sennett *Keystone Cops* series of 1919.

Show business provides two further terms, both denoting a pair of patrolmen. **Dolly Sisters** comes from the singers Janszieka (1893-1941) and Roszika (1893-1970) Deutsch, better known as Jenny and Rosie Dolly. **Gallagher and Sheehan** punned on

Gallagher and Shean, Irish/Jewish vaudeville stars, touring America from 1910-14. **Sheehan**, spelt thus, was of course Irish – there weren't many Jews on the force – but the real Al Shean was the Marx Brothers' uncle and wrote their hit show *Home Again* in 1914. Finally **five-oh** or **5-0**, currently popular on the streets of America, comes from the long-running television series *Hawaii 50*.

ANIMALS

As objects of dislike, the police have always been compared with animals. **Pigs**, **bulls** and **bears** are the most common, but others came first. The long obsolete **bandog** (C15-18, from SE *band*: chain, plus *dog*) meant first a bailiff or his assistant, and before that a large guard-dog. The obscure **bolly dog** (18C) may come from **bolly**: hobgoblin. Detectives have been known as **beagles** since the 17C, and **bloodhounds** since at least 1811. The use of **stag** is a typical slang reversal. While in nature it is the stag which is pursued, 18C villains turned the meaning around, using it first to mean enemy, then informer and finally policeman.

For the revolutionary young of the 1960s and beyond, the use of **pig** (c.1811) to mean policeman may have seemed fresh-minted, but in fact it simply revived an early 19C usage. A **China Street pig** was a Bow Street officer, and the early slang dictionary the *Lexicon Balatronicum* (1811) offers **floor the pig and bolt**: knock down the policeman and run off. The more recent **Johnny Ham** (US 1934 detective) may well claim the same origin. Certainly **cozzer** (UK: 1920s) comes from the Yiddish *chazer*: pig. Other Yiddishisms include **chapper**, possibly a pun on **copper**, and **yentzer** meaning fucker, and thus cheat, deceiver and liar.

Bull (US 1859) derives either from the German *bulle* or the Spanish *bul*, both slang terms for policemen. It appears in a number of combinations, notably **harness bull** (US 1903), **percentage bull** (a bribe-taker) **cinder bull** and **yard bull** (both railroad police) and **mother bull** and **mama bull**, two terms for police-woman, a job otherwise known by the less than inventive **copess** or **officerette**.

American again, **bear** (US c.1975), the most recent animal coinage, comes from Smokey the Bear, a cartoon figure used in US fire prevention advertising. Citizens' Band radio enthusiasts took up the term to mean state policeman, so-called for the wide-brimmed hat worn by many such officers. It has numerous variants, especially as used to mean policewoman, including **girlie bear, lady bear, mama bear, woolly bear, smokey beaver** and **mama smokey**. **Bear tracker** means detective and **baby bear** trainee. A nice variation is **goldie-locks**: a uniformed police woman. Other animals include **frog** (because he jumps on you suddenly), the derogatory **weasel** and the **roach** (fr. cockroach). One fish, the **lobster**, has been adapted from the 18C term for the red-coated British soldiery.

ACTIVITIES

As the action so the man. What police do, or are seen as doing, has created a number of names, the classic being **plod** (UK c.1981), taken from Enid Blyton's PC Plod in the stories of Noddy the Elf. The aggressive side of police activities is reflected in **door shaker, skullbuster, stick man, knock man** or **knocko, slapman** and the Aus. **walloper**, while the activities of the **man hunter** are seen in **roper** (the image is of a cowboy roping cattle), **reeler** (who reels you in) and **satch** (fr. satchel: he puts you 'in the bag'). Similar are **nab, pincher, puller, shoulder tapper** and **clap-shoulder, nipper, snatcher** and **pinch and padlock man**. The essentially underhand activities of the detective give **peeker, sneaker, split, spotter** and **sneezer**, all of which can also mean informer. The police can also take on the characteristics of body parts. They can be the **arm** or the **limb** (of the law), a **claw**, an **elbow** (US 1899), a **finger** (US 1899), or a **nose** (UK 1860). Surveillance gives one **big eyes** and **elephant's ears**. CID men are known as **brains**.

SPECIAL TERMS

Finally, a number of specialist terms. The vice squad is the **pussy posse** (US fr. **pussy**: woman as a sex object) or the **tom squad** (UK 1940s, from **tom**: prostitute). A plainclothesman hanging around lavatories in the hope of entrapping gay men is a **crapper dick** (fr. **crapper**: lavatory plus **dick***) or one of the **pretty police**. Community police, parole officers and other supposedly 'caring' figures are known as **compash** (compassionate officers), while the much derided special constable is a **hobby bobby**. As well as **bear** and **smokey** CB Radio offers **Kojak with a Kodak**, meaning a policeman manning a radar speed trap and taken from the popular 1970s television show and the make of camera. **Skipper** or **skip** means sergeant in the UK, and captain in the US, and in the latter a **rusty-gun** is a veteran.

BEGGARS AND BEGGING

Britain's recent economic woes may have brought beggars onto the streets in numbers unknown in most people's lifetimes, but the phenomenon of street begging is far from new and such linguistic authorities as Harman and Grose, and such sociologists as Henry Mayhew, whose *London Labour and the London Poor* (4 vols. 1861-62) make it clear that science of begging was a complex and multi-faceted enterprise whether in the 16th, 18th or 19th century. Indeed, Harman's *Caveat* (1567) deals almost exclusively with the character and vocabulary of what would become known by 1650 as the **canting crew**, a term based on cant, from the Latin *cantus*, meaning singing, song, or chant and as such referring to the patter of various sorts emanating from the begging classes or **crew** (a word incidentally that is barely altered in its meaning when used as a self-description by today's inner city gangs. **Canting** is used by Harman only to describe the thieves' and beggars' language — but the meaning and its origins are identical.

It is the fine-tuning of the mendicant world and the vocabulary that accompanies it that impresses the modern reader. It is also notable that certain pertinent words, notably **skipper**, **mumper** and **moocher**, have lasted until today, without much variation on the meanings they held up to four centuries ago. Taken in turn,

skipper meant sleeping rough, which in 16th century England meant in a barn, and as such probably stemmed from the Welsh *ysgubor* meaning barn; **mumper** (beggar) or **mump** (to beg) appeared c.1670, both come from the Dutch *mompen*, meaning cheat; the term was further developed (although this use has not persisted) as **mumpins**, meaning alms. **Moocher**, found in such variations as the song 'Minnie the Moocher', the New York street insult **mook**, particularly popular in Scorsese's *Mean Streets* (1973), and the everyday 'mooching around', all stem from the earlier **mooch** or **mouch**, itself rooted in Old French *muchier*: to hide or skulk. Other terms, typically **go to Bath**, still have a contemporary resonance. As a wealthy, fashionable town Bath attracted a flood of beggars in the 18C; those citizens who complain of today's invasion of **crusties** would doubtless sympathise.

THE 'CANTING CREW'

It is impossible to list every gradation of beggar, although the reader should look also at the section on THIEVES and thieving for further information. Harman, writing of the **cursetors** (fr. Latin *currere*: to run) or vagabonds of Elizabethan England, cites three chief orders of 'the unruly rabblement of rascals': **upright men**, **rogues** and **palliards**, and at the end of his work, actually lists a selection of the most notorious, or at least those who frequented what are now the Home Counties. Among such long-dead names are 'Harry Smith, hee dryveleth when he speaketh', 'Robert Browswerd, he weareth his heare long' and 'Richard Horwood, wel neer lxxx. yeare old, he will bite a vi. peny nayle asunder with his teeth and a baudy dronkard.' Although these labels, and some that follow, appear to be standard English, they were all specialist terms of their time, each pertaining to a distinctive style of beggary.

In due order, the **upright man** was a senior criminal, outranked (if at all) only by a **ruffler**. The term comes literally from his stance —he adopted no form of counterfeit physical deformity as did many of his peers – and in his pose as a solid citizen. As such he both gulled the public and commanded loyalty and financial dues from his inferiors. The **rogue** (which term held a specific cant meaning between the 16C-18C, before it was absorbed into standard English) wandered the country armed with some form of official-looking letter or other document to justify such travelling. Backed by this 'licence' he would beg for alms, often underlining his appeal with claims of illness. Sometimes he worked with a woman, a **pullet**, as a team. The **palliard** took his names from the French *paille*, or straw, upon which he slept as wandered the country, taking his nightly refuge in barns or outhouses. The antithesis of the **upright man**, he adorned himself with faked, but still convincingly hideous sores and wounds. His clothes were invariably ragged, and his patched cloak was almost a badge of office. The term emerged c.1484, alongside its standard English definition: 'a low or dissolute knave; a lewd fellow, a lecher, a debauchee'.

To these Harman adds a number of fellow villains, not all of whom were strictly beggars, although all wandered the countryside. The **ruffler**, the 'first rank of canters', posed as soldier, but actually worked as an itinerant robber; the word comes from SE *ruffle it*: to swagger and is linked to the idea of a bird ruffling up its feathers. The **hooker** or **angler**, used a hook on a stick to filch objects from market stalls, shops and passing carts, a **prigger of prauncers** was a horse thief (**prig**: steal, **prauncer**: a horse). A **frater** (Latin: brother) was a fake friar claiming to beg alms for a hospital or charitable institution; adopting a similarly religious guise an **abraham** or **abram man** or **cove**, was a 'lusty strong rogue' who posed as a poor, crazy and, through his deliberately tattered clothing, naked or 'abraham' man. **Abraham men** appeared shortly after the dissolution of the monasteries in 1538: bereft of the alms they had regularly gathered from such institutions, they were forced to beg for their subsistence. Two centuries later, the term had been adopted by those who posed as sham naval ratings, equally distressed, and equally demanding. A **fresh-water mariner**, 'their shippes were drowned in the playne of Salisbury', claimed to have suffered shipwreck or piracy; a **counterfeit crank** (fr. Dutch or German *krenk*: sickness) faked sickness, a **dommerar** or **dummerer** feigned dumbness, often claiming to have suffered at the hands of the infidel Turk who, on capturing them during a sea voyage, had torn out their tongue for denying Muhammed; a **jark**

man forged passports (for internal travelling) and a **glimmer** claimed to have lost all his, or more commonly her possessions in a fire (fr. **glim**: fire).

A more general term is **clapperdudgeon**: 'a beggar born'. The word comes from the combination of *clapper*, meaning hitter, plus *dudgeon*, the hilt of a dagger. Its origins remain a mystery, but it has been suggested that it comes from the beggar hitting his *clapdish* (a wooden dish with a lid, carried by lepers, beggars and mendicants generally, to give warning of their approach, and to receive alms) with a *dudgeon*. The later **staff striker** means much the same.

Although women are not included in his lists of names ('the number of them is great and would ask a large volume'), Harman includes a number of female beggars: a **bawdy basket** sold obscene literature (as well as pins, ballads and other goods); an **autem mort** (meaning married woman and taken from the cant terms **autem**: church and **mort**: woman) was the companion of an **upright man** – 'shee is a wyfe married at the church and they be as chaste as a cowe, [which] gooeth to bull every month, with what bull she careth not.' A **walking mort**, often accompanied by a child, claimed to be widowed and begged for her and her offspring's keep; **doxies** (fr. the Dutch *docke,* a doll) and **dells** ('a yonge wenche, able for generation, and not yet knowen by the vpright man') were simple beggars, usually alongside a man. Last came the **kynchin co** and **kynchin mort**: boys and girls brought up to beg and steal.

Uncatalogued by Harman, are further contemporary terms and occupations. **Master of the black art** meant any beggar; a **curtall** or **curtail** was noted for his characteristic short jacket (curtail), while a **Tom of Bedlam** or **Bedlam beggar**, was the genuine version of the poor, ragged madman counterfeited by the **abraham man**. His name was taken from Bedlam, by the 16th century a generic term for lunatic asylum, but originally applied specifically to the Hospital of St. Mary of Bethlehem in London, founded as a priory in 1247, with the special duty of receiving and entertaining the bishop of St. Mary of Bethlehem, and his retinue as often as they might come to England. A general hospital by 1330, it became in 1402 a hospital for lunatics; on the Dissolution of the Monasteries, it was granted to the mayor and citizens of London, and in

1547 incorporated as a royal foundation for the reception of lunatics. A **hallan shaker** (fr. Scots *hallan*: the partition of a cottage wall, especially when it cut off the front door from the fire) referred to any 'sturdy' or able-bodied (and possibly violent) beggar. To beg was to **maund**, possibly from the French *mendier*: to beg, which in turn came from the Latin *mendicus*: a beggar and as such the root of the SE *mendicant*. The Romany *mang*: to beg, has similar origins. **Strike**, which in the 18C meant borrow, meant simply steal.

EIGHTEENTH AND NINETEENTH CENTURIES

The 'canting crew', in whatever guise, persisted as the basis of professional beggary until the middle of the 18th century, with some occupational terms persisting even longer. The *New Canting Dictionary* of 1725 lists not merely Harman's core of mendicant villains, but dozens of extra criminal types, amassing a grand total of some 64 in all, although by no means all were beggars; they can be found under THIEF. Sixty years later Francis Grose, in the first edition of his own dictionary, had cut them back to 23, fourteen types of men and nine of women and children – essentially repeating Harman's categories.

The slang dictionaries of the 19C show that some new words had joined the mendicant lexicon, even if the basic methods of extracting cash from the unwary remained essentially the same. The **fresh water mariner** had become the **turnpike** or **dry land sailor**; the **palliard** had become the **scoldrum** (fr. SE *scald*: burn), equally resplendent in his faked burns, scars and wounds, often created by the deliberate burning of the body with a mixture of acids and gunpowder; the **abraham man** was now a **shallow cove, Shivering James** or **Shivering Jemmy**, all working the 'shivering dodge': appearing naked, they would be given old clothes, these were promptly sold, and the shiverer reappeared, as naked as ever. **Shallow coves** were making 10/- to 15/- a day in the 1830s. The **rogue,** armed with his faked documents had been replaced by the **silver beggar**, brandishing fake 'briefs' – 'official' papers, personal testimony and the like –to claim losses in fire, shipwreck and other alleged disasters. The **bawdy basket** had been joined by the

durrynacker, a female lace-hawker, who doubled as a fortune-teller; the term may come from the Romany *dukker.* to tell fortunes.

Other contemporary terms include the **croaker**, who whinged on about his problems; the **maunder(er)**, (a traveller, cf. **maund**); the **shyster** (possibly related to the **shicer***: an objectionable person, from the German *scheisse*: a shitter); the **goose shearer**, who shears gullible 'geese'; the **needy-mizzler**, a very shabby beggar, from *mizzle* meaning to run off (without paying). The **rampager** (fr. **ramp**: swindle), the **pike**, **piker** or **pikey** (fr. **pike**: turnpike), the **shack** (fr. **shake** or **shake-rag**) were all general terms for beggar. **Pikey** still exists, although **piker** means shirker in 20C Australia. **Cadge** (1810, from *catch*), **spring** (as in 'spring for a quid') and **mike** (a variation on **mooch**) meant beg. Australian vagabonds went **on the wallaby**: in the bush the wallaby was often the only creature to leave perceptible tracks; some led to water, others were aimless and wandering; the same thing went for the human 'wallaby' who might have been looking for food or work, or might simply have been walking at random.

TRAMPS

The line between the tramp and the beggar is thin, but if the beggars listed above are professionals, travelling the country as an adjunct to the begging that underpinned their daily life, then tramps, can perhaps be seen primarily as travellers. To some extent, therefore, the terminology reflects this difference of emphasis. The **gentleman of the pad** (fr. **pad**: road), the **land-raker**, the **scatterling**, and the **tinkler** all wandered the roads in 18th and 19th century England. **Pad** (fr. the Dutch *pad*, and Old High German *pfad,* and the cant equivalent of the SE path) is central to the begging world. The **high pad** (listed in Harman, is the highway or turnpike; the **padder** a beggar, **a rum pad** (18C, cf. **rum***) and a **footpad** both highway robbers, while a **padding crib*** or **padding ken*** was a lodging house. Their contemporary successors include the **hurricane lamp** (rhy. sl.), the **bindle stiff** (US 20C, from **bindle**: a bundle and **stiff**: a man), a **bum** (who tramps but rarely works; from the German *bummler.* loafer) and a **hobo** (who also tramps but whenever possible takes a job; the etymology remains obscure, although claims have been made for 'hoe-boy', a migrant farm-worker), the **dosser** (who sleeps rough, from 19C **doss**: sleep, itself from the Latin *dorsus*: back) and the **bag lady** (1972, originally a shopping bag lady, so called from her collection of bags with which she invariably travels). The hippie era offered a collective noun: **street people**, who wore the clothes but espoused more of a traditional begging ethic than that of the 'love and peace' generation. Love, in some debased form at least, was offered by the **gay cat**, a tramp that hangs around to pick up women.

Other modern terms include the **dero** (1970, derelict), the **glimmer**, (possibly from the 19C **glim-lurk**: the pleading for alms after suffering a supposed fire, but surely dating back to Harman's similarly named beggar); the **panhandler** (US, late 19C; the term stems from the goldfields, where hopefuls panned for gold, washing earth and rocks in perforated 'pans'), and the Yiddish **schnorrer**, from the German *schnurren*: to go begging.

THE THIEF

Like the criminal beggar the thief is responsible for a good deal of the earliest slang, or more precisely cant. As *Leathermore's Advice, or, The Nicker Nicked*, put it in 1666: 'Towards night, when ravenous Beasts usually seek their Prey, there comes in shoals of Hectors, trepanners, Guilts, Pads, Biters, prigs, Divers, Lifters, Kid-Nappers, Vouchers, Mill-kens, Pymen, Decoys, Shop-lifters, Foilers, Bulkers, Droppers, Famblers, Donnakers, Crosbyters, &c. Under the general application of Rooks.' It was ever thus and while the vocabulary may change, the larcenies remain the same.

THIEVES

Thieves in general were a central part of the **canters** or **canting crew★** of professional criminals who 'chaunt' or 'cant' the cant language of the contemporary underworld. A century later they had gained another name, relevant at least to those whose activities centred on London: **alsatians**. **Alsatia**, whether **Higher Alsatia** (Whitefriars in the City) or **Lower Alsatia** (around the Mint in Southwark), was thus named for Alsace Lorraine, the marginal, disputed border area between France and Germany. **Higher Alsatia**, its earlier manifestation, was once the lands of the Whitefriars Monastery, extending from The Temple to Whitefriars Street and from Fleet Street to the Thames. After the Dissolution of the Monasteries the area went downhill, and as allowed by Elizabeth I and James I its inhabitants claimed exemption from jurisdiction of City of London. As such the area became a centre of corruption, a refuge for villains and a no-man's-land for the law. As Lord Macaulay put it 'At any attempt to extradite a criminal, bullies with swords and cudgels, termagent hags with spits and broomsticks poured forth...and the intruder was fortunate if he escaped...hustled, stripped and jumped upon.' The privileges were abolished in 1697, but it was decades before the old habits died out.

The cross (17C, opposite of **the square** and as such another generic term for thieving) gives the **cross cove** (17C, a swindler), a **cross boy** (Aus. 19C, a crook), a **cross-biting cully** (1700, a dicing sharp), a **cross crib** (19C, a house kept by and for villains), a **cross man** (19C, thief), a **cross-mollisher** (19C, a female professional thief, from **moll***) and a **cross rattler** (19C) a fake cab which is actually used to carry off the loot from a robbery.

Other generic terms for a thief are **roberd's man** (17C), from 'roberd' or Robin Hood, a **kiddy** (18C), a **family man** (cf. **Johnson**s), a **flash cove**, **flash man** or **flash gentry** (18C). A **push** (18C) was a criminal gang, a term that has been preserved in 20C Australia, albeit usually stripped of its criminal overtones. The 19C has **family** and the US **Johnsons** or **Johnson family** (possibly from the common-ness of the surname), while the 20C has **wise guys** and **the Mob** (both specifically the Mafia). US criminals are also known collectively as **good people**, a term that may hark back to the 16C cant term **bene***, meaning good or excellent. British villains can work as a **crew** (which can also be used in an ostensibly non-criminal way of skinheads and of young blacks), a **team** (thus **team-handed**: working in a group, typically of bank robbers), a firm, and a mob (with **mob-handed**). A **made man** is a member of the US Mafia, while the US teenage street gangs of the 1950s/1960s had **debs** (girlfriends) and **coolies** (unaffiliated youths). A top criminal can be a **damber** or **dimber damber** (17C, lit. a handsome rascal), an **aaron** (19C, the Biblical Aaron was first High Priest), an **arch rogue** (18C), **arch-cove** (19C) or **arch gonnof** (19C, from the Yiddish **gonnif***: thief); a top woman criminal is an **arch dell** or **arch doxy** (both 17C); a **kite** (20C) is one who 'flies high'). An expert thief is a **boman** or **bowman** (18C, from *beau man*), a **top sawyer** (19C) or a **tradesman** (19C). Today's terms include **the Man** (although this is also a policeman and a drug dealer), **Mr Big**, a **rounder** (Canada, but US 19C, from 'going the rounds' of the criminal underworld) and one of **the Ten** (the FBI's Ten Most Wanted Criminals list).

More general terms include the 16C **prig**, **prigger**, **prigman** or **Prince Prig**; the term comes either from the Latin *pregare*: to pray, and as such underlines the contemporary role of criminal beggars, or **prig** = prick = sting = rob or cheat; **prig** meaning a carping knowall may have similar roots, but may be based on the 17C divine Richard Baxter (1615-91) who in 1684 associated it with the initial letters of PRoud IGnorance. **Prig**, in its criminal sense, could also be a synonym for the **drunken tinker**, a 16C ne'erdowell who, accompanied by his woman, wandered the country, mixing villainy and legitimate work, pursuing neither, it appears, with a great deal of energy. The 17C brings **puggard** (fr. **pug**: to tug or pull), **napper** (fr. **nap**: to grab or steal), **nimmer** (fr. **nim**: to steal; SE from 9-16C, then cant) and **pieman** or **pyman**. The **snammer** (19C) was more usually found as a **pudding-snammer**, who stole from cookshops. A **dromedary** or a **purple dromedary** was a clumsy thief, referring to the ungainliness of the creature. **Saint Peter's sons** (18C) is based on the Biblical Saint Peter 'the greatest fisherman' (cf. **angler**, **hooker**), the **fidlam-bens** (18C) would grab anything, irrespective of its value, while the **filching cove** and **filching mort** (18C) were male and female thieves, specialising in the **filch**, or long pole with which to snare items of value. **Gonef**, **gonnif**, **gonnof** and the abbreviated **gun** (all from the Yiddish *gonif*: thief) emerge in the 19C, as do **gazlon** (Yid.), **tealeaf** (rhy.sl.), **finder, geach**, (fr. Scots *geach*: to steal) **gleaner, gutter-prowler, klep** (fr. *kleptomaniac*), **nabber**, (US) and **practitioner**. **Traveller** (19C) was the self-description of beggars, vagrant thieves and other movers about, as was **commercial** (19C), borrowing from the legitimate *commercial traveller*. 20C terms include **roller** (cf. **jack-roller**), **babbler** and **babbling brook** (Aus. rhy.sl.: crook), **body, bandit, buck, face, hardhead** (Aus.), **merchant, operator** and **perp** (fr. SE *perpetrator*, as used by the police).

Small-time criminals include the **filcher** and **Hugh Prowler** (both 16C), the **sneaksman** or **sneaking budge** (17C, cf. **budge**), the **lumper** (18C), defined as 'the lowest order and more contemptible species of thieving who lurk around and grab whatever they can regardless of value, **funker** (18C, the lowest order of thieves), the **nibbler** or **nibbling cull** (19C) the **prowler** (19C, UK petty thief, US housebreaker) and the **snick fadger** (19C, from **snick**: snatch, **fadge**: farthing). 20C petty thieves include the **cruncher** and **pie-eater** (both Aus.), the **heel** and the ironically contemptuous **international milk thief, parking-meter thief** or **bandit** and the **tearaway**. In the alleged hierarchy of the US Mafia, the lowest ranks are **soldiers** or **button-men**.

A young or novice criminal has been a **Newgate bird** or **Newgate nightingale** (18C, from the prison in which they are destined to end up), a **Tyburn blossom** (18C, from the Tyburn gallows: a young thief, who will in time ripen into the mature one), **eriff** (18C) and **ziff** (19C), **JD** (juvenile delinquent), a **schoolboy** or a **virgin**. Despite constant misreadings, a **gunsel** or **gonsil** had nothing to do with guns but was a criminal's young, and possibly homosexual accomplice. Assistants and lookout men included the **snapper** or **snapper-up** (16C, then 20C US meaning plain thief), the **standing budge** (17C, fr. **budge**: to skulk), the **pushing tout** (1718, especially when operating in a **push** or crowd), the **cover** or **coverer** (19C, he covers the actual thief, pickpocket or whomever), the **whisper** (19C) and the **decker** (20C, possibly from **decko**: a glance). A **clicker** (18C) was the gang member deputed to divide up the spoils fairly; in prison jargon it meant warder: one who clicks the key, cf. **sneck drawer**). The **carrier** (17C) either carried information between gang members or carried away the proceeds of a robbery, of pick-pocketing and so on; the **swagsman** was his 19C successor (fr. 16C **swag**: a shop, and thus the shop's contents or in this case potential booty). An **earwig** (20C) is a look-out), a **seducer** (20C, Afro-American) one who provides means of making illicit cash and a **set-up man** (20C) is a planner.

THIEVES BY JOB

Many villains could be further identified by the area of theft in which they specialised. Primary among them are pickpockets, burglars and housebreakers, violent criminals, swindlers and con-men, forgers and counterfeiters. These are listed in their own discrete sub-sections. Other specialities, from cloak-snatching to grabbing goods from the back of vans, appear below, in no particular order other than the generally chronological. Among the earliest of villains, whose 'job descriptions' linked theft, swindling and beggary, were those members of the **canting crew★** listed in Harman's *Caveat*, specifically the **abraham cove, palliard, counterfeit-crank, dommerar** or **dummerer, frater, freshwater mariner, glimmerer, ruffler, upright man**, and **curtall**. They have all been dealt with properly under BEGGING. The **knight of St Nicholas** or **knight of the blade** (16C) was a wandering **ruffler★** living on his wits.

The **swigman** or **swygman** (16C) was a vagrant thief who posed as a pedlar; the term possibly originates in **swag**: a heavy pack and must be the ancestor of the 19C Australian **swagman**. The **Irish toyle** (17C) was another fake beggar, who adopted the disguise in order to gain entrance to houses which he then robbed. The **lully prigger** (16C), the **hedge creeper** (17C) and the **snow dropper** or **snow gatherer** (19C) all stole linen from hedges (where once washing was laid out to dry) or latterly from washing lines; they are the predecessors of the modern **knickers bandit** (20C), although it is sexual excitement rather than the desire to sell his booty, that primarily informs the latter.

The **ark-man, ark-pirate, ark ruff** or **ark ruffian** (18C) worked as a river thief, as did the **waterpad** or **water-sneak** (18C); the **river rat** (19C) stripped the corpses of those who drowned in

London's River Thames. The **resurrection cove** (19C) stole from graveyards and turned his grim booty over to the teaching hospitals for dissection. A **blue pigeon flyer** or **bluey-hunter** (18C) stole lead or **blue pigeon** from house roofs; the **dubber** (17C, was a lock picker, from **dub**: lock); the **cloak twitcher** (18C) stole cloaks by twitching them off wearer's back, as did the **silk-snatcher** (18C); the **sutler** (17C) stole handkerchiefs, gloves, knives, snuff- or tobacco-boxes and similar small items; the SE *sutler* sells provisions to soldiers. The **flimper** and the **jerry sneak** (19C) specialised in watches (**jerries**) although the term could also mean a henpecked husband; **onion hunters** (19C) opted for seals, and other watch-chain trinkets; the **toy getter** (19C) stole watches. The **poulterer** (19C) stole from letters – the image is one of gutting a chicken. The **jilter, jilt** or **gilt** (18C, from **jilt**: a crowbar or **gilt**: a skeleton key) or **note-blanker** (19C) worked as a sneak thief and a hotel thief. The **night bird, night-cap, night-hunter, night-poacher, night-snap, night-trader, night-walker** and **nighthawk** (all 19C) preferred to operate at night.

The 20C has the **reader** and the **slow walker** (US: both follow postmen to rob them); the **dunnigan worker** (one who robs in public lavatories, from **dunnigan***); the **shitter** (one who excretes in the place where he steals), the **nailer** (an extortionist, but also a policeman); the 19C **van-dragger** has been succeeded by the **jump-up merchant** or **jump-up man** (all of whom loot carts or trucks of their contents); the **blagger** (possibly from blackguard) was once a youthful mugger but now means thief.

HOUSEBREAKERS AND BURGLARS

17C housebreakers include the **mill ben** (fr. **mill**: chisel, **ben**: good), the **snudge** (fr. **sneak** and **budge**?; he enters a house, hides and then emerges to rob it late at night), the **darkman's budge** (a thief's accomplice who enters the house, opens it and lets the gang in) and the **glazier** or **running glazier** who goes in via a window. Entry though an open or unlocked window creates a number of terms: the **jump** (18C, he jumps through a window), the **garreteer** (19C, specialising in attics and skylights), the **par-**

lour jumper (19C), the **back-jumper** (late 19C, using the back windows) and the **fagger** (18C, and with its root in **fag**: to work hard for another, cognate with the public school term **fag**: a junior boy who works for his seniors) or **diver** (16C), a small boy who, like Oliver Twist in Dickens' eponymous novel, is put in through an otherwise impassably small window; once inside the house he either lets the gang in or passes booty out to them; a **little snakesman** (18C) performs the same service, although he enters through a drain, while the **snakesman** (19C) is his adult peer. 18C terms include **jacob** (who like his Biblical predecessor is armed with a **jacob** or ladder), a **crack** or **cracksman** (18C), and a **ken-burster** and **ken-cracker**, both from the 17C **ken-miller**, and all meaning house (**ken**) breaker. The **eves-dropper** (18C) lurked outside a house waiting for chance to break in while its owners were absent and a **skylarker** (18C) doubled as a journey-man bricklayer, using the legitimate job to facilitate the villainy: he gets up early – 'with the lark' – to spy out vulnerable houses.

A **screwsman** (19C) takes his name from the **screw** or skeleton key, while the **pannyman** (19C) derives from **panny**: house. Other 19C terms are **breaker**, **crib-man** and **crib-cracker** (fr. **crib**: house), the **creep** or **creeper** was a sneak thief, an **area-sneak** (who robbed basements, adjacent to the area), a **baster** (US), a **buster** (mid-19C) a **second-story man** or a **dancer** (a cat burglar who 'dances' along the roof and in through a convenient window; the 20C use refers to those who steal from empty offices), a **draw latch** and a **sneck drawer** (fr. 14C **sneck**: latch), both meaning latchlifter. The 20C has **flat worker** (who specialises in robbing flats) and an **in-and-out man** (a spontaneous thief).

PICKPOCKETS

Still rampant on the crowded streets of the world's great cities, the pickpocket – as well as the less dextrous **cutpurse** – is one of the oldest varieties of thief. The wide range of slang duly attests to his or her ingenuity and longevity.

The best description of a prototype pickpocketing gang can be found in Robert Greene's 'coney-catching' pamphlets of the 1590s, dealing with the fleecing of the unwary. Here, in lavish detail, he runs down the main operators: the **foist**, the **nip** and the **stall**. The **foist**, the master pickpocket, who unlike the **nip**, who uses a knife to cut the purse, uses his fingers to open it and then extract its contents, is deserving of especially lavish description: 'The Foist is so nimble-handed that he exceeds the jugler for agilitie and hath his *legiar de maine* as perfectly. Therefor an exquisite Foist must have three properties that a good Surgeon should have, and that is, an Eagles eie, a Ladies hand, and a Lions heart. An Eagles eie to spie out a purchase, to have a quick insight where the boung lies, and then a Lions heart, not to feare what the end will be, and then a Ladies hand to be light and nimble, the better and more easie to dive into any mans pocket.' The **nip**, on the other hand, was a very much inferior artist; indeed the Foist 'refuseth even to weare a knife about him, lest he be suspected to grow into the nature of the nip.' The **stall**, as one might expect, 'ran interference' for his partners, distracting the victim and making the robbery that much easier. Other 16C terms include the **figger** (fr. **fig**: to steal), the **horn-thumb** (fr. the sheath of horn worn by a cutpurse to protect his thumb) and the **snap** (a cutpurse's assistant).

Cutpurse itself emerges in the 17C, as do the synonymous **bung-napper**, **boung-napper** and **boung-nipper** (fr. **bung** or **boung**: a purse; the 20C use of **bung** means a bribe). New synonyms for **foist** include **dive** or **diver**, and **file**. The combination **bulk and file** means a pickpocket and his assistant, while **buttock and file** means a pickpocket and a whore working as a team; the pickpocket robs the client but, unlike the complete ripoff of the classic 'murphy game', the whore does satisfy her client first. The 17C **buttock and twang** have no such scruples: the whore entices the client and her accomplices beats and robs him; no sex ever takes place. A **shoulder-sham** is a pickpocket's assistant. **Cly** or **cloy** also means pickpocket, although it is as often found as a common thief in his own right. The term originated in **cly** meaning money, then the pocket in which it is kept, and finally the man who extracts it thence. The next century brings yet more terms: the **frisker** (fr. **frisk**: to search through pockets), the **clouter** (fr. **clout**: a cloth and thus handkerchief) and **fogle hunter** (both of whom specialised in **fogles** or silk handkerchiefs), the **reader-hunter** or **reader-merchant** (specialising in **readers**, or pocket books) and the **kiddy-nipper** (a variety of **cutpurse** who actually cut the pockets out of clothes to steal their contents; fr. **kiddy**: dextrous, **nipper: cutter**). A **natty lad** (fr. SE *neat*) was a young pickpocket while an **anabaptist** was a pickpocket who had been caught in the act and 'baptised' by being dumped into a pond. The religious motif continues with **groaner** (fr. his exaggeratedly enthusiastic devotions) and **autem-diver** (fr. **autem**: church, and **diver**★), both of whom exploited church congregations. Church-wardens, charged with responsibility for distributing alms to the poor were similarly named – to the poor they were as great robbers as any real villain. Their 19C equivalent is **kirk-buzzer** (fr. **kirk**: church, and **buzzer**★). **Autem**, one of the core terms of the cant vocabulary comes possibly from a church anthem or possibly from the Yiddish *a' thoumme*, meaning forbidden church, although the Yiddish may be a later coinage.

To the 19C underworld a **mobsman** described anyone who used manual dexterity for theft, a category that included both pickpockets and shoplifters. Mayhew, writing at mid-century uses the term to cover **buzzers**★, **wires**★, **prop-nailers**★ and **thimble-screwers** (proprietors of 'find the lady' games). The general vocabulary was much more extensive. Perhaps the most popular term was **buzzer**, with its variations **buzz, buz-bloke, buz-cove, buz-faker, buz-man**, all of which played on the image of a bee buzzing around a flower, waiting to extract the nectar. Terms based on buzz include a **billy buzman** (specialising in silk handkerchieves or **billies**), a **chariot buzzer** (working in the still new omnibuses or 'chariots'), a **tail buzzer** (stealing snuffboxes; from tail: posterior and referring to the back pockets) and a **moll buzzer** (who picked only women's pockets, as did the **moll tooler** or **tooler**; from **moll**: woman). The **adept** had overtones of alchemy and the occult, the **brief-snatcher** worked race-courses (fr. **brief**: either a wallet or a playing card, and referring to the illegal card games which provided opportunities for theft) the **bugger** or **bug-hunter** snatched **bugs**: breast- or tie-pins. **Cly faker, conveyancer**, (punning on the legal terminology), **hoister, wire, dip, dipper** and

dipping bloke, dummy hunter (fr. **dummy**: wallet) **finger-smith, fish hook** (fr. **fish hooks**: fingers), **fork** and **forker** (fr. **forks**: fingers), **grafter** (US), **knuck, knucker** and **knuckler** and **leather-merchant** (fr. **leather**: wallet) all meant pickpocket pure and simple. Other specialists were a **fobber** (removing small change from fob pockets), a **propnailer** (fr. prop: a tie-pin) and his 20C successor the **prop-getter** pursued pins and brooches, a **stook buzzer, stook hauler** or **wipe drawer** (fr. **stook** and **wipe**, both meaning handkerchief) stole silk handkerchieves, and a **watch maker** preferred watches; a **snatcher**, as the term implies, was a young inexperienced pickpocket.

Many 19C terms have lasted and are still used, notably **dip** and **wire**, but modernity has produced a few extras. Whether through coincidence, or through the gradually accelerating pace, the 19C's relatively leisurely **buzzer** becomes, in the 20C the **whizzer**, with its concomitant **whiz mob, whiz game** and **the whiz**, all referring to the art of pickpocketing and those who practise it. Other terms include the **bumper**, the **cannon**, the **pick** and a pair of Australianisms, the **knockabout man** and the **legshake artist**.

SWINDLERS AND CON-MEN

While Thomas Harman's *Caveat* delineated the ranks of villainous beggars, and the tricks they played on the unwary, it is in Robert Greene's *Art of Coney-Catching* (1591) and its sequels that the urban conmen and swindlers of the 16C make their first appearance as far as their language is concerned. The **coney**, meaning rabbit since the 13C (and in its Latin root *cuniculus*, an underground passage, cognate with the origins of **cunt***), was the sucker, the **coney-catcher** the swindler who, to use modern terminology, 'took' him. As Greene puts it: 'The partie that taketh up the cony, the Setter. He that plaieth the game, the Verser. He that is cosened, the Cony. He that comes into the them, the Barnacle. The monie that is wonne, the Purchase.' The makeup of the swindling team was hardly new four centuries ago, it has altered little over the years. The **setter** was the first member to meet the mark or victim; once they were talking the **verser** joined in and enticed the hapless simpleton into a game of cards, often by claiming to be a friend of one of his friends — and thus a trustworthy figure; with the victim suitably ensnared the third team member, the **barnacle**, later the **barnard**, would appear, posing as an independent individual, with no knowledge of his new companions. Together they fleeced their victim.

As well as coney-catching, Greene expounds upon the 'cross-biting law', 'cosenage by whores', or what, in modern terms would be the **badger** or **murphy game**. In this case the participants were the whore, the **traffique**, the sucker, this time termed the **simpler**, and the **cross-biter**, who beat and robbed the unfortunate punter. It was (and remains) a particularly alluring form of crime, since, unlike robbery or pickpocketing, there were few risks, given the guilt of the **simpler** who would rarely wish to admit to trafficking with a prostitute. As Greene puts it in *A Disputation* (1592), 'Crosbiting now adaies is growne to a marvellous profitable exercise, for some cowardly knaves that feare of the gallows, leave nipping and foysting, become Crosbites, knowing that there is no danger thein but a little punishment, at the most the Pillorie.'

Other 16C conmen included the **shifter**, and the **fingerer**, both of whom specialised in defrauding young and innocent visitors to taverns and inns, the former by having them pay for a lavish supper, the latter by enticing them into games of chance which, unsurprisingly, they fail to win. 17C terms include the **Chaldee** (fr. **Chaldee**: astrologer, and thus seen as being of dubious honesty), the **bilk** or **bilker** (a cheat, especially one who does so to avoid paying their debts), a **rogue*** and a **rogue and pullet** (a man and woman working as a team). The **pocket book dropper**, **gold dropper**, **sweetener** (all 17C) and their 18C successors the **dropper**, **drop cove** and **money dropper**, all pursued the same swindle: a wallet, coin or a jewel was dropped in the road, where it would be found by a potential victim. This led to an encounter, after which the victim was either lured into a game or, in the case of the (invariably fake) jewel, the conman persuaded the sucker to buy it, claiming that by rights they should share the profits, but that he, the conman, will sell his share and let the victim have the whole benefit. **Fawney-rigging** (18C, from **fawney**: a ring, itself fr. the Irish *fáin(n)e* a ring) is a similar trick, with a sham gold ring as the bait.

As Partridge notes in *Adventuring Among Words* (1961) (with a justifiable air of self-satisfaction) it is this same **fawney** that is the root of the modern phoney or fake, a term that, prior to his highlighting of what, ever since, has seemed the very obvious, had baffled generations of inventive, but inaccurate lexicographers. Synonymous terms are **ring-dropping** and **ring-falling**, with their concomitant nouns; a further term for one who drops money is a **gambler**.

The conmen of the period also include the **bite** (18C, a cheat), **leatherhead** (17C, also a thug), the **beau-trap** (17C, preying on foolish young aristocrats or beaux), a **cross cove** (18C) and his 19C peers the **cross** and **crossman**, and the **chouser** (18C) which came from **chouse**: a swindle; itself based on *chiaus* or *chaus*, a Turkish official messenger. The link here comes either from the fleecing in 1609 of of some Turkish and Persian merchants by an agent or *chiaus* of Sir Robert Shirley, or by the remark that a Turkish messenger is little better than a fool. Specialist swindlers are the **queer plunger** (18C) who plunges into water and is saved from 'drowning'; his conveniently pre-assembled 'rescuers' then claim money for saving him; the **skyfarmer** (18C) who tours the country posing as a gentleman farmer fallen on hard times, backed by suitably impressive, if counterfeit papers; the **fire prigger** (fr. **prig***) and **tinny hunter** (18C, **tinny**: fire) who rob people whose homes are burning down, while pretending to give assistance; as George Parker wrote in *A View of Society* (1781): 'No beast of prey is so noxious to Society, or so destitute of feeling, as these wretches.' The **dudder** or **whispering dudder** (18C) sold clothes (especially handkerchiefs) or **duds** (fr. 15C **dudde**: a cloak) under the pretence of their being smuggled contraband – they were not – while the **duffer** (18C) similarly gulled those whose tastes ran to 'contraband' brandy or silks (fr. **duff**: alleged contraband, which has lasted into the 20C, meaning general second-rate or broken). Like the 16C **dummerar*** the **gagger** pretended to be a deaf mute; the **christener** (18C) faked the identity marks – the 'christening' – on cheap gold and silver watches and like the earlier **Chaldee** the **cunning man** (18C) used astrology to 'help' his victims (the term also meant a judge). The **macer** or **mace cove** (18C) obtained goods on credit and never paid for them (cf. **long firm**); the term comes either from the Yiddish *mos*: to make money, or the Yiddish *masser*: a betrayer; thus to **mace**: to cheat). The **thimble-screwer** (17C) **thimble-rigger** and **thimble twister** (both 18C) were precursors of today's find the lady, three-card monte or shell-game men. 19C synonyms include the **nobbler** and **nob-pitcher** (often working in a fairground, from **nob**: to swindle), the **pea rigger** and **pea-man** and the **charley pitcher**, the last of whom, according to Mayhew, takes his name from *ceorla* or peasant to whom he 'pitches the tale'; however **charley** may simply be a generic term for peasant, or a euphemism for the derisive churl.

Aside from the plain **diddler**, the **dead nap**, the **gammoning cove** (fr. **gammon**: both a pickpocket's assistance and the cant language, and thus lies and humbug; the term possibly comes from the OE *gamen*: to game or sport with) and **flat catcher** (fr. **flatty**: an innocent or dupe) the 19C adds several new specialist terms – although the specialities in question are more predictable. Like his predecessor the **cross-biter**, the **badger** beat and robbed the clients of a confederate whore, although he was not above a little general blackmail. The **badger** could also be the whore herself. The term had existed since the 17C, although it began life describing 'a Crew of desperate Varlets, who rob and kill near any River, and then throw the dead Bodies therein'. The **panel dodger** or **panel thief** (US) worked at the **panel game**: the robbing of a whore's clients. The term comes from the **panel house**, a brothel in which the rooms were supplied with false panels that permitted access to the whore's room so that the client can be robbed or beaten up. A **bull trap** posed as a policeman to extort money (fr. **bull***: policeman); a **flying cove** promised victims of theft that for a suitable payment they could have their possessions returned; a **blackleg** or **leg** is a racecourse swindler (either from game-cocks, which have black legs, or from the black boots such swindlers always wore); the **lumberer** was a swindling tipster (the term could also mean pawnbroker; in this context the word comes from the medieval Lombard Room, where pawnbrokers and bankers stored their pledges), the **bunco-steerer** or **bunco-man** (US) pulled victims into a crooked card game (fr. **bunco**: a swindle, itself taken from *banco*, the 'bank' held by the dealer in a card game). Finally the **magsman** (possibly from Yiddish *machas*: a great man), the king of the 19C swindlers, a fashionable swell who appeared as sophisticated a figure as those on whom he preyed. **Megsman** was essentially a variation, but with less class.

Nothing really changes in the 20C but for the vocabulary. General terms include **con artist**, **bunco artist** (US) and **fleecer** (fr. SE *fleece*) while among the specialists Australia offers **illywhacker** (for which no reliable etymology exists), **ram** and its rhy. sl. synonym **amster** (**amsterdam**: **ram**), both meaning a con-man's **stall**; the West Indies have **alias man**, **ginnal** and **samfie**; the **thrower** and **slide** are members of a three-card monte team; like the older **dudder** and **duffer** the **slum hustler** sells cheap jewellery (**slum**) pretending that it has been stolen; and a **ringer** one who steals, improves and then sells cars. The **bait**, unsurprisingly, is an attractive girl used to lure victims while the **hedge** is the crowd that gathers around a street con-man. The US **grifter** is a small-change swindler and thus any small-time gambler, living primarily on his wits. The **inside man** is a modern-day **verser**, 'playing the game' rather than luring in the victim.

THE HIGHWAYMAN

The highwayman, and his distinctly less romantic peer the **footpad**, are very much a phenomenon of the 16-18C, especially the latter when such figures as Dick Turpin and 'Captain Lightfoot' (properly James Maclaine)plied their trade. The practice lingered into the early 19C, but accelerating industrialization and urban growth gradually whittled down the heaths and highways upon which a **gentleman of the road** might operate.

For doubtless self-serving reasons the names for highwayman reflect their elevated image from the start. The 16C has a **knight** and a **knight of the road** and a **high lawyer**, who could be either a highwayman or a footpad. Robert Greene, describing the 'High Law, robbing by the highway side' in 1591 sets out the gang: 'The theefe is called a High Lawier. He that setteth the watch, a Scrippet. he that standeth to watch, an Oake. He that is rob'd, the Martin.'

Scrippet possibly comes from that Latin *scripsit*: he wrote, referring to the **scrippet's** written instructions, while the **oak**, upon whose vigilance so much depended, refers to the sturdiness and value of the wood. **Footpad** itself emerges in the 17C, as do a number of terms referring to the **pad***, or road, a term based on the Dutch *pad* and Old High German *pfad* meaning road and cognate with the English path. These include **padder** and **high pad**, a term that a century earlier had meant only the highway itself, but had now been extended to the villains who exploited it. Synonymous is **high toby**, which by the 19C taken a similar journey from object to person. A 19C highwayman was a **toby gill**, **toby gloak** (**gloak**: man, with similar colloquial overtones to bloke; it comes either from the Shelta *glokh*: man or the Erse *oglak*: hero) or **toby man**. A further 17C term is **landpirate**, although this was virtually SE.

As Hollywood costume dramas have assured us, the 18C was the heyday of highwaymen and the slang acquires a suitably romantic tone. Typical are **gentleman of the road** and **gentleman of the pad**; **gentleman** (like the earlier knight) was an all-purpose appellation, meaning practitioner; thus the variation **gentleman of the green baize road**: a card-sharper. The villain could also, and perhaps more accurately, be a **gentleman's master**, referring to his temporary ascendancy over his wealthy victims. **Bridle cull** (**cully**: man, usually as fellow or chap) refers to his horse-riding while a **colt** could be either a youthful accomplice, or an innkeeper who lent him his horses. A **collector** did just that, while **Newmarket Heath Commissioner** name-checked a favoured area for robbery. A **scampsman** derived from **scamp**, the highway, while a **royal scamp** was one who never killed or injured. Other terms include **St Nicholas' clerk** or **St Nicholas' clergyman** (18C), a **spice gloak** (19C, **spice**: to rob, either fr. the German *speissen*: to eat or fr. **speak**: to arrest and thus to hold up), and a **pull up**, giving **pull up a Jack**: to stop a coach to rob it.

FORGERS AND COUNTERFEITERS

The earliest forger was the **jarkman**, cited in Harman (1567). **Jark** meant a seal (and by the 19C any trinket worn on a watch-chain) and thus the **jarkman** created any form of fake documentation: passports, licences, testimonials and the like. The contemporary **fambler** (fr. **famble**: a ring, in turn from **fam***: a hand) dealt in fake 'gold' rings. The **bene-faker** (17C, lit. 'well make') and **bene-gybe** (17C, fr. **gybe**: a counterfeit license to beg, later a fake passport) were counterfeiters, initially of documents, later of money. The **niggler** (18C) clipped money as did the contemporaneous **nigger** (although this might have been a misprint for **niggler**). The **smasher** passed counterfeit coins (fr. **smash**: counterfeit coins; by 19C **smash** was rhy. sl. for cash) as did the **queer** (fr. **queer**: bad) **shover, queer cole** (fr. 16C **cole***: money) fencer; the **queer bit** (fr. 17C **bit**: money) **maker** and **queer cole maker** actually created the fakes as did the 16C **voucher** (abbrev. of SE *avoucher*: witness) and the 19C **varnisher**, whose polishing of his bad coinage looked suspiciously like varnish. Counterfeit was **snide** (19C) and thus the **snide pitcher** distributed bad money as did the **sourplanter** (19C, from **sour**: counterfeit coins), the **shover** and the **shoful pitcher** (fr. the Hebrew *shaphell*: low or base). The **boodler**, who passed bad notes, took his name from **boodle***: money; 20C Aus. uses the same term for a corrupt politician. The **penman** and the **scratcher** created fake notes: the former so named from his drawing, the latter from the etching of the notes. Modern terminology includes the **maker** (US) and the **cobbler** (US), specialising in stocks and bonds as well as the more customary notes and passports. The **lay-down merchant** and the **slinger** distribute forged banknotes while the **kiter** (fr. **kite**: cheque) and **paper hanger** pass dud cheques.

CARDSHARPS AND GAMESTERS

Cheating, whether in games of cards or dice, was doubtless well-established by the 16C yet Greene, usually so determined in his efforts to reveal every facet of villainy, becomes strangely reticent when faced with what he calls the 'Cheting Law' and declares, 'Pardon me, Gentlemen, for although no man could better than myself discover this law and his termes, and the names of their Chetes, Bar'd-Dice, Flats, Forgers, Langrets, Gourds, demies and many other...yet for some speciall reasons, herein I will be silent.' And so he is, although one can illuminate some of the missing terminology. **Flats** are either cards or, in this context, crooked dice although other than Greene's throwaway reference neither appears until, respectively the early 19C and late 17C. **Forgers** are also crooked dice (another term apparently specific to Greene), as are **barred dice**, **langrets**, **demies** and **gourds**. In all cases one or more sides was slightly altered so as to ensure (to the sharper) a predictable roll.

Other 16C terms include the **rook** (any form of cheat, a term that survives, mainly as a verb meaning to cheat, into the 20C and comes from the allegedly thievish disposition of the bird), a pair of sharpers: the **shark** and the **cogger** (fr. **cog**: a piece of money, which as a verb means to cheat at gambling) and the **ambidexter** (a **shill** or 'house player', so called from his 'playing with both hands'). The 17C introduces **hawk**, **needle**, **needle-point** (both of which are 'sharp'), **nicker** and **nickum** (thus **nick**: to win at cards), and **wheedle** while the 18C has **picaro** and **picaroon** (both from the Spanish *picaro*: a rogue), **prinado**, which should be Spanish too but the nearest term, *prenada* (as cited in the *OED*), pregnant is hard to justify, although Partridge opts for *primada*, meaning first and thus most skillful, although there seems no real reason for the feminine '-a' ending. In the tradition of **Captain Standish*** (the penis) and **Captain Hackum*** (a thug) are **Captain Sharp** and **Captain Cheat**, both cheating bullies employed by card sharpers.

Broads is the main slang term for cards in the 19C – they have length and breadth but no depth – thus creating a **broadsman** (a sharp), the **broad cove** and **broad-faker** (professional card players) and the **broad mob**, a team of sharpers. The US **broad tosser** or **broad spieler** is a three card monte operator, whose skills (and profits) lie in his ability to deal the three cards in a sufficiently confusing manner. Other terms include the **burner** (prefiguring the 20C **burn**: to sell inferior or fake drugs) who cheats the innocent with either cards or dice, the **fiddle** and the **workman** (both sharpers), the **bonnet** and the **buttoner** (cheats' accomplices, who lure victims into the game) and the **crow**, who attests to the honesty of his confederates. The **subway dealer** (US 20C) works literally underground, a **KG** is a 'known gambler' in police terminology, a **digits dealer** is involved in the US numbers racket and an **operator** runs a gambling game. A **baglady** (a female version of the bagman: who transports bags of money, especially when making illegal payoffs) is a woman used by numbers racketeers to collect bets and pay off winners. A **crossroader** is an itinerant card sharp who travels in search of new victims for his cheating skills.

In modern US casinos an **agent** is a player-cheat who works in collusion with the staff of the casino — the croupiers, pit bosses, etc — but not with its owners; a **dice mechanic** is a professional cheat; the term, often abbreviated to **mechanic**, can also be used admiringly of a successful player whether of cards or dice. **Animals** are professional 'heavies' on the casino payroll, used to collect outstanding debts and ensure that no customers misbehave on the premises; a **capper** is a shill or a confederate of either the gambler or the casino. In and out of casinos **dice cappers** are those who make and use shaved or loaded dice, a **hand-mucker** or **hold-out man** specialises in palming cards, then holding them out of the game until they become useful to him; a **hold-out artist** is a gambler or cheat who will never admit how much money he has made out of a game and a **proposition cheat** never gives his victims even the thought of a win, taking 100% advantage in every game.

THE FENCE

While not a robber himself, the **fence**, or receiver plays a vital part in criminal life, buying the stolen property and selling it on. **Fence** itself, appears c.1698; its etymology is probably a shortening of the SE *defence*: the fence standing between the criminal and the law. The combinations **fencing cully** and **fencing master** followed soon afterwards. The **fencing-crib** was the house or room from which the fence operated; synonymous are **dollyshop** (19C, also a pawnshop), **leaving shop** (19C) and **swag shop** (early 19C, from **swag** meaning both a shop and the goods it stocks). The fence as go-between generated a number of terms: **Janusmug** (19C from Roman god Janus, who had two faces, or **mugs**), a **bag man** (20C, cf. **bag lady**), **bird dog** (20C, from the SE *bird dog*: a retriever, who fetches things) and the **placer** (20C, who places the thief's loot with a fence). Other fences include the **angling-cove** (18C, 'one who fishes in troubled waters'), the **Adam Tiler** (18C, from the German *teile: a share or slice), the* **billy fencer** (19C, specialising in stolen metal) the **father** (mid-19C, on the pattern of **uncle**: pawnbroker) and the **buyer**. The **family-man** has a similar image.

THE SHOPLIFTER

Greene has no place for shoplifters, since his real focus is swindlers, but Harman cites the **angler** and the **hooker**, both of whom, as their names imply, 'fish' for booty on market stalls or amongst shop displays. These terms were followed in the new century by the **lift** or **lifter** who, dressed a servant, would offer to carry one's bags and packages, and then run off — by the 18C he was a simple shoplifter; the **Jack in the box** or **sheep shearer**, who 'rings the changes' by bamboozling a merchant and the **budge** or **budget**, who stole cloaks from houses; by the 19C the budge was better known for sneaking into unguarded shops and stealing anything he could take. The **budge and snudge** (17C) were a team: the budge entered an open house and grabbed anything he could; he then passed it to the snudge, who took it to the fence. The **clank-napper** or **clink rigger** stole silver tankards while his 19C successor the **cat and kitten nipper** stole pewter quart (**cats**) and pint (**kittens**) pots from inns. The 18C brought the **hoist** or **hoister** (still extant, especially in Black America), the **pincher** (the 18C's **Jack in the box**), the **lob crawler** or **lob sneak** who robbed the shop till (fr. **lob**: box), his 19C successor was a **till sneak**; the **bouncer** who stole while distracting the merchant's attention with his argumentative bargaining, and the **avoirdupois-man**, who stole the brass weights from shop counters; such theft was the **avoirdupois lay**. A **bob** (18C) was that member of a shoplifting team who actually carried off their spoils. Finally the **puffer** (fr. **puff**: to praise excessively) would work in a team with a man posing as a gentlemen who would buy some goods and pay cash. At this point the **puffer**, who happened to be present, explained that the young man had recently come into a large inheritance which he was eager to squander. When, by chance, the young man returned a few days later he was thus able to secure something very expensive, this time on credit. It would not be paid. The favour was returned, by the **ferret** or **rabbit-sucker**, who would gull rich young men into running up huge bills, then dun them for their debts.

As well as the generalised **pitch fingers** (pitch is 'sticky') and **shop bouncer** (see **bouncer**) the 19C offers a number of specialist operators, stealing either from shops or from other places where goods were on display: the **bank-sneak** (US) took bonds from banks, the **pinch-gloak** took small articles from jewellers, the **pudding snammer** stole from cook shops (**snammer** from Scots *snam*: to snatch greedily) and the **sawney hunter** stole from provisioners and grocers (**sawney**: a flitch of bacon). The **scuffle hunter** was a dockside pilferer) while a **shutter racket worker** specialised in boring through a shutter, removing a pane of glass, and reaching through for anything to steal. The **dragsman** worked the **drag lay**: stealing from carts or coaches as did the **drag-sneak**; the **peter**, **peter biter**, **peter claimer**, **peter hunter** or **peter man**, stole boxes (**peters**), luggage and so on; by the 20C **peter-man** reflected the alternative definition of **peter**: a safe, and meant a safe-cracker; the **baggage smasher** (US) stole unguarded luggage from railway stations.

The 20C shoplifting team includes the **lugger** (fr. **lug**: carry off or drag) who removes the lifted goods, the **blocker** who acts suspiciously so as to divert the attention of store detectives, and the **skin worker** whose 'skin' (or hands) picks up the goods. A **stickman** is an accomplice who is passed the goods by the actual shoplifter. **Booster**, perhaps the most common contemporary term, at least in the US, refers to the boosting or lifting itself.

VIOLENCE

Many criminals are thugs, but not all thugs are criminals. For simple men of violence the reader should check INSULTS; this section looks at the terminology of those who rob with violence.

The **roarer** (17C) was a plain thug, as was the **ding-boy** (fr. **ding**: to knock down); both individuals acted as bodyguards or accomplices, providing the 'muscle' for a more skillful villain; the **circling boy** (17C) was equally tough, but restrained his aggression long enough to help lure a victim into a position where he might then be robbed, with or without violence. The 18C **bully-buck, bully-cock** or **vamper** deliberately started fights between others, so as to to rob them in the confusion; the **sneeze lurker** threw snuff in the victim's face, thus blinded he could be robbed; similar was the **amuser** who threw dust in one's eyes and then ran off; a companion would then appear, and while ostensibly offering his sympathy pick the victim's pockets; the term is a literal interpretation of **amuse**: to beguile with entertaining tales or to 'throw dust in one's eyes'. The **tripper up** (18C) robbed a person who had been deliberately tripped up by an accomplice; the **snatch cly** (**cly**: money or purse) snatched women's handbags.

More fake sympathy was offered by the **stander up** (19C) who robbed drunks under pretence of helping them up from the gutter into which they had fallen (or been pushed); the **drummer** wasted no time on sympathy, he simply robbed drunks, often after helping them to oblivion with a mickey finn or knockout draught; the **bearer-up** would knock a man's hat over his eyes, then rob him as he struggled to remove it. The garrotting team, who choked rather than actually killed their victims, consisted of the **nastyman** or **uglyman** (who actually did the choking) and the **backstall**, his accomplice. **Nastyman** soon came to mean any sort of strong-arm man, as did the **bester** (who would as well use physical threats as he would verbal patter in his efforts to swindle or rob). A **silver cooper** was a kidnapper, its original use referring to the press-gang or **crimps**, who kidnapped men to serve in the navy, whether Royal or merchant. **Snaffler** (18C), **smugger**, **snabbler**, and **snaggler** (all 19C, the last originally a stealer of geese) were all toughs, specialising in snatch-and-grab thefts, while the **bobby-twister** (19C) would stop at nothing, even killing (**twisting**) a policeman. A **bludger** (19C) used a bludgeon and could be either a violent thief or a pimp; the term prefigures its 20C Aus. use as an all-purpose insult. The last 19C term is **rampsman**, **ramper** or

ramp, all of whom are robbers with violence; **ramp** is an abbreviation of the 14C *rampant*, acting in a violent or threatening manner; in its alternative meaning of swindle (19C) ramp is the root of the 'bankers' ramp' a deliberately engineered financial crisis best-known from its use in 1932, when the Labour government accused the City of creating such a crisis for purely political reasons.

Modern terms for the criminal tough guy include the **stick-up artist**, the **git-em-up guy** (20C, a hold-up man who tells his victims 'Get 'em up!'), the **jack roller** (US), a thief who robs his intoxicated companion and the **lush** (fr. **lush**: a drunkard) **worker** (US) who steals from drunks. The **dropper**, the **hatchet man**, the **hit man** and the **trigger man** all carry and may use firearms.

LIVESTOCK THIEVES

A **buffer** (17C), **buffer napper** (17C) or **dog buffer** (18C) stole dogs (all from 16C **bufe***: a dog), while an **abacter** (fr. Latin *abigere*: to drive away) or **dunaker** (17C) preferred cows (fr. **dunnock**: a cow). **Satyrs** (18C) based on the mythological figures, lived as travelling wild men who made their money from stealing cattle. A **ticker** (fr. 17C **tick**: credit) would buy cattle (and produce) at a fair for credit and depart with the goods, he would never return with the payment; the **rank rider** (17C) did much the same with horses: they would travel from inn to inn posing as a knight's or gentlemen's servants and requesting horses for themselves and their master. They would then leave, ostensibly to meet their master. They too would never pay the bill, but take the horses to a distant fair where they could be sold. Other horse thieves included the **trailer** (16C), the **jingler** (17C) who also travelled round country fairs, the **pad borrower** (18C, from **pad**: a horse, especially a gentle one), an **ingler** (18C, from SE *ingle*: a corner, where one discusses the deal), a **chaunting cove** (19C, from **chaunt** or **chant**: to advertise – such criminals advertised their horses in the press) and a **queer prancer** (18C, either a cowardly horse stealer or an ageing whore). Sheep stealers were variously **bleating culls** (17C, from **bleating chete***: a sheep), **sheep nappers** (18C) and **fleecy-claimers** (19C), and a poultry thief was a **walking poulterer**

(18C) who stole fowls, then hawked them from door to door, a **beaker-hauler** or **beaker-hunter** (19C).

IMPRISONMENT

THE PRISON

Although Thomas Harman offers the **harmans**★ for the stocks his *Caveat* has no specific entry for prison and the earliest relevant term thus appears to be **cage** (16C). **Clink**, originally the specific name of the Southwark prison is also 16C, as is the somewhat literary **caperdochy**, **caperdocchio** or **caperdewsie**, all stemming from the king of Capadocia, allegedly rich in slaves but short on cash. The 17C offers **blockhouse**, originally a fort, **quod**, also spelt **quad** and as such probably an abbreviation of quadrangle, although the original quod referred only to Newgate; the **iron doublet**, the **shop** (shop meaning a place, as in 'all over the shop', thus the 19C **toil shop**, where one performed hard labour), the **sturrabin** or **stariben** (the Romany term for confine) and the **naskin** or **nask** with its variations the **Old Nask** (the City bridewell) the **New Nask** (the Clerkenwell jail) and **Tuttle Nask** (in Tothill Fields).

Coop is an 18C term as is the **sheriff's hotel** (cf. **Akerman's Hotel**), **rope walk** (a nickname for the Old Bailey), **bladhunk** (a Shelta term for prison), **bower** (originally Newgate, latterly found in the US and Australia for any jail) and **jigger** (a cant term for key, with a secondary meaning of whipping post). The 19C is filled with names for prison. The 18C sturrabin was abbreviated to **stir** (with a possible nod to the stirring of a prisoner's staple diet: **porridge**, itself a term for prison, although usually for the time one serves) with its rhyming synonym **Joe Gurr**. **Jug**, originally **stone jug** and as such specific to Newgate, was found on both sides of the Atlantic although **calaboose** (Spanish *calabozo*: jail) and **hoosegow** (fr. Spanish *juzgado*: a tribunal or court of justice) were strictly American. Another import, **chokey**, came from the Hindi *chauki*: a four-sided building or a shed. Another name for Newgate, the

college, entered general use, giving **college chum**, a fellow convict, while the **family hotel** referred to the **family***: the criminal underworld. **Irish theatre** (US) referred to the predominantly Irish prison officers (and possibly inmates too) while the UK **mill** abbreviated the treadmill, as well as generalising **Mill**, the old nickname for the defunct Insolvency Court; thus **go through the mill**: to be declared bankrupt. The ironic **dry room** referred to an invariably damp dungeon, the **house that Jack built** possibly related to the hangman Jack Ketch, while *reesbin* is Shelta and **raspin** Scots. **To nick** means to arrest; **nick** thus means prison.

Other terms include the **joint** (originally Anglo-Irish but since c.1880 strictly US), the **pen** (US, cf **coop**), the **pokey** (US, from the **pogey**: a workhouse and thus a local house of correction), the **slammer** (US, from the sound of cell doors), the **cross-bar hotel**, the **bucket** (Canada), **Texas steel** and the **tank**. A **boarding house** (US) popularised the old nickname for New York City's Tombs, while the **big house** originally meant workhouse in the UK, but survives as an US Federal (rather than state) institution. The early 19C prison ships, the hulks moored on the Thames, were the **boats**, the **floating academies** or **Campbell's academy**, while the **academy** alone was any prison where one did hard labour. The **lagging station** was the transit prison for those being **lagged** or tranported; the **brig**, originally **Dutch brig** (19C) was a miltary prison – the term rapidly emigrated to the US – as was the **glasshouse**, originally the glass-roofed North Camp prison at Aldershot. **Juvie** (US) is a juvenile prison.

The workhouse, a 19C institution designed to control Britain's itinerant beggars, was variously the **spinning house** or **spinniken** (fr. Dutch *spinnhuis*: a woman's house of correction), the **spring ankle warehouse** (**spring ankle**: sprained ankle, thus unable to run), **wol house** or the **pan** (possibly from Romany *pan*: to lock or bind). The casual ward where a tramp might stay for a few nights was a **strawyard**, a **spike** (fr. the hardness of the beds, the food and the treatment), a **twopenny rope** (fr. the rope strung across a room, on which bedless tramps could lean and fitfully sleep), the **teetotal hotel**, and the **trib** (fr. tribulation).

Two forms of what might be termed open-air prisons should be noted: the pillory, in which the prisoner's head and hands were secured between two sliding, lockable boards, and the stocks, which dealt with the feet, generate a number of terms. They include the **wooden ruff**, the **iron** or **wooden parenthesis**, the **penance board**, the **stoop**, the **timber**, the **Norway neckcloth** (fr. the Norway fir from which it was made), the **nut-crackers** and the **harmans** (cf. **harman beck★**). A **babe in the wood** or an **overseer** or **inspector of the pavement** was the man or woman thus imprisoned. The pillory was abandoned in the UK, other than for perjury in 1815; it was finally abolished in 1837; it survived in America, or at least in the state of Delaware, until 1905.

Other obsolete punishments give to be **tipped the scroby** (fr. scrub?) or **tipped the claws** (fr. the cat o'nine-tails) (**before breakfast**): to be whipped before the justices; to **shove the tumbler** (17C, meaning tumbril) or to **play the part of the strong man** (17C) both meant to be whipped at the cart's tail; the image is one of pushing both cart and horses. To **tease** was to flog, thus to **nap the teize** was to be flogged, although this punishment was in jail, not before the justices.

SPECIFIC PRISONS

As well as the general terms listed above, prisons have always attracted speicifc nicknames, and as noted some have gone on to become generic terms.

Newgate, London's main prison and 'a house of entertainment for rogues of every description' (Jon Bee, 1823) was variously known as the **City College** (fr. its site in Old Bailey), the **Whitt** or **Whittington College**, **Akerman's Hotel** and **Newman's Hotel** (fr. the names of various jailers), the **King's** or **Queen's Head** or **Inn**, the **stone doublet, jug, pitcher** or **tavern**. Cold Bath Fields, the harshness of which was such that Coleridge suggested that on seeing it, 'The devil was pleased, for it gave him a hint/For improving his prisons in hell', was the **Steel** the **Bastille**, the rhy. sl. **Fillet of Veal** or **Bates' Farm** or **Bates' Garden** (fr. a notorious governor). The Fleet Prison, built soon after the Norman

Conquest and a regular repository for those imprisoned for debt, was the **Never-Wag**, the **Man of War** and **Number 9**, for its address of 9, Fleet Market. The Tothill Fields House of Correction (wherein Hogarth's fictional Rake was imprisoned) was the **Tea Garden**, the **Downs**, the **Tuttle** and the **Tuttle Nask**. The King's Bench Prison in Southwark, in which literary lights Tobias Smollett and John Wilkes once suffered for their debts, was the **Park** or **Ellenborough Lodge**; the spikes that topped its walls were known as **Ellenborough's teeth**, Lord Ellenborough being Lord Chief Justice between 1802-18.

Horsemonger Lane, outside which Dickens watched a public execution, was the **Old Horse**, White Cross Street jail was **Burdon's Hotel** (fr. its jailer), the Clerkenwell House of Detention, once host to the notorious Jack Sheppard and his mistress Edgeworth Bess, was the **Tench** or the **Wells** and the **Mill Doll** was the jail at Bridge Street, Blackfriars. Outside London Melbourne's jail was **Castieu's Hotel**, that in Edinburgh was the **Ten**, the **Pen** or **Smith's Hotel**, while the Durham prison was the **Kitty**. More recently Parkhurst, Isle of Wight is **The Island**, Dartmoor **The Moor**, Wormwood Scrubs is **The Scrubs** and Pentonville **The Ville**. In America San Quentin is **Q**, the New York City jail **The Tombs**, Riker's Island, a detoxification centre for drug addicts is **The Island**, Ossining, NY is **Sing Sing** and so on. Most state and federal prisons have some kind of shorthand identification among those who are likely to suffer their attentions.

PLACES IN PRISON AND THE CELLS

Individual prison cells are a relatively new invention, brought into being by the prisons reforms of the 19C. Terms to describe them include the rhyming slang **flowery** (**flowery dell**: cell, although its earlier use in the pedlar's Lingua Franca meant no more than a room, especially a room in an inn). The 19C has **clinch, shoe, box** (the **salt box** was the condemned cell in Newgate), while the 20C **peter** starts life two centuries earlier meaning box or chest, and moves on to mean safe (19C) before adopting its current meaning. **Cheder** comes from a Hebrew term, usually meaning a classroom.

The US has **slams** (cf. **slammer**) and Australia the **slot**. The cell door is a **Rory** (rhy. sl. **Rory O'Moore**: door). The open area that runs along the landing outside the cells is known in the US as **the range**, thus to **flash the range** is to use a mirror poked through one's cell bars to survey what it happening outside. The 19C **polish the king's iron with one's eyebrow** – to look through the bars – means much the same.

The solitary confinement cells are the **block**, **chokey**, the **cooler** or **damper**, **Florida** (US), **the hole** or **Siberia** (US) and to be in solitary confinement is to be **behind one's door**, **buried** (US), **iced**, **OP** (Canada: off privilege). In UK jails those who volunteer for solitary confinement – usually sex offenders who would not survive in the larger prison population – are **on Rule 43**. The **crazy alley**, **paddy** or **pads** are the padded cells and to be **in the peek** is to be under observation. The **limbo room** (Canada) is a corporal punishment room, but **limbo**, from the Latin *limbus patrum*, has meant a prison since at least the 16C. A **drunk tank** (US, in a local prison or sheriff's office) is a lockup for drunks while the **boob** (fr. **booby hatch**: an asylum) is a detention cell.

To be locked up for the night is **carpy** (UK, from the Latin *carpe diem*: enjoy the day!), and men are variously **two-ed up**, **three-ed up** and so on, depending on the numbers forced to share a cell.

PRISONERS

Among the earliest terms for prisoner is **queer bird** (16C, fr. **queer**: bad and **bird**: man), shortly followed by **canary** or **canary-bird** (17C) which referred to the keeping of such a bird inside a **cage***; the term re-emerged in Australia in the early-19C, when, applied once more to convicts, it reflected the yellow uniforms that the newly arrived transportees wore when they landed. Other 19C terms were **government men**, the **police-van corp**s and the **devil's regiment (of the line)** (coined by Thomas Carlyle mid-19C, who further suggested that 'the post of honour due to this distinguished corps is the Van', ie. the Black Maria.) A transported felon was also a **t'other sider** or **traveller at Her Majesty's expense**.

Probably the best-known contemporary term, universal throughout the English-speaking world is **con**, an abbreviation of convict.
Goalbird is well-known as is **lag**, or **old lag**, which now means
no more than a prisoner, but originally (19C) referred to those
who received a **lagging**: transportation to Australia. **Lagging** itself
gradually altered its meaning: by the late 19C, and after transportation had ceased, it meant simply penal servitude, usually of more
than two years, and as such was to more feared than a **stretch** –
then twelve months – although the **stretch** could be compounded
as a **three stretch, five stretch** or whatever, the number denoting
the number of years. A **yardbird** comes from the prison's exercise
yard; the ironic **innocent** has been locked up and as such is
incapable of further crime.

There are also a number of specific terms for prisoners. **Fish** or
new fish is a new arrival, a **star** (UK) a first offender, while **flipflop**
(US) is a recidivist; a prisoner nearing the end of his sentence is
short (US). **Aces high**, a **real man** or a **right guy** (US) is a
popular prisoner; a **centreman** or **jointman** (Canada) sucks up
to the guards – the terms come from the centre of the jail where
the guards have their office, or **joint**: prison – and a **stoolie** (fr.
stool pigeon) is an informer; in the UK a **red band** (fr. the one
he wears) is a trusty. **Stool pigeon** itself comes from the hunters'
practice of tethering a pigeon to a stool in order to attract others.
A tough convict is variously an **atlas** (fr. the mythical giant), **OBC**
('one brutal convict') and, in the old British Borstals, a **daddy**. A
baron or **carvie** (he 'carves up' the spoils) trades in the UK prison
staple, tobacco or any other lucrative commodity. A **sweet kid** (US)
is a young homosexual while the **prison wolf** is an older one, as
is a **knight of the golden grummet** (**knight of...** dates back to
17C, while **golden grummet** means anus). The **liquid cosh** (UK)
refers to the major tranquilisers used for restraint; one who has
succumbed to prison-induced insanity is **stir-crazy** or **stir bugs**.
A **politician** is one who secures privileges and a **jailhouse lawyer**
studies law, usually to test out the institution's rules. A **wallflower**
(UK) is planning an escape; the term puns on those social wall-
flowers who want to get away from the crowd. The **lifer** is serving
life while in the US a **three-time loser** is serving mandatory life

after a third conviction; a **recluse** (US) is a long-term prisoner with no outside contacts. A child molester is a **monster, nonce** or **beast** (UK) and **short eyes** (US, from having 'eyes for' the short, i.e. children) and **shut eyes** (US, either a synonym for **short eyes**, or from the molesters instruction, 'Just shut your eyes...') .

One one has **gone up the river** (gone to jail), and begun to **do a bit** (serve a sentence), a prisoner could **blow his copper** (US, **copper*** meaning policeman, and thus a law-abiding individual or lifestyle) lose remission, possibly after **copping a heel** (US) attacking an enemy from behind. To become religious is to **get the Book** or **get the glory**; to **give (one) the office** is to initiate a newcomer (originally to tip off); anyone who wants to escape **has some rabbit** (US), if he succeeds he is **over the wall** or **hill, away**, or **on the lam**. In the claustrophobic world of jail one who invades another's privacy **plays too close**, while to **choose up** (US) is to select a homosexual partner and to **ride the deck** or **swap cans** (US, **can***: anus) is to have have anal intercourse).

PRISON OFFICERS

Of the various terms for prison officer, warder or jailer on offer, the best-known is **screw**, based on the older slang for key, and synonymous with **twirl**, which has a similar root. Variations on screw give **flue**, rhyming slang, and the **bent** or **safe screw**: a corrupt officer. Equally widespread in the US is **hack**, originally meaning a night-watchman. Other warders include the **herder** (US 20C), the 19C **dubber** and **under-dubber** or **dubsman** and **under-dubsman**, all of whom take their name from **dubs**, meaning a bunch of keys. Specific warders include the **bully beef**, **screwdriver** or **white shirt** (UK, senior officers), the **bitch's bastard** or **caser** (UK, a severe officer; **caser** is fr. **case**: a reprimand), the **light of love** (rhy. sl.: guv = governor) and the **dep** (deputy governor). **Particulars** (US) are external prison authorities. A **tube** (UK) is an officer who eavesdrops on prisoners, a **zombie** (UK) is a sour, surly officer, while the **Gabriel** (UK) is the chapel organist. A warder who suffers from **convictitis** has a paranoid fear of his charges.

The screw's primary job is to **bang up, dub up** (dub: key], **chubb** or **miln up** the prisoner (the latter pair are the names of locks); to do this he uses the **locksmith's daughter**, the **betty, blacksmith's daughter** or **wife**, the **gilkes** (a skeleton key), **Jack in the box, screw, sket** or **twirl**. A martinet may place a fellow-officer on a **ducket** (a report) or **put the block on** (UK: tighten up prison regulations); his victim will probably **get the Book** (US: to be reprimanded); to **ghost** (UK) is to move prisoners at night.

IMPRISONMENT

To send to jail is in the UK to **send down**, notably from the stairs that lead down from the dock in the Old Bailey's No. 1 court and in the US, and latterly UK too, to **send up**, an abbreviation of **send up the river**, which refers to the trip up the Hudson River to the upstate New York prison of Ossining, or Sing Sing. A 19C synonym was **hit**. To be imprisoned is to be **away, inside, in the nick, in chokey, in stir**, etc., **jugg**ed, **on jankers, on the corn** (Aus.), **under glass** or **up the river**.

Imprisonment in general can be **porridge** (which one is served on a regular basis, thus **doing one's porridge**: serving one's sentence), **time** (with its accompanying saying: 'If you can't do the time, don't do the crime'), **bird** (rhy. sl. **birdlime**: time) and **jailing** (US, thus fellow prisoners **jail** with each other). A **tubbing** (19C), a **hard bit** or **hard time** is a difficult sentence, while **first bird** (UK) is one's first sentence. **Good time** is remission, and in US jails **dead time** is any imprisonment that does not count towards the sentence. More terms include a **jacket** (fr. **jacket** meaning case file or record) and **mileage**. A criminal record is **form** (fr. the horse-racing context), **PC** (previous convictions), **previous**, a **sheet, rap sheet** or **yellow sheet** (all based on the paperwork).

Periods of imprisonment have attracted a number of names. A **tray** is three months as are **three moon**, a **nag-drag** or **drag**, a **sorrowful tale** (rhy. sl. three months jail), a **spell** and a **carpet** (the assumption was that a prisoner could weave a small carpet in three months). So too was **thirteen clean shirts**: one every week. A **dose** is four months. A **length** and a **jade** (19C) are longer, if unspecified sentences. A **stretch** is a year and **half a stretch** six months. **Nevis** and **neves** (both backsl.) and **seven pennorth** are seven months or seven years; **sixer** and **twelver** six and twelve months; a **lagging*** was any sentence of more than two years. To **do the book and cover** was to be jailed for the rest of one's natural life); to **get the knickers** or **the knickers and stockings** (both US) was to suffer a life term. To be **on track 13 and a washout** (US) was to serve a life sentence: **track 13** means bad luck, **washout** refers to the track having been washed out by rain, thus leaving no chance of turning back.

Tobacco, the staple of the prison economy, can either be **smash** (19C) or **snout** (late 19C), which comes from the then illegality of smoking: the prisoner was forced to cup the cigarette in his hand so that he might appear to be rubbing his nose — or **snout** — when actually he was taking a puff. Other bodily comforts include **pussy in a can** (US, sardines), **shit on a shingle** (chipped beef on toast) and **whodunnit** (UK: meat pie); **skilly** (19C), an abbreviation of **skilligolee**, was gruel or broth, a jail loaf is a **cob** (UK), thus **cobitis** is a general dislike of jail food, **duffer** (fr. duff) is pudding in the UK, **bread** in the US. A **scratcher** (UK) is a match and a **rim slide** (US) is a fart (fr. **rim***: the anus).

Other prison slang includes **blanket party** (US) an initiation rite in which an inmate is rolled in blankets and beaten, a **rower** (UK) is an argument (fr. row), **break** (US/UK) an escape and **outfit** an escape kit; a **cell task** (UK) is, punning on the real thing, a pin-up (the 'task' presumably masturbation). In the days of corporal punishment the cat o'nine-tails was either the **cat**, or **wicked lady**, **nine-tail bruser** or **mouser** or **number one**. A **reader** (UK) is any reading matter, a **kite** (otherwise a bouncing cheque), is any form of contraband communication or any form of prison paperwork; a **full sheet** (UK) is a complaint against an officer while a **KB** or **knockback** is a rejection — whether of that complaint, of a plea for parole or of any other request. The **hominy gazette** (Australia) means rumours; hominy grits being the basis of prison meals, when men could chatter.

A 19C US jail uniform was a **zebra** (now gone 'legit' and meaning a US football umpire), a **flying pasty** was a package of excrement

wrapped in newspaper and tossed out of one's window, the obsolete
treadmill was the **cockchafer**, the **wheel of life**, the **everlasting
staircase**, **Jack the slipper**, the **shinrapper**, the **stairs without
a landing**, the **stepper** or the **universal staircase**.

EXECUTION

The decline of capital punishment, while it may have benefited the
judicial system, at least in liberal eyes, has had one deleterious effect:
an abrupt cutting off of what was once a fecund source of slang:
the judicial execution, especially those that were carried out in
public. While the 20C does have a few terms, notably **burn**, **fry**,
sit in the hot seat, **take the juice** or **the hot squat** (all referring
to death in the electric chair) and **topping** and **swinging** (for
hanging), all of which have lasted as long as did the activities they
describe, but they are nothing compared with the substantial listings
of an earlier, bloodier era.

Public executions were instituted at Tyburn, near what is now
London's Marble Arch, in 1388. There were other sites – Tyburn
dealt only with the malefactors of the county of Middlesex – but
that jurisdiction effectively dealt with every major London villain.
As the vocabulary makes clear, this was the headquarters of judicial
death, and until 1838, when the hangman transferred his equipment to the street outside Newgate, it so remained. Public hangings,
which at their peak could attract crowds of 100,000 spectators,
including in 1849 Charles Dickens, who watched the 'turning off'
of the murderous Mr and Mrs Manning at Horsemonger Lane Jail,
continued for 30 more years. The last victim was one Michael
Barrett, a Fenian responsible for the Clerkenwell bombing of 1868.
After that, bowing to public pressure, the executions disappeared
behind the prison walls. It would be a further century before the
death penalty was abolished in Britain. In America, after a lull
during the 1960s and early 1970s, it is back in place.

Death, in the 20C, has attained a degree of taboo that was once accorded to sexuality in an earlier century. It is not merely the end of capital punishment, nor even its banishment to the **topping sheds** of Britain's prisons, that has shrunk the vocabulary. For the 17th and 18th centuries in particular, death was accepted with far fewer qualms, whether of the young, the old, and particularly of the criminal. The slang vocabulary that accrued to the topic, especially as here, in its judicial context, is literally gallows humour.

THE GALLOWS

Thomas Harman cites in 1567 **chates**, **chattes** and **chats** for the gallows; the source of all three is the Anglo-Saxon *cheat*, meaning thing. *Cheat* itself offers a number of combinations: **treyning cheat** or **trining cheat** (16C) possibly a variation on the phrase **trine to the gallows**, from *trine* (14C): to go or march, or from *trine*: triple, and thus referring to the 'triple tree.' **Hanging cheat** and **topping cheat** (fr. **top**: to hang) are both 17C, as is **nubbing cheat** (fr. **nub**: neck) which also gives **nubbing-cove**, the hangman and **nubbing-ken**, the Sessions-house.

Such terms are essentially practical; with **Tyburn tree** (17C), one moves into the area of imagery. Although hanging at Tyburn was already nearly 180 years old the first permanent gallows was not set up until June 1571. Its first victim was the 'Romish Canonical Doctor' John Story. The great **triple tree**, capable if necessary of dispatching 21 villains at a time, stands menacingly in the background of Hogarth's 1747 engraving of a public hanging. Other 'trees' include the **deadly nevergreen** (18C), the **leafless tree**, (19C), the **three trees**, the **tree with three corners** and the **tree that bears fruit all year round** (all 17C). **Abraham's balsam** (18C) was the Abraham's balm, the old name of the chaste tree, *Vitex Agnus castus*.

After trees come horses, all 17C coinages. They include a **horse foaled by an acorn** (**horse** was also the triangle or crossed halberds to which soldiers were tied for floggings), the **mare with three legs** or the **three legged** or **wooden-legged mare**.

Other terms include the 16C **ladder**, giving in **climb three trees with a ladder** and **mount the ladder**: both meaning to be hanged, and **groom of the ladder**, the hangman. **Queer 'em** and **swing** were 18C terms, while the transfer of hangings from Tyburn to Newgate where they continued, first outside and then, until the prison was demolished in 1903, behind its closed doors, is indicated in the **City stage** and the **hotel**, an abbreviation of **Akerman's Hotel***. The **crap** (19C) came from the Dutch *krap* meaning cramp or clasp, while the **derrick** (c.1600) paid homage to a contemporary Tyburn hangman. The **government signpost** (19C) pointed the rogues' path to hell, while the **door posts** were presumably those of the next world.

Moll Blood (19C) is Scots while **prop** and **stalk** (mid-19C) come from showman's jargon and can be found in Punch and Judy shows; the **stifler** (19C) gives the combinations **nab the stifler**: to be hanged and **queer the stifler**, to escape the gallows. The **fork** comes, anachronistically, from the Latin *furca*: the fork-shaped Roman gallows, while the **widow** (18C) is from the French slang, *la veuve* and the **morning drop** (19C) puns on a more healthful prescription. **Tower hill vinegar** (16C) is the swordsman's block, which was replaced with the advent of the noose, by **preaching on Tower Hill** (16C): to be hanged.

THE HANGMAN'S NOOSE

The mordant humour of the fatalistic was equally in evidence when it came to the instrument of execution: the noose. Tyburn, as ever, stands in the forefront. The 16C offered the **Tyburn tippet**, **Tyburn check** and **Tyburn pickadill***, that same form of stiff collar, originally Spanish, that would, in the following century, give a name to the London thoroughfare Piccadilly. The **Tyburn tiffany** (17C) took its name from a transparent gauze muslin, often used as a headcover.

The 16C also had **Sir Tristram's Knot** and **Sir Andrew's Knot** (referring perhaps to a pair of hanging judges, the **halter** (thus halter-sack: a gallows bird) and **neckweed**, a synonym for hemp, which was used for the rope itself. Other 'hempen' terms emerge in the 18C: the **hempen collar, hempen cravat, hempen croak**, **hempen garter, hempen necktie, hempen habeas, hempen candle** and **hempen circle**; a **hempen widow** had lost her husband to the noose, and those who **died of a hempen fever** had been hanged. Further 18C terms include the **sheriff's picture frame**, a **tight cravat** and an **anodyne necklace**, originally a form of medicinal amulet and based on the original definition of anodyne as soothing pain, in this context that of a mis-spent life. The **caudle** or, ironically, **caudle of hempseed** – originally gruel spiced with wine or ale and given to the sick, and especially to women in labour – was another form of 'painkiller'.

Finally and logically, a number of terms refer to the neck: **necklace** (17C); **scrag, scrag squeezer** and **squeezer** (all 18C) were all based on **scrag**, meaning neck; **necktie** (18C), **neckcloth** and **neck squeezer** (both 19C).

TO BE HANGED

Many terms meaning to be hanged are simply combinations of those above plus a verb. Thus one **climbs the stalk, climbs** or **leaps from the leafless** or **the triple tree, swings, is nubbed, wears hemp** or **an anodyne necklace**, a **hempen collar, cravat** and so on. Similarly one **rides the horse foaled of an acorn**, one is **stretched, topped, scragged**, and much more. There are, however, a number of new terms worthy of mention.

Perhaps the most elaborate is the 18C's **to dance** or **shake one's trotters at Beilby's ball where the sheriff plays the music** or **pays the fiddlers.** As Grose remarked in 1796 'who Mr Beilby was, or why that ceremony was so called, remains with the quadrature of the circle, the discovery of the philosopher's stone and divers other desiderate as yet undiscovered', but there exist a number of suggestions. The most obvious is that Beilby was a well-known sheriff; a second is that beilby is a mispronunciation of Old Bailey, the court in which so many villains were sentenced to death. The third, and that espoused by Eric Partridge, is that **beilby** refers to the *bilbo*, a long iron bar, furnished with sliding shackles to confine the ankles of prisoners, and a lock by which to fix one end of the bar to the floor or ground. *Bilbo* comes from the Spanish town of Bilbao, where these fetters were invented.

Dancing and kicking are twin leitmotifs of judicial extermination. One might **dance at the sheriff's ball and loll out one's tongue at the company, dance** or **cut a caper upon nothing, cut one's last fling, do the Paddington** (18C) or **Newgate** (19C) **frisk (in a hempen cravat), dance the Newgate hornpipe (without music), dance at Tuck 'em Fair** (18C, from **tuck**: to hang). Similarly one **could kick the wind (with one's heels), kick the clouds** (19C) **kick before the Hotel door** (fr. **Akerman's hotel***), **kick away the prop,** or **wag hemp in the wind. Morris** too presumably came from the dance.

Tyburn, again, has its place and 16C terms include **preach at Tyburn cross, fetch a Tyburn stretch** and **make a Tyburn show**. A **Tyburn show, Tyburn jig** or **Tyburn stretch** was a hanging, just as **Paddington Fair** was the hanging day, Tyburn being sited in what was then the village of Paddington.

The choking aspect of hanging provided some grim humour: **catch** or **nab the stifles,** (17C) to **have a hearty choke with caper sauce for breakfast** (18C, a laboured pun on artichoke) and **take a vegetable** (19C, once again an 'artichoke') **breakfast**. One could **cry cockles** (18C, from the choking noises). Other terms include to **die in ones boots** or **shoes** (two centuries before the phrase became a staple of the US Wild West), to **leave the world** or to **die with cotton in one's ears** (19C, Cotton being a Newgate chaplain), and to **die of a hempen fever** or a **hempen quinsy** (18C). One could also **marry the widow, bless the world with one's heels** (16C), **walk up ladder lane and down hemp street** (19C, nautical: hanged at the yardarm), **walk backwards up Holborn Hill,** a reference to the traditional journey to Tyburn from Newgate, which is also the origin of the phrase **go west**. One could **die in a horse's nightcap, be stabbed with a Bridport dagger** (the best variety of British hemp was grown near Bridport) or **go off with the fall of the leaf** (a pun on the leaves of the drop and the dead leaves the fall from a natural, rather than judicial 'tree'. Finally the US **lanter** (fr. the French revolutionary exhortation '*À la lanterne!*') meant to hang from a lampost, while **whittle** meant to confess on the gallows (16C, from **whiddle**: to confess, which in turn derived from **whid** meaning a cant 'word' and thus a lie). A **horse's nightcap** was the cap pulled over the condemned man's head prior to his death.

THE HANGMAN

General terms for the hangman include the **dancing master** (17C), the **cramping cull** (fr. **cull** or **cully**: a man, or, specifically, a constable), the **topsman** and the **sheriff's journeyman** (all 18C), but three individual executioners earned their own immortality and became generic terms in their own right. The most celebrated is still **Jack Ketch** (sometimes written Catch or Kitch), who was the common executioner from c.1663-1686. Partly on account of his barbarity at the executions of Lord Russell, the Duke of Monmouth, and other political offenders, and partly perhaps from the obvious links with the SE *catch*, his name became widely known. When it was given to the hangman in the puppet-play of *Punchinello*, which arrived from Italy shortly after his death, his immortality was assured. Kindred terms are **Jack Ketch's kitchen**, that room in Newgate where the hangman boiled the quarters of those dismembered for high treason and **Jack Ketch's pippin**: a candidate for the gallows.

Derrick has been cited above, while the **gregorian tree**, the gallows and the **gregory**, the hangman, come from one Gregory Brandon, who worked as executioner under James I, to be succeeded by his son Richard, better known as 'Young Gregory'.

DEATH

Amassing the terms that relate to death, dying and the various impedimenta – the coffin, the funeral and the like – it is hard to avoid the fact that as opposed to the language of judicial executions (see Execute), where the blackest of humour is constantly on display, death 'by natural causes' (or at least not at a rope's end or via some other compulsory agency) seems to give slang coiners a certain pause for reflection. Perhaps the subject is just too serious. What one finds, as will become apparent, is a good deal of material skating along the thin line that in this context at least, runs between proper slang and the kinder world of euphemism.

DEATH

Termination is the name of the game, and the words for death echo that finality. The **last farewell**, **last goodbye**, **last muster** and **last roundup** all suggest the solemnities of a final departure, as does Raymond Chandler's **long goodbye** (the title of his novel, published in 1953). Chandler also offers the **big sleep** (this eponymous novel appeared in 1939), a term that seems to reek of gangland authenticity, but which the oil executive-turned-novelist created in his own study. As in many of its terms, death-related material grabs hold of the imagery of other, livelier activities to create its purpose-built vocabulary. Thus **curtains** and the **final curtain** evoke the stage (with an unspoken '*La commedia é finita*' as a famous last word), **fadeout** comes from the movies while **lights out** evokes a dormitory or perhaps a barracks, and the **end of the ball game** the culmination of a baseball encounter. **Kiss off**, **push off** and **send off** are logical enough – each implies departure – but **kickoff** is slightly paradoxical: as much as finality it implies a beginning, it is, as it were, the start, not the end of the ball game. Only the **big chill** and **cold storage** present a genuine whiff of the morgue. As for the actual figure of death he is relatively unrepresented. The **Grim Reaper**, **Old Mr Grim** (fr. **grim**: a skeleton) and the **Old Floorer** (whence he knocks you) are the only names that slang can suggest.

THE CORPSE

'A dead wife is the best cold meat in a man's house,' declared Francis Grose in 1785 and **cold meat**, seemingly the earliest slang term for corpse is possibly the harshest. There is little euphemism there. It also led to a number of combinations: **cold meat box** (1820, a coffin), **cold meat cart** (1820, a hearse), **cold meat train** (mid-

19C), a train that stops at a cemetery, although officers at Aldershot thus christened the last train, which brought them back to barracks from a night's indulgence in London) and, during World War I, **cold meat ticket**: an identity disc (US *dogtags*) by which a corpse could be most easily identified.

Other terms for corpse included **goner** (c.1847, and imported from the US to UK), **dead meat** (mid-19C) and **croaker**, which meant a dying person, a corpse, and the doctor who had failed to save the first from becoming the second. It is as a doctor that **croaker** still exists, especially in the world of narcotics, where a **writing croaker** is a doctor who writes narcotics' prescriptions without asking questions – albeit for an inflated fee. Still in the surgery, or at least the hospital, **pickles** or **dead pickles** was what 19C medical students called the corpses brought in for dissection.

A **stiff 'un** (1823) and a **stiff** (mid-19C) have survived reasonably well, especially in the abbreviated form; the former version also described a horse which, for whatever reason, failed to run as expected. To **cut up stiff** was to leave a large estate. **Rags and bones** and **wormbait** both indicate the fate of the buried body, while a **flounder** (1870) meant a drowned man and a **dab** a drowned woman; the contemporaneous rhy. sl. **flounder and dab**, however, meant a cab.

THE CEMETERY

The cemetery became a **bone yard** or **bone orchard** during the late 19C, in time for World War I's grim nicknaming of the battle of Neuve Chapelle (1915) with the same phrase: so heavy were the casualties that it became impossible to dig into the ground without disinterring bones. Americans had **marble orchard** from the same period. The punning **landed estate** confers a degree of (spurious) dignity, while **Darby's Dyke** smacks of jail, coming as it probably does from **darby's fair**, the day a prisoner was transferred from one jail to another, to be prepared for his trial; this term, in turn, has its roots in **darbies**, meaning handcuffs. The best known of slang cemeteries, however, is the watery one: **Davy Jones' locker**. At best Davy Jones represents the spirit of the sea, at worst he is the ocean's own devil; either way it is in his 'locker' that drowned seamen are stowed. The identification was first printed by Smollett in *Peregrine Pickle* (1751). The etymology remains obscure, but Partridge suggests that 'Jones' refers to 'Jonah' whose own 'locker' was the belly of the whale; Davy, it is proposed, may have been added by Welsh sailors.

THE BURIAL

As misogynistic as ever, slang terms a funeral a **scold's cure**; the only alternative term being a **black job** (which was practiced, c.1850, by experts in the **black art**, i.e. undertaking). Burying a body is to **plant** it (18C), to **put it six feet under**, to **send home in a box** or to be **put to bed with a shovel**. Those thus interred are **taking a ground sweat** (17C) or **going to grass with their teeth upwards**. The coffin is a **six-foot bungalow, pine** or **wooden overcoat** (19C), or a **wooden kimono**. Some version of a wooden 'garment' has existed since the 18C, starting with **wooden doublet** (1761), and progressing through **wooden habeas** (18C), **wooden surtout** (1780) and **wooden ulster** (19C). In the same spirit a **wooden casement** or **wooden cravat** described the 18C pillory, while those who were buried gained a **wooden suit**. The **concrete overcoat**, a product of gangster killings and probably coined by journalists rather than the gangsters themselves, emerged in the 1920s.

TO DIE

Although the 19th century offered **go aloft, go up, join the great majority** and **join the angels** and spiritualist euphemism has **cross over**, up references to heaven are relatively rare in the list of slang terms that mean 'to die'. Gambling, sport and the sea have a far more substantial representation. The former, for instance, has to be **thrown for a loss, cash in one's chips, crap out, throw a seven, have one's chips, have one's number come up, pass in one's checks** or **chips, put one's checks in the rack, throw in one's cards, throw in one's hand** —all of which come either from cards or the game of craps dice and emerge subsequent to the mid-19C. Sport, similarly, offers **strike out**, **drop the cue**, **peg out** (19C), **hang up one's harness**, **jump the last hurdle**, **go to the races** (19C), **throw in the sponge** and **take the long count**, drawn variously on baseball, snooker, cribbage, horse-racing and boxing.

The sea is especially fertile in images of demise. Aside from the sailors' own **go to Davy Jones' locker**, a number of terms with a nautical background are equally popular amongst landlubbers. The majority come from the mid-19C, when many more sailors stood 'in peril on the sea', and they include **cut** or **slip one's cable**, **keel over**, **lose the number of one's mess**, **give up the ship**, **drop off the hook** and **sling one's hook**; drowning as such engenders **go feed the fishes** and **turn into fish food**. **Answer the last roll-call** and **answer the last muster** may have nautical origins too, although **answer the last round-up** is definitely a product of dry land —notably the American West, which is also the source of **bite** or **kiss the dust**. America too furnishes **buy the farm**, a World War II coinage which refers to the wish of US aviators to retire from combat missions, buy a farm and settle down. The term referred ironically to those whose 'retirement' came somewhat sooner than they might have desired. To **go West**, however, has nothing to do with land of cowboys and Indians; rather it refers to the last trip an 18th century villain would make, moving from his or her cell in Newgate (now the Old Bailey) westward towards the gallows at Tyburn (now Marble Arch). The term also has some flavour of the metaphorically 'setting sun' — which descends in the West. Although the majority of such under-world terms are to be found under EXECUTION, a couple of general phrases also reflect the moment of execution: **get it in the neck** (fr. an executioner's blade) and **kick the wind** (as one hangs).

The act of dying draws on a wide variety of sources for its imagery. The animal kingdom offers **hop the twig** (19C) and **go belly up** (like a dead fish), while nature has **drop off the twig** (like a leaf); domesticity, especially in the context of eating, gives **lay down one's knife and fork** (19C), **go for one's tea**, **hand in one's dinner pail** and **hang up one's hat**; **stick one's spoon in the wall** (19C) has a neat finality, but its etymology remains a mystery.

What may be the ultimate in food-related images is **kick the bucket**, which dates back to 1570 and has been accorded two, not wholly dissimilar origins. The first refers to a 16C method of slaughtering a pig: the animal is suspended from a beam by the insertion of a piece of bent wood behind the tendons of its hind legs; this piece of wood is known as a 'bucket'; the dying animal naturally kicks out at the bucket. The second is more marginal, and refers to an ostler working at an inn on the Great North Road who killed himself by hanging; to gain the necessary drop he stood on a bucket, kicking it away as required. Other metaphors are **conk out** (c.1917, like an engine), **snuff it** (hence today's supposed 'snuff movies'), **take an earth bath** (19C), **take the big jump** and **come to a sticky end** (the 'stickiness' is that of blood).

The physical act of dying is reflected in **croak** (fr. one's death rattle), **turn up up one's toes, curl up one's toes (and die)** and **cock up one's toes** (19C); resignation underlines **call it a day, call it quits, turn one's face to the wall** and **give up the ghost**, while the body's decay is echoed in **feed the worms, push** or **kick up daisies** and **kick up dust**. Departure is seen in **kick off, check out** (as in leaving a hotel), **bow out** (with a theatrical echo of **curtains**, above), **take a powder, pop off** (18C), **quit** and **slam off**. Indeed, given the essentially colloquial nature of such terms, there are few verbs for leaving that cannot (and have not) been recruited to serve as softeners for death.

Finally come **pop one's clogs** (**fr. pop**: pawn; the inference is that only in extremis would one 'pop' one's clogs, given the role they play as indispensable footwear), and **go to Peg Trantum's** (17C, but **Peg Trantum** is still extant in East Anglian dialect as a 'hoyden or tomboy'). To be dying, rather than actually dead adds a few extra phrases: to be **on one's last legs**, to have **one foot in the grave**, to have **one's number come up**, to be **pegging out**, and to be **measured for a funeral sermon**.

SUICIDE

Suicide, it might be presumed, requires even more careful euphemism, but in fact the terminology tends to the tough, often borrowing from a vocabulary more usually associated with murder: **do oneself in**, **bump oneself off**, **turn off one's lights** or **turn out one's lights**, **kiss oneself goodbye**, **wipe oneself out** and **top oneself** (19C, fr. **top**: kill, especially when the 'top' or head is either removed or placed within a hangman's noose). Other phrases include **do the Dutch** (19C, which originally meant to run away and, racial stereotyping aside, underlines the feeling that suicide is 'the coward's way out'), **take the easy way out** (cowardice again), **gorge out** (to jump from a high cliff) and **have a catfish death** (drown oneself). Perhaps the most exotic is **take a Brodie**: this refers to one Steve Brodie, a 23 year-old New York saloonkeeper who on July 23, 1886 leaped some 41.5 metres (135 feet) from the city's Brooklyn Bridge in order to win a $200 wager. He survived the fall and was scooped out of the East River by a friend in a small boat. His exploit coined two slang phrases: the first, since he survived, was 'doing a Brodie', meaning attempting a dangerous stunt. The second, perhaps boosted by the fact that the police briefly charged him with attempting suicide, was that listed above. Not everyone was impressed, anyway: the boxing champion Jim Corbett was told that Brodie had jumped *over* the bridge; when he discovered the truth he snorted, 'So? Any fool can jump *off* a bridge.'

TO BE DEAD

Death's adverbial state, 'dead', naturally modifies some of the verbs listed earlier, but takes the opportunity to expand the grim lexicon somewhat further. Those for whom **all bets are off**, who have been **put to bed with a shovel**, whose **hash is settled**, whose **number is up** and whose **race is run**, who are **out of their misery**, **down for the last count** and moved **out of the picture** have gone **belly up**, **across the river**, **pegged out**, **popped off**, **gone west**, **checked out**, **croaked**, **kicked off** and **kicked the bucket**. **All up** and **done for** they are **pushing up daisies**, **all washed up**, **wasted**, **counting worms**, **dead as a doornail**, **cold**, **scragged**, **smabbled** and **snabbled**. **Gone for six**, they're **grinning at daisy roots**, **jacked in**, **slated**, **throwing sixes** or **a seven** (a throw of twelve in craps dice is a loss, as, when trying to make a given 'point', is one of seven). They have, to return to religion, **gone trumpet-cleaning** – the trumpeter in question being the angel Gabriel. Once again, this is but a selection, the potential vocabulary is open to euphemists everywhere.

GONE FOR A BURTON

Although the *OED* pontificates that 'None of the several colourful explanations of the origin of the expression is authenticated by contemporary printed evidence.' **gone for a Burton** remains one of the most tantalising slang expressions, Britain's version of America's **OK★**, as it were, and for all the *OED*'s self-denial, a trawl through the possibilities is simply too tempting to resist.

There is no argument as regards what the phrase, used invariably in the past tense (**gone for a Burton**), meant: initially it was dead, killed either during some sortie or in a dogfight; latterly, post 1941, it came to mean missing, whether in the air or not. Although there are some claims for its existence during World War I, when **Burton** was supposedly derived from an elision of the words 'burnt 'un' (the fate of many young aviators), most lexicographers, including Partridge, an expert on every aspect of 1914–18 slang, opt for the following conflict and the magisterial *OED* offers no citation before that from the *New Statesman*, dated August 1941. From thereon in, all is confusion.

Partridge in the 7th edn. of the *DSUE*, and Paul Beale in the 8th, suggest 1. a euphemism: going for a glass of Burton ale; 2. Burton-on-Trent is rhy.sl. for went, as in 'went west' (cf. **go west**); 3. Burton ale is heavy, as is a burning aircraft as it crashes to the ground; 4. the Burton refers to the suits made by Montague Burton. This ties in neatly with descriptions of coffins as **wooden overcoats**, **wooden kimonos** and the like, but would conclusively disqualify any World War I origins, since Burtons had yet to appear on the High Street; 5. To confound the whole issue even further, during World War II the RAF used a number of billiard halls, invariably sited above Burton shops, as medical centres. Those who attended such centres had 'gone for a Burton'; the black joke was that such treatment was more likely to kill than cure.

Other suggestions, vouchsafed by correspondents to BBC Radio 4's *Enquire Within* brought up the large-scale inter-war advertising campaign for Burton's Ales (which, *pace* Partridge, were apparently not that heavy). The campaign featured on posters 'several scenes depicting a Burton Ale house in the background and a tableau in the foreground where a principal character was obviously missing. An example is a broken-down car, bonnet up, distraught lady standing beside it, male character disappearing up the road towards the pub.' The copy line for this and similar pictures was 'He's gone for a Burton'. Only after the advertising campaign was it picked up by participants in the military one.

A second correspondent noted that Montague Burton's halls were used for morse aptitude tests, not medical checkups, and going for a Burton meant failing such a test, 'made,' he noted 'more difficult by open windows and passing trams.' It was also claimed that the **burton** came from seafarers' jargon, referring to the stowing of a barrel athwart rather than fore-and-aft. Such stowage was notoriously unsafe in a rough sea, and a rolling barrel could be a genuine threat to a sailor deputed to tackle it. Thus this going for a Burton meant risking death.

INDEX

ABBREVIATIONS

AA: Afro-American
Aus.: Australian
abbrev.: abbreviation
backsl.: backslang
cf.: compare

fr.: from
Fr.: French
Gk.: Greek
Heb.: Hebrew
Lat.: Latin
orig.: originally

qv.: which see
rhy. sl.: rhyming slang
Rom.: Romany
Yid.: Yiddish
*: see further entry